Minds at War

The Poetry and Experience
of the First World War

The testimony of poets, politicians, pundits, propagandists, generals, and
ordinary people.

At the start of the twenty-first century, as mankind's dangerous
love affair with war is renewed, the message of the poets of the
First World War remains as powerful, relevant and compelling as
ever.

"War is the opposite of civilisation" - Michael Longley, Irish poet.

Minds at War

The Poetry and Experience of the First World War

Edited by David Roberts

Saxon Books

Minds at War - The Poetry and Experience of the First World War

ISBN 0 9528969 0 7

Saxon Books, 221 London Road, Burgess Hill, West Sussex RHI5 9RN
Great Britain
Phone/fax 01444 232 356
e-mail: saxonbooks@warpoetry.co.uk
Web site: www.warpoetry.co.uk

First published 1996
Second printing 1998
Third printing 1999
Fourth printing 2003

Printed and bound in Great Britain by Biddles Ltd, Guildford.

Acknowledgements

I am grateful to all who have helped me in the production of this book. I am indebted to the staffs of the Imperial War Museum Photographic Archive, the Imperial War Museum Art Department, the Imperial War Museum Reading Room, the Hulton Getty Picture Collection, the Newspaper Library, The Poetry Library, Sussex University and Brighton Libraries. The staff of Burgess Hill Library and West Sussex Library Service gave exceptional support over many months tracking down books and articles often long out of print.

I am especially appreciative of the help of friends and family: my wife, Julie, Mary Bailey, Alison Brett, Doug and Barbara Kershaw, Jan Shimmin, and Tanya Summers who gave me encouragement, helpful advice and pointed out a number of errors; Alan and Ken Shimmin for their technical assistance; Geoff Green, cartographic advice; Lorraine Roberts for typing most of this book; Gavin Roberts for his illustrations.

For readings and dates of Wilfred Owen's texts I am indebted to the poets and scholars who have worked over many decades to interpret Owen's manuscripts - especially D S R Welland, Dominic Hibberd and Jon Stallworthy.

My thanks go to all the individuals and organisations who have given me permission to use copyright material, many of whom have been generously supportive.

Poetry

Richard Aldington: *Soliloquy I, Soliloquy II*, ©The Estate of Richard Aldington. Edmund Blunden: *At Senlis Once, Come on, My Lucky Lads, Preparations for Victory, Thiepval Wood, The Zonnebeke Road,* Peters, Fraser & Dunlop Group Ltd. Vera Brittain: *August 1914, To My Brother, Perhaps . . ., Hospital Sanctuary, The Lament of the Demobilised;* by permission of Paul Berry, her literary executor. E E Cummings: *I Sing of Olaf Glad and Big*, is reprinted from *Complete poems 1904-1962* by E E Cummings, Edited by George J Firmage, reprinted by permission of W W Norton & Company Ltd, copyright© 1931, 1959, 1979, 1991 by the Trustees for the E E Cummings Trust and George James Firmage. Geoffrey Dearmer: *Two Trench Poems - The Storm Night and Ressurection*, from *A Pilgrim's Song*, Edited by Laurence Cotterell, published by John Murray (Publishers) Ltd, by permission of John Murray (Publishers) Ltd. Eva Dobell: *Pluck*, and *Night Duty* by permission of Stephen Dobell. Walter de la Mare: *Happy England:* The Literary Trustees of Walter de la Mare, and The Society of Authors as their representative. Eleanor Farjeon *Now That You Too*, from *First and Second Love,* published by Oxford, and *Peace* from *Sonnets and Poems 1918*, published by Blackwell, by permission of David Higham Associates. Gilbert Frankau: *The Deserter, Poison,* and extracts from *On Leave* and *Parting*, A P Watt Ltd on behalf of Timothy d'Arch Smith. Wilfred Gibson: *Breakfast, The Bayonet*; © Macmillan General Books, with special thanks to Mrs Dorothy Gibson. Robert Graves: *Armistice Day, A Child's Nightmare, A Dead Boche, Hate Not, Fear Not, Not Dead, Sergeant-Major Money, The Shadow of Death, Trench Life, Two Fusiliers*, from *Robert Graves, Poems About War*, Edited by William Graves, published by Cassell Publishers Ltd 1988, *Defeat of the Rebels* from *An Anthology of War Poetry*, Edited by Julian Symons, published by Penguin, 1942 – all by permission of Carcanet Press Limited, © the Executors of the Estate of Robert Graves. A P Herbert: *After the Battle*, A P Watt Ltd on behalf of Crystal Hale and Jocelyn Herbert. Teresa Hooley: *A War Film*, Random House UK Ltd. David Jones: extract from *In Parenthesis* published by Faber and Faber Ltd, 1937, by permission of Faber and Faber Ltd. Winifred Letts: *What Reward?* from *The Spires of Oxford*, published by E P Dutton, 1917, by permission of John Murray Publishers Ltd. Rose Macaulay: *Many Sisters to Many Brothers*, from *Poems of Today*, Sidgwick and Jackson, 1919, by permission of Peters, Fraser and Dunlop. John Masefield: *August 1914*, The Society of Authors as the literary representative of the Estate of John Masefield. Alfred Noyes: *The Victory Ball*, by permission of John Murray (Publishers) Ltd. Herbert Read: *The Execution of Cornelius Vane, The Happy Warrior, My Company, A Short Poem for Armistice Day, To a Conscript of 1940*, by permission of David Higham Associates. Siegfried Sassoon: *Absolution, Attack, Banishment, Christ and the Soldier, Counter Attack, Died of Wounds, Does it Matter? Dreamers, The General, The Great Men, The Hero, In the Church of St Ouen, I Stood With the Dead, The Kiss, Lamentations, The March Past, Memorial Tablet, A Mystic as Soldier, Night Attack, The One-legged Man, On Passing the New Menin Gate, Peace, The Poet as Hero, Prelude: the Troops, Reconciliation, Remorse, Suicide in the Trenches, Survivors, A Testament, "They", To Any Dead Officer, To My Brother, Vicarious Christ*, by permission of George Sassoon. Osbert Sitwell: *The Next War*, and *The End*, David Higham Associates. Robert Service: *The Volunteer*, by permission of M William Krasilovsky, New York.

Prose

Vera Brittain: extracts from *Testament of Youth*, published by Victor Gollancz Ltd 1933, by permission of Paul Berry, Literary Executor and Victor Gollancz Ltd. Rupert Brooke: extracts from letters published in *The Letters of Rupert Brooke,* edited by Sir Geoffrey Keynes, published by Faber and Faber Ltd 1968, by permission of the publisher. Malcolm Brown: extracts from *Tommy Goes to War*, published by J M Dent, 1978 by permission of the publisher. Eleanor Farjeon: extracts from *Edward Thomas the Last Four Years*, published by Oxford University Press 1958, and 1979, by permission of David Higham Associates. Robert Graves: extracts from *Goodbye to All That*, published byJonathan Cape Ltd,1929, and Penguin Books, 1960, by permission of Carcanet Press Limited, © the Executors of the Estate of Robert Graves. Lyn Macdonald: Extracts from *The Roses of No Man's Land*, published by Michael Joseph Ltd, 1980, © Lyn Macdonald, and extracts from *Voices and Images of the Great War*, published by Michael Joseph Ltd, 1988, © Lyn Macdonald, by permission of Penguin Books Ltd. Michael Moynihan: extracts from *People* at War 1914-1918, published by David and Charles 1973, by permission of the publisher. Wilfred Owen: extracts from letters from *Wilfred Owen: Collected Letters*, edited by Harold Owen and John Bell, © Oxford University Press 1967 by permission of Oxford University Press. Herbert Read: extracts from *Annals of Innocence and Experience*, published by Faber and Faber by permission of David Higham Associates. Erich Maria Remarque: extracts from *All Quiet on the Western Front*, translated by A W Wheen, published by Putnam and Co 1929, by permission of the estate of the author, the translator and The Bodley Head. Siegfried Sassoon: extracts from *Siegfried Sassoon Diaries 1915-1918*, edited by Rupert Hart-Davis, published by Faber and Faber Ltd, and extracts from *Memoirs of a Fox-hunting Man*, published by Faber and Faber Ltd, by permission of the publisher. George Bernard Shaw: extracts from *Common Sense About the War*, published by *The New Statesman*, 1914, by Permission of *New Statesman and Society*. H G Wells: extracts from *Mr Britling Sees it Through* 1916, *The War That Will End Wars* 1914, *Experiment in Autobiography* 1934 by permission of A P Watt Ltd on behalf of the Executors of the Estate of H G Wells.

Illustrations

CONTENTS

War Poets on War Poetry and War Poets

All a poet can do today is warn. That is why the true poet must be truthful.

Wilfred Owen

. . . He's shed
All fear, all faith, all hate, all hope.

Robert Graves

THE POET AS HERO

You've heard me, scornful, harsh, and discontented,
Mocking and loathing War: you've asked me why
Of my old, silly sweetness I've repented –
My ecstasies changed to an ugly cry.

You are aware that once I sought the Grail,
Riding in armour bright, serene and strong;
And it was told that through my infant wail
There rose immortal semblances of song.

But now I've said good-bye to Galahad,
And am no more the knight of dreams and show:
For lust and senseless hatred make me glad,
And my killed friends are with me where I go.
Wound for red wound I burn to smite their wrongs;
And there is absolution in my songs.

Siegfried Sassoon, 1916

. . . there's things in war one dare not tell
poor father sitting safe at home, who reads
of dying heroes and their deathless deeds.

Siegfried Sassoon, 1918

HERE DEAD WE LIE

Here dead we lie
Because we did not choose
To live and shame the land
from which we sprung.

Life, to be sure,
is nothing much to lose,
But young men think it is,
And we were young.

A E Housman

INTRODUCTION

ESSENTIAL VOICES OF THE FIRST WORLD WAR

We well see what we are doing.

Thomas Hardy, *Men Who March Away*, September, 1914.

We might not have had the war, and then the world would not have been made safe for democracy, nor would militarism have been overthrown.

Bertrand Russell, *The Harm That Good Men Do*, 1935.

The First World War was one of mankind's greatest tragedies – and the poets were those most gifted to express the experience of those traumatic years. Then brave men rushed to fight for what they saw as a great and honourable cause, only to find themselves in a quagmire of mass murder. The world became suddenly more uncertain, more out-of-control, more dangerous, more godless than it had ever seemed before; and at the centre of the problem was modern man himself, unleashing power and destruction which he could neither understand nor handle.

The war shattered personal, and national self-confidence; intensified our sense of human vulnerability and insecurity; made people ponder the concept of civilisation and doubt the idea of progress; weakened or destroyed faith in religion, and "authority" – especially military and national leaders. It brought the distress of the deaths or maiming of millions of men to millions of families and so broke up a pattern of parenting which each generation had learned from the previous – with repercussions for succeeding generations. Women took on new roles. The press developed unjustifiable power to influence events and almost control the mind of the masses and the behaviour of some politicians. Arms industries expanded, siphoning off the wealth of nations, learning how to fuel future wars. Innocence had gone: an age of cynicism had arrived.

The First World War was a war of delusions, euphemism and bitter ironies. Heads of state and politicians, posturing and bluffing, found that it was easy to talk themselves into a war, and almost impossible to talk themselves out of it. Rhetoric and double-talk blossomed from politicians, newspapers, posters, pulpits and poets. It was so pervasive that clear thought and common sense were overwhelmed. – The loftiest ideals were used to justify behaviour that was evil in the extreme. Soldiers were shot for refusing to fight for freedom. Self-preservation justified self-destruction. The love of one's fellow man justified destroying him. – The words "Human Civilisation" seemed to have lost their meaning.

The experience of the front line war poets was more overwhelming, more prolonged and more intense than for any previous generation of soldiers. Few can be unimpressed by their suffering, their endurance, by the appalling tragedy which was their lot. Yet, in spite of the extremity of their experience, it was permeated by universal emotions and problems which have faced everyone throughout time. Each one of us must sooner or later cope with conflicting duties, psychological pressures, moral dilemmas, guilt, tests of courage, suffering, loss of friends, bereavement, the dead – face death itself, and contemplate the meaning of life.

But the poets spoke of new, peculiarly twentieth century things, too. Men found themselves to be driven cogs in vast, insensitive, impersonal machines, stripped of will, morality, and dignity. They were victims of the grossest abuses by the countries which they served and so often loved. Paradoxically, many, in finding themselves to be players in highly motivated teams, found a greater sense of comradeship and purpose than they ever found in a world at peace. Even protesting poets with pacifist beliefs were, at times, whole-hearted members of a fighting brotherhood, willing, not only to make the supreme sacrifice, but also willing to commit the supreme crime.

Of course, most of the poets showed no grasp of power politics, the relentless pressure of arms industry economics and propaganda, no understanding of causes or cures for the war. They spoke simply as human beings caught up in bewildering and shocking events. As human beings they recorded their experiences and moral responses. They spoke of the problems of modern warfare conducted by "advanced" and "civilised" nations. The poets' words are a warning, unheeded and unanswered. Since their time warfare has "progressed," becoming more technological, more cruel, more destructive. A man on a battlefield at the end of the twentieth century counts for even less than the soldier of World War One. He is merely the software of battle.[1]

1 John Keegan's expression.

ESSENTIAL POETRY OF THE FIRST WORLD WAR[1]

Thousands of poems were written during the war. In selecting "essential" poems I have tried, first, to include most of the poems which are widely regarded as amongst the greatest; second, to include poems which, because of their quality or because they struck a deep chord with their contemporary readers, became famous. These include Rupert Brooke's five sonnets, collectively known as *1914*, John McCrae's *In Flanders Fields* (perhaps the most famous poem of the war), and Alan Seeger's *Rendezvous with Death* (perhaps the the most famous American poem of the war). These groups are essential because they would be found in any good anthology of First World War poetry.

Third, certain physical, mental and emotional experiences of the war were the focus of many poems. These are the "essential" themes around which the poems have been gathered, and a number of rarely seen poems have been added to these groupings because they explore the themes or contrast with the better-known poems.

The first poems of the First World War were embodiments of ideas, and ideals prevalent in the poetry of Empire, patriotism and heroism, which were popular before the outbreak of the war. Some of the best-loved and most influential of these pre-war poems are included as vital to an appreciation of the ethos and poetry of August 1914.

A further category of First World War poetry, which is usually neglected in anthologies, is presented here: poetry by those living in Britain – including many women poets, and the propagandist poets who wrote to rouse the reluctant populace to warlike action.

Finally, I have taken the opportunity to include some of the war poetry of Robert Graves which he suppressed for over half a century, and the poetry of some who are among the best-known writers of prose.

CONTEXT

To approach a full appreciation of these poems it is necessary to know something of the context in which they were written. What were the circumstances and conditions out of which such agonised writing sprang? How did the poets become involved in a monumental human disaster? – Why did nations send men to the hell of the trenches? Why did

1   Readers who wish to go straight to particular poems, or find material on the individual poets, are referred to the indexes and *Brief Lives*.

millions actually *volunteer* to fight? Just what went on in the minds of millions of decent, educated, intelligent and caring people – including the poets – that led them to enter and continue the war, carrying through a sustained and massively organised outrage against fellow human beings, suffering grievously themselves or dying, and sowing the seeds for the next war? When armchair poets, with grandiloquent cliché, tell us that "they died that we might live" it seems worth asking for the facts of the matter. Was *that* the motive that drove men to risk all? Was the result of their deaths the giving of life to others? – When Owen complained that soldiers "died as cattle" was that poetic exaggeration or a realistic assessment of the facts? Were Owen, Sassoon, and other war poets critical of the war, exceptional in their attitudes? Were their attitudes to politicians, the press and the generals justified? – What compelled so many to feel that they must record their thoughts, feelings and experiences?

In providing some historical background to the war I have tried particularly to explore what went on in the minds of people, to seek to understand, above all, their motivations. The events and personalities recorded have been selected either because they seemed to have the greatest impact on people's thinking, or because they were especially relevant to certain poems. I have tried to give some account of the way poetry, fiction and newspapers were used deliberately to create the psychological climate of war-readiness, fear and hatred — and the way they were used to promote ideals of heroism, patriotism and sacrifice, the concepts of a fight of Good against Evil and a need to "crush militarism for ever" to carry the war on to its bitter end. In this, poets were sometimes active in helping to create and develop the psychological climate. All were influenced by it.

Some poets wrote their poetry partly out of an anger with the press and the distorted, cosy pictures the press created of the soldiers' lot. Sassoon condemned the Northcliffe press and in his poem, *Fight to the Finish*, fantasized about returning soldiers bayonetting the "Yellow-Pressmen." Owen's plea for the truth was probably a reaction against "press-lies", and his poem, *Smile, Smile, Smile*, was written in direct response to an article in the *Daily Mail*.

A desire to respond to what the poets believed were the attitudes of civilians, was another stimulus to their poetry – evident, for example, in the bitter didacticism of Owen's *Dulce et Decorum Est* and *Apologia pro Poemate Meo*. "Cursed are dullards whom no cannon stuns," he moans in the last verse of *Insensibility*. Sassoon rails against, "the callous complacency of those at home," and the "smug-faced crowds."

The war poets, as all poets, brought, to everything they wrote, their education, their life experience, their character. Sometimes it has been possible to fill in a little of this background. They wrote in the context of momentous events and intense national feelings. But more importantly, poets wrote mainly in response to personal experiences, and their letters, diaries and biographies often illuminate their poems. Some examples: Rupert Brooke's and Edward Thomas's selfless heroism takes on a new meaning in the light of their mental instability. It is easier to appreciate the irony in Charles Sorley's *All the Hills and Vales* when we know of his inner conflict – the discrepancy between his actions and his convictions; it may help us to detect the mindless violence in Julian Grenfell's *Into Battle* – a poem which is an enthusiastic celebration of army life – when we know that he appeared to take pleasure in killing people; and Eleanor Farjeon's poem, about seeing her soldier "boyfriend" on his last leave before embarking for France and the front line, is made more moving, I feel, by a fuller knowledge of the circumstances and occasion on which it is based.

Not all the war poetry included here is written from personal experience, and the hollowness of some of it is explained by the fact that it was written in direct response to governmental requests – even though most authors no doubt sincerely believed in the ideas they expressed. – It is especially sad to see a great writer like Thomas Hardy struggling to make a series of propaganda points in some of his poems and sacrificing intellectual and literary judgement in pursuit of his narrow aim. – Other poets who accepted invitations from politicians to write for the promotion of the war include Bridges, de la Mare, Kipling, Newbolt, Watson and Seaman.

THE PLACE OF PROSE

Prose has become an ancillary feature of this volume in meeting the need to provide contexts for poems. It seemed best, wherever possible, to let people of the war years express their observations and ideas themselves. A few of the prose extracts are already well-known, including Churchill's obituary for Rupert Brooke, Haig's *Backs to the Wall* message and the *Quaker Peace Testimony*. But the witness of politicians, generals, ordinary soldiers, nurses, and reports of journalists help to enlarge our understanding of matters and circumstances which concerned the poets.

Some of the best-known prose writers, including H G Wells and Arnold Bennett, were major voices helping to develop the war fever which gripped the country and was a factor in the willingness of many poets to volunteer. A few writers, among them Bertrand Russell and George Bernard Shaw, offered criticism of the war, though their views tended not to appear in the most popular papers. – A letter by Shaw, written in September 1914 and turned down by *The Times,* was offered to the

Liberal *Manchester Guardian* (now *The Guardian*). The editor, C P Scott, whilst admitting he agreed with every word in the letter, refused to print it. He saw the need for national unity as overriding.

Other prose writers were able to reflect on the war and its effects on the young participants in a way which no poet accomplished. Vera Brittain is outstanding in this respect. She had faced the realities of war as a nurse in military hospitals, and suffered deeply felt personal losses. She wrote her *Testament of Youth* some years after the war, in the early 1930's.

Sometimes prose is so beautifully written, and conveys such an intense emotion, that it becomes pure poetry. (And conversely, of course, writing which has the outward form of poetry is often total dross.) Consider, for example, the soliloquy of Remarque's soldier in *All Quiet on the Western Front*, stunned and empty, as he views himself and his future at the end of the war. This passage, in A W Wheen's translation, both impressive and moving, is prose beyond the normal bounds of prose. (Page 362.)

The prose written by the poets themselves is often fascinating to read. For example, Sassoon's diaries and Owen's letters are sometimes more revealing than their poems; Owen's letters often give accounts of events which later feature in his poems, and it can be rewarding to compare the two versions. His letter showing his anguish, as a Christian turned murderer, is as powerful as many of his poems. Sorley's analysis of the psychological pressures on young men and his personal feelings as the war started, throws light on the phenomenon of young men swarming to die for England.

THE SPECIAL SIGNIFICANCE OF THE POETRY

The First World War bore no comparison with any previous human experience. – The scale of it was unprecedentedly vast – involving not only enormous armies, but the mobilisation of whole nations. In tens of thousands men were ordered to advance with the prospect of imminent death and hurl themselves into the abyss. – Machines, high explosives and gas created a power to destroy human life which was superhumanly effective and placed protagonists at a distance, even out of sight of each other. The enemy was faceless. The war was impersonal, inhuman. The conditions were beyond all expectation.

In totality the First World War is beyond the comprehension or exposition of a single human being. The biographies of the war, the diaries, the histories, novels, films, museums, cemeteries and monuments all contribute to our grasp of it, but the poetry of the First World War has a special significance. Written, in the main, by soldiers who had experienced the burning centre of the action, and in language which is intensely conceived, it encapsulates and communicates much of what is humanly important and deeply moving of that vast war experience.

With so little time to set down their searing thoughts, writers took to the short poem as the ideal medium of expression. Like eye-witnesses in sensational TV news bulletins from centres of disaster they made their hasty reports. – The stunning blows of fate, the traumas of front line experience, the fears, the physical and moral nightmares, the sense of loss and bewilderment, the scenes which the war caused to be played and replayed repeatedly in the minds of soldiers, and civilians – all these the poets set down in stark and urgent honesty. Admittedly they often wrote some distance from situations or occasions they recalled, but their writing was the distillation of intense thought and unparalleled experience, which gripped their minds, demanding to be exorcised. – A few, writing months and even years after their experiences, did attempt longer poems, notably Herbert Read, David Jones , and Edmund Blunden.

Time has already begun to sift the poetic outpourings of the war, but the appreciation of poetry is a strange business – far from objective. We are all helplessly influenced by our feelings towards a poet's ideas. As a result, the appreciation of poetry is subject, not only to personal attitudes, but very largely to fashion, and the enormous reversals in esteem which First World War poets have experienced, illustrate this – telling us as much about the ethos of the war years and the present day as about literary merit. – Readers will form their own opinions of each poem.

Whilst trying to select poems that might be called essential I have inevitably concentrated on what seems to me to be "the greatest and the best" poetry, but I have included some lesser, though rewarding, poetry, and some which has an interest for the light it throws on situations, beliefs and attitudes – for example, the work of the Begbies, Watson, Bridges, and Newbolt. There are also some deservedly forgotten poems, in fact truly vomitorial verse, which are included partly as literary curiosities.

If these awful poems had been merely bad they could have been left in peace. But they have importance because during the war they were amongst the most popular verses in print, and for anyone curious about what was going on in people's heads they are vitally relevant. There is also the point that some of the better poetry was written partly as a reaction against popular verse. It is therefore helpful as a means to understanding the better poetry. (The best-known instance, perhaps, is Owen's *Dulce et Decorum Est* which he originally intended to dedicate to Jessie Pope.)

Now Rupert Brooke's reputation is only a pale shadow of what it was in the First World War. Once the darling of the Establishment he was the most celebrated poet of the time. Today, though the quality of his poetic talent is still recognised, the emptiness and confusion of the ideas which he adorned in mellifluous and grandiloquent rhetoric in his famous *1914* sonnets, can be seen for what they are: the brilliantly heroic and selfless front which concealed a tragically lost young man.

The reputations of other poets have undergone similar radical reappraisals. At the extremes we have two poets: Wilfred Owen and John Oxenham. During the war Oxenham was easily the most popular poet with both soldiers and civilians. He claimed to have sold over a million copies of his war verse. His hymn, *For the Men at the Front,* sold eight million copies. (Page 215.)

Owen had only five poems published during his life-time and those near the end. As a poet he was unknown outside a tiny group of poet friends. For years after his death he was rejected by the literary establishment. Not until 1967 was he even mentioned in *The Oxford Companion to English Literature*.

Oxenham's popularity may be accounted for only by the fact that he was in tune with the most popular attitudes and images of soldiers. His verses spoke of the comfort and blessings of God as if Oxenham knew His every thought: soldiers were fighting for Good against Evil, fighting for Right, Christianity, God's Kingdom; they were martyrs and saints; they died as Christ died; they died that we might live; they were innocents who, it seemed, never did any wrong, never killed.

His language is often crudely simple and inappropriate, for example, using frisky rhythms at odds with its tragic subject matter and more suited to tales of Rupert Bear than the life and death struggles of soldiers and nations. Read, for example, the poem of ten men fighting till all were killed, and then happily received into Heaven. This is *Ten Men in a Crater Hole*. (Page 214.)

In contrast stands the poetry of Wilfred Owen, who is today, after Shakespeare, the most studied poet in English classrooms. His mastery of language was remarkable. – At his best he was sensitive to the resonances of every image, every syllable, the music of every line; his structures – whether simple, novel, or complex – were appropriate or cogent; his choice of words, deeply considered. The central strength of his poetry came from his desperate personal experience, and his burning passion to set on record the soldier's suffering, his suffering. He wrote with integrity and unsurpassed power of the horrors of war, the soldier's experience, his spiritual condition, his anguish. He is one of England's greatest poets.

The story of Siegfried Sassoon's reputation is exceptional among war poets, for although today he is certainly one of the most impressive and important he was already establishing a reputation and a following during the war. Some of his poems were readily published, chiefly by the *Cambridge Magazine*. He was, therefore, unlike so many of the soldier poets, writing directly for a public. In May 1917 his volume, *The Old Huntsman* was published and sold well, though not as well as Brooke's *1914 and Other Poems*, which was reprinted, on average, every eight weeks from May 1915 to October 1918. Sassoon's volume of war poetry, *Counter-Attack and Other Poems,* was published in June 1918 and this was followed with *War Poems* in October 1919. – He was exceptional, too, in that he attempted to influence the political situation. It is strange that so few poets sought political change.

Between Oxenham and Owen lies a range of war poets who may be grouped in various ways – professional poets and amateurs; those who were taught and thought in medieval ways – of valour, chivalry, heroism, honour, noble sacrifice and duty and often wrote with Biblical language and the language of nineteenth century hymns; those who leapt on a bandwagon of popular ideas writing loud clichés to please the crowd; imagists, Georgians, simple versifiers, innovators. But the most striking division is between those who wrote from experience, from the heart, from personal conviction: and those who wrote from the armchair, relying on inadequate imagination.

The armchair poets often showed a strange inability to grasp the nature of the war. This is partly because of the way censorship and propaganda confused people's understanding of what was happening, and because much of the poetry was written as actual propaganda – and as such took a narrow view of truth and reality.

But there were scores of poets who wrote directly from experience. Theirs is poignant and moving poetry, written by men and women at times of extreme personal crisis – shocked and bewildered, seeking a meaning and purpose for suffering; parting from a loved one who might soon be killed; trying to cope with bereavement; young men writing their final thoughts in anticipation of their imminent slaughter; contemplating with horror their own behaviour; visualising a future emptied of friends and loved ones. – Those who wrote so directly about such experiences are the principal poets of this book – the ones whose work stands as the great poetry of the Great War.

1

THE SPIRIT OF WAR IS NATIVE TO THE BRITISH

The British Empire is built up on good fighting by its army and its navy: the spirit of war is native to the British.

The Morning Post[1]

I see the Junker and Militarists of England and Germany jumping at the chance they have longed for in vain for many years of smashing one another and establishing their own oligarchy as the dominant military power in the world.

George Bernard Shaw

Count the life of battle good, and dear the land that gave you birth.

Henry Newbolt

What could bring millions of men to rush to abandon their homes and families, risk their lives, and kill others simply in response to advertisements and stories in newspapers? How had the minds of the British been prepared so that without hesitation young men would make a gigantic sacrificial leap in response to a mere request, and others would cheer them on their way?

EDUCATION FOR MILITARISM

For governments to take whole nations to war it is necessary for them to have the support of a large part of their populations. The British at home had grown accustomed to British conquests overseas. They were no more than dimly conscious of the bloodshed and violence these conquests required, having never come face to face with the reality of war. In the late nineteenth century the great increase in public awareness of

1   Quoted in a letter from I J C Brown in *New Age*, 10 December, 1914.

British exploits overseas was made possible by the increase in elementary education which, for the first time, enabled most sections of the population to read newspapers. A popular press soon grew up which fanned the nation into enthusiasm for the colonial conquests which they interpreted for their readers. Millions believed that rather than spreading exploitation or destroying social organisation, the conquests represented the bringing of civilisation to an uncivilised world. It created both national self-confidence and a sense of righteousness about military power. Sometimes, of course, it was true that the British placed great emphasis on ruling through traditional native institutions, but nevertheless military violence was frequently employed as in 1879 and 1893 when the British ruthlessly put down Zulu and Matabele resistance in Africa.

By 1914 Britain ruled four hundred million people outside its own border. France ruled fifty million and Germany and Italy about fourteen million each.

In the double-think of the times military aggression was equated with Christian self-sacrifice and the heroism of ancient warriors. These ideas were fostered through teaching in schools – especially public schools where, in the words of Vera Brittain, their "tradition stood for militaristic heroism unimpaired by the damping exercise of reason."[1]

POETRY FOR MILITARISM

Henry Newbolt, who went on to promote ideas of warrior heroism through his poetry, and as a propagandist at the Ministry of Information, certainly loved these ideas which he absorbed in his days at school. In his prep school in Caistor, Lincolnshire, his headmaster would interrupt stories of the heroes of Ancient Greece to give the class up to the minute news of real life "heroic deeds" of the British army in Africa.

"The young of my generation," he later wrote, "had neither cruel experience nor dark apprehension to weaken them. We expected fighting and we prepared for it: but we felt as mighty as the heroes and heroines in the great sagas and trusted ourselves to Destiny with incredible confidence."

In our present age of disillusion there are no heroes. Few modern school children relate to the concept of hero, having been brought up in an atmosphere of cynicism fostered especially by the popular press.

1   Vera Brittain, *Testament of Youth*, p100.

Yet at the start of the twentieth century the spirit of hero worship flour-
ished and was evident in the popular poetry of the period. *Admirals All*
was the title poem from Newbolt's best-selling collection of poetry and
celebrated the heroes of Britain's naval successes. It was published
seventeen years before the First World War, and sold twenty-one thousand copies in its first year. In it, *Vitai Lampada (The Torch of Life)*
famously linked the ideas of war and duty with sportsmanship.

In *Clifton Chapel* Newbolt linked ideas of heroic death with God,
school, brotherhood and loving the game (of war) "beyond the prize".
Clifton Chapel, and Clifton College, at which Newbolt was a student
along with Field Marshal Sir Douglas Haig, certainly succeeded in
transmitting this ethos, for three thousand of Clifton College's former
students fought in the war, of whom five hundred were killed.

Rudyard Kipling, one of the most popular writers of his day, also
celebrated England's soldiers, and linked God with England's conquests
(*A Song of the English* and *Hymn Before Action*). In *A Song of the White
Men* he associated "the white men" with war, conquest and purification.

How militarist ideas were accepted into the minds of young public
schoolboys is evident in Charles Sorley's poem, *A Call to Action* which
he wrote when he was seventeen.

PRELUDE TO HOSTILITIES –
IMAGES OF ENGLAND, EMPIRE, AND WARFARE

VITAI LAMPADA *

There's a breathless hush in the Close to-night –
Ten to make and the match to win –
A bumping pitch and a blinding light,
An hour to play and the last man in.
And it's not for the sake of a ribboned coat,
Or the selfish hope of a season's fame,
But his Captain's hand on his shoulder smote –
"Play up! play up! and play the game!"

The sand of the desert is sodden red, –
Red with the wreck of a square that broke; –
The Gatling's* jammed and the Colonel dead,
And the regiment blind with dust and smoke.

The river of death has brimmed his banks,
And England's far, and Honour a name,
But the voice of a schoolboy rallies the ranks:
"Play up! play up! and play the game!"

This is the word that year by year,
While in her place the School is set,
Every one of her sons must hear,
And none that hears it dare forget.
This they all with a joyful mind
Bear through life like a torch in flame,
And falling fling to the host behind –
"Play up! play up! and play the game!"

Henry Newbolt, June 1892

* VITAI LAMPADA - the torch of life
* Gatling – a hand-cranked early machine gun

From ADMIRALS ALL

Admirals all, they said their say
(The echoes are ringing still),
Admirals all, they went their way
To the haven under the hill.
But they left us a kingdom none can take,
The realm of the circling sea,
To be ruled by the rightful sons of Blake
And the Rodneys yet to be.

Admirals all, for England's sake,
Honour be yours and fame!
And honour, as long as waves shall break,
To Nelson's peerless name!

Henry Newbolt, 1892

CLIFTON CHAPEL

This is the Chapel: here, my son,
Your father thought the thoughts of youth,
And heard the words that one by one
The touch of Life has turned to truth.
Here in a day that is not far
You too may speak with noble ghosts
Of manhood and the vows of war
You made before the Lord of Hosts.

To set the cause above renown,
To love the game beyond the prize,
To honour, while you strike him down,
The foe that comes with fearless eyes;
To count the life of battle good,
And dear the land that gave you birth,
And dearer yet the brotherhood
That binds the brave of all the earth.

My son, the oath is yours: the end
Is His, Who built the world of strife,
Who gave His children Pain for friend,
And Death for surest hope of life.
To-day and here the fight's begun,
Of the great fellowship you're free;
Henceforth the School and you are one,
And what You are, the race shall be.

God send you fortune: yet be sure,
Among the lights that gleam and pass,
You'll live to follow none more pure
Than that which glows on yonder brass:
"Qui procul hinc", the legend's writ, –
The frontier-grave is far away –
"Qui ante diem periit:
*Sed miles, sed pro patria."**

Henry Newbolt

*Qui procul hinc, qui ante diem periit: sed miles, sed pro patria. –   He who died so
far from home, died before his time: but he was a soldier, and it was for his country he
died.

"Yonder brass" was one of Newbolt's poetic inventions. No such brass
or inscription exists in Clifton Chapel.

FAREWELL

Mother, with unbowed head
Hear thou across the sea
The farewell of the dead,
The dead who died for thee.
Greet them again with tender words and grave,
For, saving thee, themselves they could not save.

To keep the house unharmed
Their fathers built so fair,
Deeming endurance armed
Better than brute despair,
They found the secret of the word that saith,
"Service is sweet, for all true life is death."

So greet thou well thy dead
Across the homeless sea,
And be thou comforted
Because they died for thee.
Far off they served, but now their deed is done
For evermore their life and thine are one.

Henry Newbolt, January 1910.
Reprinted in *The Times,* 23 September 1914.

HYMN BEFORE ACTION

The earth is full of anger,
The seas are dark with wrath,
The Nations in their harness
Go up against our path:
Ere yet we loose the legions –
Ere yet we draw the blade,
Jehovah of the Thunders,
Lord God of Battles, aid!

High lust and froward bearing,
Proud heart, rebellious brow –
Deaf ear and soul uncaring,
We seek Thy mercy now!
The sinner that forswore Thee,
The fool that passed Thee by,
Our times are known before Thee –
Lord, grant us strength to die!

For those who kneel beside us
At altars not Thine own,
Who lack the lights that guide us,
Lord, let their faith atone!
By honour bound they came;
Let not Thy Wrath befall them,
But deal to us the blame.

From panic, pride and terror,
Revenge that knows no rein –
Light haste and lawless error,
Protect us yet again.
Cloak Thou our undeserving,
Make firm the shuddering breath,
In silence and unswerving
To taste Thy lesser death.

Ah, Mary pierced with sorrow,
Remember, reach and save
The soul that comes tomorrow
Before the God that gave!
Since each was born of woman,
For each at utter need –
True comrade and true foeman –
Madonna, intercede!

E'en now their vanguard gathers,
E'en now we face the fray –
As Thou didst help our fathers,
Help Thou our host to-day.
Fulfilled of signs and wonders,
In life, in death made clear –
Jehovah of the Thunders,
Lord God of Battles, hear!

Rudyard Kipling, 1896

From A SONG OF THE ENGLISH

Fair is our lot –
O goodly is our heritage!
(Humble ye, my people, and be fearful in your mirth!)
For the lord our God Most High
He hath made the deep as dry,
He hath smote for us a pathway to the ends of all the Earth!

Rudyard Kipling, 1893
Reprinted in *The Morning Post*, 10 August 1914.

An Englishman bestrides Africa like a Colossus, confident, arrogant, controlling it all with a gently held string, inviting our admiration. – Cecil Rhodes in a *Punch* cartoon of 1892.

A SONG OF THE WHITE MEN

Now, this is the cup the White Men drink
When they go to right a wrong,
And that is the cup of the old world's hate –
Cruel and strained and strong.
We have drunk that cup – and a bitter, bitter cup –
And tossed the dregs away.
But well for the world when the White Men drink
To the dawn of the White Man's day!

Now, this is the road that the White Men tread
When they go to clean a land –
Iron underfoot and levin* overhead
And the deep on either hand.
We have trod that road – and a wet and windy road –
Our chosen star for guide.
Oh, well for the world when the White Men tread
Their highway side by side!

Now, this is the faith that the White Men hold
When they build their homes afar –
"Freedom for ourselves and freedom for our sons
And, failing freedom, War."
We have proved our faith – bear witness to our faith,
Dear souls of freemen slain!
Oh, well for the world when the White Men join
To prove their faith again!

Rudyard Kipling, 1899

* levin – lightning

The heyday of Empire. – The status of white men, as defined and accepted by white men.

From A CALL TO ACTION

A thousand years have passed away,
Cast back your glances on the scene,
Compare this England of today
With England as she once has been.

Fast beat the pulse of living then:
The hum of movement, throb of war
The rushing mighty sound of men
Reverberated loud and far.

They girt their loins up and they trod
The path of danger, rough and high;
For Action, Action was their god,
"Be up and doing," was their cry.

***

It needs no thought to understand,
No speech to tell, nor sight to see
That there has come upon our land
The curse of Inactivity.

***

We, dull and dreamy, stand and blink,
Forgetting glory, strength and pride,
– Half-listless watchers on the brink,
– Half-ruined victims of the tide.

***

Soon after lunch we take a chair,
And light a comforting cigar,
And muse with languid, mild, despair
Upon the state in which things are.

***

Yes, still we ponder, pry, infer,
Decide – and do not DO the same;
Still shrink from action, still prefer
To watch, instead of play, the game.

***

For we have utterly forgot
One great unanswerable fact:
We are not tools, but craftsmen – not
Machines to think, but men to Act!

A few have learned the lesson: they
Can never know the good they do;
They help their brethren on their way,
They fight and conquer:– all too few.

Charles Sorley, age 17.
Written at Marlborough College, October 1912

HOW HAD ENGLAND'S GERMAN FRIEND BECOME HER ENEMY?

> Mankind, we saw too late, had been guilty of an incalculable folly in permitting private men to make a profit out of the dreadful preparations for war. But the evil was started; the German imagination was captured and enslaved. On every other European country that valued its integrity was thrust the overwhelming necessity to arm and drill . . . Money was withdrawn from education, from social progress, from every kind of happiness; life was drilled and darkened.
>
> H G Wells [1]

The British people had become mentally prepared to think of the Germans as their natural enemies long before the outbreak of the war. In 1870/71 the British were shocked by the success of the German invasion of France and seizure of Alsace and Lorraine. The Germans had clearly become a power to be reckoned with. After this there were a number of international squabbles over colonial and trading activities. Whilst the British were the dominant coloniser of the world, the Germans were beginning to challenge British supremacy.

For example, in 1882 the Germans demanded that the British should cease competition with them to build railways in Turkey. In 1896 the Germans sent a well-publicised telegram to Paul Kruger, President of the Transvaal, congratulating him on resistance against the British. In Britain this caused a great public feeling of anger against the Germans. In 1890, when Germany's industry was already far more developed than Britain's, the German Emperor, Kaiser William II – nephew of King Edward VII and grandson of Queen Victoria – ordered the expansion of the German navy to overcome its great inferiority to the British navy. It is said that the move was made out of vanity but many in Britain saw it as an aggressive move and some sections of the British press encouraged this idea, demanding, and getting, vast amounts of money spent on building new battleships. This was especially so in 1909 and 1910 when the First Sea Lord, Admiral Sir John Fisher, fed a good deal of confidential information to his "beloved friend," J L Garvin, the influential editor of *The Observer*.

In spite of this, Britain still sought friendship with Germany. The two countries were each other's best customers, after all. In 1901 Joseph Chamberlain, Secretary for the Colonies, had sought an alliance with Germany and warned, "We should prefer adherence to Germany and

1   *The War That Will End War*, 1914, p 11.

The Triple Alliance. But if this proves impossible then we, too, contemplate a rapprochement with France and Russia."

Friendship with France did not exist at this time, but Chamberlain opened negotiations with the French. They had been particularly irritated by Britain's presence in Egypt which they wanted for themselves, but a deal was struck (April 1904) in which the French agreed to accept the British occupation of Egypt in return for Britain accepting the French "right" to occupy Morocco if she could achieve this. Edward VII's visit to Paris also helped to create a thaw in French-British relations.

German distrust of the British was fuelled by Admiral Sir John Fisher's public pronouncements about a preventive war against Germany and "smashing the German fleet." Could Germany do any other than prepare for war? – The Kaiser seemed to welcome the idea. On 31st October 1905 he wrote to Chancellor von Bulow, "First shoot the Socialists down, behead them, render them impotent – if necessary per bloodbath – and then war abroad!"[1]

The disputes between the two nations gave militarists and arms manufacturers on both sides opportunities to increase their influence and power. By 1914 H G Wells felt able to write,

> All Europe has for more than half a century bent more and more wearily under a perpetually increasing burden of armaments. For many years Europe has been an armed camp, with millions of men continually under arms, with the fear of war universally poisoning its life . . . with everything pinched but its equipment for war. It would be foolish to fix the blame for this on any particular nation . . . But we English do assert that it is the Government of the German Emperor which has for the last forty years taken the lead and forced the pace in these matters.[2]

George Bernard Shaw saw matters differently.

> We began it; and if they met us more than half-way, as they certainly did, it is not for us to reproach them.[3]

---

1   Quoted by Basil Liddell Hart, in *History of the First World War*, p12.
2   *The War That Will End War*, p74/75.
3   *Common Sense About The War*, p5.

FICTION, AND PRESS PROPAGANDA
BEFORE THE WAR

> We cannot shout for years that we are the boys of the bulldog
> breed, and then suddenly pose as gazelles.
>
> George Bernard Shaw[1]

The Germans had their censored and subsidised press and their
militarist propagandists who promoted the idea of a "British threat" and
the need to arm. These included Admiral von Tirpitz, General Frie-
drich von Bernhardi, and the historian, Heinrich von Treitschke.

In England a vigorous anti-German campaign began in 1871 with a work
of fiction. The story was *The Battle of Dorking* which was written
anonymously and enjoyed enormous popularity. It was the first suggestion that England's natural enemy was Germany and told of a German invasion of Britain. As the Germans had just invaded France it was
easy to make the threat seem real.

In 1914 Shaw recalled this publication. "The lead given by *The Battle
of Dorking,*" he wrote, "was taken up by articles in the daily press and
magazines," and he listed other contributors to the propaganda: Mr
Robert Blatchford, Mr Garvin, Admiral Maxse, Mr Newbolt, Mr
Rudyard Kipling, *The National Review*, Lord Roberts and Mr Wells
with his *War in the Air.* [2]

Other fiction contributed to the anti-German campaign. *How the
Germans Took London* appeared in 1900. In 1903 came Erskine
Childers' *Riddle of the Sands* which described a German plan to invade
England. In this, his hero, Davies, foresees the likelihood of a war with
Germany – "the war that he felt was bound to come". And, in a
passage revealing respect, admiration and fear of Germany, refers
to "the strength and wisdom of her rulers, her dream of a Colonial Empire . . . our great trade rival of the present, our great naval rival of the
future, she grows and strengthens and waits, an ever more formidable
factor in the future of our delicate network of Empire, sensitive as
gossamer to external shocks . . . and we aren't ready for her." His
scaremongering went further. "We have a small army, dispersed over
the whole globe, and administered on a gravely defective system . . .
co-operation between the army and navy is not studied and practised;
much less do there exist any plans, worthy of the name, for the
repulse of an invasion."

---

1   Also p5.
2   *Common Sense About The War*, p4.

In 1904, in Germany, *Der Weltkrieg,* which told of a German conquest of Britain, was a best seller.

From 1893 onwards, Alfred Harmsworth – who became Lord Northcliffe – used his newspapers to promote his views, including the ones he was most passionate about: the threat of Germany, and Britain's need to develop her defences, especially her navy. In 1905 Harmsworth commissioned William Le Queux to write a serial for the *Daily Mail*, entitled *The Invasion*. Harmsworth was able to provide assistance from his ardent pro-conscription friend, Earl Roberts, and the *Daily Mail*'s naval expert, H W Wilson. The serial was an enormous success. It was published in 1906 in book form, translated into twenty-seven languages, and sold over a million copies.

Le Queux opens his book with the words of a speech made in the House of Lords by Earl Roberts. "I sometimes despair of the country ever becoming alive to the danger and unpreparedness of our position until too late to prevent some fatal catastrophe. . . History tells us in the plainest terms that an Empire which cannot defend its own possessions must inevitably perish." Le Queux continued, "The purpose of this book is to illustrate our utter unpreparedness for war from a military standpoint; to show how England can successfully be invaded by Germany."

As a further step in his campaign which promoted hatred and fear of Germany, Harmsworth, in 1908, had taken on J L Garvin to edit the Sunday paper, *The Observer,* and boost its flagging sales. The target was to raise sales from 20,000 per issue to 50,000. Garvin had already established an outstanding reputation as a critic of Germany. In fact, he had actually been singled out by the Kaiser for criticism in 1905 when Garvin was a columnist for the *Daily Telegraph*, and also wrote under a number of pseudonyms for various other publications. The Kaiser accused him of "a continual and systematic poisoning of the wells" and "the most unheard of and shameless lies against Germany and colonies and against myself." [1]

In 1910 Harmsworth commissioned Robert Blatchford to write a series of articles for the *Daily Mail*. The first article began, "I write these articles because I believe that Germany is deliberately preparing to destroy the British Empire." [2] The campaign which Harmsworth, Garvin, Roberts, Le Queux and others waged was strikingly successful: considerable military preparations were made.

1   *The Observer and J L Garvin,* A M Gollin, p13.
2   *Keep the Home Fires Burning,* Cate Haste, p18.

Between 1905 and 1912 the Territorial Army, the Officers' Training Corps and the British Expeditionary Force were created. The B E F was specifically created and trained for a war in Europe. War plans were prepared which detailed all the actions that needed to be taken by every Government department in the event of a war. "Mobilisation was frequently practised from 1908 onwards and mobilisation tables, railway timetables and shipping dispositions constantly revised and improved in the light of experience." [1]

The incessant promotion of anti-German ideas over many years created indelible impressions in the minds of the British public. People who, without newspapers and popular fiction, would have been indifferent to Germany were now filled with misgivings. The minds of people in Britain were thoroughly prepared to adopt a hostile attitude to Germany. When the German invasion of Belgium came it triggered an instant and overwhelming response. Suddenly, ideas which people had doubted for so long were, apparently, proved to be true. They were ready to believe the worst.

PACIFISM

There was an international pacifist movement, especially large in Germany, which might have acted and spoken more effectively against a European war; and international socialism might have ensured that the workers of all European nations would refuse to kill each other. But the press was not owned by pacifists, and, in the event, the leadership was unable to handle the situation with sufficient speed to achieve the mass-communication necessary. There were so very few days in which to react to a rapid chain of events that led to multiple declarations of war. And pacifist sentiments evaporated suddenly in the first days of August.

At the end of July 1914, in France, as war fever gripped the country, and three million reservists were called up to prepare for war, one of the most important and influential pacifist Socialist leaders, Jean Jaurès, was assassinated.

In keeping with the Resolution of the Socialist International Conference of 1907 Keir Hardie, the first English Socialist member of Parliament, addressed a rally in Trafalgar Square calling for a general strike if war were declared. The appeal of patriotism, racial hatred, and war, however, far outweighed the appeal of workers of the world uniting in peace.

1   *Britain and the Great War 1914-1918,* J M Bourne.

2

WHAT ENGLAND WANTS IS A WAR

Punch, 5 August 1914

Many people would sooner die than think. –

Bertrand Russell.

THE RUSH TO WAR

If human beings were truly rational they would think long and hard before embarking on anything so costly, in terms of life and resources, as a war. They would pursue to the utmost extremity their efforts to settle disputes without resorting to war. Strangely, though, human beings, even with modern awareness of the dangers of war, seem actually keen to get involved in military aggression. Those who remember the Falklands War will recall how in 1982 not one person in a thousand in Britain could confidently say where the Falkland Islands were – yet when the British task force landed in defence of the 1,800 Falkland Islanders, 8,000 miles from Britain, a London Weekend Television poll showed that seventy-six per cent of the population favoured the assault and fifty-three per cent considered that a successful operation was worth Britain sustaining heavy casualties.

Four days after the outbreak of the Gulf War, in January 1991, *The Sunday Times* reported that eighty per cent of of those questioned in their survey were in favour of Britain fighting on behalf of Kuwait, and sixty per cent believed the liberation of Kuwait was worth the loss of the lives of British servicemen.

A pro-war mood developed within Britain with similar astonishing speed at the outbreak of the First World War, before most people were aware of the events that led to the declaration of war, and certainly before they had begun to imagine the consequences. On 23rd July 1914 the Austro-Hungarian government sent an ultimatum to Serbia. On 28th July Austro-Hungary, without justification, declared war on Serbia. On 30th July Russia decided to move armies up to its western borders as a gesture of solidarity with the Serbs. Germany offered, in return for British neutrality, to refrain, in the event of victory, from annexing French territory in Europe, and similarly pledged to respect Dutch and Belgian integrity. Germany then took fright at Russian troop movements and declared war on Russia on 1st August. At this time Edward Grey, the British Foreign Secretary, urged that Britain should remain neutral. On the 2nd, Germany decided to put into action a plan prepared more than a decade earlier to attack France by advancing through Belgium. This was "necessary" because France had a treaty with Russia and if Russia invaded Germany then France would be sure to come to the aid of her ally. Hence the need for a pre-emptive strike against France. Because of international agreements, guaranteeing the neutrality of Belgium, Britain declared war on Germany at 11.05pm on 4th August. – There were other motives, too, behind Britain's declaration of war.

Thus, in four days, Britain moved from neutrality to what was recognised as "the greatest catastrophe that has ever befallen the continent of Europe at one blow." The words are Sir Edward Grey's, quoted in *The Times* of 1st August 1914. On the same page *The Times* acknowledged that "The conflict which seems to be at hand must have worldwide results, and cannot, in any sense be regarded as affecting the Continent of Europe alone."

The Nation, a liberal weekly newspaper, reflected what it saw of public opinion. On Saturday 1st August it said, "There has been no crisis in which the public opinion of the British people has been so definitely opposed to war as it is at this moment." Yet one week later it said, "There are great masses of opinion in this country which hoped that this country might have avoided intervention. But the feeling is unanimous that the struggle must now be carried on with the utmost energy, not indeed until Germany is crushed, but until German aggression is defeated and German militarism broken."

It is doubtful if the public at large had really grasped what the few days of international yo-yo diplomacy meant. Vera Brittain, a member of an educated middle-class family, remarked in her autobiography that on the 3rd August she considered that, "the events in the newspapers seemed too incredible to be taken seriously," and went out to play tennis.

The New Age (a weekly review of politics, literature and art) warned, a few weeks later that, "We should not, of course, think of turning to the daily press for anything but the most distorted reflection of the mind of the country. The art of suggesting the false and suppressing the true is carried to its highest degree of perfection in the newspapers of London. But, while the papers only pretend to interpret the spirit of the people, they do set forth in grim earnest the beliefs, desires and prejudices of what we may, for the sake of convenience, call the governing classes."

John Galsworthy, popular novelist and member of the "governing classes" showed in his diary how many of the more politically aware reacted to the start of the war, though his pacifist inclinations were probably not typical.

> Monday August 3rd . . . a miserable anxious day, ourselves hovering on the verge of this war. The question of Belgian neutrality to the fore. If Germany will not respect it we shall be in. I hate and abhor war of all kinds, I despise and I loathe it. And the thought of the million daily acts of its violence and hateful brutishness keeps riving my soul.

> Tuesday August 4th . . . We are in! . . . The horror of the thing keeps coming over one in waves; and all happiness has gone out of life. I can't keep still and I can't work . . . If this war is not the death of Christianity it will be odd.

> Being personally of a humane and peaceful and more or less contemplative composition, I feel in it all that is antagonistic to myself and consequently hateful to me. Which feeling does not, however, blind me to the recognition that certain guarantees laboriously secured (as they thought) by men for their common advance towards unattainable Perfection – such as Treaty Rights and Decency towards the Weak – have got to be fought for when they are commonly assailed. And so to me the war is for England a hateful expedient to avoid an even more hateful end . . . If I weren't married and old and blind and bald and game in the shoulder I believe these atrocities would make me go and forswear all my convictions and commit some.[1]

He was 47 at the outbreak of the war.

Might cannot be right

For Galsworthy, as for most Englishmen, what offended him most was the dreadful injustice of a small, inoffensive country being bullied by an army, five million strong, highly trained, and superbly equipped. He wrote:

> The impossibility of considering any Peace proposals now is the impossibility of allowing the semblance of a German military

1   Quoted by D G Wright in *The Great War and Government Propaganda* in *Literature and History*, VIII, Spring, 1978, p84, 85.

victory to go forth into the world and down the ages as the
victory of 'Might is Right.'₁

BRAVO, BELGIUM!

This cartoon encapsulates the British perception of Germany as the big bully and
Belgium as the brave little victim. – *Punch* ,12 August 1914.

1   Galsworthy, quoted by Wright, p86.

In *Punch* on 5th August was a satirical story by A. A. Milne, entitled *Armageddon*. It was from the mouth of his character Porkins, in the bar of his golf club, that he put the words, "What England wants is a war. (Another whisky and soda, waiter.) We're getting flabby . . . The lower classes seem to have no sense of discipline nowadays. We want a war to brace us up." By the end of the story (one year later) the hundred thousandth English soldier had been killed. – Apparently it wasn't just the Foreign Secretary who knew what the horrific consequences of the war might be.

In the first week of August, Owen Seaman, the editor of *Punch*, had not clarified his response to the war, for this was the last note of criticism of it that occurred in *Punch*'s pages. From the next issue onwards *Punch* adopted a policy of solid support for the war. It encouraged enlistment by making light of the soldiers' "hardships," and preaching the necessity and righteousness of the war.

THE FLOOD OF PRO-WAR VERSE BEGINS

The first jolly angry verse of the war to appear in print was William Watson's *To the Troubler of the World,* which appeared in *The Times* on 6th August, followed quickly by the lofty patriotism of Bridges' *Wake Up England*, and Binyon's *Now in Thy Splendour*. – The tone of the press was set, and the flood of verse had begun.

TO THE TROUBLER OF THE WORLD

At last we know you, War-lord. You, that flung
The gauntlet down, fling down the mask you wore,
Publish your heart, and let its pent hate pour,
You that had God for ever on your tongue.
We are old in war, and if in guile we are young,
Young also is the spirit that evermore
Burns in our bosom ev'n as heretofore,
Nor are these thews unbraced, these nerves unstrung.
We do not with God's name make wanton play;
We are not on such easy terms with Heaven;
But in Earth's hearing we can verily say,
"Our hands are pure; for peace, for peace we have
striven."
And not by Earth shall he be soon forgiven
Who lit the fire accurst that flames today.

William Watson,
The Times, 6 August 1914

WAKE UP, ENGLAND

Thou careless, awake!
Thou peace-maker, fight!
Stand, England, for honour,
And God guard the Right!

Thy mirth lay aside,
Thy cavil and play:
The foe is upon thee,
And grave is the day.

The monarch Ambition
Hath harnessed his slaves;
But the folk of the Ocean
Are free as the waves.

For Peace thou art armed
Thy Freedom to hold:
Thy Courage as iron,
Thy Good-faith as gold.

Through Fire, Air, and Water
Thy trial must be:
But they that love life best
Die gladly for thee.

The Love of their mothers
Is strong to command:
The fame of their fathers
Is might to their hand.

Much suffering shall cleanse thee:
But thou through the flood
Shalt win to Salvation,
To Beauty through blood.

Up, careless, awake!
Ye peacemakers, Fight!
ENGLAND STANDS FOR HONOUR.
GOD DEFEND THE RIGHT!

Robert Bridges,
The Times, 8 August 1914

NOW IN THY SPLENDOUR

Now in thy splendour go before us,
Spirit of England, ardent-eyed!
Enkindle this dear earth that bore us,
In the hour of peril purified.

The cares we hugged drop out of vision,
Our hearts with deeper thoughts dilate.
We step from days of sour division
Into the grandeur of our fate.

For us the glorious dead have striven;
They battled that we might be free.
We to that living cause are given,
We arm for men that are to be.

Among the nations noblest chartered,
England recalls her heritage.
With her is that which is not bartered,
Which force can neither quell nor cage.

For her immortal stars are burning,
With her, the hope that's never done,
The seed that's in the Spring's returning,
The very flower that seeks the sun.

We fight the fraud that feeds desire on
Lies, in a lust to enslave or kill,
The barren creed of blood and iron,
Vampire of Europe's wasted will.

Endure, O Earth! and thou, awaken,
Purged by this dreadful winnowing-fan,
O wronged, untameable, unshaken
Soul of divinely suffering man!

Laurence Binyon, *The Times*, 11 August 1914

PRO PATRIA*

England, in this great fight to which you go
Because where Honour calls you, go you must,
Be glad, whatever comes, at least to know
You have your quarrel just.

Peace was your care; before the nations' bar
Her cause you pleaded and her ends you sought
But not for her sake, being what you are,
Could you be bribed and bought.

Others may spurn the pledge of land to land,
May with the brute sword stain a gallant past;
But by the seal to which *you* set your hand,
Thank God, you still stand fast!

Forth, then, to front that peril of the deep
With smiling lips and in your eyes the light,
Stedfast and confident, of those who keep
Their storied scutcheon bright.

And we, whose burden is to watch and wait –
High-hearted ever, strong in faith and prayer,
We ask what offering we may consecrate,
What humble service share?

To steel our souls against the lust of ease;
To find our welfare in the general good;
To hold together, merging all degrees
In one wide brotherhood;-

To teach that he who saves himself is lost;
To bear in silence though our hearts may bleed;
To spend ourselves, and never count the cost,
For others' greater need;-

To go our quiet ways, subdued and sane;
To hush all vulgar clamour of the street;
With level calm to face alike the strain
Of triumph or defeat;-

This be our part, for so we serve you best,
So best confirm their prowess and their pride,
Your warrior sons, to whom in this high test
Our fortunes we confide.

Owen Seaman,   *Punch*, 12 August 1914

*Pro patria - for one's country

AUGUST, 1914

How still this quiet cornfield is tonight!
By an intenser glow the evening falls,
Bringing, not darkness, but a deeper light;
Among the stalks a partridge covey calls.

The windows glitter on the distant hill;
Beyond the hedge the sheep-bells in the fold
Stumble on sudden music and are still;
The forlorn pinewoods droop above the wold.

An endless quiet valley reaches out
Past the blue hills into the evening sky;
Over the stubble, cawing, goes a rout
Of rooks from harvest, flagging as they fly.

So beautiful it is, I never saw
So great a beauty on these English fields,
Touched by the twilight's coming into awe,
Ripe to the soul and rich with summer's yields

   *   *   *   *   *

These homes, this valley spread below me here,
The rooks, the tilted stacks, the beasts in pen,
Have been the heartfelt things, past-speaking dear
To unknown generations of dead men,

Who, century after century, held these farms,
And, looking out to watch the changing sky,
Heard, as we hear, the rumours and alarms
Of war at hand and danger pressing nigh.

And knew, as we know, that the message meant
The breaking off of ties, the loss of friends,
Death, like a miser getting in his rent,
And no new stones laid where the trackway ends.

The harvest not yet won, the empty bin,
The friendly horses taken from the stalls,
The fallow on the hill not yet brought in,
The cracks unplastered in the leaking walls.

Yet heard the news, and went discouraged home,
And brooded by the fire with heavy mind,
With such dumb loving of the Berkshire loam
As breaks the dumb hearts of the English kind,

Then sadly rose and left the well-loved Downs,
And so by ship to sea, and knew no more
The fields of home, the byres, the market towns,
Nor the dear outline of the English shore,

But knew the misery of the soaking trench,
The freezing in the rigging, the despair
In the revolting second of the wrench
When the blind soul is flung upon the air,

And died (uncouthly, most) in foreign lands
For some idea but dimly understood
Of an English city never built by hands
Which love of England prompted and made good.

*   *   *   *   *

If there be any life beyond the grave,
It must be near the men and things we love,
Some power of quick suggestion how to save,
Touching the living soul as from above.

An influence from the Earth from those dead hearts
So passionate once, so deep, so truly kind,
That in the living child the spirit starts,
Feeling companioned still, not left behind.

Surely above these fields a spirit broods
A sense of many watchers muttering near
Of the lone Downland with the forlorn woods
Loved to the death, inestimably dear.

A muttering from beyond the veils of Death
From long-dead men, to whom this quiet scene
Came among blinding tears with the last breath,
The dying soldier's vision of his queen.

All the unspoken worship of those lives
Spent in forgotten wars at other calls
Glimmers upon these fields where evening drives
Beauty like breath, so gently darkness falls.

Darkness that makes the meadows holier still,
The elm-trees sadden in the hedge, a sigh
Moves in the beech-clump on the haunted hill,
The rising planets deepen in the sky,

And silence broods like spirit on the brae,
A glimmering moon begins, the moonlight runs
Over the grasses of the ancient way
Rutted this morning by the passing guns.

John Masefield

VERITAS VICTRIX*

The Mill of Lies is loud,
Whose overseer, Germania's Over-lord,
Hath overmuch adored
The Over-sword,
And shall be overthrown, with the overproud.

Praised be the overwatching Heavens, that though
Falsehood her blare of brass may pitch yet higher,
Truth hath her trumpets also, and these of gold,
And she can blow
Longer than any liar,
Fronting the sun, high on her mountains old.

William Watson, *The Times*, 10 September 1914

*Veritas Victrix - truth victorious

This American recruiting poster, from 1917, shows how the monster image of Germany crossed the Atlantic.

3

EARLY ENTHUSIASM FOR THE WAR

I find myself enthusiastic for this war against Prussian militarism. We are, I believe, assisting at the end of a vast intolerable oppression upon civilisation.

H G Wells[1]

There is an accumulative cruelty in a number of men, though none in particular is ill-natured.

Rudyard Kipling

At moments of crisis people's natural mode of expression is cliché.

John Galsworthy

War . . . can so easily be gilt with romance and heroism and solemn national duty and patriotism and the like by persons whose superficial literary and oratorical talent covers an abyss of Godforsaken folly.

George Bernard Shaw[2]

A War To End War

After long years of lethargy, our country was once more about to assert her authority as one of the greatest, some said THE greatest of world powers. We had been too modest, too lenient, they said, and see what had come of it; now, once for all, we must give such small upstarts a lesson . . . It was really a war to prevent future wars.

Flora Thompson[3]

1 *The War That Will End War,* p29.
2 *Common Sense About the War,* p24.
3 Writing about the Boer War (1899-1902) in *Heatherley.*

Crowds gather in Trafalgar Square to celebrate the news of the declaration of war.

A Sporting War From The Start

"England enters reluctantly upon the greatest of wars, united and resolved to do her duty. What the people of these islands now want is their
orders . . . Englishmen will be true to the great traditions of their race."
So said Sir Edward Grey, the English Foreign Secretary, in his speech
to Parliament announcing and justifying his commitment of Britain to
war. It was greeted rapturously. *The Morning Post* of August 4th reported,

> Members rose from their seats, cheered and cheered again, and
> wildly waved hats and handkerchiefs. It was as though a thrill of
> responsive sympathy had struck the whole House – a feeling that
> we really meant to "play the game" as it ought to be played and
> stand by our friends.

On the 5th, *The Morning Post* claimed, "Within a month from today
victory will have declared itself."

The Prime Minister's Statement

On 7th August, 1914, (three days after Britain joined the war)
Asquith, the Prime Minister, said in Parliament to loud cheers:

I do not think any nation ever entered into a great conflict –
and this is one of the greatest that history will ever know – with
a clearer conscience or stronger conviction that it is fighting not
for aggression, not for the maintenance of its own selfish ends,
but in defence of principles, the maintenance of which is vital
to the civilisation of the world.

We have a great duty to perform; we have a great truth to fulfil;
and I am confident Parliament and the country will enable us to
do it.

THE MOBILISATION OF PUBLIC OPINION

It *may* be a tremendous catastrophe in one sense, but in another
it is a huge step forward in human life. It is the end of forty years
of evil suspense. It is crisis and solution. . . Now suddenly we
face an epoch . . . This is the end and the begining of an age. This
is something far greater than the French Revolution or the Ref-
ormation . . . and we live in it.

Mr Britling in *Mr Britling Sees It Through* by H G Wells.[1]

It seems generally agreed to describe the state of mind in which
our nation has entered the struggle as one of cool and calm
determination. . . But it would be a mistake to ignore the intensity of feeling which is gathering, because it has not yet caught
up the swift current of events, and is not yet, as it were,
mobilised.

The Nation, 15 August 1914

It was not long, however, before public opinion was mobilised and a
wave of enthusiasm and patriotism swept the country. Newspapers,
posters, poetry, speeches and music hall songs proclaimed the need to
fight – and with minds already conditioned to the ideas of fighting,
and dying, and already seeing Germany as the enemy, there was a
flood of young men besieging the recruiting offices in an effort to join
the army.

---

1   Set in 1914; first published in 1916. Book 2, chapter 1, section 6.

Recruiting offices were overwhelmed with volunteers.

A MUSIC HALL SONG

. . .Now your country calls you
To play your part in war
And no matter what befalls you
We shall love you all the more.

So come and join the forces
As your fathers did before.
Oh we don't want to lose you
But we think you ought to go
For your king and your country
Both need you so.

We shall want you and miss you
But with all our might and main
We shall cheer you
Thank you, kiss you
When you come back again.

Another song proclaimed:

> We don't want to fight
> But by Jingo if we do,
> We've got the ships;
> We've got the men;
> We've got the money, too.

One soldier explained it this way:

> We had been brought up to believe that Britain was the best
> country in the world and we wanted to defend her.The history
> taught us at school showed that we were better than other people
> (didn't we always win the last war?) and now all the news was
> that Germany was the aggressor and we wanted to show the
> Germans what we could do.

> Private George Morgan,
> 16th Battalion, West Yorkshire Regiment[1]

Volunteers

Lord Kitchener who, as the newly appointed Minister for War, was put
in charge of recruiting a large army to fight the war, asked the country
to give him 100,000 volunteers. His advertisements billed the conflict
as "the greatest war in the history of the world."

Those who first rushed to join wondered if they would be in time. Everyone was sure of an easy victory. The newspapers encouraged recruiting with the confident prediction that it would "all be over by
Christmas."

Within about eighteen months Kitchener had not 100,000 volunteers,
but two million. Wars run, not on reason, but on adrenalin, base emotion, hype, and herd instinct.

HAPPY IS ENGLAND NOW

> There is not anything more wonderful
> Than a great people moving towards the deep
> Of an unguessed and unfeared future; nor
> Is aught so dear of all held dear before
> As the new passion stirring in their veins
> When the destroying Dragon wakes from sleep.

---

1   *Tommy Goes to War*, edited by Malcolm Brown. p21.

Happy is England now, as never yet!
And though the sorrows of the slow days fret
Her faithfullest children, grief itself is proud.
Ev'n the warm beauty of this spring and summer
That turns to bitterness turns then to gladness
Since for this England the beloved ones died.

Happy is England in the brave that die
For wrongs not hers and wrongs so sternly hers;
Happy in those that give, give, and endure
The pain that never the new years may cure;
Happy in all her dark woods, green fields, towns,
Her hills and rivers and her chafing sea.

Whate'er was dear before is dearer now.
There's not a bird singing upon his bough
But sings the sweeter in our English ears:
There's not a nobleness of heart, hand, brain,
But shines the purer; happiest is England now
In those that fight, and watch with pride and tears.

John Freeman, 1914

HAPPY ENGLAND

Now each man's mind all Europe is;
Courage and fear in dread array
Daze each true heart; O grave and wise,
Abide in hope the judgement day.

This war of millions in arms
In myriad replica we wage;
Unmoved, then, Soul by earth's alarms
The dangers of the dark engage.

Remember happy England: keep
For her bright cause thy latest breath.
Her peace that long hath lulled to sleep
May now exact the sleep of death.

Her woods and wilds, her loveliness,
With harvest now are richly at rest;
Safe in her isled securities
Thy children's heaven is her breast:

> O what a deep, contented night
> The sun from out her Eastern seas
> Would bring the dust which in her sight
> Had given its all for these!
>
> Walter de la Mare
> First published in *The Times Literary Supplement,*
> 27 August 1914.

Happy for Some

With day after day of blue skies and wonderful summer sunshine, in the golden summer of 1914, the English countryside was seen and enjoyed at its best. For poets with minds filled with such images it was easy to think of England as an ideal and idyllic country – and forget the short-comings.

The "land of the free" in 1914 had moved towards democracy, but no woman had the vote, and, of the men, only those who were house own-ers. In all, out of 25 million adults, only 8 million men had the vote.[1]

For the working class (about 17 million workers) hours were often long, wages poor, and conditions harsh. Improvements were gradually taking place, though. The Shop Hours Act, for example, guaranteed shop work-ers a minimumum of half a day's holiday each week.

There was a good deal of overcrowding in working class homes which often lacked basic amenities. Henry Asquith reckoned in 1913 that the country was short of between 100,000 and 120,000 houses. Few working class houses had their own water supply. In York, in a survey carried out in 1901 by Seebohm Rowntree, only one working class house in five had its own water supply – and bathrooms were practically unheard of in working class homes.[2]

From the start of the twentieth century unemployment had been growing in Britain. Widescale hardship was so apparent that charities were set up by the Lord Mayor of London and the Queen "to alleviate the suffer-ing of the poor, starving unemployed." On 1st January 1908 official statistics put the number of paupers in England and Wales at 928,671.[3]

---

1   *The Deluge, British Society and the First World War*, Arthur Marwick, p23.
2   Marwick, p24, 25.
3   *Ourselves, 1900-1930*, Irene Clephane, p40.

A Holy War

Robert Bridges wrote to *The Times* on 1st September declaring that the war was "primarily a holy war."

> Those who fight for them will fight for "the devil and all his works," and those who fight against them will be fighting in the holy cause of humanity and the law of love. If the advocacy of their bad principles and their diabolical conduct do not set the whole world against them, then the world is worse than I think. My belief is that there are yet millions of their own countrymen who have not bowed the knee to Satan, and who will be as much shocked as we are; and that this internal moral disruption will much hamper them.
>
> The infernal machine which has been scientifically preparing for the last 25 years is now on its wild career like one of Mr Wells's inventions, and wherever it goes it will leave desolation behind it and put all material progress back for at least half a century. There was never anything in the world worthier of extermination, and it is the plain duty of all civilised nations to unite to drive it back into its home and exterminate it there.

AUGUST 1914

Use me, ENGLAND,
In thine hour of need,
Let thy ruling
rule me now in deed.

Sons and brothers
Take for armoury,
All love's jewels.
Crushed, thy warpath be.

Thou has given
Joyous life and free,
Life whose joy now
Languishes for thee.

Give then, England,
If my life thou need,
Gift yet fairer,
Death, thy life to feed.

"By the author of *Charitesse.*"
First published in *The Times Literary Supplement*,
3 September 1914.

FALL IN

What will you lack, sonny, what will you lack
When the girls line up the street,
Shouting their love to the lads come back
From the foe they rushed to beat?

Will you send a strangled cheer to the sky
And grin till your cheeks are red?
But what will you lack when your mate goes by
With a girl who cuts you dead?

Where will you look, sonny, where will you look
When your children yet to be
Clamour to learn of the part you took
In the war that kept men free?
Will you say it was naught to you if France
Stood up for her foe or bunked?
But where will you look when they give the glance
That tells you they know you funked?

How will you fare, sonny, how will you fare
In the far-off winter night,
When you sit by the fire in an old man's chair
And your neighbours talk of the fight?
Will you slink away, as it were from a blow,
Your old head shamed and bent?
Or – say I was not with the first to go,
But I went, thank God, I went?

Why do they call, sonny, why do they call?
For the men who are brave and strong?
Is it naught to you if your country fall?
And Right is smashed by Wrong?
Is it football still and the picture show,
The pub and the betting odds,
When your brothers stand to the tyrant's blow
And England's call is God's?

Harold Begbie

GERMAN ROLE IN THE DEVELOPMENT OF WAR FEVER IN BRITAIN

The greatest stimulation for support for the war came from the biggest public relations blunder of all time – the German invasion of neutral Belgium and the brutal crushing of Belgian resistance.

International agreement on some aspects of conducting warfare had been reached in discussions at The Hague in 1907. By these "conventions" it was not allowable to move troops across neutral countries – which was Germany's first offence against Belgium. If such an act took place then resistance to such movements could not be regarded as hostile acts. The Germans did regard resistance as hostile acts.

The German Military Governor of Belgium, Field Marshal Baron von der Goltz, warned the citizens of Belgium that, "It is the stern necessity of war that the punishment for hostile acts falls, not only on the guilty, but on the innocent as well."

Later he warned, "In future, villages in the vicinity of places where railway and telegraph lines are destroyed will be punished without pity (whether they are guilty or not of the acts in question). With this in view hostages have been taken in all villages near the railway lines which are threatened by such attacks. Upon the first attempts to destroy lines of railway, telegraph or telephone, they will be immediately shot."[1]

He was speaking in early October, 1914, and was undoubtedly rather desperate: over 2000 miles of Belgian track (out of a total of 2,500 miles) had been wrecked, and 26,000 German construction workers were labouring to carry out repairs.

But reprisals had already started – including the execution in Dinant of 612 men, women and children on 23rd August.

British newspapers reported fully the plight of the Belgian people, but, as if the truth were not bad enough, they added numerous stories of atrocities which the Germans were supposed to have carried out – such as the spearing of babies, the cutting off of a woman's breasts, and children's hands.

The Gentle German,
by Edmund J Sullivan
in *The Kaiser's Garland*.

1   *First World War*, Martin Gilbert, p88.

It is no exaggeration to say that the invasion of Belgium shocked the nation and turned against the German people most of those who considered themselves to be pacifists, and those who desired friendship with them.

WRITERS ENLISTED IN THE SECRET WAR PROPAGANDA BUREAU

Clearly, writers in the same frame of mind as John Galsworthy and Robert Bridges needed little encouragement to write supporting the war effort. However, the Government did not leave the matter to chance. At the end of August Sir Edward Grey and Lloyd George took the initiative in setting up a department of propaganda, The Secret War Propaganda Bureau, whose offices were established in Wellington House, Buckingham Gate, London. The Bureau was put in the hands of Charles Masterman, a member of the Cabinet.

One of his first ideas was to encourage sympathetic, famous, and influential writers to use their pens in support of the war effort and in particular to spread the "British viewpoint" in America where there was little understanding of the British Government's actions.

He called a meeting of "well-known men of letters" at Wellington House on 2nd September 1914. To this day no official departmental papers relating the activities of the Wellington House Propaganda Department are available in the Public Records Office, but from the personal papers of some participants quite a lot is known. Those present included Thomas Hardy (then 74), H G Wells, Arnold Bennett, John Galsworthy, John Masefield, Robert Bridges (the Poet Laureate), Conan Doyle, Owen Seaman (Editor of Punch), J M Barrie, G K Chesterton, Israel Zangwill, G M Trevelyan and Gilbert Murray. Rudyard Kipling, unable to attend, sent a message of support. Laurence Binyon was soon to be associated with the group.

From this distinguished literary gathering there was one significant absentee: George Bernard Shaw. He was far too clever, too independent and far too inclined to speak his mind to make the meeting positive and harmonious. He believed the Admiralty, the Foreign Office and Sir Edward Grey the Foreign Secretary had for years wanted a war with Germany. He was critical of both British and German militarism, although, having voiced his criticisms, he solidly backed the British war effort. "There is no alternative," he wrote.

Inspired by the meeting, many of those present rapidly set to work to provide the literary help requested by the Government. – Hardy's poem was quickly taken up by the British and American press: published in

The Times Literary Supplement, on 10th September, and *The New York Times* on 11th September.

MEN WHO MARCH AWAY
(Song of the Soldiers)

What of the faith and fire within us
Men who march away
Ere the barn-cocks say
Night is growing gray,
Leaving all that here can win us;
What of the faith and fire within us
Men who march away?

Is it a purblind prank, O think you,
Friend with the musing eye,
Who watch us stepping by
With doubt and dolorous sigh?
Can much pondering so hoodwink you!
Is it a purblind prank, O think you,
Friend with the musing eye?

Nay. We well see what we are doing,
Though some may not see–
Dalliers as they be–
England's need are we;
Her distress would leave us rueing:
Nay. We well see what we are doing,
Though some may not see!

In our heart of hearts believing
Victory crowns the just,
And that braggarts must
Surely bite the dust,
Press we to the field ungrieving,
In our heart of hearts believing
Victory crowns the just.

Hence the faith and fire within us
Men who march away
Ere the barn-cocks say
Night is growing gray,
Leaving all that here can win us;
Hence the faith and fire within us
Men who march away.

Thomas Hardy, 5 September 1914

Crowds turned out to cheer the soldier heroes on their way.

FOR THE FALLEN

With proud thanksgiving, a mother for her children,
England mourns for her dead across the sea.
Flesh of her flesh they were, spirit of her spirit,
Fallen in the cause of the free.

Solemn the drums thrill: Death august and royal
Sings sorrow up into immortal spheres.
There is music in the midst of desolation
And a glory that shines upon our tears.

They went with songs to the battle: they were young,
Straight of limb, true of eye, steady and aglow.
They were staunch to the end against odds uncounted:
They fell with their faces to the foe.

They shall grow not old, as we that are left grow old:
Age shall not weary them, nor the years condemn.
At the going down of the sun and in the morning
We will remember them.

They mingle not with their laughing comrades again;
They sit no more at familiar tables of home;
They have no lot in our labour of the day-time;
They sleep beyond England's foam.

But where our desires are and our hopes profound,
Felt as a well-spring that is hidden from sight,
To the innermost heart of their own land they are known
As the stars are known to the Night;

As the stars that shall be bright when we are dust,
Moving in marches upon the heavenly plain;
As the stars that are starry in the time of our darkness,
To the end, to the end they remain.

Lawrence Binyon
Published in *The Times*, 21 September, 1914.

FOR ALL WE HAVE AND ARE

For all we have and are,
For all our children's fate,
Stand up and take the war.
The Hun is at the gate!
Our world has passed away,
In wantonness o'erthrown.
There is nothing left today
But steel and fire and stone!

Though all we knew depart,
The old Commandments stand:–
"In courage kept your heart,
In strength lift up your hand."

Once more we hear the word
That sickened earth of old:–
"No law except the Sword
Unsheathed and uncontrolled."
Once more it knits mankind,
Once more the nations go
To meet and break and bind
A crazed and driven foe.

Comfort, content, delight,
The age's slow-bought gain,
They shrivelled in a night.
Only ourselves remain

To face the naked days
In silent fortitude,
Through perils and dismays
Renewed and re-renewed.

Though all we made depart,
The old Commandments stand:–
"In patience keep your heart,
In strength lift up your hand."

No easy hope or lies
Shall bring us to our goal,
But iron sacrifice
Of body, will, and soul.
There is but one task for all –
One life for each to give.
What stands if Freedom fall?
Who dies if England live?

Rudyard Kipling, 1914

Official employment for famous writers

From the Government's point of view the Wellington House meeting proved highly successful. Most of the writers present supported the Government throughout the war. Some went on the Government's payroll. John Masefield was sent on a pro-war lecture tour of America and was paid to write *Gallipoli*, mainly with the idea of influencing American readers. (He also, good man that he was, served with the Red Cross in France and on board a hospital ship at Gallipoli.) Newbolt was commissioned to write the naval history of the war. Conan Doyle was commissioned to write *British Campaigns in France and Flanders* which took him six volumes to cover. Robert Nichols worked for the Ministry of Information. Government influence on the 400 million people of the colonies was taken care of by Rudyard Kipling. Arnold Bennett, turning his prolific journalist's pen to whole-hearted patriotism was fed ideas and information by Wellington House and later became Director of British propaganda to France. For the last few weeks in the war he was in charge of Britain's entire propaganda organisation.

Whilst H G Wells did not maintain his uncritical support throughout the war he was certainly fulsome at the outset. Even before the Wellington House meeting (but following an evening with Lloyd George), he had written his article famously entitled, *The War That Will End War*. In September he expanded this to a pamphlet and in October published it in book form for sale in Britain and the United States. It went through three printings that month. In it he declared:

> It was possible to argue that to be prepared for war was the way to keep the peace. But now everyone knows better. The war has come. Preparation has exploded . . . Our men must die, in heaps, in thousands; we cannot delude ourselves with dreams of easy victories.
>
> Out of it all must come one universal resolve. . . there must be no more buying and selling of guns and warships and war machines. There must be no more gain in arms.
>
> The Krupp concern and the tawdry Imperialism of Berlin are linked like thief and receiver. . . It is from Berlin that the intolerable pressure to arm and still to arm has come . . .It was useless to dream even of disarmament while these people could still go on making the material uncontrolled, waiting for the moment of national passion, feeding the national mind with fears and suspicions through their subsidised Press.
>
> The defeat of Germany may open the way to disarmament and peace throughout the earth . . . Never was war so rigthteous as war against Germany now. Never has any state in the world so clamoured for punishment. . . Every sword that is drawn against Germany is a sword drawn for peace.

Wells's title – *The War That Will End War* – became a catch-phrase, a major justifying idea for the war. George Bernard Shaw had a pithy response to its central idea. "Disarmament is all nonsense: nobody is going to disarm after this experience."

In 1917 the work of the Bureau was taken over by a new "Department of Information". H G Wells worked with its head, the novelist, Colonel John Buchan, and then in 1918, with Lord Beaverbrook (later to become the owner of the *Daily Express*) at the Ministry of Information, which took over from Buchan's Department.

Thomas Hardy

Thomas Hardy did his best to support the war effort by writing patriotic verse. Some idea of the nature and strength of his feelings may be gleaned from the fact that, with Henry Newbolt, Edmund Gosse and others, he joined the "Fight for Right Movement" whose manifesto stated,

> The spirit of the Movement is essentially the spirit of Faith: Faith in the good of man; Faith therefore in ourselves, Faith in the righteousness of our Cause, Faith in the ultimate triumph of Right; but with this Faith the understanding that Right will

only win through the purification, the efforts and the sacrifices of men and women who mean to make it prevail.[1]

Hardy was determined to give the war his full support. At the age of
seventy-four, sometimes, easily to Hardy poetry came not. Yet onward
he wrote it. No soothe was his intent.

ENGLAND TO GERMANY IN 1914

"O England, may God punish thee!"
– Is it that Teuton genius flowers
Only to breathe malignity
Upon its friend of earlier hours?
– We have eaten your bread, you have eaten ours,
We have loved your burgs, your pines' green moan,
Fair Rhine-stream, and its storied towers;
Your shining souls of deathless dowers
Have won us as they were our own:

We have nursed no dreams to shed your blood,
We have matched your might not rancorously
Save a flushed few whose blatant mood
You heard and marked as well as we
To tongue not in their country's key;
But yet you cry with face aflame,
"O England, may God punish thee!"
And foul in onward history,
And present sight, your ancient name.

Thomas Hardy, Autumn 1914

A RESPONSE TO BELGIUM'S AGONY

Over a million refugees fled from Belgium in the first two months of
the war. A hundred thousand arrived in Britain.

ON THE BELGIAN EXPATRIATION

I dreamt that people from the Land of Chimes
Arrived one autumn morning with their bells,
To hoist them on the towers and citadels
Of my own country, that the musical rhymes

---

1   Imperial War Museum pamphlet, *The Fight for Right Movement.*

Rung by them into space at meted times
Amid the market's daily stir and stress,
And the night's empty star-lit silentness,
Might solace souls of this and kindred climes.

Then I awoke; and lo, before me stood
The visioned ones, but pale and full of fear:
From Bruges they came, and Antwerp, and Ostend.

No carillons in their train. Foes of mad mood
Had shattered these to shards amid the gear
Of ravaged roof, and smouldering gable-end.

Thomas Hardy, 18 October 1914

AN APPEAL TO AMERICA ON BEHALF OF THE BELGIAN DESTITUTE

Seven millions stand
Emaciate, in that ancient Delta-land:–
We here, full-charged with our own maimed and dead
And coiled in throbbing conflicts slow and sore,
Can poorly soothe these ails unmerited
Of souls forlorn upon the facing shore!–
Where naked, gaunt, in endless band on band
Seven millions stand.

No man can say
To your great country that, with scant delay,
You must, perforce, ease them in their loud need:
We know that nearer first your duty lies;
But – is it much to ask that you let plead
Your lovingkindness with you – wooing-wise –
Albeit that aught you owe, and must repay,
No man can say?

Thomas Hardy, December 1914

Belgian refugees arriving at Victoria Station, London, October 1914.

Ford Madox Ford's poem, *Antwerp,* T S Eliot regarded as the best poem of the First World War.

ANTWERP

1

Gloom!
An October like November;
August a hundred thousand hours
And all September,
A hundred thousand, dragging sunlit days,
And half October like a thousand years . . .
And doom!
That then was Antwerp . . . In the name of God,
How could they do it?
Those souls that usually dived
Into the dirty caverns of mines;
Who usually hived
In whitened hovels; under ragged poplars;
Who dragged muddy shovels, over the grassy mud,
Lumbering to work over the grassy sods . . .

Those men there, with the appearances of clods
Were the bravest men that a usually listless priest of God
Ever shrived . . .
And it is not for us to make them an anthem.
If we found words there would come no wind that would fan them
To a tune that the trumpets might blow it,
Shrill through the heaven that's ours or yet Allah's
Or the wide halls of any Valhallas.
We can make no such anthem. So that all that is ours
For inditing in sonnets, pantoums, elegiacs, or lays
Is this:
 "In the name of God, how could they do it?"

II

For there is no new thing under the sun,
Only this uncomely man with a smoking gun
In the gloom . . .
What the devil will he gain by it?
Digging a hole in the mud and standing all day in the rain by it
Waiting his doom,
The sharp blow, the swift outpouring of the blood,
Till the trench of grey mud
Is turned to a brown purple drain by it.
Well, there have been scars
Won in many wars . . .
Punic, Lacedaemonian, wars of Napoloen, wars for faith, wars for
     honour, for love, for possession,
But this Belgian man in his ugly tunic,
His ugly round cap, shooting on, in a sort of obsession,
Overspreading his miserable land,
Standing with his wet gun in his hand . . .
Doom!
He finds that in a sudden scrimmage,
And lies, an unsightly lump on the sodden grass . . .
An image that shall take long to pass!

III

For the white-limbed heroes of Hellas ride by upon their horses
For ever through our brains.
The heroes of Cressy ride by upon their stallions;
And battalions and battalions and battalions –
The Old Guard, the Young Guard, the men of Minden and of
Waterloo,
Pass, for ever staunch,
Stand for ever true;

And the small man with the large paunch,
And the grey coat, and the large hat, and the hands behind
the back,
Watches them pass
In our minds for ever . . .
But that clutter of sodden corpses
On the sodden Belgian grass –
That is a strange new beauty.

IV

With no especial legends of marchings or triumphs or duty,
Assuredly that is the way of it,
The way of beauty . . .
And that is the highest word you can find to say of it.
For you cannot praise it with words
Compounded of lyres and swords,
But the thought of the gloom and the rain
And the ugly coated figure, standing beside a drain,
Shall eat itself into your brain.
And that shall be an honourable word,
As honourable as the mention of the many-chorded lyre,
And his old coat shall seem as beautiful as the fabrics woven
in Tyre.

V

And what in the world did they bear it for?
I don't know.
And what in the world did they dare it for?
Perhaps that is not for the likes of me to understand.
They could very well have watched a hundred legions go
Over the fields and between their cities
Down into more southerly regions.
They could very well have let the legions pass through their
woods,
And have kept their lives and their wives and their children
and cattle and goods.
I don't understand.
Was it just love of their land?
Oh poor dears! Can any man so love his land?
Give them a thousand thousand pities
And rivers and rivers of tears
To wash off the blood from the cities of Flanders.

VI

This is Charing Cross;
It is midnight;
There is a great crowd
And no light. A great crowd, all black that hardly whispers aloud.
Surely, that is a dead woman – a dead mother!
She has a dead face;
She is dressed all in black;
She wanders to the bookstall and back,
At the back of the crowd;
And back again and again back,
She sways and wanders.

This is Charing Cross;
It is one o'clock.
There is still a great crowd, and very little light;
Immense shafts of shadows over the black crowd
That hardly whispers aloud . . .
And now! . . That is another dead mother,
And there is another and another and another . . .
And little children, all in black,
All with dead faces, waiting in all the waiting-places,
Wandering from the doors of the waiting-room
In the dim gloom.
These are the women of Flanders.
They await the lost.
They await the lost that shall never leave the dock;
They await the lost that shall never again come by the train
To the embraces of all these women with dead faces;
They await the lost who lie dead in trench and barrier and foss,
In the dark of the night.
This is Charing Cross; it is one of the clock;
There is very little light.

There is so much pain.

L'ENVOI
And it was for this that they endured this gloom;
This October like November,
And August like a hundred thousand hours,
And that September,
A hundred thousand dragging sunlit days,
And half October like a thousand years . . .
Oh poor dears!

Ford Madox Ford

A REMARKABLE LETTER OF SUPPORT FOR THE WAR

On 18th September 1914 a striking letter appeared in *The Times*. Its heading:

BRITAIN'S DESTINY AND DUTY
Declaration by Authors
A Righteous War

It was signed by fifty-two writers, and was another outcome of the Wellington House meeting where its content was discussed. The letter had been prepared by Gilbert Murray, (who had advocated neutrality as the war approached). The letter had been checked by Owen Seaman and Anthony Hawkins. – It began,

> The undersigned writers, comprising amongst them men and women of the most divergent political and social views, some of them having been for years ardent champions of good will towards Germany, and many of them extreme advocates of peace, are nevertheless agreed that Great Britain could not without dishonour have refused to take part in the present war.

It concluded,

> Many of us have dear friends in Germany, many of us regard German culture with the highest respect and gratitude; but we cannot admit that any nation has the right by brute force to impose its culture upon other nations, nor that the iron military beaurocracy of Prussia represents a higher form of human society than the free constitutions of Western Europe.

> Whatever the world-destiny of Germany may be, we in Great Britain are ourselves conscious of a destiny and a duty. That destiny and duty, alike for us and for all the English-speaking race, call upon us to uphold the rule of common justice between civilised peoples, to defend the rights of small nations and to maintain the free and law-abiding ideals of Western Europe against the rule of "Blood and Iron" and domination of the whole Continent by a military caste.

> For these reasons and others the undersigned feel bound to support the cause of the Allies with all their strength, with a full conviction of its righteousness and with a deep sense of its vital import to the future of the world.

The signatories included:

J M Barrie, Arnold Bennett, Laurence Binyon, Robert Bridges, Arthur Conan Doyle, H A I Fisher, John Galsworthy, H Rider Haggard, Thomas Hardy, Jerome K Jerome, Rudyard Kipling, John Masefield, Gilbert Murray, Henry Newbolt, Eden Phillpotts, Arthur Pinero, Arthur Quiller-Couch, Owen Seaman, G M Trevelyan, H G Wells, Israel Zangwill.

RUPERT BROOKE – THE HERO POET

"All that one could wish England's noblest sons to be"

Rupert Brooke, in 1914, was a greatly admired young man. He was good-looking, charming, charismatic. Many who met him testify to his striking physical presence. "A young Apollo", Frances Cornford called him. He had friends in high places: Winston Churchill, First Lord of the Admiralty; and he spent a week over Christmas 1914 recovering from flu at 10 Downing Street, being nursed by the Prime Minister's daughter. He was the most famous young poet of his time. Shortly after the end of the year he finished his set of five sonnets. These resounding, assertive poems glorified England and the idea of dying for England. Within a few months they were to rank among the most praised and widely read poems of their day.

In spite of his apparently boundless confidence in the justness of the British cause and the joyful opportunity that the war offered for heroic self-sacrifice – which was Brooke's public image, his feelings when war was declared were quite different. The outbreak of war threw him into mental and emotional confusion. His essay, *An Unusual Young Man*,[1] supposedly about a friend, but clearly about himself, is revealing. He acknowledged that his kindly feelings towards Germany, which he had developed during his time there, must now be turned into hatred, and he realised "with increasing resentment . . . that he might have to volunteer for military training and service." – "He vaguely imagined a series of heroic feats, vast enterprise, and the applause of crowds." – He felt a reverence for England and the landscapes he knew, and imagined himself looking down on them to the accompaniment of hymn tunes.

"To his great disgust, the most commonplace sentiments found utterance in him. At the same time he was extraordinarily happy." He was also, "feeling a little frightened, and more than a little unwell . . . He felt the triumphant helplessness of a lover. . ."

---

1   *The New Statesman*, 29 August, 1914.

He associated his feeling of "ignorant helplessness" with two past crises in his life: the death of his father, and the mental breakdown that occurred when he believed his relationship with his girlfriend, Katherine Cox, had come to an end. "His mind fluttered irascibly . . . and wandered out for a time into fantasy. . . Now, as then, his mind had been completely divided into two parts; the upper running about aimlessly from one half-relevant thought to another, the lower unconscious half, labouring with some profound and unknowable change."

In early August, along with several university friends, he put his name down to join the Artists' Rifles, but on August 24th he dropped out.

In a letter, dated 15th-17th August, to Lady Eileen Wellesley he described his doubts this way,

> I find in myself two natures. . . There's half my heart which is normal and English . . . But the other half is a wanderer and a solitary, selfish, unbound, and doubtful. Half my heart is of England, the rest is looking for some home I haven't yet found. So, when this war broke, there was part of my nature and desires that said, 'Let me alone. What's all this bother? I want to work. I've got ends I desire to reach. If I'd wanted to be a soldier I should have been one. But I've found myself other dreams.'

For a time he tried to get a job as a war correspondent and then started "offering himself with a vague persistence" to the army, getting himself put on waiting lists.

Winston Churchill, who was then First Lord of the Admiralty, personally encouraged him to join the Royal Naval Division, which he did on 27th September. Shortly after this he went with the navy and witnessed the unsuccessful defence of Antwerp against the Germans.

For seven days in October 1914 Rupert Brooke was in Belgium with his brigade of the Royal Naval Division, virtually untrained but in charge of a platoon. Their mission was to assist the Belgians in the defence of Antwerp. On the 7th they moved close to the action near Fort Number Seven. The Germans were using some of their biggest artillery pieces to destroy the city – firing 12", 16" and 17" shells. Neither the Belgians nor the English could match this fire-power and within a matter of hours Brooke's brigade was ordered to withdraw,– and, in fact, retire from the scene and return to England.

He had been, in his own words, "barely under fire," but he had witnessed a city being destroyed, and a civilian population in desparate flight as his brigade overtook the refugees to catch trains to Bruges.

He wrote to his friend, Cathleen Nesbitt:

> We got to a place called Vieux Dieux . . . passing refugees and Belgian soldiers by millions. Every mile the noise got louder, immense explosions and detonations . . . five or six thousand British troops, a lot of Belgians, guns going through, transport wagons, motor cyclists. . . staff officers. . . An extraordinary thrilling confusion.

To another friend, Russell Loines, he wrote, at Christmas, 1914:

> Antwerp that night was like several different kinds of hell – the broken houses, the dead horses lit up by an infernal glare. The refugees were the worst sight. The German policy of frightfulness has succeeded so well, that out of that city of half a million, when it was decided to surrender Antwerp, not ten thousand would stay . . . I'll never forget that white-faced, endless procession in the night . . . the old men crying, and the women with hard drawn faces. What a crime!
> It's all a terrible tragedy. And yet, in it's details, it's great fun. And – apart from the tragedy – I've never felt happier or better in my life than in those days in Belgium. And now I've a feeling of an anger of a seen wrong – Belgium – to make me happier and more resolved in my work. I know that whatever happens, I'll be doing some good, fighting to prevent *that*.

Unfortunately for Brooke, during his time in Belgium, he experienced a serious misfortune – a manuscript he was working on went missing. However, he claimed compensation from The Admiralty and on the proceeds was able to dine at the Carlton Grill in London's West End on New Year's Eve with his friends: Edward Marsh (Secretary of Winston Churchill), Arthur Asquith (son of the Prime Minister), and Violet Asquith (the Prime Minister's daughter).

With his Antwerp experience in mind, unshaken by news of heavy losses on the Western Front in the first months of the war, and with an admiration of military heroism, developed at public school, he wrote his series of five sonnets entitled *1914*.

1914

I. PEACE

Now, God be thanked Who has matched us with His hour,
And caught our youth, and wakened us from sleeping,
With hand made sure, clear eye, and sharpened power,
To turn, as swimmers into cleanness leaping,
Glad from a world grown old and cold and weary,
Leave the sick hearts that honour could not move,
And half-men, and their dirty songs and dreary,
And all the little emptiness of love!

Oh! we, who have known shame, we have found release there,
Where there's no ill, no grief, but sleep has mending,
Naught broken save this body, lost but breath;
Nothing to shake the laughing heart's long peace there
But only agony, and that has ending;
And the worst friend and enemy is but Death.

II. SAFETY

Dear! of all happy in the hour, most blest
He who has found our hid security,
Assured in the dark tides of the world at rest,
And heard our word, "Who is so safe as we?"
We have found safety with all things undying,
The winds, and morning, tears of men and mirth,
The deep night, and birds singing, and clouds flying,
And sleep, and freedom, and the autumnal earth.

We have built a house that is not for Time's throwing.
We have gained a peace unshaken by pain for ever.
War knows no power. Safe shall be my going,
Secretly armed against all death's endeavour;
Safe though all safety's lost; safe where men fall;
And if these poor limbs die, safest of all.

III. THE RICH DEAD

Blow out, you bugles, over the rich Dead!
There's none of these so lonely and poor of old,
But, dying, has made us rarer gifts than gold.
These laid the world away; poured out the red
Sweet wine of youth; gave up the years to be
Of work and joy, and that unhoped serene,
That men call age; and those who would have been,
Their sons, they gave, their immortality.

Blow, bugles, blow! They brought us, for our dearth,
Holiness, lacked so long, and Love, and Pain.
Honour has come back, as a king, to earth,
And paid his subjects with a royal wage;
And Nobleness walks in our ways again;
And we have come into our heritage.

IV. THE DEAD

These hearts were woven of human joys and cares,
Washed marvellously with sorrow, swift to mirth.
The years had given them kindness. Dawn was theirs,
And sunset, and the colours of the earth.
These had seen movement, and heard music; known
Slumber and waking; loved; gone proudly friended;
Felt the quick stir of wonder; sat alone;
Touched flowers and furs and cheeks. All this is ended.

There are waters blown by changing winds to laughter
And lit by the rich skies, all day. And after,
Frost, with a gesture, stays the waves that dance
And wandering loveliness. He leaves a white
Unbroken glory, a gathered radiance,
A width, a shining peace, under the night.

V.THE SOLDIER

If I should die, think only this of me:
That there's some corner of a foreign field
That is for ever England. There shall be
In that rich earth a richer dust concealed;
A dust whom England bore, shaped, made aware,
Gave, once, her flowers to love, her ways to roam,
A body of England's, breathing English air,
Washed by the rivers, blest by suns of home.

And think, this heart, all evil shed away,
A pulse in the Eternal mind, no less
Gives somewhere back the thoughts by England given;
Her sights and sounds; dreams happy as her day;
And laughter, learnt of friends; and gentleness,
In hearts at peace, under an English heaven.

Rupert Brooke
December,1914, January 1915

THE SPECIAL PLACE OF BROOKE'S SONNETS

These five sonnets had an importance in the First World War that went far beyond poetry. They expressed with elegance, eloquence and appealing imagery the ideals of magnanimous self-sacrifice in war. They were turned from fanciful logic-defying verse to key expressions of national will by the promotional powers of the establishment. – There was something in them which galvanised the attention of the conditioned minds of early 1915, and Brooke may be given the credit for his ability to express a national mood so effectively.

At a time when tens of thousands of men accepted that they should risk their lives fighting England's enemy these complex effusions of picturesque imagery and high sounding sentiment mesmerised and confused readers with the idea that death – without any suggestion of Heaven – is a wonderful opportunity and reward. Had they simply been published in *New Numbers* (a poetry magazine, with a circulation of about eight hundred, run by Brooke and his friends) their influence would have been minimal, but their rapturous patriotism was a gift to national leaders and propagandists.

In his sermon on Easter Sunday, 4th April, in St Paul's Cathedral, Dean Inge quoted *The Soldier*. This in itself amounted to little, but the sermon was reported in *The Times*. Then, following Brooke's timely death on 23rd April, the First Lord of the Admiralty himself wrote a glowing promotional obituary in *The Times*.

Rupert Brooke – by Winston Churchill

> Rupert Brooke is dead. A telegram from the Admiral at Lemnos tells us that his life has closed at the moment when it seemed to have reached its springtime. A voice had become audible, a note had been struck, more true, more thrilling, more able to do justice to the noblity of our youth in arms engaged in this present war than any other, more able to express their thoughts of self-surrender, and with a power to carry comfort to those who watch them so intensely from afar. The voice has been softly stilled. Only the echoes and the memory remain; but they will linger.

> During the last few months of his life, months of preparation in gallant comradeship and open air, the poet-soldier told with all the simple force of his genius the sorrow of youth about to die, and the the sure triumphant consolations of a sincere and valiant spirit. He expected to die; he was willing to die for the dear England whose beauty and majesty he knew; and he advanced towards the brink in perfect serenity, with absolute conviction of the rightness of his country's cause and a heart devoid of hate for fellow-men.

The thoughts to which he gave expression in the very few incomparable war sonnets which he has left behind will be shared by the many thousands of young men moving resolutely and blithey forward into this, the hardest, the cruellest, and the least-rewarding of all wars that men have fought. They are a whole history and revelation of Rupert Brooke himself. Joyous, fearless, versatile, deeply instructed, with classic symmetry of mind and body, ruled by high undoubting purpose, he was all that one could wish England's noblest sons to be in days when no sacrifice but the most precious is acceptable, and the most precious is that which is most freely proffered.

The words, "If I should die" tuned in to thoughts in every soldier's head, and the reward, patriotic and modest, (decomposing to "a richer dust . . . which is for ever England") somehow in the dizzy cold-sweat of the times seemed, to simple Englishmen, quite adequate. His verse sold copiously throughout the war.

Brooke's life-diminishing ideas and Churchill's obituary enshrined the belief, already widely accepted, that patriotism meant a willingness, or even a desire, to die for one's country. How sad that patriotism was not seen as a desire to live for one's country! The sick philosophy infected the mind of the nation. Most significantly and harmfully these ideas were prevalent in the top echelons of military leadership where the quality of fighting units was measured by the number of losses they sustained – an unsuccessful attack in which few casualties were sustained clearly showed that the soldiers were not trying hard enough.[1]

The puzzle of Brooke's sonnets

Modern readers of these celebrated sonnets may find Brooke's enthusiasm to die for his country and his resounding patriotism difficult to understand. – A pure and total identification with his country may be the only explanation we need. However, other factors may be relevant and the following may offer partial explanations of his attitudes.

Suicidal depression?

That someone should find death such an attractive proposition suggests a corresponding disaffection with life.

Brooke had suffered from suicidal depression two years before writing the sonnets. At that time he had been overworking on a thesis for some weeks and had then been distressed to find one of his girlfriends,

---

1   *Butchers and Bunglers of World War One,* John Laffin. p95.

Katherine (Ka) Cox, flirting with another man, the painter, Henry Lamb. This triggered a nervous breakdown. Brooke took to his bed and virtually gave up eating. He wrote six letters "in case of his death." The one to Katherine ended, "It is a good thing I die. Goodbye child."

While convalescing at Easter, in Lyndhurst in the New Forest, he wrote to his old friend Hugh Dalton,

> Friend of my laughing, careless youth, where are those golden hours now? Where now the shrill mirth of our burgeoning intellects? And by what dubious and deleterious ways am I come down to this place of shadows and eyeless pain ? In truth, I have been for some months in Hell. I have been very ill. I am very ill. In all probability I shall be very ill. It is thought by those that know me best (viz. myself) that I shall die. Nor do I greatly want to live, the savour of life having oddly left it, and my mind being worn and flabby, a tenth of anything it used to be.
>
> Boys laugh at me in the street. But that is partly, also, on account of my manner. For I am more than a little gone in my head, since my collapse.

His suicidal depression lasted, in its severest form for nine months. By July, 1912, he was writing to his girlfriend, Noel Olivier, (with whom he had been in love for four years) in increasingly obsessive and desperate language, eventually threatening to kill himself if she didn't marry him.

> The procession of hopeless hours – That's what's so difficult to face; – That's why one wants to kill oneself. (29 July.)
>
> I feel it very probable that I shall smash up altogether this autumn. I think a great deal and very eagerly of killing myself if this present state goes on... You mustn't kill me. I must marry you. (28 August.)

He wanted Noel to go camping with him.

> And, by God, if I do kill myself, I'd like to do it with one fairly decent memory just behind. . . I'm in a most bloody hell still.
> (5 September.)

A few weeks before he began writing the *1914* sonnets he again seemed less than positive about his life. In a letter to Katherine Cox on 3rd September, 1914, when the call to volunteer to fight for England was loud in every young man's ears, he wrote,

Don't seem to myself to do very much with my existence. And I don't know of anything I very much want to do with it.

In December he was writing the sonnets. On the third he wrote to an old friend , Jacques Raverat,

I'm largely dissatisfied with the English, just now. The good ones are all right. . . But there's a ghastly sort of apathy over half the country. And I really think large numbers of male people don't want to die; which is odd.

Two days later he wrote to a girl friend, the actress, Cathleen Nesbitt,

My dearest, I'm in a state of extreme depression. I was innocu- lated against typhoid (second time) yesterday; and it is a process which induces fever and despair.

In the remaining weeks of his life he mentions in a number of letters to friends his sense of failure and how death will be a benefit to him.

Lack of sincerity?

There is a possiblity that Brooke may not have written in absolute sincerity. In reviewing Brooke's first volume of poetry, *Poems 1911* Edward Marsh (Brooke's close friend and promoter) noted that,

A too conscientious critic might argue that he is not sincere, that he rides round the world as though it were a circus, crashing through the emotions as if through paper hoops.[1]

And Brooke himself said –   in a letter to his publisher, Frank Sidg- wick,

I occasionally feel, like Ophelia, that I've turned "thought and affliction, passion, hell itself . . . to flavour and pretti- ness"[2]

The words of Edward Thomas, in his role as critic, writing in *The Daily Chronicle* about Brooke's first published volume of poetry, may well apply to the sonnets:

1   *The Splendour and the Pain,* John Frayn Turner, p89.
2   *Collected Poems of Rupert Brooke,* 1929, the introductory *Memoir* by Edward Marsh.

He is full of . . . contempt, self-contempt, and yet arrogance too.
He revels chiefly what he desires to be and be thought.[1]

Commercially motivated?

Writing to Maurice Brown, who had literary connections in Chicago
– the home of *Poetry* magazine – Brooke described the poems as "honest but too crude stuff" and asked Brown to send the poems to *Poetry.* "I want to get gold for it from the Yanks."[2]

The financial exploitation of his talents had been an idea of his, not
unreasonable, for a number of years. In 1911, in conversation with his
friend, Sybil Pye, he had stated that it was one of his aims to have, "an
artistic eye in a business head."[3]

A student friend of Brooke had told Marsh, "The real foundation of his
(Brooke's) character was a hard business faculty." Brooke had thought
of numerous ideas to promote the Georgian Anthology. Perhaps he
should have been in advertising.

He loved paradox and dangerous sounding ideas?

He was perhaps carried away rather with the effect of his words and
just pushed ideas on. He enjoyed paradox.

As a schoolboy he had written, "I love to think of myself seated on the
greyness of Lethe's banks, and showering ghosts of epigrams and shadowy paradoxes upon the assembled wan-eyed dead." [4]

Hysteria and panic?

Brooke's statements written when he learned he was to go into action
in the Aegean and perhaps fight against the Turks take his ideas up a
stage higher in enthusiasm than even the sonnets, and gives further
indication of the workings of his mind. His education – the stories
of Homer in particular – influenced his concepts of war and heroism.
He suggests the ideas have been with him since childhood and sees
himself as a Greek hero of old:

1   Quoted in *Rupert Brooke, His Life and Legend,* John Lehman.
2   Turner, p149.
3   *Life and Letters,* Sybil Pye.
4   Marsh's *Memoir.*

It's too wonderful for belief. I had not imagined fate could be so benign . . . Do you think perhaps the fort on the Asiatic coast will want quelling . . . and they'll make a sortie and meet us on the plains of Troy? Will Hero's tower crumble under the 15-inch guns? . . . Oh God! I've never been quite so pervasively happy in my life, I think.   Never quite so pervasively happy: like a stream flowing entirely to one end. I suddenly realise that the ambition of my life has been - since I was two - to go on a military expedition against Constantinople.

There is a breathless, orgasmic quality to the writing and at the same time the ideas are juvenile – a long way removed from a mature consideration of going into action. In fact, Brooke knew the risks. He had learned, before finishing his sonnets that a seventy-five per cent casualty rate was expected on the Gallipoli campaign which he was to be involved in. In this letter, as with the sonnets, he seems to be meeting a crisis with hysterical enthusiasm and pretence. He has no ideas of his own for coping with the dangers that confront him and he falls back on the ideas with which his education has prepared his mind.

With his sonnets published in his poetry magazine, *New Numbers,* Brooke sailed for the Mediterranean and the Gallipoli encounter on 1st March 1915.

In April he spent some time in Egypt where he was slightly unwell. He suffered from sunstroke, and a mosquito bite which was soon to turn septic.

Whilst his ship was anchored off the Greek island of Skyros Brooke became ill with acute blood-poisoning. Within three days he had lost consciousness and died – on 23rd April. His friends, Arthur Asquith and Denis Browne, had been by his side in his final hours.

He was buried on Skyros that same evening, by moonlight, in a beautiful olive grove which he had admired only a few days earlier. At six the next morning the friends who had buried him sailed for Gallipoli.

Siegfried Sassoon on Brooke

Rupert Brooke was miraculously right when he said, "Safe shall be my going, Secretly armed against all death's endeavour; Safe though all safety's lost". He described the true soldier-spirit – saint and hero like Norman Donaldson and thousands of others who have been killed and died happier than they lived.

Sassoon's diary, 1 April 1916. Immediately after this entry he wrote the poem, *Peace*, which is printed on page 134 .

Michael (gloomily). "MUMMY, I DO HOPE I SHAN'T DIE SOON."
Mummy. "DARLING! SO DO I – BUT WHY?
Michael. "IT WOULD BE TOO AWFUL TO DIE A CIVILIAN." – *Punch,* 9 December 1914

WHY DID YOUNG MEN RUSH TO RISK THEIR LIVES?

According to Bertrand Russell,

> At all times, except when a monarch could enforce his will, war has been facilitated by the fact that vigorous males, confident of victory, enjoyed it, while their females admired them for their prowess.[1]

According to George Bernard Shaw,

> Men flock to the colours by instinct, by romantic desire for adventure, by the determination not, as Wagner put it, "to let their lives be governed by fear of the end," by simple destitution through unemployment, by rancour and pugnacity excited by the inventions of the press, by a sense of duty inculcated in platform orations which would not stand half an hour's discussion, by the incitements and taunts of elderly non-combatants and maidens with a taste for mischief, and by the verses of poets jumping at the cheapest chance in their underpaid profession.[2]

1   In his essay, *The Case for Socialism,* in volume of essays, *In Praise of Idleness,* p91.
2   *Common Sense About the War,* p14.

Our way of getting an army able to fight the German army is to declare war on Germany just as if we had such an army, and then trust to the appalling resultant peril and disaster to drive us into wholesale enlistment.[1]

War propaganda, fanning the fire of the easily aroused natural feelings of male aggression – and removing the restraints of Christian or civilised codes of conduct, succeeded amazingly.

NEW RECRUITS TAKING THE OATH.
Obviously these young men have thoroughly considered the detail and implications of the international situation before offering their lives in the defence of their country.

THE OATH: I . . . . swear by Almighty God that I will be faithful and bear true Allegiance to His Majesty King George the Fifth, and that I will honestly and faithfully defend His Majesty . . . in Person, Crown, and Dignity against all enemies, and will obey and observe all orders of His Majesty, and of the Generals and Officers set over me. So help me God.

1   *Common Sense*, p13.

The call of adventure, patriotism, racial hatred, and the excitement of aggression

The romance of it . . . the mystery and uncertainty of it . . . the glowing enthusiasm and lofty idealism of it: of our own free will we were embarked on this glorious enterprise, ready to endure any hardship and make any sacrifice, inspired by a patriotism newly awakened by the challenge to our country's honour.

Private W T Colyer, First Battalion, Artist's Rifles[1]

THE INCORRIGIBLES

New Arrival at the Front. "WHAT'S THE PROGRAMME?"

Old Hand. "WELL, YOU LAY DOWN IN THIS WATER, AND YOU GET PEPPERED ALL DAY AND ALL NIGHT, AND YOU HAVE THE TIME OF YOUR LIFE!"

New Arrival. "SOUNDS LIKE A BIT OF ALL RIGHT. I'M ON IT!"

It was all such fun. – *Punch,* 7 October 1914.

1   Tommy Goes to War, Malcolm Brown, p43.

Motivations for joining the army varied greatly. – Ronald Blythe interviewed many farm workers for his book *Akenfield*. Leonard Thompson told him, "I returned to my old farm at Akenfield for 11 shillings a week, but I was unsettled. When the farmer stopped my pay because it was raining and we couldn't thrash, I said to my seventeen-year-old mate, 'Bugger him. We'll go and join the army.'"

POETS PREPARED TO FIGHT

Siegfried Sassoon

Siegfried Sassoon, who was to become very bitter about the war as time went on, was the first of the well-known war poets to sign up in response to the actions of Germany. (Osbert Sitwell and Julian Grenfell were already serving as established professional soldiers at this time.) He had his medical inspection on 1st August 1914, and was in uniform the day after Britain declared war on Germany.

His key motivation for joining up is not clear. In his *Memoirs of a Fox-hunting Man* he gives us a few clues.

> The war was inevitable and justifiable. Courage remained a virtue . . . I had serious aspirations to heroism . . . My one idea was to be first in the field. In fact I made quite an impressive inward emotional experience of it. . . My gesture was, so to speak, an individual one, and I gloried in it.

Financial considerations may have been a factor. Shortly after enlisting he records,

> Most of the letters I had received since enlisting had been bills. But they no longer mattered. If the War goes on till next spring, I ruminated, I shall be quite rich. Being in the army was economical, at any rate!

As a keen horseman his strongest incentive may have come from the loss of the centre of his life, his horse.

> For forty-five months he had been my most prized possession in the world.

Sassoon had been forced, like thousands of other horse owners, to sell his horse to the army – in his case for "a perfunctory fifty pounds." Yet in the army he continued , for some time, to ride his own horse.

> For me, so far, the War had been a mounted infantry picnic in perfect weather . . . And I was agreeably relieved of all sense of personal responsibility.

He was, however, thinking seriously about what the war meant. His first war poems, not surprisingly, are in keeping with the popular spirit of the times. His bitterness and hostility to the war did not begin until early 1916.

ABSOLUTION

The anguish of the earth absolves our eyes
Till beauty shines in all that we can see.
War is our scourge; yet war has made us wise,
And, fighting for our freedom, we are free.

Horror of wounds and anger at the foe,
And loss of things desired; all these must pass.
We are the happy legion, for we know
Time's but a golden wind that shakes the grass.

There was an hour when we were loth to part
From life we longed to share no less than others.
Now, having claimed this heritage of heart,
What need we more, my comrades and my brothers?

Siegfried Sassoon,   April-September 1915

TO MY BROTHER

Give me your hand, my brother, search my face;
Look in these eyes lest I should think of shame;
For we have made an end of all things base.
We are returning by the road we came.

Your lot is with the ghosts of soldiers dead,
And I am in the field where men must fight.
But in the gloom I see your laurell'd head
And through your victory I shall win the light.

Siegfried Sassoon, 18 December 1915

Siegfried Sassoon's younger brother, Hamo, had been buried at sea on 1st November 1915, after being mortally wounded at Gallipoli. He was twenty-eight.

A TESTAMENT

If, as I think, I'm warned to pack and go
On a longer journey than I've made before,
I must be taking stock of what I leave,
And what I stand to lose, of all my store,

Cries for completion. Things, that made me weep
For joy of loveliness, come shining back
Dazzling my spirit that prepares for sleep.

Hushed is the house that once was full of songs.
In stillness rich with music that has been,
I wait death's savage hour that shall deliver
My soul and leave the soaring night serene.

There was a narrow path from glade to glade
Threading the golden forest, like a story
Planned to no certain close; a path that went
From morning to a sundown spilt with glory:

My home was safe among the slender trees;
There, on the blossomed slopes of time and sense,
Birds flocked and days came delicate and cold;
But now the tempest stoops to bear me hence.

The arches of air are mighty songs
That tell me of a wide-flung radiance spread
Across the world; my feet roam with the tides,
And I am crowned with the triumphant dead.

Siegfried Sassoon, Montagne, 1 January 1916

Robert Graves

I had just finished Charterhouse and gone up to Harlech, when
England declared war on Germany. A day or two later I decided
to enlist. In the first place, though the papers predicted only a
very short war – over by Christmas at the outside – I hoped
that it might last long enough to delay my going to Oxford in
October, which I dreaded. Nor did I work out the possibilities of
getting actively engaged in the fighting, expecting garrison service at home, while the regular forces were away. In the second
place, I was enraged to read of the Germans' cynical violation
of Belgian neutrality.[1]

Graves might have hesitated more than most. His mother was German,
and as a child, he had spent five summer holidays at his grandfather's
house in Germany. As he remarked to friends in the trenches a few
months later, "I have three or four uncles sitting somewhere opposite,
and a number of cousins, too. One of those uncles is a general."

1   *Goodbye To All That*, p60.

THE SHADOW OF DEATH

Here's an end to my art!
I must die and I know it,
With battle murder at my heart –
Sad death for a poet!

Oh my songs never sung,
And my plays to darkness blown!
I am still so young, so young,
And life was my own.

Some bad fairy stole
The baby I nursed:
Was this my pretty little soul,
This changeling accursed?

To fight and kill is wrong –
To stay at home is wronger:
Oh soul, little play and song,
I may father no longer!

Robert Graves, May 1915

Gilbert Frankau

In his semi-autobiographical novel, *Peter Jackson, Cigar Merchant*, explaining why his hero joined the army, Frankau wrote, "My dear fellow I was at Eton and *one does, don't you know, one just does*."[1]

Julian Grenfell – A soldier in love with war

Grenfell loved the army, his fellow officers, his dogs and fighting. He wrote,

> I adore war. It's like a big picnic without the objectlessness of a picnic. I've never been so well or happy. No one grumbles at one for being dirty.

> The war just suits my stolid health, and stolid nerves, and barbaric disposition. The fighting excitement vitalises everything, every sight and word and action. . .

> One loves one's fellow-man so much more when one is bent on killing him.

1   *Peter Jackson, Cigar Merchant*, p198.

Grenfell's speciality, he revealed in a letter to his parents, was stalking
German snipers and shooting them from very close range.

INTO BATTLE

The naked earth is warm with spring,
And with green grass and bursting trees
Leans to the sun's gaze glorying,
And quivers in the sunny breeze;

And life is colour and warmth and light,
And a striving evermore for these;
And he is dead who will not fight;
And who dies fighting has increase.

The fighting man shall from the sun
Take warmth, and life from the glowing earth;
Speed with the light-foot winds to run,
And with the trees to newer birth;
And find, when fighting shall be done,
Great rest, and fullness after dearth.

All the bright company of Heaven
Hold him in their high comradeship,
The Dog-Star, and the Sisters Seven,
Orion's Belt and sworded hip.

The woodland trees that stand together,
They stand to him each one a friend;
They gently speak in the windy weather;
They guide to valley and ridge's end.

The kestrel hovering by day,
And the little owls that call by night,
Bid him be swift and keen as they,
As keen of ear, as swift of sight.

The blackbird sings to him, "Brother, brother,
If this be the last song you shall sing,
Sing well, for you may not sing another;
Brother, sing."

In dreary, doubtful waiting hours,
Before the brazen frenzy starts,
The horses show him nobler powers;
O patient eyes, courageous hearts!

And when the burning moment breaks,
And all things else are out of mind,
And only joy of battle takes
Him by the throat, and makes him blind,

Through joy and blindness he shall know,
Not caring much to know, that still
Nor lead nor steel shall reach him, so
That it be not the Destined Will.

The thundering line of battle stands,
And in the air Death moans and sings;
But Day shall clasp him with strong hands,
And Night shall fold him in soft wings.

Julian Grenfell

The day this poem was published in *The Times,* May 1915, Grenfell's death was announced. He had died from wounds on April 30th.

Herbert Read

In August 1914, Read was a member of Leeds University Officer Training Corps which he had joined without any serious motive. He simply enjoyed the physical diversion. – Of that time he wrote:[1]

Politically I was a pacifist, and regarded the war as a conflict between rival imperial powers which would bring destruction to the peoples engaged. I hoped that the war would be stopped by international working-class action, and the failure of the responsible leaders to bring about a stoppage was my first lesson in political disillusionment. But fundamentally – that is to say ethically – I could not claim to be a pacifist. It must be remembered that in 1914 our conception of war was completely unreal. We had vague childish memories of the Boer War, and from these and a general diffusion of Kiplingesque sentiments, we managed to infuse into war a decided element of adventurous romance. War still appealed to the imagination.

To this romantic illusion must be added, in my case, a state of uncertainty about the future. Though I was ambitious and full of determination, I had no precise career marked out: I was to be a free-lance of some sort, and a free-lance finds a very appropriate place in the army. The war meant a decision: a crystalisation of

---

1   *Annals of Innocence and Experience, p140.*

vague projects: an immediate acceptance of the challenge of life. I did not hesitate.

He was commissioned in the Yorkshire Regiment (the Green Howards) in January 1915.

As the months went by, I was to see all the proud pretensions which men had acquired from a conventional environment sink into insignificance before the basic facts of body and spirit. In my own case I was to discover, with a sense of self-confidence wholly new to me, that I could endure the experience of war, even at its worst. This was far from claiming that I was fearless: the first days in the trenches, the first bombardment or attack was a draining sickness of the spirit. But I presently recovered, as from a plunge into a cold sea.[1]

Isaac Rosenberg

Isaac Rosenberg had tried repeatedly to get work in which he could use his considerable artistic skills and failed. "I could not get the work I thought I might so I have joined their Bantam Battalion," he wrote. He had been told that half his pay could be sent to his mother.

Wilfred Owen

At the outbreak of the war Wilfred Owen was twenty-one. He was living in France, at Bagnères-de-Bigorre, six miles from the foot of the Pyrenées and twelve from Lourdes, earning his living as a private tutor, teaching English to French children. His distance from the action and the media diffused the effect of the war on him. Also, the influence of the fifty-nine-year-old French pacifist poet, Laurence Tailhade, whom he met at this time, may have reduced his enthusiasm for war. The result was that for many months he rarely mentioned the war in his numerous personal letters.

However, he was not immune to its effects, for in September he visited a local hospital with his friend, Doctor Sauvaître, to see the French and German war wounded who were being brought in. To "educate" his brother, Harold, "to the actualities of war" he described in detail and with a certain relish, some of the wounds and operations he saw – completing the letter with little sketches of injuries.

Nevertheless, he did write one pro-war poem at that time: *The Ballad of Purchase Money* which contains this verse:

1   *Annals*, p143.

O meet it is and passing sweet
To live in peace with others,
But sweeter still and far more meet
To die in war for brothers.

MANY WOMEN WANTED TO DIE FOR ENGLAND

MANY SISTERS TO MANY BROTHERS

When we fought campaigns (in the long Christmas rains)
With soldiers spread in troops on the floor,
I shot as straight as you, my losses were as few,
My victories as many, or more.
And when in naval battle, amid cannon's rattle,
Fleet met fleet in the bath,
My cruisers were as trim, my battleships as grim,
My submarines cut as swift a path.
Or, when it rained too long, and the strength of the strong
Surged up and broke a way with blows,
I was as fit and keen, my fists hit as clean,
Your black eye matched my bleeding nose.
Was there a scrap or ploy in which you, the boy,
Could better me? You could not climb higher,
Ride straighter, run as quick (and to smoke made you sick)
 . . . But I sit here and you're under fire.

Oh it's you that have the luck, out there in blood and
muck:
You were born beneath a kindly star;
All we dreamt, I and you, you can really go and do,
And I can't, the way things are.
In a trench you are sitting, while I am knitting
A hopeless sock that never gets done.
Well, here's luck, my dear – and you've got it, no fear;
But for me .... a war is poor fun.

Rose Macaulay

THE END OF ENTHUSIASM FOR THE WAR

Soldiers who enlisted in the first weeks of the war really had no conception of the carnage they were volunteering for, but intelligent people
soon realised what the war meant for the ordinary soldier. Well's *The
War That Will End War*, published in its extended form in October, 1914
stated that "Already there is hideous butchery," and warned, "through
this war we have to march through pain, through agonies of the spirit,
worse than pain, through seas of blood and filth."

In spite of his undoubted awareness of the nature of the war, Edward Thomas, nevertheless, made up his mind to go and fight.

Edward Thomas was called to death

At thirty-seven, Edward Thomas was older than most of the early volunteers, and he was not in the first rush of men to join. He deliberated endlessly about what action he should take. He was by nature indecisive, given to moods of great depression and irritability. Death attracted him as a release from his misery. He had once attempted suicide. His enlistment echoed his suicide attempt.

His wife, Helen, described the occasion in her autobiography– the worrying times she had when Edward disappeared for days on end, and, when at home, his days of silence and brooding despair. He had a "terrible haggard greyness of face" and would fling himself in his chair without speaking or looking at her. Once, in one of these moods, his daughter had cried at his harsh words. He couldn't bear the cry, seized a revolver which he kept in a drawer and walked out of the house. Helen watched him go up the hill and disappear into the trees, thinking that she might never see him again. She wanted to be alone to listen but the questions and chatter of the children had to be attended to. She prayed that they both might be released from their agony. The afternoon passed.

She was in the kitchen, ironing, when he returned. He did not look at her. She asked if she should make the tea.

"Please" he replied. And in his voice, she said, she was aware of all he had suffered and had overcome.[1]

He wrote his own, fictionalised, third-person account of this event in his short story *The Attempt*. It provides an insight into the workings of his mind.

> Why should he live who had the power to draw such a cry from that sweet mouth? So he used to ask in the luxurious self-contempt which he practised. He would delay no more. He had thought before of cutting himself off from the power to injure his child and the mother of his child. But they would suffer; also, what a rough edge would be left to his life, inevitable in any case, perhaps, but not lightly to be chosen. On the other hand, he could not believe that they would ever be more unhappy than they often were now; at least, the greater poverty which his death would

1   *World Without End,* Helen Thomas, 1931.

probably cause could not well increase their unhappiness; and settled misery or a lower plane of happiness was surely preferable to a state of faltering hope at the edge of abysses such as he often opened for them. To leave them and not die . . . such a plan had none of the gloss of heroism and the kind of superficial ceremoniousness which was unconsciously much to his taste. But on this day the arguments for and against a fatal act did not weigh with him. He was called to death.

He was called to death, but hardly to an act which could procure it. Death he had never feared nor understood; he feared very much the pain and the fear that would awake with it. He had never in his life seen a dead human body or come in any way near death. Death was an idea tinged with poetry in his mind – a kingly thing which was once only at a man's call. After it came annihilation. To escape from the difficulty of life, from the need of deliberating on it, from the hopeless search for something that would make it possible for him to go on living like anybody else without questioning, he was eager to hide himself away in annihilation, just as, when a child, he hid himself in the folds of his mother's dress or her warm bosom, where he could shut out everything. . . There was also an element of vanity in his project; he was going to punish himself and in a manner so extreme that he was inclined to be exalted by the feeling that he was now about to convince the world he had suffered exceedingly. . . There was little in him left to kill.[1]

Thomas always had financial worries. After the outbreak of the war he was very tempted for a long time to take up the invitation of his friend, the American poet, Robert Frost, to go to America. But after some time he applied for a clerical job at the War Office, and saw his name added to a long list of applicants.

He described his eventual enlistment as, "Not a desperate nor purposed resolution but the natural culmination of a long series of moods and thoughts." [2]

Thomas had a deep love of the English countryside. He walked thousands of miles in it, and had a remarkable knowledge of the natural world. Yet his enlisting was a conscious sacrifice of things he loved, in return for a contentment to be given by Fate. It was coldly calculated. He was playing Russian roulette. The following poem he wrote the day of his enlistment.

1   *Edward Thomas, Selected Poems and Prose*, edited by David Wright, p91, 92.
2   Quoted in *Edward Thomas, a Critical Biography*, William Cook, p225.

FOR THESE

An acre of land between the shore and the hills,
Upon a ledge that shows my kingdoms three,
The lovely visible earth and sky and sea
Where what the curlew needs not, the farmer tills:

A house that shall love me as I love it,
Well-hedged, and honoured by a few ash trees
That linnets, greenfinches, and goldfinches
Shall often visit and make love in and flit:

A garden I need never go beyond,
Broken but neat, whose sunflowers every one
Are fit to be the sign of the Rising Sun:
A spring, a brook's bend, or at least a pond:

For these I ask not, but, neither too late
Nor yet too early, for what men call content,
And also that something may be sent
To be contented with, I ask of Fate.

Edward Thomas
14 July 1915

In the last four years of his life one of Thomas's closest friends was Eleanor Farjeon. She was a frequent visitor to his family home, and went on numerous walks with him. He called on her quite often; she typed all of his poetry for him and sent it off to potential publishers, who rejected it. Eleanor had fallen in love with Edward Thomas early in their acquaintance. He, whatever his feelings for Eleanor, was devoted to his wife, Helen. Eleanor never dared to express her feelings for Edward because she feared it would instantly bring about the end of their relationship.

He told her he was enlisting in a letter to her on 15th July 1915. Shortly after this he called to see Eleanor at her family home. She later wrote,

> I rose as he came into the room. He bent his head, and for the only time in our four years of friendship we kissed spontaneously. He sat down saying, "I've joined up."
>
> "I don't know why, but I'm glad," I said.
>
> "I am too," he said, "and I don't know why either."
>
> Before long I did know why. Self torment had gone out of him, and I was glad because of that.

As a tribute to the country he loved, Thomas compiled an anthology of writing which to him expressed the best qualities of England. In it – *This England*, 1915 – he described his reasons for fighting.

> It seemed to me that either I had never loved England, or I had loved it foolishly, aesthetically, like a slave, not having realised that it was not mine unless I were willing and prepared to die rather than leave it.

RAIN

Rain, midnight rain, nothing but the wild rain
On this bleak hut, and solitude, and me
Remembering again that I shall die
And neither hear the rain nor give it thanks
For washing me cleaner than I have been
Since I was born into this solitude.
Blessed are the dead that the rain rains upon:
But here I pray that none whom once I loved
Is dying to-night or lying still awake
Solitary, listening to the rain,
Either in pain or thus in sympathy
Helpless among the living and the dead,
Like a cold water among broken reeds,
Myriads of broken reeds all still and stiff,
Like me who have no love which this wild rain
Has not dissolved except the love of death,
If love it be for what is perfect and
Cannot, the tempest tells me, disappoint.

Edward Thomas

NO ONE CARES LESS THAN I

"No one cares less than I,
Nobody knows but God,
Whether I am destined to lie
Under a foreign clod,"
Were the words I made to the bugle call in the morning.

But laughing, storming, scorning,
Only the bugles know
What the bugles say in the morning,
And they do not care, when they blow
The call that I heard and made words to early this morning.

Edward Thomas, 25-26 May 1916.

4

EARLY DOUBTS ABOUT THE WAR

We are within measurable, or imaginable, distance of a real Armageddon . . . Happily there seems to be no reason why we should be anything more than spectators. - Henry Asquith, Prime Minister, in a letter to Venetia Stanley, 24 July 1914

It is safe to say that there has been no crisis in which the public opinion of the English people has been so definitely opposed to war as it is at this moment. - *The Nation*, 1 August 1914

It can but end in the greatest catastrophe that has ever befallen the continent of Europe at one blow. - Edward Grey, English Foreign Secretary, 1914. Quoted in *The Times*, 1 August 1914

This war is really the greatest insanity in which white races have ever been engaged. - Admiral von Tirpitz, Grand Admiral of the German Navy, Letter to his wife, 4 October 1914[1]

NO RULER OR LEADER WANTED WAR

I cannot recall any discussion on the subject in the Cabinet until the Friday evening (24 July, 1914) before the final declaration of war by Germany. We were much more concerned about the imminent threat of civil war in the North of Ireland . . .

In looking back on those few eventful days one feels like recalling a nightmare and after reading most of the literature explaining why the nations went to war, and who was responsible, the impression left on my mind is one of utter chaos, confusion, feebleness and futility, especially of a stubborn refusal to look at the rapidly approaching cataclysm. The nations backed their machine over the precipice. Amongst the rulers and statesmen who alone could give the final word which caused the great armies to spring

1 *The First World War*, Martin Gilbert, p88.

from the ground and march to and across frontiers, one can see now clearly that not one of them wanted war; certainly not on this scale.

David Lloyd George[1]

The Tsar Telegraphs the Kaiser

In this most serious moment I appeal to you to help me. An ignoble war has been declared to a weak country. The indignation in Russia shared fully by me is enormous. I foresee that very soon I shall be overwhelmed by the pressure brought upon me and be forced to take extreme measures which will lead to war. To try and avoid such a calamity as a European war, I beg you in the name of our old friendship to do what you can to stop your allies from going too far.

Nicky, 28 July 1914

The Kaiser Telegraphs the Tsar

With regard to the hearty and tender friendship which binds us both from long ago with firm ties, I am exerting my utmost influence to arrive at a satisfactory understanding with you. I confidently hope you will help me in my efforts to smooth over difficulties that still arise.   Your very sincere and devoted friend and cousin.

Willy, 28 July 1914

No Reason for War

On that same day the Kaiser read Serbia's note, in which she accepted all but two of Austria's demands - the two which violated her independence. He wrote,

A brilliant performance for a time limit of only forty-eight hours . . . a great moral victory for Vienna; but with it every reason for war drops away. . . On the strength of this I should never have ordered mobilisation.

Unfortunately he had agreed full support for Austro-Hungary who, on that day, at 11am, declared war on Serbia.[2]

---

1 *War Memoirs*, p33/34.
2 *History of the First World War*, Basil Liddell Hart, p20.

The opinions of the city, the Liberal Party, and the Prime Minister

The Prime Minister, Henry Asquith, wrote daily to Venetia Stanley to keep her informed of the often highly confidential developments of Government business and of his affection for her.

On 30th and 31st of July he reported to her that the city wanted Britain to keep out of the war "at almost all costs."

On Sunday 1st of August he told her that the bulk of the Liberal Party wanted Britain "*in no circumstances*" to intervene against Germany. The Cabinet still hoped to avoid war, and as a last, forlorn move Asquith, and a few colleagues, had, in the early hours of Sunday morning drafted "a direct personal appeal" from the King to the Tsar to halt Russian mobilisation. He had then, at 1.30am, driven to Buckingham Palace by taxi. "The poor King was hauled out of bed." Sitting bleary-eyed in his brown dressing gown the King had agreed to the message, suggesting only changing it to open "My Dear Nicky," and to end "Georgie" to make it sound more personal. (The Tsar and the King were cousins.)

The day had been an unhappy one for Asquith. "I can honestly say that I have never had a more bitter disappointment," he told Venetia. It was not the drift to war that most upset him, but the fact that war discussions prevented him from seeing her. "All these days have been sustained by the thought that when today came I should see your darling face and be with you." The pressure of Government business prevented him from seeing her for a further week.[1]

A Nation's First Duty

> A nation's first duty is to its own people. We are asked to intervene in the Continental war because unless we do we shall be "isolated." The isolation which will result for us if we keep out of this war is that, while other nations are torn and weakened by war, we shall not be . . . It is now universally admitted that our last Continental war – the Crimean War – was a monstrous error and miscalculation. Would this intervention be any wiser or likely to be better in its results?
>
> Norman Angel, in *The Times,* 2 August 1914.
> Two days before Britain's declaration of war.

---

[1]   *H H Asquith, Letters to Venetia Stanley*, p136-140.

Britain mobilises

Shortly after midnight of 2nd August Asquith wrote out the authority to mobilise the army, though not to send forces to France. Haldane took the note to the War Office mid-morning on the 3rd and instructions reached the army on 4th August. The Cabinet ordered troops to France on 6th August.

THE ULTIMATUM TO GERMANY

David Lloyd George:

> On Sunday, the 2nd of August, the omens were not propitious. There were clear indications that the German forces were massing on the Belgian frontier. Germany had appealed to Belgium for permission to march through her territories to attack France. Belgian Ministers hesitated, but the answer given by Belgium's heroic King constitutes one of the most thrilling pages of history. The British Government, on hearing the news, issued an ultimatum to Germany warning her that unless by twelve o'clock on August 4th assurances were received from Germany that the neutrality of Belgium would be treated as inviolate, Britain would have no alternative but to take steps to enforce that treaty. Would Germany realise what war with Britain meant, arrest the progress of her armies, change her strategy, and perhaps consent to a parley? How much depended upon the answer to these questions! We could suspect then what it meant: we know now. There were many of us who could hardly believe that those responsible for guiding the destiny of Germany would be so fatuous as deliberately to provoke the hostility of the British Empire with its inexhaustible reserves and with it's grim tenacity of purpose once it engaged in a struggle.[1]

The Bells Of Doom – 4th August 1914

> It was a day full of rumours and reports, throbbing with anxiety. Hour after hour passed and no sign came from Germany. There were only disturbing rumours of further German movements towards the Belgian line.   The evening came.   Still no answer. Shortly after nine o'clock I was summoned to the Cabinet Room for an important consultation. There I found Mr Asquith, Sir Edward Grey, and Mr Haldane all looking very grave. Mr M'Kenna arrived soon afterwards. A message from the German Foreign Office to the German Embassy in London had been intercepted.

1   *War Memoirs*, p44.

It was not in cipher. It informed the German Ambassador that the British Ambassador in Berlin had asked for his passports at 7 pm and declared war. A copy of this message was passed onto me, and I have it still in my possession.

We were at a loss to know what it meant. It looked like an attempt on the part of the Germans to anticipate the hour of the declaration of war in order to effect some coup either against British ships or British coasts. Should this intercept be treated as the commencement of hostilities, or should we wait until we either heard officially from Germany that our conditions had been rejected or until the hour of the ultimatum had expired? We sat at the green table in the famous room where so many historic decisions had been taken in the past. It was not then a very well-lighted room, and my recollection is that the lights had not all been turned on, and in the dimness you might imagine the shades of the great British statesmen of the past taking part in a conference which meant so much to the Empire, to the building up of which they had devoted their lives – Chatham, Pitt, Fox, Castlereagh, Canning, Peel, Palmerston, Disraeli, Gladstone. In that simple unadorned, almost dingy room they also had pondered over the problems which had perplexed their day. But never had they been confronted with so tremendous a decision as that with which British Ministers were faced in these early days of August, 1914.

And now came the terrible decision: should we unleash the savage dogs of war at once, or wait until the time limit of the ultimatum had expired, and give peace the benefit of even such a doubt as existed for at least another two hours? We had no difficulty in deciding that the Admiralty was to prepare the fleet against any sudden attack from the German flotillas and to warn our coasts against any possible designs from the same quarter. But should we declare war now, or at midnight? The ultimatum expired at midnight in Berlin. That was midnight according to Central Europe time: it meant eleven o'clock according to Greenwich time. We resolved to wait until eleven. Would any message arrive from Berlin before eleven informing us of the intention of Germany to respect Belgian neutrality? If it came there was still a faint hope that something might be arranged before the marching armies crashed into each other.

As the hour approached a deep and tense solemnity fell on the room. No one spoke. It was like awaiting the signal for the pulling of a lever which would hurl millions to their doom – with just a chance that a reprieve might arrive in time. Our eyes wandered anxiously from the clock to the door, and from the door to the clock, and little was said.

"Boom!" The deep notes of Big Ben rang out into the night, the first strokes in Britain's most fateful hour since she arose out of the deep. A shuddering silence fell upon the room. Every face was suddenly contracted in a painful intensity. "Doom!" "Doom!" the hammer of destiny. What destiny? Who could tell? We had challenged the most powerful military empire the world has yet brought forth.

We knew what brunt Britain would have to bear. Could she stand it? There was no doubt or hesitation in any breast. But let it be admitted without shame that a thrill of horror quickened every pulse. Did we know that before peace would be restored to Europe we should have to wade through four years of the most concentrated slaughter, mutilation, suffering, devastation, and savagery which mankind has ever witnessed? That twelve millions of the gallant youth of the nations would be slain, that another twenty millions would be mutilated? That Europe would be crushed under the weight of a colossal war debt? That only one empire would stand the shock? The three other glittering empires of the world would have been flung to the dust, and shattered beyond repair? That revolution, famine and anarchy would sweep over half Europe, and that their menace would scorch the rest of this hapless continent?

Has the full tale yet been told? Who can tell? But had we foreseen it all on the 4th August we could have done no other.

David Lloyd George[1]

Love and War

We are on the eve of horrible things. I wish you were nearer my darling: wouldn't it be a joy if we could spend Sunday together? I love you more than I can say.

Henry Asquith to Venetia Stanley, 4th August

A REVERSAL OF VALUES

13th August, 1914 – Bertrand Russell (who was later dismissed from his post at Cambridge University and sent to prison for his views about the war) writing in *Nation*,

A month ago Europe was a peaceful comity of nations; if an Englishman killed a German, he was hanged. Now if an Englishman kills a German, of if a German kills an Englishman, he is a

---

1   War Memoirs, p42-48.

patriot, who has deserved well of his country. We scan the newspapers with greedy eyes for news of slaughter, and rejoice when we read of innocent young men, blindly obedient to the word of command, mown down in thousands by the machine-guns of Liège.

Those who saw the London crowds, during the nights leading up to the Declaration of War saw a whole population, hitherto peaceable and humane, precipitated in a few days down the steep slope to primitive barbarism, letting loose, in a moment, the instincts of hatred and blood lust against which the whole fabric of society has been raised . . .

And all this madness, all this rage, all this flaming death of our civilisation and our hopes, has been brought about because a set of official gentlemen, living luxurious lives, mostly stupid, and all without imagination or heart, have chosen that it should occur rather than that any one of them should suffer some infinitesimal rebuff to his country's pride.

Walter Rathenau

Rathenau was in charge of Germany's procurement of raw materials throughout the war and proposed in a letter to the Chancellery on 10th October 1914, that Germany should make peace immediately based on Germany's evacuation of Belgium, reconciliation with France and the creation of a European Economic System combining Germany, Austria, France and Belgium. He proposed the same ideas eight years later as Foreign Minister, before his assassination.[1]

EARLY DOUBTS OF SOLDIER POETS

Charles Hamilton Sorley

Charles Sorley, eight years younger than Rupert Brooke, was a rare person in those emotional times. He was able to think independently and, to a large degree, rationally.

Two things helped him to take a more independent line of thought. First, he was a Scot, and did not identify himself with England and her hopes and fears. And second, up to the declaration of war he had spent 1914 in Germany, living in Schwerin in Mecklenberg with a doctor and his wife and then in Jena. He had developed a great liking for German

1   *First World War*, Martin Gilbert. p88.

people and an admiration for their culture. In February 1914 he reported that he was out walking with the doctor's wife when he heard some German soldiers singing something glorious and senseless about the Fatherland.

> And when I got home, I felt I was a German, and proud to be a German; when the tempest of the singing was at its loudest, I felt perhaps I could die for Deutschland - and I have never had an inkling of that feeling about England, and never shall.

When war was declared Sorley was still in Germany. He was arrested in Trier and put in prison for eight hours. On his release he returned to Cambridge and joined the army at the first opportunity.

He hated the jingoism which he found everywhere.

> England, I am sick of the sound of the word. In training to fight for England, I am training to fight for that deliberate hypocrisy, that terrible middle-class sloth of outlook and appalling "imaginative indolence" that has marked us out from generation to generation.

Sorley despised himself for submitting to the pressure of public opinion.

> What a worm one is under the cartwheels - big, careless lumbering cartwheels of public opinion. I might have been giving my mind to fight against Sloth and Stupidity: instead, I am giving my body (by a refinement of cowardice) to fight against the most enterprising nation in the world.

He also wrote, a few days after his arrival in Cambridge:

> Isn't all this bloody? I am full of mute and burning rage and annoyance and sulkiness about it. I could wager that out of twelve million eventual combatants there aren't twelve who really want it.

Not surprisingly, Sorley did not like Brooke's sonnets.

> He is far too obsessed with his own sacrifice, regarding the going to war of himself (and others) as a highly intense, remarkable sacrificial exploit, whereas it is merely the conduct demanded of him (and others) by the turn of circumstances, where non-compliance with this demand would have made life intolerable . . . He has clothed his attitude in fine words, but he has taken the sentimental attitude.

Sorley's keen intelligence and remarkable poetic achievements mark him out as one of the greatest losses of the war. He was killed at the age of twenty.

A HUNDRED THOUSAND MILLION MITES

A hundred thousand million mites we go
Wheeling and tacking o'er the eternal plain,
Some black with death – and some are white with woe.
Who sent us forth? Who takes us home again?

And there is sound of hymns of praise – to whom?
And curses – on whom curses? – snap the air.
And there is hope goes hand in hand with gloom,
And blood and indignation and despair.

And there is murmuring of the multitude
And blindness and great blindness, until some
Step forth and challenge blind Vicissitude
Who tramples on them: so that fewer come.

And nations, ankle-deep in love or hate,
Throw darts or kisses all the unwitting hour
Beside the ominous unseen tide of fate;
And there is emptiness and drink and power.

And some are mounted on swift steeds of thought
And some drag sluggish feet of stable toil.
Yet all, as though they furiously sought,
Twist turn and tussle, close and cling and coil.

A hundred thousand million mites we sway
Writhing and tossing on the eternal plain,
Some black with death – but most are bright with Day!
Who sent us forth? Who brings us home again?

Charles Sorley, September 1914

ALL THE HILLS AND VALES

All the hills and vales along
Earth is bursting into song,
And the singers are the chaps
Who are going to die perhaps.

O sing, marching men,
Till the valleys ring again.
Give your gladness to earth's keeping,
So be glad, when you are sleeping.

Cast away regret and rue,
Think what you are marching to.
Little live, great pass.
Jesus Christ and Barabbas
Were found the same day.
This died, that went his way.

So sing with joyful breath.
For why, you are going to death.
Teeming earth will surely store
All the gladness that you pour.

Earth that never doubts nor fears,
Earth that knows of death not tears,
Earth that bore with joyful ease
Hemlock for Socrates,
Earth that blossomed and was glad
'Neath the cross that Christ had,
Shall rejoice and blossom too
When the bullet reaches you.

Wherefore, men marching
On the road to death, sing!
Pour your gladness on earth's head,
So be merry, so be dead.

From the hills and valleys earth
Shouts back the sound of mirth,
Tramp of feet and lilt of song
Ringing all the road along.
All the music of their going,
Ringing swinging glad song-throwing,
Earth will echo still, when foot
Lies numb and voice mute.

On, marching men, on
To the gates of death with song.
Sow your gladness for earth's reaping
So you may be glad, though sleeping.
Strew your gladness on earth's bed,
So be merry, so be dead.

Charles Sorley

So happy to be going to war. Charles Sorley found the jubilation of soldiers a very strange phenomenon. – Members of D Company, 10th Battalion Royal Fusiliers at Colchester in 1914.

TO GERMANY

You are blind like us. Your hurt no man designed,
And no man claimed the conquest of your land.
But gropers both through fields of thought confined
We stumble and we do not understand.
You only saw your future bigly planned,
And we, the tapering paths of our own mind.
And in each other's dearest ways we stand,
And hiss and hate. And the blind fight the blind.

When it is peace, then we may view again
With new-won eyes each other's truer form
And wonder. Grown more loving-kind and warm
We'll grasp firm hands and laugh at the old pain,
When it is peace. But until peace, the storm
The darkness and the thunder and the rain.

Charles Sorley

Isaac Rosenberg

Because of a chest complaint Rosenberg was on holiday in Africa in August 1914. When war was declared he wrote to his friend Edward Marsh, "By the time you get this the war will only just have begun, I'm afraid. Europe will have stepped into its bath of blood."

Although he was unsuited to military service – being very small, very absent-minded and having weak lungs – he volunteered to fight at the end of October,1915, two months before conscription was brought in.

His first attempt was to join the Royal Army Medical Corps as a stretcher bearer, but he was rejected because he was so tiny. In late December he wrote to Edward Marsh,

> I never joined the army from patriotic reasons. Nothing can justify war. I suppose we must all fight to get the trouble over.

ON RECEIVING NEWS OF WAR

Snow is a strange white word.
No ice or frost
Has asked of bud or bird
For Winter's cost.

Yet ice and frost and snow
From earth to sky
This Summer land doth know.
No man knows why.

In all men's hearts it is.
Some spirit old
Hath turned with malign kiss
Our lives to mould.

Red fangs have torn His face.
God's blood is shed.
He mourns from His lone place
His children dead.

O! ancient crimson curse!
Corrode, consume.
Give back this universe
Its pristine bloom.

Isaac Rosenberg, Capetown, 1914

Wilfred Owen – "My life is worth more than my death to Englishmen."

When Owen, living in France, first mentioned the war in one of his letters it was near the end of August.

> The war affects me less than it ought. . . I can do no service to anybody by agitating for news or making dole over the slaughter . . . I feel my own life all the more precious and more dear in the presence of this deflowering of Europe.

On 2nd December 1914 he wrote to his mother,

> The *Daily Mail* speaks very, movingly about the "duties shirked" by English young men. I suffer a good deal of shame. But while those ten thousand lusty louts go on playing football I shall go on playing with my little axiom:- that my life is worth more than my death to Englishmen.

1914

> War broke: and now the Winter of the world
> With perishing great darkness closes in.
> The foul tornado, centred at Berlin,
> Is over all the width of Europe whirled,
> Rending the sails of progress. Rent or furled
> Are all Art's ensigns. Verse wails. Now begin
> Famines of thought and feeling. Love's wine's thin.
> The grain of human Autumn rots, down-hurled.
>
> For after Spring had bloomed in early Greece,
> And Summer blazed her glory out with Rome,
> An Autumn softly fell, a harvest home,
> A slow grand age, and rich with all increase.
> But now, for us, wild Winter, and the need
> Of sowings for new Spring, and blood for seed.

> Wilfred Owen
> Drafted in southern France in late 1914.

Eventually, on 15th May 1915, Owen returned to England and encountered all the psychological pressures to enlist. His brother Harold, wrote of this experience:

> being branded with lack of courage and the ostracism which would follow – this prospect and all its consequences he found appalling, and much more frightening than the horrid thought of army discipline.

He returned to France on 11th June, and came back to England on 14th September to enlist. This he finally did on 21st October.

His chief pleasure in being a soldier was in wearing the uniform and basking in the admiration of small boys.

> Walking abroad, one is the admiration of all little boys, and meets an approving glance from every eye of eld.

Letter to his mother, 2 November, 1915.

AN AMERICAN VIEWPOINT – AMERICAN POETS IN *POETRY* MAGAZINE, CHICAGO, NOVEMBER 1914

Whilst the voices of protest were well submerged, and awareness of the reality of war was all but obliterated from general consciousness in Britain, across the Atlantic the situation and the role of poets seemed very clear. Alice Corbin, writing in the Chicago magazine, *Poetry*, introducing a selection of war poems written in response to "the supreme crisis of the twentieth century," said that the patriotic poems of Kipling, Hardy, Bridges and Masefield were "inadequate" and "lacked conviction." She continued,

> Varying degrees of right and wrong, included in a greater wrong, can count for little with disillusioned minds. War has actually lost its illusion and its glamour. Some shreds of illusion may cling to the individual experience; the elemental sense of tragedy may lift the unforgivable facts to the height of emotional elo- quence, but of what worth is this eloquence beside the collective naked waste?
>
> The American feeling about the war is a genuine revolt against war, and we have believed that *Poetry* might help to serve the cause of peace by encouraging the expression of the spirit of protest.
>
> No future historian of the United States will be able to use quotations from her twentieth-century poets in support of an imperial policy of conquest and slaughter.

IF WAR IS RIGHT

> If war is right, then God is might
> And every prayer is vain:
> Go raze your temples from the hills –
> Red death is in the plain.

If war is right, then God is might,
And every prayer is vain:
Look not for Christ upon the hills –
He lies among the slain.

Parke Farley,
November 1914, *Poetry* magazine, Chicago

RESPONSES TO PRO-WAR POETRY

Not every reader of the patriotic press was insensitive to the quality of the "poetry," or admired the heroic diction or agreed with the sentiments of the poetry which appeared in it during the war. For example, take the next two responses from *New Age*, a weekly review of politics, literature and art.

WILLIAM WATSON, WAR-EATER

We heard him shout, with gas and clinkers crammed,
Atrocious sonnets on Abdul the Damned,
(His cue he cribbed from Milton at his ease –
You know that sonnet on the Piedmontese:)
Then came a silence – the gas-fire died down,
And granny Bridges got the Laureate's crown.
Watson was dumb, we knew his shot was sped,
But Watson barren is not Watson dead.
Once more he clamours loudly from his hearse
And makes war viler with his verse and worse,
Once more our blatant, beefy bard explodes
In sonnets, jingo jingles and in odes.
This apoplectic patriot, fierce and hot,
Plasters the saffron press with smoking rot;
He buries (rigged with pseudo-Shakespeare rhymes)
The Kaiser, and he barks from out *The Times* –
(So much per bark), or snorting through the nose,
Follows the odorous breeze that Harmsworth blows.
Behold him swelling as he sits and strums
His rusty harp and all his fingers thumbs.
The muddy brain, inflamed by clots of gore,
The stall of Pegasus, the pressmen's roar,
Breaks headlong from its Milton-Wordsworth pose –
And lo! a deluge of truncated prose.
Upon the prongs of his decrepit quill
He pitchforks "Huns" to hell and sputters:
"Kill!" From the black bastions of the Northcliffe flung,
Flaps the pink banner of his ranting tongue.
In Northcliffe's styes, in North Seas foul with ink,
We hear his mines explode, we smell the stink.

We mark the fellow, purple-jowled and solemn,
Sniping at morn and eve in every column,
(So much per snipe) we hear him ramp and rave
O'er Wilhelm's, like the ass o'er Bahram's grave.
To far America he sends his yelp,
And blackguards Britain by a cry for "Help!"
Fame, fill him up with thistles and with hay,
O hasten, Peace, your mute but glorious day
When sons of Wat, unlunged, shall cease to bray.

Atilla. Published in *New Age*, 17 December 1914.

A BALLADE FOR PATRIOTIC POETS

I wondered, after reading Noyes and Co.,
If I could write a patriotic fake;
So had a glance or two at *Westward Ho!*
To catch the spirit of the times of Drake.
He made the Spaniards reel and no mistake;
For fighting he was always in good form.
I see – on deeps they played as on a lake –
The ships of England riding out the storm.

So down the stream of ancient years I go
Until I reach the dashing days of Blake.
(I fear Bechofer's pen may lay me low,
But, as a Briton, all the chances take)
Well, Blake was he who made the Dutchmen quake;
In fancy I can see our fleets re-form;
And view, as through a mist that's half opaque,
The ships of England riding out the storm.

We cannot all go out to fight the foe;
But we can sing until the critics shake,
And Deutschland totters to her overthrow
By reason of the burning words we spake.
With powerful pen we will the Kaiser break;
And while we keep in England, smug and warm,
We'll watch in dreams (while sailors are awake)
The ships of England riding out the storm.

Poets, who sing your songs for England's sake!
I'd like to see you all in uniform;
And manning, with your precious lives at stake,
The ships of England riding out the storm.

Vectis, *New Age*, 24 December, 1914

IF I SHOULD DIE, BE NOT CONCERNED TO KNOW

If I should die, be not concerned to know
The manner of my ending, if I fell
Leading a forlorn charge against the foe,
Strangled by gas, of shattered shell.
Nor seek to see me in this death-in-life
Mid shirks and curses, oaths and blood and sweat,
Cold in the darkness, on the edge of strife,
Bored and afraid, irresolute, and wet.

But if you think of me, remember one
Who loved good dinners, curious parody,
Swimming, and lying naked in the sun,
Latin hexameters and heraldry,
Athenian subtleties of $\delta\eta\zeta$ and $\pi o\iota\zeta$
Beethoven, Botticelli, beer and boys.

Phillip Bainbrigge

"THE GREATER GAME"
Mr Punch (to Professional
Association Player). "NO
DOUBT YOU CAN MAKE
MONEY IN THIS FIELD,
BUT THERE'S ONLY ONE
FIELD TODAY WHERE
YOU CAN GET HONOUR"

Punch, 21 October, 1914

5

TRENCH WARFARE

BLOCH'S PREDICTION

> At first there will be increased slaughter on so terrible a scale as
> to render it impossible to get troops to push the battle to a
> decisive issue. They will try to, thinking they are fighting
> under old conditions, and they will learn such a lesson that they
> will abandon the attempt. The war, instead of being a hand-
> to-hand contest in which the combatants measure their physical
> and moral superiority, will become a kind of stalemate, in which,
> neither army being able to get to the other, both armies will be
> maintained in opposition to each other, threatening each other,
> but never being able to deliver a final and decisive blow. Every-
> body will be entrenched in the next war; the spade will be as
> indispensable to the soldier as his rifle.

> Ivan Bloch (a Polish banker) in *War in the Future*, 1897

The war, which was not over by Christmas, as the newspapers had
predicted, developed in unexpected ways. The British commanders,
in creating and dominating the British Empire, had been used to
sending armies of men armed with modern weapons against natives
armed with spears. In such conditions the British cavalry could sweep
forward with devastating effect.

But in France the British army faced a modern power with highly
disciplined troops, and weapons which were equal to, or superior to,
its own.

As advancing troops could be mown down by a barrage of machine-gun
fire, an alternative method of fighting had to be worked out on the spot.
Men simply dug deep trenches. In these they lived, and from them they
made their periodic attacks.

The German enemy took a similar approach, though applied slightly
more intelligence, retiring to the highest ground around, and leaving the
swamps to the English. In such places the Germans often turned their

trenches into bunkers up to 30 feet (almost 10 metres) deep, securely
built of concrete, and comfortably furnished.

Behind the trenches were the reserves, the supplies, casualty clearing
stations, and field hospitals, and the commanders. The headquarters
were at a safe distance from the war zone. For the Battle of the Somme,
Field Marshal Haig conducted the action from Montreuil, fifty miles
from the front line.

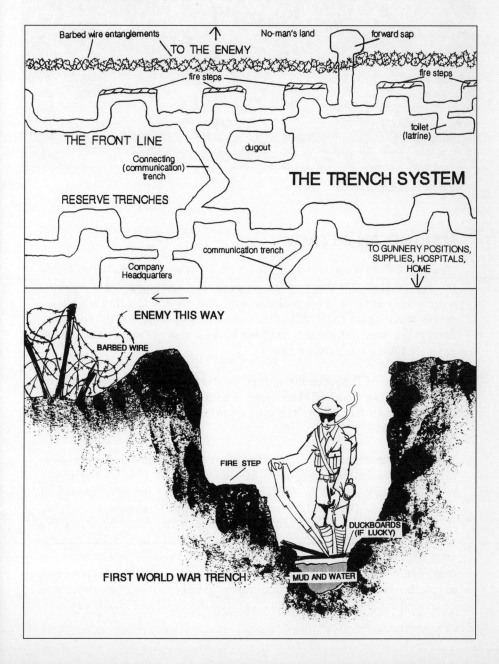

A 9.2 inch field gun in action.

MAKING AN ATTACK

Usually, before a major attack, the massive long range guns fired onto the enemy lines for many hours or even day and night for a week or more. This gave the enemy the warning he needed to bring up his reserves and prepare to fight, but the intention was to demolish the enemy front lines, their inhabitants, and the barbed wire entanglements which protected them from foot soldiers.

In the Battle of Passchendaele three thousand heavy guns fired for ten days delivering four and three quarter tons of explosive for every yard of the German front line. The cost of the shells used was twenty-two million pounds.

After the bombardment, in an attempt to overwhelm the enemy, hundreds, and sometimes thousands of men would be ordered out of the trenches ("going over the top") to advance across the open ground of no-man's land. They walked in a line, shoulder to shoulder, carrying their rifles with bayonets fixed, into a blaze of fire from the rifles and machine guns of the enemy. – After many months of unhappy experience with this approach looser formations were used. A further improvement came when Field Marshal Haig, who considered the machine gun a "much over-rated weapon" and allowed only two per battalion, was overruled by Lloyd George who increased the supply of these weapons.

THE NOISE OF THE BIG GUNS BEFORE AN ATTACK

The noise is terrific, as we are just in front of the guns, the shells passing right over us. I cannot describe the noise accurately; it is a series or succession of huge bangs, developing at times into a continuous roar . . . The whole air throbs with sound . . . It seems to come in huge sudden stabs.

Major Walter Vignoles[1]

The noise was so great it could be heard in England. As a treat, children in Sussex were taken on the Downs to listen to the roar of guns in France 100 miles, and more, away. The bombardment that preceded the Battle of the Somme could be heard in London.

THIEPVAL WOOD

The tired air groans as the heavies swing over, the river-hollows boom;
The shell fountains leap from the swamps, and with wild-fire and fume
The shoulder of the chalk down convulses.
Then jabbering echoes stampede in the slatting wood,
Ember-black the gibbet trees like bones or thorns protrude
From the poisonous smoke –   past all impulses.
To them these silvery dews can never again be dear,
Nor the blue javelin-flame of thunderous noons strike fear.

Edmund Blunden, September 1916

MANIAC EARTH!

Maniac Earth! howling and flying, your bowel
Seared by the jagged fire, the iron love
The impetuous storm of savage love.
Dark Earth! dark heaven, swinging in chemic smoke
What dead are born when you kiss each soundless soul
With lightning and thunder from your mined heart,
Which man's self dug, and his blind fingers loosed.

Isaac Rosenberg

1   *Tommy Goes to War*, p138.

Maniac Earth! was originally the ninth stanza of Rosenberg's *Dead Man's Dump*. It was omitted from his final version of that poem, presumably because it broke up the flow of ideas.

GREAT GUN

On seeing a piece of our heavy artillery brought into action.

Be slowly lifted up, thou long black arm,
Great Gun, towering towards Heaven, about to curse;
Sway steep against them, and for year's rehearse
Huge imprecations like a blasting charm!
Reach at that Arrogance which needs thy harm,
And beat it down before its sins grow worse.
Spend our resentment, canon, – yea, disburse
Our gold in shapes of flame, our breaths in storm.

Yet, for men's sakes whom thy vast malison
Must wither innocent of enmity,
Be not withdrawn, dark arm, thy spoilure done,
Safe to the bosom of our prosperity.
But when thy spell be cast complete and whole,
May God curse thee, and cut thee from our soul!

Wilfred Owen. Revised at Scarborough, May 1918.

PREPARATIONS FOR VICTORY

My soul, dread not the pestilence that hags
The valley; flinch not you, my body young,
At these great shouting smokes and snarling jags
Of fiery iron; as yet may not be flung
The dice that claims you. Manly move among
These ruins, and what you must do, do well;
Look, here are gardens, there mossed boughs are hung
With apples whose bright cheeks none might excel,
And there's a house as yet unshattered by a shell.

"I'll do my best," the soul makes sad reply,
"And I will mark the yet unmurdered tree,
The token of dear homes that court the eye,
And yet I see them not as I would see.
Hovering between, a ghostly enemy.
Sickens the light, and poisoned, withered, wan,
The least defiled turns desperate to me.
The body, poor unpitied Caliban,
Parches and sweats and grunts to win the name of Man.

Days or eternities like swelling waves
Surge on, and still we drudge in this dark maze;
The bombs and coils and cans by strings of slaves
Are borne to serve the coming day of days;
Pale sleep in slimy cellars scarce allays
With its brief blank the burden. Look, we lose;
The sky is gone, the lightless, drenching haze
Of rainstorm chills the bone; earth, air are foes,
The black fiend leaps brick-red as life's last picture goes.

Edmund Blunden

Losses out of proportion

The losses involved in the trench-jumping operations now going
on on both sides are enormous and out of proportion to the ground
gained. When our new armies are ready. . . it seems folly to send
them to Flanders . . . where they will "chew barbed wire", or be
wasted in futile frontal attacks.

Henry Asquith, in a letter to Venetia Stanley, 30th December 1914

THIRD BATTLE OF YPRES – ALSO KNOWN AS THE BATTLE OF PASSCHENDAELE

Battles were not one day affairs that settled matters quickly, but would
go on for months with bombardments, poison gas, massive bombs placed
in tunnels under enemy positions, flame-throwers – and, eventually,
tanks, too – with numerous attacks and counter attacks by the infantry,
hideous death tolls and appalling suffering; and after all this the gains
or losses of territory were usually pathetically small.

The Third Battle of Ypres, 31st July to 10th November 1917, began as
an Allied attack which attempted to push back the Germans to the Channel coast in order to free the ports of Ostend and Zeebrugge forty miles
away and prevent their use by German submarines, though these ports
were, in fact, little used by submarines. In just over three months they
advanced five miles, when the Canadians gained the little village of
Passchendaele. Chief of British Military Intelligence, General Sir John
Charteris wrote on 7th November:

We have now got to where, with good weather, we should have
been in September. . . It is a rather barren victory. . . almost lives
and labour thrown away.[1]

1   *History of World War One*, edited by A J P Taylor, p211

The Allied losses were 265,423. German losses 206,000. The area was regained by the Germans five months later. – Total losses in dead, wounded and missing for the battleground east of Ypres, an area six miles by twelve, for the years 1914 -1918, were 1,700,000.

ATTACK

At dawn the ridge emerges massed and dun
In wild purple of the glow'ring sun,
Smouldering through spouts of drifting smoke that shroud
The menacing scarred slope; and, one by one,
Tanks creep and topple forward to the wire.
The barrage roars and lifts. Then, clumsily bowed
With bombs and guns and shovels and battle-gear,
Men jostle and climb to meet the bristling fire.
Lines of grey, muttering faces, masked with fear,
They leave their trenches, going over the top,
While time ticks blank and busy on their wrists,
And hope, with furtive eyes and grappling fists,
Flounders in mud. O Jesus, make it stop!

Siegfried Sassoon

COUNTER-ATTACK

We'd gained our first objective hours before
While dawn broke like a face with blinking eyes,
Pallid, unshaved and thirsty, blind with smoke.
Things seemed all right at first. We held their line,
With bombers posted, Lewis guns well placed,
And clink of shovels deepening the shallow trench.
The place was rotten with dead; green clumsy legs
High-booted, sprawled and grovelled along the saps
And trunks, face downward, in the sucking mud,
Wallowed like trodden sand-bags loosely filled;
And naked sodden buttocks, mats of hair,
Bulged, clotted heads slept in the plastering slime.
And then the rain began, – the jolly old rain!

A yawning soldier knelt against the bank,
Staring across the morning blear with fog;
He wondered when the Allemands would get busy;
And then, of course, they started with five-nines
Traversing, sure as fate, and never a dud.
Mute in the clamour of shells he watched them burst
Spouting dark earth and wire with gusts from hell,
While posturing giants dissolved in drifts of smoke.

He crouched and flinched, dizzy with galloping fear,
Sick for escape, – loathing the strangled horror
And butchered, frantic gestures of the dead.

An officer came blundering down the trench:
"Stand-to and man the fire step!" On he went . . .
Gasping and bawling, "Fire-step . . . counter-attack!"
Then the haze lifted. Bombing on the right
Down the old sap: machine guns on the left;
And stumbling figures looming out in front.
"O Christ, they're coming at us!" Bullets spat,
And he remembered his rifle . . . rapid fire . . .
And started blazing wildly . . . then a bang
Crumpled and spun him sideways, knocked him out
To grunt and wriggle: none heeded him; he choked
And fought the flapping veils of smothering gloom,
Lost in a blurred confusion of yells and groans . . .
Down, and down, and down, he sank and drowned,
Bleeding to death. The counter-attack had failed.

Siegfried Sassoon

TRENCH LIFE

Fear never dies, much as we laugh at fear
For pride's sake and for other cowards' sakes,
And when we see some new Death, bursting near,
Rip those that laugh in pieces, God! it shakes
Sham fortitude that went so proud at first,
And stops the clack of mocking tongues awhile
Until (O pride, O pride!) at the next shell-burst
Cowards dare mock again and twist a smile.

Yet we who once, before we came to fight,
Drowned our prosperity in a waste of grief,
Contrary now find such perverse delight
In utter fear and misery, that Belief
Blossoms from mud, and under the rain's whips,
Flagellant-like we writhe with laughing lips.

Robert Graves

GERMAN MACHINE GUNNERS COULD NOT BELIEVE THEIR EYES

Many Germans thought the way the British made their attacks, walking forward into the German guns, was amazing. One wrote in his diary,

> We were very surprised to see them walking. We had never seen that before . . . The officers went in front. I noticed one of them walking calmly, carrying a walking stick. When we started firing we just had to load and reload. They went down in their hundreds. You didn't have to aim. We just fired into them.

The Battle of Loos – September 1915

> Ten ranks of extended line could clearly be distinguished, each one estimated at more than a thousand men, and offering such a target as had never been seen before, or even thought possible. Never had the machine-gunners such straightforward work to do nor done it so unceasingly. The men stood on the firestep, some even on the parapets, and fired exultantly into the mass of men advancing across the open grassland. As the entire field of fire was covered with the enemy's infantry the effect was devastating and they could be seen falling in hundreds.
>
> Regimental Diarist, German XV Reserve Regiment[1]

In the Battle of Loos 8,246 British soldiers (out of nearly 10,000) were killed or wounded in just 200 minutes.

We advanced in line . . .

> As the hands of my watch whirled round I busied myself with totally unnecessary enquiries and admonitions amongst the troops in order to keep my mind free from fear. Then from my wrist in lines of fire flashed 1.45, and feeling icy from head to foot I took my troops out, and through the ominous silence of the bright midday. We advanced in line . . . An instant later, with one mighty crash, every gun spoke. Dozens of machine guns burst into action and the barrage was laid. Instantaneously the enemy barrage crashed upon us, and even as I rose, signalling my men to advance, I realized that the Germans must have known of our attack and waited at their guns. Shells were pouring on to the St Julien-Triangle Road as we advanced, and through the clouds of smoke and fountains of water I saw ahead the lines of figures

1   Quoted by John Laffin in *Butchers and Bunglers of World War One ,* p34.

struggling forward through the mud . . .   I saw, with a sinking
heart, that the lines had wavered, broken, and almost disappeared.
I was dazed, and straining my eyes through the murk of battle I
tried to distinguish our fellows, but only here and there was a
figure moving.

From the diary of a young officer, Captain Edwin Vaughan[1]

Wilfred Owen on "going over the top"

The sensations of going over the top are about as exhilarating as
those dreams of falling over a precipice, when you see the rocks
at the bottom surging up to you . . . There was an extraordinary
exultation in the act of slowly walking forward, showing ourselves openly. There was no bugle and no drum for which I was
sorry . . . Then we were caught in a tornado of shells. The various
"waves" were all broken up and we carried on like a crowd
moving off a cricket field. When I looked back and saw the
ground all crawling and wormy with wounded bodies, I felt no
horror at all but only an immense exultation at having got through
the barrage.

Letter to his brother, Colin, 14th May, 1917

SPRING OFFENSIVE

Halted against the shade of a last hill,
They fed, and lying easy, were at ease;
And, finding comfortable chests or knees
Carelessly slept.
                    But many there stood still
To face the stark, blank sky beyond the ridge,
Knowing their feet had come to the end of the world.

Marvelling they stood, and watched the long grass swirled
By the May breeze, murmurous with wasp and midge,
And though the summer oozed into their veins
Like an injected drug for their bodies' pains,
Sharp on their souls hung the imminent ridge of grass,
Fearfully flashed the sky's mysterious glass.

---

1   *Some Desperate Glory*, Edwin Campion Vaughan, p221, 222.

Hour after hour they ponder the warm field -
And the far valley behind, where buttercups
Had blessed with gold their slow boots coming up;
When even the little brambles would not yield,
But clutched and clung to them like sorrowing hands;
They breathe like trees unstirred.

Till like a cold gust thrills the little word
At which each body and its soul begird
And tighten them for battle. No alarms
Of bugles, no high flags, no clamorous haste –
Only a lift and flare of eyes that faced
The sun, like a friend with whom their love is done.
O larger shone that smile against the sun, –
Mightier than his whose bounty these have spurned.

So, soon they topped the hill, and raced together
Over an open stretch of herb and heather
Exposed. And instantly the whole sky burned
With fury against them; earth set sudden cups
In thousands for their blood; and the green slope
Chasmed and deepened sheer to infinite space.

Of them who running on that last high place
Breasted the surf of unseen bullets, or went up
On the hot blast and fury of hell's upsurge,
Or plunged and fell away past this world's verge,
Some say God caught them even before they fell.

But what say such as from existence' brink
Ventured but drave too swift to sink,
The few who rushed in the body to enter hell,
And there out-fiending all its fiends and flames
With superhuman inhumanities,
Long-famous glories, immemorial shames –
And crawling slowly back, have by degrees
Regained cool peaceful air in wonder. —
Why speak not they of comrades that went under?

Wilfred Owen, July – September 1918

COME ON, MY LUCKY LADS

O rosy red, O torrent splendour
Staining all the Orient gloom,
O celestial work of wonder –
A million mornings in one bloom!

What, does the artist of creation
Try some new plethora of flame,
For his eye's fresh fascination?
Has the old cosmic fire grown tame?

In what subnatural strange awakening
Is this body, which seems mine?
These feet towards that blood-burst making,
These ears which thunder, these hands which twine

On grotesque iron? Icy-clear
The air of a mortal day shocks sense,
My shaking men pant after me here.
The acid vapours hovering dense,

The fury whizzing in dozens down,
The clattering rafters, clods calcined,
The blood in the flints and the trackway brown –
I see I am clothed and in my right mind;

The dawn but hangs behind the goal,
What is that artist's joy to me?
Here limps poor Jock with a gash in the poll,
His red blood now is the red I see,

The swooning white of him, and that red!
These bombs in boxes, the craunch of shells,
The second-hand flitting round; ahead!
It's plain we were born for this, naught else.

Edmund Blunden [1]

SOLDIERING

AUGUST 1914

What in our lives is burnt
In the fire of this?
The heart's dear granary?
The much we shall miss?

---

1   This poem is also known as *Zero*.

Three lives hath one life–
Iron, honey, gold.
The gold, the honey gone–
Left is the hard and cold.

Iron are our lives
Molten through our youth.
A burnt space through ripe fields,
A fair mouth's broken tooth.

Isaac Rosenberg

INSPECTION

'You! What d'you mean by this?' I rapped.
'You dare come on parade like this?'
'Please, Sir, it's – ''Old yer mouth,' the segeant snapped.
'I takes 'is name, Sir?' – 'Please, and then dismiss.'

Some days 'confined to camp' he got,
For being 'dirty on parade'.
He told me, afterwards, the damnèd spot
Was blood, his own. 'Well blood is dirt,' I said.

'Blood's dirt,' he laughed, looking away,
Far off to where his wound had bled
And almost merged for ever into clay.
'The world is washing out its stains,' he said.
'It doesn't like our cheeks so red:
Young blood's its great objection.
But when we're duly white-washed, being dead,
The race will bear Field Marshal God's inspection.'

Wilfred Owen

SERVITUDE

If it were not for England, who would bear
This heavy servitude one moment more?
To keep a brothel, sweep and wash the floor
Of filthiest hovels were noble to compare
With this brass cleaning life. Now here, now there
Harried in foolishness, scanned curiously o'er
By fools made brazen by conceit, and store
Of antique witicisms thin and bare.

Only the love of comrades sweetens all,
Whose laughing spirit will not be outdone.

As night-watching men wait for the sun
To hearten them, so wait I on such boys
As neither brass nor Hell-fire may appal,
Nor guns, nor sergeant-major's bluster and noise.

Ivor Gurney

NIGHT PATROL

"Over the top! The wire's thin here, unbarbed
Plain rusty coils, not staked, and low enough:
Full of old tins, though. – When you're through, all three,
Aim quarter left for fifty yards or so,
Then straight for that new piece of German wire;
See if it's thick, and listen for a while
For sounds of working; don't run any risks;
About an hour; now, over!"
                    And we placed
Our hands on the topmost sand-bags, leapt, and stood
A second with curved backs, then crept to the wire,
Wormed ourselves tinkling through, glanced back, and dropped.
The sodden ground was splashed with shallow pools,
And tufts of crackling cornstalks, two years old,
No man had reaped, and patches of spring grass,
Half-seen, as rose and sank the flares, were strewn
With the wreck of our attack: the bandoliers,
Packs, rifles, bayonets, belts, and haversacks,
Shell fragments, and the huge whole forms of shells
Shot fruitlessly – and everywhere the dead.
Only the dead were always present – present
As a vile sickly smell of rottenness;
The rustling stubble and the early grass,
The slimy pools – the dead men stank through all,
Pungent and sharp; as bodies loomed before,
And as we passed, they stank; then dulled away
To that vague foetor, all encompassing,
Infecting earth and air. They lay, all clothed,
Each in some new and piteous attitude
That we well marked to guide us back; as he,
Outside our wire, that lay on his back and crossed
His legs Crusader-wise; I smiled at that,
And thought of Elia* and his Temple Church.
From him, a quarter left, lay a small corpse,
Down in a hollow, huddled as in bed,
That one of us put his hand on unawares.
Next was a bunch of half a dozen men
All blown to bits, an archipelago

Of corrupt fragments, vexing to us three,
Who had no light to see by, save the flares.
On such a trail, so lit, for ninety yards
We crawled on belly and elbows, till we saw,
Instead of lumpish dead before our eyes,
The stakes and crosslines of the German wire.
We lay in shelter of the last dead man,
Ourselves as dead, and heard their shovels ring
Turning the earth, their talk and cough at times.
A sentry fired and a machine-gun spat;
They shot a flare above us, when it fell
And spluttered out in the pools of No Man's Land,
We turned and crawled past the remembered dead;
Past him and him, and them and him, until,
For he lay some way apart, we caught the scent
Of the Crusader and slid past his legs,
And through the wire and home, and got our rum.

Arthur Graeme West

* Charles Lamb

BREAK OF DAY IN THE TRENCHES

The darkness crumbles away.
It is the same old druid Time as ever,
Only a live thing leaps my hand,
A queer sardonic rat,
As I pull the parapet's poppy
To stick behind my ear.
Droll rat, they would shoot you if they knew
Your cosmopolitan sympathies.
Now you have touched this English hand
You will do the same to a German
Soon, no doubt, if it be your pleasure
To cross the sleeping green between.
It seems you inwardly grin as you pass
Strong eyes, fine limbs, haughty athletes,
Less chanced than you for life,
Bonds to the whims of murder,
Sprawled in the bowels of the earth,
The torn fields of France.
What do you see in our eyes
At the shrieking iron and flame
Hurled through still heavens?
What quaver –   what heart aghast?
Poppies whose roots are in man's veins
Drop, and are ever dropping;

But mine in my ear is safe –
Just a little white with the dust.

Isaac Rosenberg
June 1916

DREAMERS

Soldiers are citizens of death's grey land,
Drawing no dividend from time's tomorrows.
In the great hour of destiny they stand,
Each with his feuds, and jealousies, and sorrows.
Soldiers are sworn to action; they must win
Some flaming, fatal climax with their lives.
Soldiers are dreamers; when the guns begin
They think of firelit homes, clean beds and wives.

I see them in foul dug-outs, gnawed by rats,
And in the ruined trenches, lashed with rain,
Dreaming of things they did with ball and bats,
And mocked by hopeless longing to regain
Bank-holidays, and picture shows, and spats,
And going to the office in the train.

Siegfried Sassoon, Craiglockhart 1917

A SOLDIER'S JOB IS TO KILL

Extracts from a First World War Army Training Manual.

Guiding rule number 8 for weapons training

The sporting spirit and desire to play for his side, or team, or
regiment is inherent in every individual of the British race. This
should be fostered and made use of by the instructor.

In an assault all ranks go forward to kill, and only those who have
developed skill and strength by constant and continuous training
will be able to kill.   –   If possible, the point of the bayonet
should be directed against an opponent's throat, as the point will
enter easily and make a fatal wound on entering a few inches, and,
being near the eyes, makes an opponent flinch. Other vulnerable,
and usually exposed parts are the face, chest, lower abdomen and
thighs, and the region of the kidneys when the back is turned.
Four to six inches penetration is sufficient to incapacitate and
allow for a quick withdrawal, whereas if a bayonet is driven home
too far it is often impossible to withdraw it. In such cases a round
should be fired to break up the obstruction

The spirit of the bayonet must be inculcated into all ranks so that in the attack they will go forward with that aggressive determination and confidence which ensures the success of an assault.

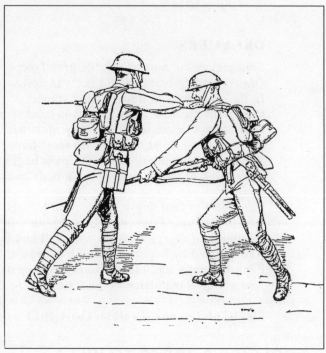

From an army training manual.
"Lesson 6.
Method of injuring an opponent: 35. The horizontal butt stroke – Step in and swing the *toe of the butt* at the opponent's jaw."

HOW SIEGFRIED SASSOON CAME TO WRITE *THE KISS*

Sassoon was at an army training school in 1916 and attended a lecture on the use of the bayonet given by a major who "spoke with homicidal eloquence." The major's ideas were based on the training manual quoted above. He told his audience that the bullet and bayonet were brother and sister. Sassoon originally wrote *The Kiss* he said, "as a sort of exercise – in Anglo-Saxon words, as far as I could manage it – after being disgusted by the barbarities of the famous bayonet fighting lecture. To this day I don't know what made me write it, for I never felt I could have stuck a bayonet into anyone, even in self-defence. The difficulty is that it [the poem] doesn't show any sign of satire." [1]

---

1   Quoted in the Preface to *Men Who March Away*, edited by I M Parsons.

THE KISS

To these I turn, in these I trust -
Brother Lead and Sister Steel.
To his blind power I make appeal,
I guard her beauty clean from rust.

He spins and burns and loves the air,
And splits a skull to win my praise;
But up the nobly marching days
She glitters naked cold and fair.

Sweet Sister, grant your soldier this:
That in good fury he may feel
The body where he sets his heel
Quail from your downward darting kiss.

Siegfried Sassoon

ARMS AND THE BOY

Let the boy try along this bayonet blade
How cold steel is, and keen with hunger for blood;
Blue with all malice, like a madman's flash;
And thinly drawn with famishing for flesh.

Lend him to stroke these blind, blunt bullet-leads,
Which long to nuzzle in the hearts of lads,
Or give him cartridges whose fine zinc teeth
Are sharp with sharpness of grief and death.

For his teeth seem for laughing round an apple.
There lurk no claws behind his fingers supple;
And God will grow no talons at his heels,
Nor antlers through the thickness of his curls.

Wilfred Owen, May 1918

ORDERS: TAKE NO PRISONERS

From a letter from Private A H Hubbard [1]: We had strict orders not to take prisoners, no matter if wounded. My first job was when I finished cutting some of their wire away, to empty my magazine on three Germans that came out of their deep dugouts,

---

1   7 July 1916, *Tommy Goes To War*, edited by Malcolm Brown, p167.

bleeding badly, and put them out of their misery. They cried for mercy, but I had my orders . . .

Robert Graves claimed that German patrols, coming across a wounded enemy soldier, would ususally cut his throat with a bowie-knife, whereas the British would normally use a cosh to smash his skull. Rescue was hazardous because the cries of a wounded man would draw attention, and fire, to the patrol.

TRAINING

In the summer of 1918 Wilfred Owen was training troops in England.

> For 14 hours yesterday I was at work – teaching Christ to lift his cross by numbers, and how to adjust his crown; and not to imagine he thirst until after the last halt. I attended his Supper to see that there were no complaints; and inspected his feet that they should be worthy of the nails. I see to it that he is dumb, and stands at attention before his accusers. With a piece of silver I buy him every day, and with maps I make him familiar with the topography of Golgotha.
>
> Letter to Osbert Sitwell, July 1918

SUPPRESSION OF THOUGHT IN SOLDIERS

> Independent thinking is not encouraged in a professional Army. It is a form of mutiny. Obedience is the supreme virtue. Theirs is not to reason why. Orders are to be carried out and not canvassed. Criticism is insubordination. The object of discipline is to accustom men to respond to a command instantly, by instant action, without thought of effect or consequence. There were many intelligent officers and men who knew that the orders given them during the War were utterly stupid and must have been given by Staffs who had no understanding of the conditions. But orders were orders. And with their men they went to a doom they foresaw as inevitable. Such an instinctive obedience to the word of command is essential to the efficiency of a body of men who have to face terror, death or mutilation in the discharge of their terrible duties.
>
> Lloyd George [1]

1   *War Memoirs,* p2041.

If only, I used to think, we poor bloody soldiers could walk out, walk home, and leave the politicians to make the best of a quarrel we did not understand and which had no interest for us! But though I believe these were the sentiments of nine men out of ten, there was no possibility of proceeding to action. A soldier is part of a machine: once the machine is in movement, he functions as part of a machine, or simply gets killed. There is very little scope for individual initiative, for non-cooperation.

Herbert Read[1]

Training for bravery

After a dinner party at St Omer in northern France on 4th December 1914, at which King George V was one of the guests, Haig wrote in his diary,

The King seemed very cheery but inclined to think that all our troops are by nature brave and is ignorant of all the efforts which commanders must make to keep up the 'morale' of their men in war, and of all the training which is necessary in peace in order to enable a company for instance to go forward as an organised unit in the face of almost certain death.

Later the King expressed the opinion that the award of the Victoria Cross was appropriate for carrying a wounded man out of battle. Haig explained to the King the steps he had to take to stop this kind of bravery getting out of hand.

As a matter of fact we have to take special precautions during a battle to post police, to prevent more unwounded men than are necessary from accompanying a wounded man back from the firing line! [2]

DEATH'S MEN

Under a grey October sky
The little squads that drill
Click arms and legs mechanically,
Emptied of ragged will!

Of ragged will that frets the sky
From crags jut ragged pines,
A wayward immortality,
That flies from Death's trim lines.

1   *Annals of Innocence and Experience*, p 153.
2   *Private Papers*, p79.

The men of death stand trim and neat,
Their faces stiff as stone,
Click, clack, go four and twenty feet
From twelve machines of bone.

"Click, clack, left, right, form fours, incline,"
The jack-box sergeant cries;
For twelve erect and wooden dolls
One clockwork doll replies.

And twelve souls wander 'mid still clouds
In a land of snow-drooped trees,
Faint, foaming streams fall in grey hills
Like beards on old men's knees.

Old men, old hills, old kings and beards
Cold stone-grey still cascades
Hung high above this shuddering earth
Where the red blood sinks and fades.

Then the quietness of all ancient things,
Their round and full repose
As balm upon twelve wandering souls
Down from the grey sky flows.

The rooks from out the tall gaunt trees
In shrieking circles pass;
Click, clack, click, clack, go Death's trim men
Across the Autumn grass.

W J Turner

THE TARGET

I shot him, and it had to be
One of us! 'Twas him or me.
"Couldn't be helped," and none can blame
Me, for you would do the same.

My mother, she can't sleep for fear
Of what might be a-happening here
To me. Perhaps it might be best
To die, and set her fears at rest.

For worst is worst, and worry's done.
Perhaps he was the only son . . .
Yet God keeps still, and does not say
A word of guidance any way.

Well, if they get me, first I'll find
That boy, and tell him all my mind,
And see who felt the bullet worst,
And ask his pardon, if I durst.

All's tangle. Here's my job.
A man might rave, or shout, or sob;
And God He takes no sort of heed.
This is a bloody mess indeed.

Ivor Gurney

In the mind of all the English soldiers there is absolutely no hate for the Germans, but a kind of brotherly though slightly contemptuous kindness − as to men who are going through a bad time as well as ourselves.

Ivor Gurney, letter to Marion Scott, 17 February 1917

Herbert Read on avoiding killing

During the whole war I never deliberately or consciously killed an individual man, with the possible exception of the one who was accompanying a German officer in [a] raid . . . I fired in self-defence, at an advancing mass of men; but I never in cold blood selected my mark, with the intention of bringing to an end a human life.[1]

THE HAPPY WARRIOR

His wild heart beats with painful sobs
his strain'd hands clench an ice cold rifle
his aching jaws grip a hot parch'd tongue
his wide eyes search unconsciously.

He cannot shriek.

Bloody saliva
dribbles down his shapeless jacket.

---

1   *Annals of Innocence and Experience,* p 153.

I saw him stab
and stab again
a well-killed Bosche.

This is the happy warrior,
this is he . . .

Herbert Read

ATROCITIES

REMORSE

Lost in the swamp and welter of the pit,
He flounders off the duck-boards; only he knows
Each flash and spouting crash, – each instant lit
When gloom reveals the streaming rain. He goes
Heavily, blindly on. And, while he blunders,
"Could anything be worse than this?" – he wonders,
Remembering how he saw those Germans run,
Screaming for mercy among the stumps of trees:
Green-faced, they dodged and darted: there was one
Livid with terror, clutching at his knees . . .
Our chaps were sticking 'em like pigs . . .
"Oh Hell!" He thought – "there's things in war one dare
not tell Poor father sitting safe at home, who reads
Of dying heroes and their deathless deeds."

Siegfried Sassoon, February 1918

Sassoon as a soldier

> The number of Germans whom I killed or caused to be killed
> could hardly be compared with his (Sassoon's) wholesale slaugh-
> ter. In fact, Siegfried's unconquerable idealism changed direc-
> tion with his environment: he varied between happy warrior and
> bitter pacifist.
>
> Robert Graves, *Goodbye to All That*

Siegfried Sassoon's Diary – attitudes to killing and death

March 31st 1916

> Last night, warmer and lovely with stars, found me creeping about
> in front of our wire with Corporal O'Brien. Got quite near the
> German wire but couldn't find the sap which had been mentioned.

Out about an hour and a half; great fun. To-night I'm going to try and spot one of their working-parties and chuck some bombs at them. Better to get a sling at them in the open – even if on one's belly – than to sit here and have a great thing drop on one's head. I found it most exhilarating – just like starting for a race. Great thing is to get as many sensations as possible. No good being out here unless one takes the full amount of risks, and I want to get a good name in the Battalion, for the sake of poetry and poets, whom I represent.

April 1st 1916

I used to say I couldn't kill anyone in this war; but, since they shot Tommy[1], I would gladly stick a bayonet into a German by daylight.

April 4th 1916

I want to smash someone's skull; I want to have a scrap and get out of the war for a bit or for ever. Sitting in a trench waiting for a rifle-grenade isn't fighting: war is clambering out of the top trench at 3 o' clock in the morning with a lot of rum-drugged soldiers who don't know where they're going – half of them to be blasted with machine-guns at point-blank range – trying to get over the wire which our artillery have failed to destroy. I can't get my own back for Hamo and Tommy that way. While I am really angry with the enemy, as I am lately, I must work it off, as these things don't last long with me as a rule. If I get shot it will be rotten for some people at home, but I am bound to get it in the neck sometime, so why not make a creditable show, and let people see that poets can fight as well as anybody else? And death is the best adventure of all – better than living idleness and sinking into the groove again and trying to be happy. Life is precious to us all now; too precious to keep long.

---

1   Lieutenant David Thomas.

PEACE

Down glaring dusty roads, a sanctuary of trees,
Green for my gaze and cool, and hushed with pigeon's croon:
Chill pitcher'd water for my thirst; and sweet as these,
Anger grown tired of hate, and peace returning soon.

In my heart there's cruel war that must be waged
In darkness vile with moans and bleeding bodies maimed;
A gnawing hunger drives me, wild to be assuaged,
And bitter lust chuckles within me unashamed.

Come back to heal me when my feckless course is run,
Peace, that I sought in life; crown me among the dead;
Stoop to me like a lover when the fight is done;
Fold me in sleep; and let the stars be overhead.

Siegfried Sassoon, 2 April 1916

Atrocities? What atrocities? – Robert Graves's views

Propaganda reports of atrocities were, it was agreed, ridiculous . . .
We no longer believed the highly-coloured accounts of German
atrocities in Belgium; knowing the Belgians now at first-hand.
By atrocities we meant, specifically, rape, mutilation and torture
– not summary shootings of suspected spies, harbourers of spies,
francs-tireurs, or disobedient local officials. If the atrocity list
had to include the accidental-on-purpose bombing or machine-
gunning of civilians from the air, the Allies were now committing
as many atrocities as the Germans. French and Belgian civilians
had often tried to win our sympathy by exhibiting mutilations of
children – stumps of hands and feet, for instance – repre-
senting them as deliberate, fiendish atrocities when as likely as
not, they were merely the result of shell-fire. We did not believe
rape to be any more common on the German side of the line than
on the Allied side. And since a bully-beef diet, fear of death, and
absence of wives made ample provision of women necessary in
the occupied areas, no doubt the German army authorities provided brothels in the principal French towns behind the line, as
the French did on the Allied side. We did not believe stories of
women's forcible enlistment in these establishments. "What's
wrong with the voluntary system?" we asked cynically.

As for atrocities against soldiers – where should one draw the
line? The British soldier, at first, regarded as atrocious the use
of bowie-knives by German patrols. After a time, he learned to
use them himself; they were cleaner killing weapons than revolv-
ers or bombs. The Germans regarded as equally atrocious the
British Mark VII rifle bullet, which was more apt to turn on

striking than the German bullet. For true atrocities, meaning personal rather than military violation of the code of war, few opportunities occurred – except in the interval between the surrender of prisoners and their arrival (or non-arrival) at headquarters. Advantage was only too often taken of this opportunity. The conductors would report on arrival at headquarters that a German shell had killed the prisoners; and no questions would be asked. We had every reason to believe that the same thing happened on the German side, where prisoners, as useless mouths to feed in a country already short of rations, would be even less welcome.[1]

FRIENDSHIP, LOVE, AND SEX

Diary of Siegfried Sassoon, 1 April 1916: Someone told me a year ago that love, sorrow, and hate were things I had never known (things which every poet *should* know!). Now I've known love for Bobbie and Tommy, and grief for Hamo[2] and Tommy, and hate has come also, and the lust to kill.

TWO FUSILIERS

And have we done with War at last,
Well, we've been lucky devils both,
And there's no need of pledge or oath
To bind our lovely friendship fast,
By firmer stuff
Close bound enough.

By wire and wood and stake we're bound,
By Fricourt and by Festubert,
By whipping rain, by the sun's glare,
By all the misery and loud sound,
By a Spring day,
By Picard clay.

Show me the two so closely bound
As we, by the wet bond of blood,
By friendship blossoming from mud,
By Death: we faced him, and we found
Beauty in Death,
In dead men, breath.

Robert Graves

1   *Goodbye to All That*, P152-154.
2   Bobby Hanmer; Hamo was Sassoon's brother.

APOLOGIA PRO POEMATE MEO*

I, too, saw God through mud, –
The mud that cracked on cheeks when wretches smiled.
War brought more glory to their eyes than blood,
And gave their laughs more glee than shakes a child.

Merry it was to laugh there –
Where death becomes absurd and life absurder.
For power was on us as we slashed bones bare
Not to feel sickness or remorse of murder.

I, too, have dropped off Fear –
Behind the barrage, dead as my platoon,
And sailed my spirit surging light and clear
Past the entanglement where hopes lay strewn;

And witnessed exultation –
Faces that used to curse me, scowl for scowl,
Shine and lift up with passion of oblation,
Seraphic for an hour; though they were foul.

I have made fellowships –
Untold of happy lovers in old song.
For love is not the binding of fair lips
With the soft silk of eyes that look and long,

By Joy, whose ribbon slips, –
But wound with war's hard wire whose stakes are strong;
Bound with the bandage of the arm that drips;
Knit in the webbing of the rifle-thong.

I have perceived much beauty
In the hoarse oaths that kept our courage straight;
Heard music in the silentness of duty;
Found peace where shell-storms spouted reddest spate.

Nevertheless, except you share
With them in hell the sorrowful dark of hell,
Whose world is but the trembling of a flare
And heaven but as the highway for a shell,

You shall not hear their mirth:
You shall not come to think them well content
By any jest of mine. These men are worth
Your tears. You are not worth their merriment.

Wilfred Owen, November, December 1917

*APOLOGIA PRO POEMATE MEO – Justification for my poetry

Did the exploding of millions of tons of explosives bring about climatic change? — There was certainly exceptional rainfall during the war which led to dreadful problems with mud. A trench like this was a common sight.

MY COMPANY

I

You became
In many acts and quiet observances
A body and a soul, entire.

I cannot tell
What time your life became mine:
Perhaps when one summer night
We halted on the roadside
In the starlight only,
And you sang your sad home-songs,

Dirges which I standing outside you
Coldly condemned.

Perhaps, one night, descending cold
When rum was mighty acceptable,
And my doling gave birth to sensual gratitude.

And then our fights: we've fought together
Compact, unanimous;
And I have felt the pride of leadership.

In many acts and quiet observances
You absorbed me:
Until one day I stood eminent
And I saw you gathered round me,
Uplooking,
And about you a radiance that seemed to beat
With variant glow and to give
Grace to our unity.

But, God! I know that I'll stand
Someday in the loneliest wilderness,
Someday my heart will cry
For the soul that has been, but that now
Is scatter'd with the winds,
Deceased and devoid.

I know that I'll wander with a cry:
"O beautiful men, O men I loved,
O whither are you gone, my company?"

II

My men go wearily
With their monstrous burdens.
They bear wooden planks
And iron sheeting
Through the area of death.

When a flare curves through the sky
They rest immobile.

Then on again,
Sweating and blaspheming –
"Oh, bloody Christ!"

My men, my modern Christs,
Your bloody agony confronts the world.

III

A man of mine
                    lies on the wire.
It is death to fetch his soulless corpse.

A man of mine
                    lies on the wire;
And he will rot
And first his lips
The worms will eat.

It is not thus I would have him kiss'd,
But with the warm passionate lips
Of his comrade here.

IV

I can assume
A giant attitude and godlike mood,
And then detachedly regard
All riots, conflicts and collisions.

The men I've lived with
Lurch suddenly into a far perspective;
They distantly gather like a dark cloud of birds
In the autumn sky.

Urged by some unanimous
Volition of fate,
Clouds clash in opposition;
The sky quivers, the dead descend;
Earth yawns.

They are all of one species.

From my giant attitude,
In godlike mood,
I laugh till space is filled
With hellish merriment.

Then again I resume
My human docility,
Bow my head
And share their doom.

Herbert Read

Officer and men

Between the company officer and his men there is every opportunity for the development of a relationship which abolishes all class distinctions and which can have a depth of understanding and sympathy for which I know no parallel in civilian life.

Herbert Read[1]

IN MEMORIAM

Private D. Sutherland killed in action in the German trench, May 16th, 1916, and the others who died.

So you were David's father,
And he was your only son,
And the new-cut peats are rotting
And the work is left undone,
Because of an old man weeping,
Just an old man in pain,
For David, his son David,
That will not come again.

Oh, the letters he wrote you,
And I can see them still,
Not a word of the fighting
But just the sheep on the hill
And how you should get the crops in
Ere the year get stormier,
And the Bosches have got his body,
And I was his officer.

You were only David's father,
But I had fifty sons
When we went up in the evening
Under the arch of the guns,
And we came back at twilight –
O God! I heard them call
To me for help and pity
That could not help at all.

Oh, never will I forget you,
My men that trusted me,
More my sons than your fathers',
For they could only see
The little helpless babies

1   *Annals of Innocence and Experience,* p 156.

And the young men in their pride.
They could not see you dying,
And hold you while you died.

Happy and young and gallant,
They saw their first-born go,
But not the strong limbs broken
And the beautiful men brought low,
The piteous writhing bodies,
They screamed "Don't leave me, sir,"
For they were only your fathers
But I was your officer.

E A Mackintosh

BOY LOVES GIRL

One of the extraordinary things about the poetry of the First World War
written by men is that hetero-sexual love, girlfriends, wives and families
almost never feature.

Whilst poetry of the war extended its range to reveal more of the suffering of war than previously, it remained quiet on the actual sexual
behaviour of many soldiers. This behaviour contrasted with the images
of soldiers presented by the media in Britain.

OH LOVERS PARTED

Oh lovers parted,
Oh all you lonely over all the world,
You that look out at morning empty-hearted,
Or you, all night turning uncomforted . . .
Would God, would God, you could be comforted . . .
                . . . eyes that weep,
And a long time for love; and, after, sleep.

Rupert Brooke
(a fragment found near the end of his notebook after his death.)

A French woman tolerates a Christmas kiss from an English soldier.

From PARTING

Times more than once, all ways about the world,
Have I clasped hands; waved sorrowful good-bye;
Watched far cliffs fading, till my sea-wake swirled
To mingle bluely with a landless sky:
Then – even as the sea-drowned cliffs behind –
Felt sorrow drowning into memory;
And heard, in every thrill of every wind,
New voices welcoming across the sea.

Until it seemed nor land nor love had power
To hold my heart in any firm duress:
Grieving, I sorrowed but a little hour;
Loving, I knew desire's sure faithlessness:

Until, by many a love dissatisfied,
Of each mistrustful and to each untrue,
I found – as one who, having long denied,
Finds faith at last – this greater Love, in you.

Parting? We are not parted, woman mine!
Though hands have clasped, though lips have kissed good-bye;
Though towns glide past, and fields, and fields of brine –

My body takes the warrior-way, not I.
I am still with you; you with me; one heart;
One equal union, soul to certain soul:
Time cannot sever us, nor sorrow part,
Nor any sea, who keep our vision whole.

Gilbert Frankau

ON LEAVE

I came from the City of Fear,
From the scarred brown land of pain,
Back into life again . . .
And I thought, as the leave-boat rolled
Under the veering stars –
Wind a-shriek in her spars –
Shivering there, and cold,
Of music, of warmth , and of wine –
To be mine
For a whole short week . . .
And I thought, adrowse in the train,
Of London, suddenly near;
And of how – small doubt – I should find
There, as of old,
Some woman – foolishly kind:
Fingers to hold,
A cheek,
A mouth to kiss – and forget,
Forget in a little while,
Forget
When I came again
To the scarred brown land of pain,
To the sodden things and the vile,
And the tedious battle-fret.

From *Meeting,* Gilbert Frankau, Flanders, 1916

A soldiers' song

APRÈS LA GUERRE

To the tune of *Sous les Ponts de Paris*

Après la guerre finie,
Soldat anglais parti.
Mamzelle Fransay bokoo pleuray,
Après la guerre finie.

Après la guerre finie,
Soldat anglais parti.
Mamzelle in the family way,
Après la guerre finie.

Aprè la guerre finie,
Soldat anglais parti.
Mamzelle can go to hell,
Après la guerre finie.

Red and blue lamps

The battalion's sole complaint against Montagne was that women were not so complaisant in that part of the country as around Béthune. The officers had the unfair advantage of being able to borrow horses and ride into Amiens. There was a "Blue Lamp" at Amiens, as at Abbeville, Le Havre, Rouen, and all the large towns behind the lines: the Blue Lamp reserved for officers, the Red Lamp for men. Whether, in the careful maintenance of discipline, the authorities made any special provision for warrant-officers, and whether the Blue Lamp women had to show any particular qualifications for their higher social ranking, are questions I cannot answer. I remained puritanical, except in language, throughout my overseas service.

Robert Graves, *Goodbye to All That* [1]

Young lad in Béthune

Eighteen-year-old Bert Chaney was billeted in Béthune. One day he saw a long queue of soldiers outside a building in the town.

Thinking there might be a concert or cinema – we called them living pictures at that time – I asked what was going on. "A bit

1   p150/151.

of a grumble and a grunt," I was told. "Only costs two francs."
Puzzled, I asked what that meant. "Cor blimey, lad. Didn't you
learn anything at all where you come from?" They thought me a
proper mug. Fancy a lad like me, and a Cockney at that, not
knowing what that meant – and didn't I know what a red lamp
stood for? These places, I was told, were not for young lads like
me, but for married men who were missing their wives.

One day I looked inside and saw a large room with a long bar
down one side, the room crowded with men, with the girls standing on the stairs leaning over the banister, presumably waiting for
the next customer. They all wore voluminous dressing-gowns
and anything less likely to excite a man would be hard to imagine.
A leg might be showing, or even a bare shoulder, to give the
impression they had nothing on underneath. To my young eyes
they all looked like disapproving mothers watching with distaste
the antics of their young offspring below.

Bert Chaney [1]

Robert Graves reports a chat with the enemy

One night at Cuinchy we had orders from divisional headquarters
to shout across No Man's Land and make the enemy take part in
a conversation. The object was to find out how strongly the
German front trenches were manned after dark. A German-speak-
ing officer in the company among the brick-stacks shouted
through a megaphone: "Wie Geht's Ihnen Kameraden?"

Somebody shouted back in delight: "Ach, Tommee, hast du denn
deutsch gelernt?"

Firing stopped, and a conversation began across the fifty yards or
so of No Man's Land. The Germans refused to disclose what
regiment they were, or talk any military shop.

One of them shouted out: "Les sheunes madamoiselles de La
Bassée bonnes pour coucher avec. Les madamoiselles de Béthune
bonne aussi, hein?"

Our spokesman refused to discuss sex.

Venereal disease

In the months before the Battle of the Somme the Rev John Stanhope
Walder was:

1   *A Lad Goes to War* in *People at War 1914-1918,* edited by Michael Moynihan, p 107.

dismayed by the steady stream of patients to the hospital's isolation camp who had contracted venereal diseases including "old offenders who often sought to justify themselves" and "a sadly large proportion of officers, some of them completely broken, others more callous than any of the men. . . I do not want to strike a hopeless note," he told his fellow-clergy, "but it is undoubtedly true that apart from the fear of death, there is not much that makes for Christian living among our soldiers now in France."[1]

From 1914 to 1918, 153,531 British and Empire soldiers in France and Belgium were admitted to hospital with gonorrhoea, syphilis or other forms of venereal disease. In 1916 such cases represented 19.24 per cent of all admissions to hospital, but the peak period for cases of venereal diseases was in 1918 when 60,099 cases were treated in France. This was in spite of the fact that the worried army had punished VD victims by disallowing leave for a whole year after release from hospital (a rule introduced in January 1917) and the placing of all brothels out of bounds to all soldiers from April 1918. [2]

BROTHERS IN ARMS

Consideration from the Germans during the Battle of Loos

After the first disastrous day of the Battle of Loos the Germans took pity on their enemy and ceased firing to allow the British to recover their wounded. Survivors worked throughout the night in complete safety, managing to gather all the wounded and most of the dead by the time dawn came.

HATE NOT, FEAR NOT

Kill if you must, but never hate:
Man is but grass and hate is blight,
The sun will scorch you soon or late,
Die wholesome then, since you must fight.

Hate is a fear, and fear is rot
That cankers root and fruit alike,
Fight cleanly then, hate not, fear not,
Strike with no madness when you strike,

1   *People at War 1914-1918*, edited by Michael Moynihan, P71.
2   *A Nation in Arms*, Peter Simpkins (contributor), p185/186.

Fever and fear distract the world,
But calm be you though madmen shout,
Through blazing fires of battle hurled,
Hate not, strike, fear not, stare Death out!

Robert Graves

RELIGION

WILFRED OWEN'S DISILLUSIONMENT

Christian Duty

I am more and more Christian as I walk the unchristian ways of
Christendom. Already I have comprehended a light which never
will filter into the dogma of any national church: namely that one
of Christ's essential commands was: Passivity at any price! Suffer dishonour and disgrace; but never resort to arms. Be bullied,
be outraged, be killed; but do not kill. It may be chimerical and
an ignominious principle, but there it is. It can only be ignored:
and I think pulpit professionals are ignoring it very skilfully and
successfully indeed. . .

Am I not myself a conscientious objector with a very seared
conscience?

Christ is literally in no man's land. There men often hear His
voice: Greater love hath no man than this, that a man lay down
his life – for a friend.

Is it spoken in English only, and French?

I do not believe so.

Thus you see how pure Christianity will not fit in with pure
patriotism.

Wilfred Owen, in a letter c.16th May 1917.

AT A CALVARY NEAR THE ANCRE

One ever hangs where shelled roads part.
In this war He too lost a limb,
But his disciples hide apart;
And now the soldiers bear with Him.

Near Golgotha strolls many a priest,
And in their faces there is pride
That they were flesh marked by the Beast
By whom the gentle Christ's denied.

The scribes on all the people shove
And bawl allegiance to the state,
But they who love the greater love
Lay down their life; they do not hate.

Wilfred Owen

Notes: THE ANCRE - Wilfred Owen was serving near the river Ancre in January, 1917. CALVARY – site of the crucifixion of Christ. In France there are thousands of "Calvaries", crosses bearing images of Christ – situated, usually, at cross roads. Many were damaged in the war (some soldiers even used them for target practice) so it was not uncommon to see a Christ figure which had "lost a limb." GOLGOTHA is another name for Calvary. HIDE APART – when Christ was crucified his disciples fled into hiding. BEAR WITH HIM – carry Christ's cross, and/or humour Him. FLESH-MARKED – suffering from small wounds (no doubt true of some priests who ventured too close to the fighting), but additionally, the Devil was believed to leave his fingermarks on his followers. THE BEAST – Germany (the cause of the small wounds), also, a name for the Devil and for war itself. – The priests were serving the Devil, war, by opposing the Devil, Germany, and in so doing were denying Christ's teachings: "love one another," and "love your enemies."

In a rather disjointed letter dated 31st March, 1918, which was written when Owen was recovering from shell-shock, he wrote his version of a famous quotation from St John's Gospel.

God so hated the world that he gave several millions of English begotten sons, that whosoever believeth in them should not perish, but have a comfortable life.

The original version reads, "For God so loved the world, that he gave his only begotten Son, that whosoever believeth in him should not perish, but have eternal life." (*John* 3, v 16.)

GREATER LOVE

Red lips are not so red
As the stained stones kissed by the English dead.
Kindness of wooed and wooer
Seems shame to their love pure.
O Love, your eyes lose lure
When I behold eyes blinded in my stead!

Your slender attitude
Trembles not exquisite like limbs knife-skewed,
Rolling and rolling there
Where God seems not to care;
Till the fierce Love they bear
Cramps them in death's extreme decrepitude.

Your voice sings not so soft, –
Though even as wind murmuring through raftered loft, –
Your dear voice is not dear,
Gentle, and evening clear,
As theirs whom none now hear,
Now earth has stopped their piteous mouths that coughed.

Heart, you were never hot,
Nor large, nor full like hearts made great with shot;
And though your hand be pale,
Paler are all which trail
Your cross through flame and hail:
Weep, you may weep, for you may touch them not.

Wilfred Owen

THE PARABLE OF THE OLD MAN AND THE YOUNG

So Abram rose, and clave the wood and went,
And took the fire with him and a knife.
And as they sojourned both of them together,
Isaac the first-born spake and said, My Father,
Behold the preparations, fire and iron,
But where the lamb for this burnt offering?
Then Abram bound the youth with belts and straps,
And builded parapets and trenches there,
And stretched forth the knife to slay his son.
When lo! an Angel called him out of heaven,
Saying, Lay not thy hand upon the lad,
Neither do anything to him, thy son.
Behold! Caught in a thicket by its horns,
A ram. Offer the Ram of Pride instead.

But the old man would not so, but slew his son,
And half the seed of Europe, one by one.

Wilfred Owen

GOD, HOW I HATE YOU

God! how I hate you, you young cheerful men,
Whose pious poetry blossoms on your graves
As soon as you are in them . . .
                    Hark how one chants –
"O happy to have lived these epic days" –-
"These epic days!" And *he'd* been to France,
And seen the trenches, glimpsed the huddled dead
In the periscope, hung on the rusty wire:
Choked by this sickly foetor, day and night
Blown down his throat: stumbled through ruined hearths,
Proved all that muddy brown monotony
Where blood's the only coloured thing. Perhaps
Had seen a man killed, a sentry shot at night,
Hunched as he fell, his feet on the firing-step,
His neck against the back slope of the trench,
And the rest doubled between, his head
Smashed like an eggshell and the warm grey brain
Spattered all bloody on the parados . . .
Yet still God's in His Heaven, all is right
In this best possible of worlds . . . God loves us,
God looks down on this our strife
And smiles in pity, blows a pipe at times
And calls some warriors home . . .
                    How rare life is!
On earth, the love and fellowship of men,
Men sternly banded: banded for what end?
Banded to maim and kill their fellow men –
For even Huns are men. In Heaven above
A genial umpire, a good judge of sport
Won't let us hurt each other! Let's rejoice
God keeps us faithful, pens us still in fold.
Ah, what a faith is ours (almost it seems,
Large as a mustard seed) – we trust and trust,
Nothing can shake us! Ah how good God is
To suffer us to be born just now, when youth
That else would rust, can slake his blade in gore
Where very God Himself does seem to walk
The bloody fields of Flanders He so loves.

Arthur Graeme West

West's doubts

West was an atheist who found the Christian God, that his fellow soldiers believed in, incomprehensible. He was a man full of doubts. He
volunteered to fight, and later trained as an officer. He was puzzled
by fellow officers whom he described as "worthy and unselfish. . . not
aggressive or offensively military. . . almost the best value in the upper
class that we have. . ." He couldn't understand how they could, "give
so much labour and time to the killing of others, though to the plain
appeals of poverty and inefficiency in government, as well national
as international, they are so absolutely heedless. How is it that as much
blood and money cannot be poured out when it is a question of
saving and helping mankind rather than of slaying them?"

He toyed with the idea of refusing to fight but lacked the courage to do
so. "No one is willing to revise his ideas or make clear to himself
his motives for joining the war; even if anybody feels regret for having
enlisted, he does not like to admit it to himself. Why should he?
Every man, woman and child is taught to regard him as a hero." [1]

TO ANY DEAD OFFICER

Well, how are things in Heaven? I wish you'd say,
Because I'd like to know that you're all right.
Tell me, have you found everlasting day,
Or been sucked in by everlasting night?
For when I shut my eyes your face shows plain;
I hear you make some cheery old remark –
I can rebuild you in my brain,
Though you've gone out patrolling in the dark.

You hated tours of trenches; you were proud
Of nothing more than having good years to spend;
Longed to get home and join the careless crowd
Of chaps who work in peace with Time for friend.
That's all washed out now. You're beyond the wire:
No earthly chance can send you crawling back;
You've finished with machine-gun fire –
Knocked over in a hopeless dud-attack.

---

1   Quoted by Tim Cross, in *The Lost Voices of World War One*, p68.

Somehow I always thought you'd get done in,
Because you were so desperate keen to live:
You were all out to try and save your skin,
Well knowing how much the world had got to give.
You joked at shells and talked the usual "shop,"
Stuck to your dirty job and did it fine:
With "Jesus Christ! When *will* it stop?
Three years . . . It's hell unless we break their line."

So when they told me you'd been left for dead
I wouldn't believe them, feeling it *must* be true.
Next week the bloody Roll of Honour said
"Wounded and missing" – (That's the thing to do
When lads are left in shell-holes dying slow,
With nothing but blank sky and wounds that ache,
Moaning for water till they know
It's night, and then it's not worth while to wake!)

Good-bye, old lad! Remember me to God,
And tell Him that our Politicians swear
They won't give in till Prussian Rule's been trod
Under the Heel of England . . . Are you there? . . .
Yes . . . and the War won't end for at least two years;
But we've got stacks of men . . . I'm blind with tears,
Staring into the dark. Cheero!
I wish they'd killed you in a decent show.

Siegfried Sassoon, Mid-June 1917

A MYSTIC AS SOLDIER

I lived my days apart,
Dreaming fair songs for God;
By the glory in my heart
Covered and crowned and shod.

Now God is in the strife,
And I must seek Him there,
Where death outnumbers life,
And fury smites the air.

I walk the secret way
With anger in my brain.
O music through my clay,
When will you sound again?

Siegfried Sassoon, November 1916

VICARIOUS CHRIST

The Bishop of Byegumb was an old friend of our General;
In fact he knew him out in the Soudan.
He preached to our Brigade; and the impression that he made
Was astounding; he was such a Christian man.

He compared us to the martyrs who were burnt alive and
strangled;
O, it made us love the war – to hear him speak!
"The Americans," he said, "are coming over in large numbers;"
"And the Huns are getting weaker every week."

The Bishop of Byegumb has preached on Victory, I am certain,
(Though I haven't seen it mentioned in the Press).
But when I was his victim, how I wished I could have kicked
him,
For he made me love Religion less and less.

Siegfried Sassoon

"THEY"

The Bishop tells us: "When the boys come back
They will not be the same; for they'll have fought
In a just cause: they lead the last attack
On Anti-Christ; their comrades' blood has bought
New right to breed an honourable race,
They have challenged Death and dared him face to face."

We're none of us the same!" the boys reply.
"For George lost both his legs; and Bill's stone blind;
Poor Jim's shot through the lungs and like to die;
And Bert's gone syphilitic: You'll not find
A chap who's served that hasn't found *some* change."
And the Bishop said: "The ways of God are strange!"

Siegfried Sassoon, 31 October 1916

CHRIST AND THE SOLDIER

I

The straggled soldier halted – stared at Him –
Then clumsily dumped down upon his knees,
Gasping, "O blessed crucifix, I'm beat!"
And Christ, still sentried by the seraphim,
Near the front-line, between two splintered trees,
Spoke him: "My son, behold these hands and feet."

The soldier eyed Him upward, limb by limb,
Paused at the Face; then muttered, "Wounds like these
Would shift a bloke to Blighty just a treat!"
Christ, gazing downward, grieving and ungrim,
Whispered, "I made for you the mysteries,
Beyond all battles moves the Paraclete."*

II

The soldier chucked his rifle in the dust,
And slipped his pack, and wiped his neck, and said –
"O Christ Almighty, stop this bleeding fight!"
Above that hill the sky was stained like rust
With smoke. In sullen daybreak flaring red
The guns were thundering bombardment's blight.

The soldier cried, "I was born full of lust,
With hunger, thirst, and wishfulness to wed.
Who cares today if I done wrong or right?"
Christ asked all pitying, "Can you put no trust
In my known word that shrives each faithful head?
Am I not resurrection, life and light?"

III

Machine-guns rattled from below the hill;
High bullets flicked and whistled through the leaves;
And smoke came drifting from exploding shells.
Christ said, "Believe; and I can cleanse your ill.
I have not died in vain between two thieves;
Nor made a fruitless gift of miracles."

The soldier answered, "Heal me if you will,
Maybe there's comfort when a soul believes
In mercy, and we need it in these hells.

But be you for both sides? I'm paid to kill
And if I shoot a man his mother grieves.
Does that come into what your teaching tells?"

A bird lit on the Christ and twittered gay;
Then a breeze passed and shook the ripening corn.
A Red Cross wagon bumped along the track.
Forsaken Jesus dreamed in the desolate day –
Uplifted Jesus, Prince of Peace forsworn –
An observation post for the attack.

"Lord Jesus, ain't you got no more to say?"
Bowed hung that head below the crown of thorns.
The soldier shifted, and picked up his pack,
And slung his gun, and stumbled on his way.
"O God," he groaned, "why ever was I born?" . . .
The battle boomed, and no reply came back.

Siegfried Sassoon, 5 August 1916

*Paraclete: the Holy Ghost as comforter or advocate

Siegfried Sassoon to Felicitas Corrigan, 28 June 1962.

Christ and the Soldier will probably make you say, like Alice,
"Curiouser and curiouser." Proof, anyhow, that I wasn't pagan-
minded in 1916. But how write that and go through the whole
war without saying a prayer? My only religion was my vocation
as a poet, and my resolve to do my duty bravely. I don't think I
quite knew what I was trying to say. I suppose that behind it was
the persistent anti-parson mentality – and it was difficult to
swallow their patriotic pietism, which seemed unreal to many of
us front-liners. But apparently a little of the reality came through
to me in that tentative poem. (I made a few alterations when I
rediscovered it in one of my war note-books, but nothing which
affects its significance.)

IN THE CHURCH OF ST OUEN

Time makes me be a soldier. But I know
That had I lived six hundred years ago
I might have tried to build within my heart
A church like this, where I could dwell apart
With chanting peace. My spirit longs for prayer;
And, lost to God, I seek him everywhere.
Here, where the windows burn and bloom like flowers,
And sunlight falls and fades with tranquil hours,

I could be half a saint, for like a rose
In heart-shaped stone the glory of Heaven glows.
But where I stand, desiring yet to stay,
Hearing rich music at the close of day,
The Spring Offensive (Easter is its date)
Calls me. And that's the music I await.

Siegfried Sassoon, Rouen, 4 March 1917

Soldiers' attitudes to religion

Robert Graves doubted that as many as one soldier in a hundred had any religious feeling.

Attitudes to Anglican priests were particularly derogatory as they were under instructions to keep clear of the front lines. Soldiers interpreted this as weakness. In contrast, the Catholic priests earned the soldiers' respect as they went gladly everywhere they were able, including the front lines, to comfort the dying and give extreme unction.

Fatalism, and loss of individuality – Herbert Read recorded these observations:

> Faith was of many kinds. But essentially it was simply a level condition of the mind. It might be Christian – sometimes was, I observed. But more often it was just fatalistic, and by fatalism I mean a resolve to live in peace of mind, in possession of mind, despite any physical environment. Such was the faith, or philosophy, that belonged to a great body of men, and was held in very different degrees of intellectuality and passion. In some – they were the majority – it was a reversion to a primitive state of belief. Every bullet has its billet. What's the use of worryin'? But in others it was a subtler form of consciousness. The war seemed to annihilate all sense of individuality. The mass of it was so immense that oneself as a separate unit could not rationally exist. But there is a sense in which the death of individuality means the birth of personality. This truth is the basis of all sacrifice and martyrdom. A saint may die for his faith, but only because that faith is an expression of his personality. And so in the presence of danger, and in the immediate expectation of death, one can forget the body and its fears and exist wholly as a mind.[1]

1   *Annals of Innocence and Experience*, p 148.

AFTER BATTLE

AFTER THE BATTLE

So they are satisfied with our Brigade,
And it remains to parcel out the bays!
And we shall have the usual Thanks Parade,
The beaming General, and the soapy praise.

You will come up in your capricious car
To find your heroes sulking in the rain,
To tell us how magnificent we are,
And how you hope we'll do the same again.

And we, who knew your old abusive tongue,
Who heard you hector us a week before,
We who have bled to boost you up a rung –
A KCB perhaps, perhaps a Corps –

We who must mourn those spaces in the mess,
And somehow fill those hollows in the heart,
We do not want your Sermon on Success,
Your greasy benisons on Being Smart.

We only want to take our wounds away.
To some warm village where the tumult ends,
And drowsing in the sunshine many a day,
Forget our aches, forget that we had friends.

Weary we are of blood and noise and pain;
This was a week we shall not soon forget;
And if, indeed, we have to fight again,
We little wish to think about it yet.

We have done well; we like to hear it said.
Say it, and then, for God's sake, say no more.
Fight, if you must, fresh battles far ahead,
But keep them dark behind your chateau door!

A P Herbert

Haig on his troops after the Battle of the Somme

That these troops should have accomplished so much under such
conditions, and against an Army and a nation whose chief concern
for so many years has been preparation for war, constitutes a feat
of which the history of our nation records no equal. The difficulties and hardships cheerfully overcome, and the endurance, determination and invincible courage shown in meeting them, can

hardly be imagined by those who have not had personal experience of the battle, even though they have themselves seen something of war.

AT SENLIS ONCE

O how comely it was and how reviving,
When with clay and with death no longer striving
Down firm roads we came to houses
With women chattering and green grass thriving.

Now though rains in a cataract descended,
We could glow, with our tribulation ended –
Count not days, the present only
Was thought of; how could it ever be expended?

Clad so cleanly, this remnant of poor wretches
Picked up life like the hens in orchard ditches,
Gazed on the mill-sails, heard the church-bell,
Found an honest glass all manner of riches.

How they crowded the barn with lusty laughter,
Hailed the pierrots and shook each shadowy rafter,
Even could ridicule their own sufferings,
Sang as though nothing but joy came after!

Edmund Blunden

A GREAT LEADER

THE GENERAL

"Good-morning, good morning!" the General said
When we met him last week on our way to the line.
Now the soldiers he smiled at are most of 'em dead,
And we're cursing his staff for incompetent swine.
"He's a cheery old card," grunted Harry to Jack
As they slogged up to Arras with rifle and pack.

But he did for them both by his plan of attack.

Siegfried Sassoon, Denmark Hill Hospital, April 1917.

During and since the war many British generals have been criticised for their wanton spending of soldier's lives, but Field Marshal Haig, as the British Commander-in-Chief for most of the war, carries greatest responsibility. Of course death and suffering have to be accepted in any

war but the safeguarding of the lives of as many of his men as possible-
seems never to have been one of his concerns.

Haig's Biography – The Most Admired General – War as it should be

Haig was, in reality, by far the most popular British Commander
within at any rate living memory. He probably never even realised that simple fact himself. Nevertheless it is perfectly true.
He was an embodiment, somehow, of all that the soldier expected
his officer to be; aloof in a sense, yet impressing the soldier to
mutter:
"He don't say much but he thinks a h–l of a lot."

Haig's personal appearance was always in his favour. Nothing
the private admires more than a well-groomed officer, and he was
always that. After the War he put on weight, but the campaigning
Haig was a near approach to the "beau ideal," the typical cavalry
officer.

He had a personal escort, following the example of his predeces-
sor in the command, consisting of a full troop of his own regiment. They were easily the smartest thing in France. Not a
buckle out of place, stripes of gold for the N.C.O.'s, great silver
"skulls and crossbones," they would clatter down the French
roads, breathing something of the lost romance of war, something
which seemed to hearten poor tired beggars in their mud and rags.
It might have been thought that such would have been scoffed at
as "feather-bed soldiers," but such was not the case. They were
accepted as the incarnation in some sense of the spirit of war, war
as it should be, a serious dispute between gentlemen who, although they have passed the arbitration stage must come to blows,
yet have not forgotten that they are gentlemen.

Sir George Arthur [1]

Haig according to his son

To picture him as a hard, unfeeling man is wrong, because I know
there was a nature full of warmth and feeling and sensibility lying
behind his reserve. The sufferings of his men during the Great
War caused him great anguish. I believe that he felt that it was
his duty to refrain from visiting the casualty clearing stations
because these visits made him physically ill.

---

[1]   In *Lord Haig*, p77, 79, 80.

Haig and Lloyd George did not always agree, and ultimately despised each other. "I gave LG a good talking to on several questions he raised, and I felt I got the better of the arguments. . . Quite a pleasant little man, but I should think most unreliable." – Diary of Lord Haig, 5 November, 1917.

THE MARCH-PAST

In red and gold the Corps-Commander stood,
With ribboned breast puffed out for all to see:
He'd sworn to beat the Germans, if he could;
For God had taught him strength and strategy.
He was our leader, and a judge of Port –
Rode well to hounds, and was a damned good sort.

"Eyes right!" We passed him with a jaunty stare.
"Eyes front!" He'd watched his trusted legions go.
I wonder if he guessed how many there
Would get knocked out of time in next week's show.
"Eyes right!!" The corpse-commander was a Mute;
And Death leered round him, taking our salute.

Siegfried Sassoon, 25 December 1916

Lloyd George on Haig

There was no conspicuous officer in the Army who seemed to be better qualified for the Highest Command than Haig. That is to say, there was no outstanding General as fit for so overwhelming a position . . . I have no doubt these great men would have risen to the occasion, but such highly gifted men as the British Army possessed were consigned to the mud by orders of men superior in rank but inferior in capacity, who themselves kept at a safe distance from the slime which they had chosen as the terrain where their plans were to operate . . .

Some of the assaults on impossible positions ordered by our Generals would never have been decreed if they had seen beforehand with their own eyes the hopeless slaughter to which their orders doomed their men.

SHOCK GERMAN BREAKTHROUGH

Bolstered with troops, released by the cessation of fighting with Russia, the Germans planned a brilliant breakthrough for the Spring of 1918.

They attacked on the 21st March near St Quentin. From observations of troop movements Haig must have known that this attack was being prepared, but his main concentration of troops remained in the north and he did not immediately call on available French troops for help. After a four and a half hour barrage, from 6000 German heavy guns, wave after wave of German troops rushed forwards, annihilating some British battalions.

On the third day of the battle, when the Germans had advanced many miles on a wide front, Haig left his chateau to see what had happened. On the fourth day he recalled some troops from the north to lend assistance.

Two days later Haig agreed that Field MarshalFoch should become Commander-in-Chief of the Allied Armies in France.

On 9th April the Germans attacked on a thirty mile front in the north, against a weary Portuguese division. The Germans had soon advanced five miles and Passchendaele, which had been captured at such appalling costs, was abandoned by the British.

Haig was beginning to sense defeat. The Germans had advanced as much as forty miles in places, pushing through and far beyond the area they had lost in the Battle of the Somme. In a bid to rally the troops he issued, on 12th April, his famous "Backs-to-the-wall" order of the day.

With our backs to the wall – Haig's Order of the Day

Three weeks ago to-day the enemy began his terrific attacks against us on a fifty-mile front. His objects are to separate us from the French, to take the Channel Ports, and to destroy the British Army.

In spite of throwing already 106 divisions into the battle, and enduring the most reckless sacrifice of human life, he has, as yet made little progress towards his goals.

We owe this to the determined fighting and self-sacrifice of our troops. Words fail me to express the admiration which I feel for the splendid resistance offered by all ranks of our Army under the most trying circumstances.

Many amongst us now are tired. To those I would say that victory will belong to the side which holds out the longest. The French Army is moving rapidly and in great force to our support.

There is no other course open to us but to fight it out. Every position must be held to the last man; there must be no retirement. With our backs to the wall, and believing in the justice of our cause, each one of us must fight on to the end. The safety of our homes and the freedom of mankind depend alike upon the conduct of each one of us at this critical moment.

D Haig, Field Marshal, Thursday 11th April 1918

A SPORTING WAR –   PLAYING THE GAME

All's fair in love and war.

Francis Edward Smedley, 1818 - 1864

To the British press, and the many it influenced, war was a game. It required selfless team work, courage, a willingness to play by the rules.

War was an opportunity for heroism, self-sacrifice, patriotism, an opportunity to fight for civilisation, democracy, freedom. It was the greatest game of life that any man could take part in.

As it was being refereed by the British – by the politicians and the newspapers – certain rules could be broken and no-one would comment. When the other side broke a rule then howls of protest were unleashed. It was allowable to take charge of a quarter of the earth's population using fire power against spears and bows because that, it was understood, was to bring superior civilisation to the world. It was allowable to blockade German ports to bring starvation to the German people, and continue this action for months after the war was over. It was acceptable for Britain to bomb Germany but not the other way round. Submarines, used by the Germans to sink ships were an unacceptable evil, as was the laying of mines in waters outside an enemy's three mile limit. – (The Germans were indiscriminate in the use of these tactics and sank hundreds of neutral, merchant, and passenger ships.) The sinking of the *Lusitania* is the most famous of all First World War sinkings because it was an "innocent" passenger liner. In fact, its cargo included substantial amounts of ammunition.

The use of poison gas had been outlawed by the First Hague Peace Conference of 1899, so there was a cry of "foul" when the Germans used 168 tonnes of chlorine gas at Langemarck near Ypres, on 22 April 1915. The next day Kitchener asked the British Cabinet permission for the British army to use poison gas, which it did, for the first time, on 25th September in the Battle of Loos. A hundred and fifty tons of chlorine were released, killing six hundred German soldiers.

A German cartoon celebrating the first use of gas in war. The caption read: Spring storms; German poison vapours in Flanders. The gentle breezes are awake. Now must everything give way to them.
– The cartoon appeared on the front page of *The Daily Mirror,* 14 May 1915.

Thomas Hardy accused the Germans of fighting dishonourably with Zeppelins, aeroplanes and submarines in *Then and Now*.

THEN AND NOW

When battles were fought
With a chivalrous sense of Should and Ought,
In spirit men said,
"End we quick or dead,
Honour is some reward!
Let us fight fair – for our own best or worst;
So, Gentlemen of the Guard,
Fire first!"

In the open they stood,
Man to man in his knightlihood:
They would not deign
To profit by a stain
On the honourable rules,
Knowing that practise perfidy no man durst
Who in the heroic schools
Was nurst.

But now, behold, what
Is warfare wherein honour is not!
Rama laments
Its dead innocents:
Herod breathes: "Sly slaughter
Shall rule! Let us, by modes once called accurst,
Overhead, under water,
Stab first."

Thomas Hardy, 1915

And in *Often When Warring* Hardy commends an enemy soldier who,
in the thick of battle, pauses to show kindness – sportsmanship of old.

OFTEN WHEN WARRING

Often when warring for he wist not what,
An enemy-soldier, passing by one weak,
Has tendered water, wiped the burning cheek,
And cooled the lips so black and clammed and hot;

Then gone his way, and maybe quite forgot
The deed of grace amid the roar and reek;
Yet larger vision than loud arms bespeak
He there has reached, although he has known it not.

For natural mindsight, triumphing in the act
Over the throes of artificial rage,
Has thuswise muffled victory's peal of pride,
Rended to ribands policy's specious page
That deals but with evasion, code, and pact,
And war's apology wholly stultified.

Thomas Hardy, 1915

But it fell to the British to perform the most sporting act of the whole war, and it occurred at the moment of our greatest danger in the Battle of the Somme, when Captain Wilfred Nevill of the East Surrey Regiment organised a combined football competition and advance across no-man's land into a hail of machine-gun fire. He gave two footballs to his men with the challenge to be the first to dribble a ball to the German front line. He himself was killed before they reached the German trenches.

The event was reported in British newspapers as an act of heroism. The Germans used the reports to show the stupidity of the British. The event is celebrated in Claude Burton's poem, *The Game* and R Caton Woodville's drawing.

THE GAME

On through the hail of slaughter
Where gallant comrades fall,
Where blood is poured like water,
They drive the trickling ball.
The fear of death before them
Is but an empty name;
True to the land that bore them
The Surreys play the game!

On without check or falter,
They press towards the goal;
Who falls on freedom's altar
The Lord shall rest his soul
But still they charge, the living,
Into that hell of flame;
Ungrudging in the giving,
Our soldiers play the game!

And now at last is ended
The task so well begun.
Though savagely defended
The lines of death are won.
In this their hour of glory,
A deathless place they claim
In England's splendid story,
The men who played the game!

Claude Burton

6

WAITING AND SUFFERING

WE HAVE A RENDEZVOUS WITH DEATH

RENDEZVOUS

I have a rendezvous with Death
At some disputed barricade,
When Spring comes back with rustling shade
And apple-blossoms fill the air –
I have a rendezvous with Death
When Spring brings back blue days and fair.

It may be he shall take my hand
And lead me into his dark land
And close my eyes and quench my breath –
It may be I shall pass him still.
I have a rendezvous with Death
On some scarred slope of battered hill,
When Spring comes round again this year
And the first meadow-flowers appear.

God knows 'twere better to be deep
Pillowed in silk and scented down,
Where love throbs out in blissful sleep,
Pulse nigh to pulse, and breath to breath,
Where hushed awakenings are dear . . .
But I've a rendezvous with Death
At midnight in some flaming town,
When Spring trips north again this year,
And I to my pledged word am true,
I shall not fail that rendezvous.

Alan Seeger

NOON

It is midday: the deep trench glares . . .
A buzz and blaze of flies . . .
The hot wind puffs the giddy airs . . .
The great sun rakes the skies.

No sound in all the stagnant trench
Where forty standing men
Endure the sweat and grit and stench,
Like cattle in a pen.

Sometimes a sniper's bullet whirs
Or twangs the whining wire
Sometimes a soldier sighs and stirs
As in hell's frying fire.

From out a high cool cloud descends
An aeroplane's far moan . . .
The sun strikes down, the thin cloud rends . . .
The black spot travels on.

And sweating, dizzied, isolate
In the hot trench beneath,
We bide the next shrewd move of fate
Be it of life or death.

Robert Nichols

RETURNING, WE HEAR THE LARKS

Sombre the night is.
And though we have our lives, we know
What sinister threat lurks there.

Dragging these anguished limbs, we only know
This poison-blasted track opens on our camp –
On a little safe sleep.

But hark! joy – joy – strange joy.
Lo! heights of night ringing with unseen larks.
Music showering our upturned list'ning faces.

Death could drop from the dark
As easily as song –
But song only dropped,
Like a blind man's dreams on the sand
By dangerous tides,
Like a girl's dark hair for she dreams no ruin lies there,
Or her kisses where a serpent hides.

Issaac Rosenberg, 1917

SORLEY'S CHANGING MOODS

On 12th July, 1915, Charles Sorley boasted in an upbeat verse,

And now the fight begins again,
          The old war joy, the old war pain.
          Sons of one school across the sea
          We have no fear to fight . . .

But on 5th October, eight days before he was killed in the Battle of Loos, he wrote, "I dread my own censorious self in the coming conflict. – I also have great physical dread of pain . . . Pray that I ride my frisky nerves with a cool and steady hand when the time arrives."

ZERO MINUS SEVEN MINUTES

But they already look at their watches and it is zero minus
seven minutes.
Seven minutes to go . . and seventy times seven times to
the minute
this drumming of the diaphragm.
From deeply inward thumping all through you beating
no peace to be still in
and no one is there not anyone to stop
can't anyone –   someone turn off the tap
or won't any one before it snaps.

Racked out to another turn of the screw
the acceleration heightens;
the sensibility of these instruments to register,
fails;
needle dithers disorientate.
The responsive mercury plays laggard to such fevers – you
simply can't take any more in.
And the surfeit of fear steadies to dumb incognition, so that
when they give the order to move upward to align with "A,"
hugged already just under the lip of the acclivity inches below
where his traversing machine-guns perforate to powder
white –
white creature of chalk pounded
and the world crumbled away
and get ready to advance
you have not capacity for added fear only the limbs are leaden
to negotiate the slope and rifles all out of balance, clumsied
with long auxiliary steel
seem five times the regulation weight –
it bitches the aim as well;
　　　　　　　　　　　and we ourselves as those small
cherubs, who trail awkwardly the weapons to the God in
　　　　　　　　　　　Fine Art works.

The returning sun climbed over the hill, to lessen the
shadows of small and great things; and registered the
minutes to zero hour. Their saucer hats made dial for
his passage: long thin line of them, virid domes of them,

cut elliptical with light
as cupola on Byzantine wall,
stout turrets to take the shock
and helmets of salvation.
Long side by side lie like friends lie
on daisy-down on warm days
cuddled close down kindly close with the mole
in down and silky rodent,
and if you look more intimately all manner of small creatures,
created-dear things creep about quite comfortably
yet who travail until now
beneath your tin-hat shade.
                              He bawls at ear-hole:
Two minutes to go.
                    Minutes to excuse me to make excuse.

Responde mihi?
                    for surely I must needs try them
so many, much undone
and lose on roundabouts as well and vari-coloured polygram
to love and know
                    and we have a little sister
whose breasts will be as towers
and the gilly-flowers will blow next month
below the pound
with Fred Karno billed for *The Holloway*.

He's getting it now more accurately and each salvo brackets more
narrowly and a couple right in, just as
"D" and "C" are forming for the second wave.

Wastebottom married a wife on his Draft-leave but the
whinnying splinter razored diagonal and mess-tin
fragments drove inward and toxined underwear.
He maintained correct alignment with the others, face
down, and you never would have guessed.

Perhaps they'll cancel it.
O blow fall out the officers cantcher, like a wet afternoon
or the King's Birthday.*
Or you read it again many times to see if it will come
different:
you can't believe the Cup wont pass from
or they wont make a better show
in the Garden.
Won't forbid the banns
or God himself will stay their hands.
It just can't happen in our family

even though a thousand
and ten thousand at thy right hand.

Talacryn doesn't take it like Wastebottom, he leaps up &
says he's dead, a-slither down the pale face – his limbs
a-girandole at the bottom of the nullah,
but the mechanism slackens, unfed
and he is quite still
which leaves five paces between you and the next live
one to the left.
Sidle over a bit toward where '45 Williams, and use all
      your lungs:
Get ready me china-plate –   but he's got it before he can
hear you, but it's a cushy one and he relaxes to the
morning sun and smilingly, to wait for the bearers.

Some of yer was born wiv jam on it
clicked lucky and favoured
                              pluckt brand from burning
and my darling from unicorn horn with only a minute to go,
whose wet-nurse cocked a superstitious eye to see his
happy constellation through the panes.

But it isn't like that for the common run and you have
no mensuration gear to plot meandering fortune-graph nor
know whether she were the Dark or the Fair left to the
grinding.

Last minute drums its taut millenium out
you can't swallow your spit
and Captain Marlowe yawns a lot
and seconds now our measuring-rods with no Duke Josue
nor conniving God
to stay the Divisional Synchronisation.

So the fullness of time
when pallid jurors bring the doomed
      mooring cables swipe slack-end on
      barnacled piles,
and the world falls apart at the last to siren screech
and screaming vertical steam in conformity with the
Company's Sailings and up to scheduled time.

David Jones (from *In Parenthesis*)

---

* A bugle call during field exercises meant an early end – possibly because of bad
weather. In normal circumstances the King's Birthday was a holiday for soldiers.

PAIN

Pain, pain continual; pain unending;
Hard even to the roughest, but to those
Hungry for beauty . . . Not the wisest knows,
Nor most pitiful-hearted, what the wending
Of one hour's way meant. Grey monotony lending
Weight to the grey skies, grey mud where goes
An army of grey bedrenched scarecrows in rows
Careless at last of cruellest Fate-sending.
Seeing the pitiful eyes of men foredone.
Or horses shot, too tired merely to stir,
Dying in shell-holes both, slain by the mud.
Men broken, shrieking even to hear a gun.
Till pain grinds down, or lethargy numbs her.
The amazed heart cries out angrily on God.

Ivor Gurney

PREPARING TO DIE

I am now dead . . . The last letter of Glyn Rhys Morgan

Whilst waiting for an attack to begin soldiers were often asked to write letters to be sent home in the event of their deaths.

My Dear Dad

> This letter is being written on the eve of going "over the top." It is only because I know by this time what are the odds against returning unhurt that I write it. It will only be sent in the event of my being killed in action.

> You, I know, my dear Dad, will bear the shock as bravely as you have always borne the strain of my being out here; yet I should like if possible, to help you to carry on with as stout a heart as I hope to "jump the bags."

> I believe I have told you before that I do not fear Death itself; the Beyond has no terror for me. I am quite content to die for the cause for which I have given up nearly three years of my life and I only hope that I may meet Death with as brave a front as I have seen other men do before.

> My one regret is that the opportunity has been denied me to repay you to the best of my ability for the lavish kindness and devotedness which you have shown me. I had hoped to do so in the struggle of Life. Now, however, it may be that I have done so in the struggle between Life and Death, between England and

Germany, Liberty and Slavery. In any case, I shall have done my duty in my little way.

Well, Dad, please carry on with a good heart, then I shall be content.

Goodbye, dearest of fathers, goodbye E - - - and G - - -. May you all reap benefits of this great war and keep happy and cheery through life.

Your affectionate son and brother,

Glyn

Glyn Rhys Morgan was killed on 1st August 1917, two days after writing this letter. He was 21.

BEFORE ACTION

By all the glories of the day
And the cool evening's benison,
By that last sunset touch that lay
Upon the hills when day was done,
By beauty lavishly outpoured
And blessings carelessly received,
By all the days that I have lived
Make me a soldier, Lord.

By all of man's hopes and fears,
And all the wonders poets sing,
The laughter of unclouded years,
And every sad and lovely thing;
By the romantic ages stored
With high endeavour that was his,
By all his mad catastrophes
Make me a man, O Lord.

I, that on my familiar hill
Saw with uncomprehending eyes
A hundred of Thy sunsets spill
Their fresh and sanguine sacrifice,
Ere the sun swings his noonday sword
Must say goodbye to all of this; –
By all delights that I shall miss,
Help me to die, O Lord.

W N Hodgson

Written two days before his death on the first day of the Battle of the Somme, 1 July 1916.

PRELUDE: THE TROOPS

Dim, gradual thinning of the shapeless gloom
Shudders to drizzling daybreak that reveals
Disconsolate men who stamp their sodden boots
And turn dulled, sunken faces to the sky
Haggard and hopeless. They, who have beaten down
The stale despair of night, must now renew
Their desolation in the truce of dawn,
Murdering the livid hours that grope for peace.

Yet these who cling to life with stubborn hands,
Can grin through storms of death and find a gap
In the clawed, cruel tangles of his defence.
They march from safety, and the bird-sung joy
Of grass-green thickets, to the land where all
Is ruin, and nothing blossoms but the sky
That hastens over them where they endure
Sad, smoking, flat horizons, reeking woods,
And foundered trench-lines volleying doom for doom.

O my brave brown companions, when your souls
Flock silently away, and the eyeless dead
Shame the wild beast of battle on the ridge,
Death will stand grieving in that field of war
Since your unvanquished hardihood is spent.
And through some mooned Valhalla there will pass
Battalions and battalions, scarred from hell;
The unreturning army that was youth;
The legions who have suffered and are dust.

Siegfried Sassoon

THE WINTER OF EARLY 1917

In France it was the coldest winter anyone could remember, with the landscape covered in deep snow and ponds frozen ten inches thick. In Paris a temperature of minus 14 degrees Celsius was registered. It was impossible to keep soldiers out in the open in front line trenches for more than forty-eight hours at a time before taking a turn in the warmth and comfort of billets. Without this, whole armies would have died of exposure.

Even so, soldiers suffered severely from frostbite, bronchitis, pneumonia, and rheumatism.

Trench feet, frostbite, rheumatism, and bronchitis

Some of the trench feet and frostbite cases were so bad that they had to be sent home. We had a tremendous number of frostbite cases at the beginning of 1917 . . . Their feet were absolutely white, swollen up, dead. Some of their toes dropped off with it, and their feet looked dreadful. We would say, "I'll stick a pin in you. Can you feel it?" Whenever they did feel the pin-prick we knew that life was coming back, and then we'd see a little bit of pink come up and everybody in the ward would cheer. It was very painful for them when the feeling started to come back, and some of them had to have crutches. They couldn't walk at all, because they simply couldn't feel their feet.

Kathleen Yarwood, VAD, Dearnly Military Hospital, Rochdale

All that winter we took in bronchitis and rheumatism cases. Some of the bronchitis patients were as bad as the men who were gassed, but the rheumatism cases really were the worst. It was pathetic to see these young men absolutely crippled with rheumatism, sometimes doubled up as if they were men of eighty instead of boys in their twenties . . .

They suffered terrible pain with it.

Sister Mary Stollard, QAIMNS,
Beckett's Park Military Hospital, Leeds[1]

Wilfred Owen – the trenches in bleak winter conditions

I have no mind to describe all the horrors of this last tour. But it was almost wusser than the first, because in this place my platoon had no dug-outs, but had to lie in the snow under the deadly wind. By day it was impossible to stand up or even crawl about because we were behind only a little ridge screening us from the Bosche's periscope.

We had five Tommy's cookers between the platoon, but they did not suffice to melt the ice in the water-cans. So we suffered cruelly from thirst.

The marvel is that we did not all die of cold. As a matter of fact, only one of my party actually froze to death before he could be got back, but I am not able to tell how many have ended up in hospital. I had no real casualties from shelling, though for ten minutes every hour whizz-bangs fell a few yards short of us. Showers of soil rained on us, but no fragments of shell could find us . . .

We were marooned in a frozen desert.

There was not a sign of life on the horizon and a thousand signs of death.

Not a blade of grass, not an insect;   once or twice a day the shadow of a big hawk scenting carrion . . .

I suppose I can endure cold, and fatigue, and the face-to-face death, as well as another; but extra for me there is the universal pervasion of Ugliness. Hideous landscapes . . . everything un- natural, broken, blasted; the distortion of the dead, whose unburiable bodies sit outside the dug-outs all day and all night, the most execrable sights on earth. In poetry we call them most glorious. But to sit with them all day, all night . . . and a week later to come back and find them still sitting there, in motionless groups, THAT is what saps the "soldierly spirit".

Letter to his mother, 4 February, 1917

1   Quoted by Lynn Macdonald, *The Roses of No Man's Land*.

EXPOSURE

Our brains ache, in the merciless iced east winds that knive us . . .
Wearied we keep awake because the night is silent . . .
Low, drooping flares confuse our memory of the salient . . .
Worried by silence, sentries whisper, curious, nervous,
But nothing happens.

Watching, we hear the mad gusts tugging on the wire,
Like twitching agonies of men among its brambles.
Northward, incessantly, the flickering gunnery rumbles,
Far off, like a dull rumour of some other war.
What are we doing here?

The poignant misery of dawn begins to grow . . .
We only know war lasts, rain soaks, and clouds sag stormy.
Dawn massing in the east her melancholy army
Attacks once more in ranks on shivering ranks of grey,
But nothing happens.

Sudden successive flights of bullets streak the silence.
Less deathly than the air that shudders black with snow,
With sidelong flowing flakes that flock, pause, and renew,
We watch them wandering up and down the wind's
nonchalance,
But nothing happens.

Pale flakes with fingering stealth come feeling for our faces.
We cringe in holes, back on forgotten dreams, and stare, snow-dazed,
Deep into grassier ditches. So we drowse, sun-dozed,
Littered with blossoms trickling where the blackbird fusses.
Is it that we are dying?

Slowly our ghosts drag home: glimpsing the sunk fires, glozed
With crusted dark-red jewels; crickets jingle there;
For hours the innocent mice rejoice: the house is theirs;
Shutters and doors, all closed; on us the doors are closed.
We turn back to our dying.

Since we believe not otherwise can kind fires burn;
Nor ever suns smile true on child, or field, or fruit.
For God's invincible spring our love is made afraid;
Therefore, not loath, we lie out here; therefore were born,
For love of God seems dying.

Tonight, this frost will fasten on this mud and us,
Shrivelling many hands, puckering foreheads crisp.
The burying-party, picks and shovels in shaking grasp,
Pause over half-known faces. All their eyes are ice,
But nothing happens.

Wilfred Owen

THE ZONNEBEKE ROAD

Morning, if this late withered light can claim
Some kindred with that merry flame
Which the young day was wont to fling through space!
Agony stares from each grey face.
And yet the day is come; stand down! stand down!
Your hands unclasp from rifles while you can;
The frost has pierced them to the bended bone?
Why see old Stevens there, that iron man,
Melting the ice to shave his grotesque chin!
Go ask him, shall we win?
I never liked this bay, some foolish fear
Caught me the first time that I came here;
That dugout fallen in awakes, perhaps,
Some formless haunting of some corpse's chaps.
True, and wherever we have held line,
There were such corners, seeming-saturnine
For no good cause.
                    Now where Haymarket starts,

That is no place for soldiers with weak hearts;
The minenwerfers have it to the inch.
Look, how the snow-dust whisks along the road
Piteous and silly; the stones themselves must flinch
In this east wind; the low sky like a load
Hangs over, a dead weight. But what a pain
Must gnaw where its clay cheek
Crushes the shell-chopped trees that fang the plain –
The ice-bound throat gulps out a gargoyle shriek.
That wretched wire before the village line
Rattles like rusty brambles or dead bine,
And there the daylight oozes into dun;
Black pillars, those are trees where roadways run.
Even Ypres now would warm our souls; fond fool,
Our tour's but one night old, seven more to cool!
O screaming dumbness, O dull clashing death,
Shreds of dead grass and willows, homes and men,
Watch as you will, men clench their chattering teeth
And freeze you back with that one hope, disdain.

Edmund Blunden

IF I SHOULD DIE – RUPERT BROOKE'S ACTUAL THOUGHTS AS HE FACED DEATH

Brooke's letters, written after the outbreak of war, reveal a great deal about the turbulent state of his mind – sometimes positive, sometimes frightened and confused. They reveal his concerns and beliefs, his immaturity. He regretted that his life had no clear direction, that he had little he could describe as an achievement. He was worried, even guilty about the nature of his character.

The first three letters below were written as Brooke prepared himself to take part in the relief of Antwerp. In the remaining letters – from the last eight months of his life – he keeps in touch with friends, furthers his romances, is attracted to, and repelled by marriage, wishes he had a son, expresses depression and then a sort of stunned awareness that his life is almost over, regrets his slight accomplishments, wants to cover up two of his relationships, and, on the whole, appears to see death as a solution to his problems. – In his final letter, like Wilfred Owen, sensing his end is near, he writes to his mother to assure her that he is happy and well, and quite safe. – The following are extracts only, from each letter.

To Lady Eileen Wellesley, 14 September 1914

My dear,

So you puzzled your foolish but lovely head to know what I meant by saying I was "horrible". Well, I am horrible. And occasionally it comes over me that I am. And then I feel – for a few moments – wretched . . . I think one of the things that appals me is my extraordinary selfishness: . . I mean, I just enjoy things as they come, & don't think or care how they affect other people. That my gentle and adorable child, is why I felt uneasy & frightened about you, at first. I knew how often I did harm to people, through carelessness & selfishness . . . Oh, I'm rather a horror. A vagabond, drifting from one imbecility to another. You don't know how pointless and undependable and rotten a thing you've got hold of . . . Well, child, if you're happy with me: that's something, isn't it? I'm certainly happy with you. We can have fun togther, can't we? And supposing I go off & get blown to pieces – what fools we should feel if we hadn't had fun – if we'd forgone our opportunities – shouldn't we? . . I kiss you good night . . . All heaven be about you. – Rupert

To Cathleen Nesbitt, September 1914

Dear love,

I adore you. I love you in every other way: and I worship the goodness in you . . . It comes on me more and more dazzlingly how infinitely you're the best thing in my life: and that I might live a million years, and never find anything so glorious as you, for me to adore and pray to, nor anything so good in me as my love for you.

Child, oh my dear, it's very wonderful when we're together; and it's wonderful how strongly I lean on you and am thrilled by you, and live for you and hold you when we're apart . . . Cathleen if you knew how I adore you, and fight towards you. I want to cut away the evil in me, and be wholly a thing worthy of you. Be good to me, child. I sometimes think you can make anything in the world of me.

Dear love, I feel so happy in this new safety and brightness.

I kiss you, my dear and holy one. – Rupert

To Lady Eileen Wellesley, 23 September 1914

I'd rather like to see you. Are you very majestic & cool & competent? Do you conceal your Rabelaisian mind? – Rupert

To EJ Dent, 5 November, 1914

. . . It's a bloody thing, half the youth of Europe blown through pain to nothingness, in the incessant mechanical slaughter of these modern battles. I can only marvel at human endurance. . .

To Mrs Rosalind Toynbee (Rosalind Murray), 20 November, 1914

. . . I hope I get through. I'll have such a lot to say and do afterwards. Just now I'm rather miserable: because most of my school friends are wounded, or "wounded and missing" or dead. . .

To Dudley Ward, 15 December, 1914

If I knew I'd be shot I'd marry in a flash – oh any of two or three ladies – and do my best to leave a son. . .

I agonise at night. At times I want to wire almost anybody, "Will you be my widow?" And later, I sigh that I'll be free and the world before me, after the war.

It's partly dependent on my premonition. If I think I'll survive, I plump for freedom. When I feel I'll be killed (which is my general feeling and deepest), I have a revulsion towards marriage.

A perplexing world.

To Dudley Ward, 10 January,1915

. . .We're to be here till the middle of March, AT LEAST. . . It's TOO bloody, to have three more months of life, when one hoped for three weeks. . .

To Violet Asquith, 8 March 1915

. . . Do not care much what happens to me or what I do . . .

 Somewhere, I think, there's bad luck about me.

There's a very bright sun, and a lot of comedy in the world; so perhaps there's some point in my not getting shot. But also there's a point in my getting shot. Anyway you're very good to me. . .

Good-bye,   – Rupert.

To Edward Marsh, 9 March 1915

My dear, – This is very odd. But I suppose I must imagine my non-existence, & make a few arrangements.

You are to be my literary executor. . . You must decide everything about publication. Don't print much bad stuff. . . There's nothing much to say. . .

You've been good to me. I wish I'd written more. I've been such a failure.

Best love & good-bye,   – Rupert.

To Katharine Cox, 10 March 1915

Dear child,

I suppose you're about the best I can do in the way of a widow . . . My dear, my dear you did me wrong: but I have done you a very great wrong. Every day I see it greater.

You were the best thing I found in life. If I have memory, I shall remember . . . It's a good thing I die.

Good-bye, child. – Rupert.

To Dudley Ward (Envelope marked "If I die to be sent to Dudley Ward"), 17 March 1915

My dear Dudley,

You'll already have done a few jobs for me. Here are some more.

My private papers and letters I'm leaving to my mother, and when she dies, to Ka.[1]

But I want you, now . . . to go through my letters . . . and destroy all those from (a) Elizabeth van Rysselberghe[2] . . . (b) Lady Eileen Wellesley: . . .

It's odd, being dead . . .

Be good to Ka. Give Jacques and Gwen my love.

---

1   Ka: Katherine Cox.
2   Elizabeth van Rysselberghe was a Flemish sculptress whom Brooke met at a party in Munich. She claimed that they had an affair.

Try to inform Taata[1] of my death. Mlle Taata, Hotel Tiare, Papeete, Tahiti. It might find her. Give her my love . . .

The realisation of failure makes me unpleasantly melancholy. Enough.

Good luck and all love to you and Anne.

Call a boy after me. – Rupert.

To Jacques Raverat [and Gwen], 18 March 1915

My dear,   –   I turn to you. Keep the innumerable flags flying. I've only two decent reasons for being sorry for dying – (several against) – I want to destroy some evils, and to cherish some good. Do it for me. You understand. I doubt if anyone else does – almost.

Best love to you both,   – Rupert.

To his mother, his last letter, 20 April 1915

Dear Mother,

Still aboard[2], and still in the peacefullest surroundings . . .

Ian Hamilton,[3] asked me if I'd like to be attached to his staff as a sort of "galloper" and odd-jobber – "A D C" . . . But I'd made up my mind to see at any rate some of a campaign in my present capacity: and I'm very happy as I am, with several people I like: and it wouldn't be fair to my company to leave it suddenly at the last moment like this, with a gap it couldn't fill, out here . . .

However, I gather we're pretty well as safe as if we were all Staff officers, so all's well. There's no further news . . .

Best love,   Rupert.

---

1   A Tahitian girl Brooke had an affair with early in 1914, while on his round-the-world tour.
2   Aboard the *Grantully Castle*, anchored off the Greek island of Skyros, awaiting orders to sail for Gallipoli.
3   Ian Hamilton was Sir Ian Hamilton, the commander of the Gallipoli Campaign whom Brooke had met socially.

RUPERT BROOKE'S LAST POEM

As Rupert Brooke and his friends sailed towards Gallipoli he watched
them with a detached gaze that saw them turning into ghosts before
his eyes: and then, at the last moment, he accepted, simply, that he
might share their fate. – In this, his last, barely finished poem, all his
posturing and rhetoric have gone, and, at last, he coldly faces reality
and death.

SOON TO DIE

I strayed about the deck, an hour, to-night
Under a cloudy moonless sky; and peeped
In at the windows, watched my friends at table,
Or playing cards, or standing in the doorway,
Or coming out into the darkness. Still
No one could see me.

        I would have thought of them –
Heedless, within a week of battle – in pity,
Pride in their strength and in the weight and firmness
And link'd beauty of bodies, and pity that
This gay machine of splendour 'ld soon be broken,
Thought little of, pashed, scattered . . .

        Only, always,
I could but see them – against the lamplight – pass
Like coloured shadows, thinner than filmy glass,
Slight bubbles, fainter than the wave's faint light,
That broke to phosphorus out in the night,
Perishing things and strange ghosts – soon to die
To other ghosts – this one, or that, or I.

Rupert Brooke, April 1915

7

HOME FRONT

WARS ARE WON ON THE HOME FRONT

Governments have the entire responsibility for the home front. That front is always underrated by generals in the field. And yet that is where the Great War was won and lost. The Russian, Bulgarian, Austrian and German home fronts fell to pieces before their armies collapsed. The averting of that great and irrevocable catastrophe is the concern of the Government. Great care must be taken of the condition and susceptibilities of the population at home, who make it possible to maintain, to reinforce and to equip armies.

All the suffering is not in the trenches. The most poignant suffering is not on the battlefield, but in the bereft hearths and hearts in the homeland. If, in addition to the anguish of grief, women have to witness the pinched faces and waning strength of their children, there will soon be trouble in the nation behind the line, and if men home on leave have to carry back these unnerving memories to the trenches their will to fight on is enfeebled. That is what accounted for the sudden breakdown in the German resistance in November, 1918. The ration allowance for each British household was cut down to the lowest minimum compatible with health. Anything lower would have made trouble. But there was no privation. In Germany and Austria children died of hunger.

Lloyd George[1]

BRITAIN TRANSFORMED

The war was far across the sea, but life, work and thought in Britain were totally transformed and dominated by the war as soon as people could grasp that it had started.

1 *War Memoirs,* p 2032, 2033.

The first signs of war were met with raised eyebrows and a shrug of incomprehension. On 3rd August 1914 Vera   Brittain wrote in her diary, "I do not know how we all managed to play tennis so calmly and take quite an interest in the result. I suppose it is because we all know so little of war that we are indifferent." [1]

Germany invaded Belgium on the 3rd of August. In Britain orders went out at 4pm on the 4th, to call up reservists, and make preparations for a war in Europe.

> After that events moved, even in Buxton, very quickly . . . My parents rushed over in the car to familiar shops in Maccles-field and Leek where they laid in stores of cheese, bacon and butter under the generally   shared impression   that by next week we might all be besieged by Germans.   Wild rumours circulated from mouth to mouth; they were more plentiful than the newspapers, over which a free fight broke out on the station platform every time a batch came in by train from London or Manchester . . . One or two Buxton girls were hurriedly married to officers summoned to unknown destinations. Pan-demonium swept over the town. Holiday trippers wrestled with one another for the *Daily Mail;* habitually quiet and respectable citizens struggled like wolves for the provisions in the food shops and vented upon the distracted assistants their dismay at learning that all prices had suddenly gone up.
>
> Vera Brittain [2]

Instant action

Within forty-eight hours of the declaration of war three hundred and fifty troop trains had arrived at Southampton which was the principal port for embarkation to France. Huge amounts of equipment, guns, ammunitions, food, wagons, and thousands of horses were soon on their way. Thousands of telegrams were sent to reservists ordering them to report for duty immediately. The telegrams had all been written by March 1914 and only required dating and dispatching on the day of mobilisation. Within hours of the declaration of war, offices, farms, factories, homes – the whole work and social scene was changed be-yond recognition.

---

1   *Testament of Youth*, p94.
2   P96.

JOINING THE COLOURS
(West Kents, Dublin, August 1914)

There they go marching all in step so gay!
Smooth-cheeked and golden, food for shells and guns.
Blithely they go as to a wedding day,
The mothers' sons.

The drab street stares to see them row on row
On the high tram-tops, singing like the lark
Too careless-gay for courage, singing they go
Into the dark.

With tin whistles, mouth-organs, any noise,
They pipe the way to glory and the grave;
Foolish and young, the gay and golden boys
Love cannot save.

High heart! High courage! The poor girls they kissed
Run with them: they shall kiss no more, alas!
Out of the mist they stepped – into the mist
Singing they pass.

Katharine Tynan

SING A SONG OF WAR-TIME

Sing a song of War-time,
Soldiers marching by,
Crowds of people standing,
Waving them "Good-bye."
When the crowds are over,
Home we go to tea,
Bread and margarine to eat,
War economy!

If I ask for cake, or
Jam of any sort,
Nurse says, "What! in War-time?
Archie, cert'nly not!'"
Life's not very funny
Now, for little boys,
Haven't any money,
Can't buy any toys.

Mummy does the house-work,
Can't get any maid,
Gone to make munitions,
'Cause they're better paid,
Nurse is always busy,
Never time to play,
Sewing shirts for soldiers,
Nearly ev'ry day.

Ev'ry body's doing
Something for the War,
Girls are doing things
They've never done before,
Go as bus conductors,
Drive a car or van,
All the world is topsy-turvy
Since the War began.

Nina Macdonald

WAR GIRLS

There's the girl who clips your ticket for the train,
And the girl who speeds the lift from floor to floor,
There's the girl who does a milk-round in the rain,
And the girl who calls for orders at your door.

Strong, sensible, and fit,
They're out to show their grit,
And tackle jobs with energy and knack.
No longer caged and penned up,
They're going to keep their end up
Till the khaki soldier boys come marching back.

There's the motor girl who drives a heavy van,
There's the girl who cries "All fares, please!" like a man,
And the girl who whistles taxis up the street.
Beneath each uniform
Beats a heart that's soft and warm,
Though of canny mother-wit they show no lack;
But a solemn statement this is,
They've no time for love and kisses
Till the khaki soldier boys come marching back.

Jessie Pope

Women in munitions

947,000 women were employed in munitions work. – Three hundred workers lost their lives from T N T poisoning and from explosions during the war. – Factory work for women was not an innovation of the war. As an indication of their growing role in industry, by 1900 there were 100,000 women in Britain who were members of trade unions (mainly workers in cotton mills). By 1914 there were 360,000 women members of trade unions.

WOMEN AT MUNITION MAKING

Their hands should minister unto the flame of life,
Their fingers guide
The rosy teat, swelling with milk,
To the eager mouth of the suckling babe
Or smooth with tenderness,
Softly and soothingly,
The heated brow of the ailing child.
Or stray among the curls
Of the boy or girl, thrilling to mother love.
But now,
Their hands, their fingers
Are coarsened in munition factories.
Their thoughts, which should fly
Like bees among the sweetest mind flowers,
Gaining nourishment for the thoughts to be,
Are bruised against the law,
"Kill, kill."
They must take part in defacing and destroying the natural body
Which, certainly during this dispensation
Is the shrine of the spirit.
O God!
Throughout the ages we have seen,
Again and again
Men by Thee created
Cancelling each other.
And we have marvelled at the seeming annihilation
Of Thy work.
But this goes further,
Taints the fountain head,
Mounts like a poison to the Creator's very heart.
O God!
Must It anew be sacrificed on earth?

Mary Gabrielle Collins

MUNITION WAGES

Earning high wages? Yus,
Five quid a week,
A woman, too, mind you,
I calls it dim sweet.

Ye' are asking some questions –
But bless yer, here goes:
I spends the whole racket
On good times and clothes.

Me saving? Elijah!
Yer do think I'm mad.
I'm acting the lady,
But – I ain't living bad.

I'm having life's good times.
See 'ere, it's like this:
The 'oof come o' danger,
A touch-and-go bizz.

We're all here today, mate,
Tomorrow – perhaps dead,

If Fate tumbles on us
And blows up our shed.

Afraid! Are yer kidding?
With money to spend!
Years back I wore tatters,
Now – silk stockings, mi friend!

I've bracelets and jewellery,
Rings envied by friends;
A sergeant to swank with,
And something to lend.

I drive out in taxis,
Do theatres in style.
And this is my verdict –
It is jolly worth while.

Worth while, for tomorrow
If I'm blown to the sky,
I'll have repaid mi wages
In death – and pass by.

Madeline Ida Bedford

AS THE TEAM'S HEAD-BRASS

As the team's head-brass flashed out on the turn
The lovers disappeared into the wood.
I sat among the boughs of the fallen elm
That strewed an angle of the fallow, and
Watched the plough narrowing a yellow square
Of charlock. Every time the horses turned
Instead of treading me down, the ploughman leaned
Upon the handles to say or ask a word,
About the weather, next about the war.
Scraping the share he faced towards the wood,
And screwed along the furrow till the brass flashed
Once more.
              The blizzard felled the elm whose crest
I sat in, by a woodpecker's round hole,
The ploughman said. "When will they take it away?"
"When the war's over." So the talk began –
One minute and an interval of ten,
A minute more and the same interval.
"Have you been out?" "No." "And don't want to, perhaps?"
"If I could only come back again, I should.
I could spare an arm. I shouldn't want to lose
A leg. If I should lose my head, why, so,
I should want nothing more . . . Have many gone
From here?" "Yes." "Many lost?" "Yes, a good few.
Only two teams work on the farm this year.
One of my mates is dead. The second day
In France they killed him. It was back in March,
The very night of the blizzard, too. Now if
He had stayed here we should have moved the tree."
"And I should not have sat here. Everything
Would have been different. For it would have been
Another world." "Ay, and a better, though
If we could see all all might seem good." Then
The lovers came out of the wood again:
The horses started and for the last time
I watched the clods crumble and topple over
After the ploughshare and the stumbling team.

Edward Thomas

IN MEMORIAM
(Easter, 1915)

The flowers left thick at nightfall in the wood
This Eastertide call into mind the men,
Now far from home, who, with their sweethearts,
should
Have gathered them and will do never again.

Edward Thomas, 6 April 1915

Easter 1915

Upon the battlefield and ocean the purpose of the God of Battles
marches swiftly towards its majestic fulfilment. Soon the long
night of death and agony will break into the glory of the Resurrection morn. . . As we take stock on the morrow of victory, we
shall find that nothing of real value to the human race has been
destroyed. Our dead heroes will have won immortality. Civilisation will have gained new vitality. Humanity will have entered
upon a richer heritage. In the fierce furnace of destruction only
the dross will have perished.

Horatio Bottomley
From his Easter message in the *Sunday Pictorial,* 4 April 1915.

YOUR COUNTRY NEEDS YOU

Patriots always talk of dying for their country, and never of
killing for their country.

Bertrand Russell

There were initial spontaneous floods of volunteers and enthusiasm for
the war. Fifteen per cent of all recruitment in the war took place in the
first two months, but the flow of recruits never returned to anything like
this level. Fewer men enlisted in October than in the first four days of
September.[1] But for months recruitment remained at a very high level,
stimulated by sympathy for the plight of Belgium – with thousands
of Belgian refugees in London by October 1914, and the steady stream
of provocative actions made directly against the citizens of Britain.

---

1   Ian Beckett in *A Nation in Arms,* p7.

Kitchener was a national hero - the Commander-in-Chief of the British Army that won the Boer War. He was appointed Secretary for War from 7th August, 1914. His face on this poster drew an overwhelming response in new recruits to the British Army.

"Our gallant boys!"

Those gallant boys of whom we, their mothers, and, I venture to think, the whole British nation are justly proud . . .

If my own son can best serve England at this juncture by giving his life for her, I would not lift one finger to bring him home. If any act or word of mine should interfere with or take from him his grandest privilege, I could never look him in the face again.

Mrs Berridge
in *The Morning Post,* 30 September, 1914.

THE TWO MOTHERS

"Poor woman, weeping as they pass,
Yon brave recruits, the nation's pride,
You mourn some gallant boy, alas!
Like mine who lately fought and died?"

"Kind stranger, not for soldier son,
Of shame, not grief, my heart will break,
Three stalwarts have I, but not one
Doth risk his life for England's sake!"

Matilda Betham-Edwards

THE CALL

Who's for the trench –
Are you, my laddie?
Who'll follow French –
Will you, my laddie?
Who's fretting to begin,
Who's going out to win?
And who wants to save his skin –
Do you, my laddie?

Who's for the khaki suit –
Are you, my laddie?
Who longs to charge and shoot –
Do you, my laddie?
Who's keen on getting fit,
Who means to show his grit,
And who'd rather wait a bit –
Would you, my laddie?

Who'll earn the Empire's thanks –
Will you, my laddie?
Who'll swell the victor's ranks –
Will you, my laddie?
When that procession comes,
Banners and rolling drums –
Who'll stand and bite his thumbs –
Will you, my laddie?

Jessie Pope

THE GOODLY COMPANY

Thou with us, and we with Thee,
Maketh goodly company,
Proof against all villainy,
Strong to vanquish tyranny;
Thou with us, and we with Thee,
Maketh goodly company.

Who would fight a goodly fight
Must have cause both just and right,
Then, with God's good oversight,
He in mail of proof is dight;
Who would fight a goodly fight
Must have cause both just and right.

Who would God upon his side,
And with Him would be allied,
By God's will his course must guide;
Fully then he's fortified,
Who hath God upon his side,
And with Him is close allied.

John Oxenham

AWAKE

Death hunts for us beneath the seas,
Death hawks at us amidst the air.
Awake, O slumberers lulled in ease!
Up and prepare!

Shall England bow her head at last,
The badge of vassalage to wear?
Awake – the hour for sleep is past;
Up and prepare!

Know you what fate on Belgium fell,
You that have wives and daughters fair?
Shall they, too, feed the lusts of Hell?
Up and prepare!

What sound is this that rises o'er
The squadron tramp, the bugle's blare?
'Tis Doom, knocking at England's door!
Up and prepare!

Arm as your sires were proud to arm,
Dare as your brothers yonder dare!
In mart and mine and forge and farm,
Up and prepare!

William Watson

The need for more soldiers

It was easy for continental countries to find men for their armies. The
soldiers were all there on the orders of their governments. The British
army consisted entirely of volunteers. As hundreds of thousands
of men were killed and wounded more and more volunteers were needed.
The height limit was reduced and the upper age limit increased.
The flow of recruits continued but it was not sufficient.

TO THE SHIRKER: A LAST APPEAL

Now of your own free choice, while the chance is yours
To share their glory who have gladly died
Shielding the honour of our island shores
And that fair heritage of starry pride, –
Now, 'ere another evening's shadow falls,
Come, for the trumpet calls.

What if tomorrow through the land there runs
This message for an everlasting stain? –
"England expected each of all her sons
To do his duty – but she looked in vain;
Now she demands, by order sharp and swift,
What should have been a gift."

For so it must be, if her manhood fail
To stand by England in her deadly need;
If still her wounds are but an idle tale
The word must issue which shall make you heed;
And they who left her passionate pleas unheard
Will *have* to hear that word.

And, losing your free choice, you also lose
Your right to rank on Memory's shining scrolls,
With those, your comrades, who made haste to choose
The willing service asked of loyal souls:
From all who gave such tribute of the heart
Your name will stand apart.

I think you cannot know what meed of shame
Shall be their certain portion who pursue
Pleasure "as usual" while their country's claim
Is answered only by the gallant few.
Come, then, betimes, and on her altar lay
Your sacrifice today!

Owen Seaman. Published in *Punch*, 11 November 1914.

Conscription

If the war was to be continued the Government had only one choice: to
introduce conscription, which it did in January 1916 with the Military
Service Act – calling up all unmarried men aged 18-41 (except those
in exempted occupations). On 26th April the Act was extended to include married men.

THE VOLUNTEER

Sez I: My Country Calls? Well, let it call.
I grins perlitely and declines with thanks.
Go let 'em plaster every blighted wall,
'Ere's *one* they don't stampede into the ranks.
Them politicians with their greasy ways;
Them empire-grabbers – fight for 'em? No fear!
 I've seen this mess a-comin' from the days
Of Algyserious and Aggydear*
 I've felt me passion rise and swell,
But . . . wot the 'ell, Bill? Wot the 'ell?

Sez I: If they would do the decent thing,
And shield the missis and the little'uns,
Why, even *I* might shout God save the King,
And face the chances of them 'ungry guns.
But we've got three, another on the way;
It's that wat makes me snarl and set me jor:
The wife and nippers wot of 'em, I say,
If I gets knocked out in this blasted war?
Gets proper busted by a shell,
But...wot the 'ell, Bill? Wot the 'ell?

Ay, wot the 'ell's the use of all this talk?
Today some boys in blue* was passin' me,
And some of 'em had no legs to walk,
And some of 'em they'ad no eyes to see.
And – well, I couldn't look 'em in the face,
And so I'm goin, goin' to declare
I'm under forty-one and take me place
To face the music with the bunch out there.
A fool you say! Maybe you're right.
I'll 'ave no peace unless I fight.
I've ceased to think; I only know
I've gotta go, Bill, gotta go.

Robert Service

* The Algeciras Conference of 1906 and the Agadir Crisis of 1911. International
diputes between France, Germany and Great Britain – potentially explosive, which
nevertheless had peaceful outcomes.

* A blue uniform was worn by war-wounded convalescents.

Conscientious objection

The Military Service Act put many who opposed the war into a position
of direct personal conflict with the Government. Exemption was allowed on grounds of conscience and unsympathetic tribunals were set
up to assess those who claimed conscience as a reason for not fighting.
– Lloyd George promised the conscientious objectors, "a rough time."
However, such was the decline in enthusiasm for the war there were
three quarters of a million claims for exemption.   Of these the tribunals
accepted 16,500 as conscientious objectors. The great majority of these
accepted some form of alternative service, but, over one thousand refused all forms of service. These were imprisoned and most were brutally treated, resulting in physical and mental abuse and the deaths of
some seventy men in prison. Abuse began gently.

A simple way to convert a pacifist

> Some of the early batches, when nothing could be done with them,
> were taken singly and run across the yard to special rooms – airy
> enough, but from which they could see nothing. They were fed on
> bread and water and some of them presently came round. I had
> them placed in special rooms, nude, but with their full army kit
> on the floor for them to put on as soon as they were so minded.
> There were no blankets or substitutes for clothing left in the
> rooms which were quite bare. Several of the men held out naked
> for several hours but they gradually accepted the inevitable.
> Forty of the conscientious objectors who passed through my
> hands are now quite willing soldiers.

> From *The Daily Express*, 4 July, 1916. Lieutenant Colonel
> Reginald Brooke, Commander of Military Detention Barracks,
> Wandsworth.

Other newspapers campaigned against conscientious objectors, too.
Quakers were prominent in promoting conscientious objection, and
were thus the butt of Harold Begbie's verse.

A CHRISTIAN TO A QUAKER

> I much regret that I must frown
> Upon your cocoa nibs; *
> I simply hate to smite you down
> And kick you in the ribs;

> But since you will not think as I,
> It's clear you must be barred,
> So in you go (and may you die)
> To two years hard.

We are marching to freedom and to love;
We're fighting every shape of tyrant sin;
We are out to make it worth
God's while to love the earth,
And damn it, you won't join in!

To drive you mad, as I have done,
Has almost made me sick.
To torture Quakers like a Hun
Has hurt me to the quick.
But since your logic wars with mine
You're something I must guard,
So in you go, you dirty swine,
To two years hard.

We are marching to destroy the hosts of hate:
We've taken, every man, a Christian vow;
We are out to make war cease,
That men may live at peace,
And, damme, you're at it now!

Harold Begbie

*Cocoa nibs – a reference to Cadbury, a prominent Quaker family.

The Quaker Peace Testimony – George Fox to Charles II, 1661 – the principal statement of British Quakers on war, current from 1661 to the present day

We utterly deny all outward wars and strife and fighting with outward weapons, for any end or under any pretence whatsoever. And this is our testimony to the whole world. The spirit of Christ, by which we are guided, is not changeable, so as once to command us from a thing as evil and again to move unto it; and we do certainly know, and so testify to the world, that the spirit of Christ, which leads us into all Truth, will never move us to fight and war against any man with outward weapons, neither for the kingdom of Christ, nor for the kingdoms of this world.

From *Christian Faith and Practice in the Experience of the Society of Friends.* [1]

---

1   Published by The Yearly Meeting of the Religious Society of Friends. Now published as *Quaker Faith and Practice.*

Making a wrong choice

When D H Lawrence , then 31, was called up for military service he was delighted that he failed the medical examination. He wrote to Catherine Carswell on July 9th, 1916.

My Dear Catherine,

> I never wrote to tell you that they gave me a complete exemption from all military service, thanks be to God. That was a week ago last Thursday. I had to join the Colours in Penzance, be conveyed to Bodmin (60 miles), spend a night in barracks with all the other men, and then be examined. It was experience enough for me, of soldiering. I am sure I should die in a week, if they kept me. It is the annulling of all one stands for, this militarism, the nipping of the very germ of one's being. I was very much upset. The sense of spiritual disaster everywhere quite terrifying. One was not sure whether one survived or not. Things seem very bad.

> Yet I liked the men. They all seemed so decent. And yet they all seemed as if they had chosen wrong. It was the underlying sense of disaster that overwhelmed me. They are all so brave, to suffer, but none of them brave enough, to reject suffering. They are all so noble, to accept sorrow and hurt, but they can none of them demand happiness. Their manliness all lies in accepting calmly this death, this loss of integrity. They must stand by their fellow man: that is the motto.

> This is what Christ's weeping over Jerusalem has brought us to, a whole Jerusalem offering itself to the Cross. To me, this is infinitely more terrifying than Pharisees and Publicans and Sinners, taking their way to death. This is what the love of our neighbour has brought us to, that, because one man dies, we all die.

"YOU'RE IN FOR MURDER? FUNNY, I'M IN FOR REFUSING TO!"

TOMMIES IN THE TRAIN

The sun shines,
The coltsfoot flowers along the railway banks
Shine like flat coin which Jove in thanks
Strews each side the lines.

A steeple
In purple elms, daffodils
Sparkle beneath; luminous hills
Beyond –   and no people.

England, O Danaë
To this spring of cosmic gold
That falls on your lap of mould! –
What then are we?

What are we
Clay-coloured, who roll in fatigue
As the train falls league after league
From our destiny?

A hand is over my face,
A cold hand. –
I peep between the fingers
To watch the world that lingers
Behind, yet keeps pace.

Always there, as I peep
Between the fingers that cover my face!
Which then is it that falls from its place
And rolls down the steep?

Is it the train
That falls like a meteorite
Backward into space, to alight
Never again?

Or is it the illusory world
That falls from reality
As we look? Or are we
Like a thunderbolt hurled?

One or another
Is lost, since we fall apart
Endlessly, in one motion depart
From each other.

D H Lawrence

A national change of mood

By December 1916 the Asquith administration, having failed to win the
war, was ousted, and the new coalition government of David Lloyd
George trembled in the face of the anti-war feeling which was taking
hold of the country. In Lloyd George's own words,

> Terrible losses without appreciable results had spread a general
> sense of disillusionment and war weariness throughout the na-
> tion. . . Ministers who held key positions in the British Cabinet
> which resigned in December, 1916, were advising their colleagues
> that we could not carry on the War for many more months. . .
> Discontent was spreading rapidly in our workshops. The pacifist
> movement was growing in the country. Crowded meetings were
> held in the towns and industrial centres demanding that the war
> should be brought to an end. . . Even distinguished statesmen like
> Lord Lansdowne were advising negotiations for an early settle-
> ment. Men of high standing and of unchallengeable patriotism
> were privately urging the Lansdowne appeal on the Government.[1]

From the first days of the war the government had accepted that support
for the war would not, of itself, last – and that support would have to
be actively encouraged.

The work of the Secret War Propaganda Bureau had played an important part, even though its main focus of attention was America and
other foreign countries. (See chapter 3.) By June 1915 two and a half
million copies of books, pamphlets and speeches had been distributed
in a number of languages.

For the first time a film unit had been set up to further the cause of
propaganda. Now, in response to the growing clamour of protest, the
Propaganda Bureau and its successors the Department, and then Ministry of Information, turned increasing attention to encouraging support
on the home front.

Hundreds of patriotic organisations had spontaneously sprung up on the
initiative of individuals. The *Fight for Right Movement* which Thomas
Hardy joined has already been mentioned.

In June 1917 the Government decided to take further steps to counter-
act pacifist propaganda and to promote, "inflexible determination to
continue to a victorious end the struggle in maintenance of those ideals

1   *The Truth About the Peace Treaties*, David Lloyd George, p51, 55, 56.

of Liberty and Justice which are the common and sacred cause of the Allies." [1]

It therefore brought into being the National War Aims Committee. This was an all-party committee financed, initially, from the funds of political parties, but in November it received £240,000 from the government.

The committee organised hundreds of meetings throughout the country addressed by politicians, authors and other volunteers; commissioned articles for the press, posters, postcards, banners, cartoons and hundreds of thousands of leaflets. In spite of the idealistic sounding aims of the NWAC what it really did was to promote racial hatred. The propaganda stressed the viciousness of the Germans, and the "danger" of a negotiated peace − in other words the Government wanted to crush Germany utterly so that it could impose terms of settlement entirely to the benefit of the British side.

Eventually, even loyal supporters of the Government and the war were belatedly questioning its purpose.

H G Wells accused the National War Aims Committee of doing nothing except "antagonizing our people against anything and everything German," and being "totally unconstructive about the war aims or what was to happen after the war."

Poets against objectors

Even though joining the army had become compulsory for all men aged eighteen to forty-one in April 1916, the number applying for exemption inspired poets to renew their calls to fight. This was especially so after the German breakthrough in the Spring of 1918 when losing the war looked a serious possibility for the Allies.

•

A CALL TO NATIONAL SERVICE

Up and be doing, all who have a hand
To lift, a back to bend. It must not be
In times like these that vaguely linger we
To air our vaunts and hopes; and leave our land

1   *Struggle 1914-1918*, E Wrench, p112.

Untended as a wild of weeds and sand.
– Say, then, "I come!!" and go, O women and men
Of palace, ploughshare, easel, counter, pen;
That scareless, scathless, England still may stand.

Would years but let me stir as once I stirred
At many a dawn to take the forward track,
And with a stride plunged on to enterprise,

I now would speed like yester wind that whirred
Through yielding pines; and serve with never a slack,
So loud for promptness all around outcries!

Thomas Hardy, March 1917

A OUTRANCE *

The foe has flung his gage,
His hands clutch at the spoil,
Not ours his wrath to assuage,
Not ours, his sins to assoil.
His challenge must be met,
His haughtiness brought low.
On guard! The lists are set.
Stand fast! The trumpets blow.

So stand that none shall flinch
From the last sacrifice,
A life for every inch,
For every yard its price.
See – our twin banners dance,
Linked till the long day's close –
The Fleur-de-lis of France
Beside the English Rose.

With these to guard her gates
Against the foeman's power,
Undaunted, Freedom waits
The issue of the hour.
Her knights are in the field,
His blade each warrior draws.
Their pride – a stainless shield:
Their strength – a righteous cause.

F W D Bendall, 21 March 1918

*To the bitter end

Military Service Act 1918

In April 1918 the original Act was extended to include men aged 41 to 50, authorised the extension of the age limit to 56, and the bringing of conscription to Ireland.

JUSTICE

Across a world where all men grieve
And grieving strive the more,
The great days range like tides and leave
Our dead on every shore.
Heavy the load we undergo,
And our own hands prepare,
If we have parley with the foe,
The load our sons must bear.

Before we loose the word
That bids new worlds to birth,
Needs must we loosen first the sword
Of Justice upon earth;
Or else all else is vain
Since life on earth began,
And the spent world sinks back again
Hopeless of God and Man.

A people and their King
Through ancient sin grown strong,
Because they feared no reckoning
Would set no bound to wrong;
But now their hour is past,
And we who bore it find
Evil Incarnate held at last
To answer to mankind.

For agony and spoil
Of nations beat to dust,
For poisoned air and tortured soil
And cold, commanded lust,
And every secret woe
The shuddering waters saw –
Willed and fulfilled by high and low –
Let them relearn the Law.

That when the dooms are read,
Not high nor low shall say –
"My haughty or my humble head
Has saved me in this day."

That, till the end of time,
Their remnant shall recall
Their fathers' old, confederate crime
Availed them not at all.

That neither schools nor priests,
Nor Kings may build again
A people with the heart of beasts
Made wise concerning men.
Whereby our dead shall sleep
In honour, unbetrayed,
And we in faith and honour keep
That peace for which they paid.

Rudyard Kipling, October 1918

THE ENGAGED IMAGINATIONS

It is clear that not only did everyone think of their relations, friends
and acquaintances engaged in the fighting in France but a great many
were out there imaginatively, living through the experience – none
more so than Wilfrid Wilson Gibson who tried to enlist four times,
failing on each occasion because of poor eyesight. Eventually he did
get into the army and served his time at an army supplies depot in Sy-
denham working as a loader and packer. He never saw action. Thirty-
two of his poems were published in a collection entitled *Battle* in
1915, and his poems were very popular.

Most of the other writers in this section are non-combatants too, but
Vera Brittain knew from first hand experience the fighting realities
of war. She worked as a nurse in military hospitals in France, Malta and
England.

TO THE VANGUARD

Oh, little mighty Force that stood for England!
That, with your bodies for a living shield,
Guarded her slow awaking, that defied
The sudden challenge of tremendous odds
And fought the rushing legions to a stand –
Then stark in grim endurance held the line.
O little Force that in your agony
Stood fast while England girt her armour on,
Held high our honour in your wounded hands,
Carried our honour safe with bleeding feet –
We have no glory great enough for you,
The very soul of Britain keeps your day!
Procession? – Marches forth a Race in Arms;

And, for the thunder of the crowd's applause,
Crash upon crash the voice of monstrous guns,
Fed by the sweat, served by the life of England,
Shouting your battle-cry across the world.

Oh, little mighty Force, your way is ours,
This land inviolate your monument.

Beatrix Brice-Miller

AUGUST 1914

God said: "Men have forgotten Me;
The souls that sleep shall wake again,
And blinded eyes be taught to see."

So, since redemption comes through pain,
He smote the earth with chastening rod,
And brought destruction's lurid reign;

But where His desolation trod,
The people in their agony
Despairing cried: "There is no God!"

Vera Brittain, 1914

WONDER

If God is thrilled by a battle cry,
If He can bless the moaning fight,
If, when the trampling charge goes by
God Himself is the leading knight;
If God laughs when the guns thunder,
If He yells when the bullet sings —
Then, bewildered, I but wonder
The God of Love can love such things!

*   *   *   *   *   *

The white gulls wheeling over the plough,
The sun, the reddening trees —
We, being enemies, I and thou —
There is no meaning in these.
There is no flight on the wings of Spring,
No scent in the summer rose,
The roundelays that the blackbirds sing —
There is no meaning in those!

If you must kill me – why the lark,
The hawthorn bud, and the corn?
Why do the stars bedew the dark?
Why is the blossom born?
If I must kill you – why the kiss
Which made you? There is no why!
If it be true we were born for this –
Merciless God, good-bye!

John Galsworthy

AN IRISH AIRMAN FORESEES HIS DEATH

I know that I shall meet my fate
Somewhere among the clouds above;
Those that I fight I do not hate,
Those that I guard I do not love;
My country is Kiltartan Cross,
My countrymen Kiltartan's poor,
No likely end could bring them loss
Or leave them happier than before.
Nor law, nor duty bade me fight,
Nor public men, nor cheering crowds,
A lonely impulse of delight
Drove to this tumult in the clouds;
I balanced all, brought all to mind,
The years to come seemed waste of breath,
A waste of breath the years behind
In balance with this life, this death.

W B Yeats

Yeats's poem was inspired by the death of his friend, Major Robert Gregory, who was shot down on the Italian Front on 23 January, 1918. Kiltartan was a ruined church near Robert Gregory's – and Yeats's – home, a few miles north of Gort, County Galway.

BREAKFAST

We ate our breakfast lying on our backs
Because the shells were screeching overhead.
I bet a rasher to a loaf of bread
That Hull United would beat Halifax
When Jimmy Stainthorpe played full-back instead
Of Billy Bradford. Ginger raised his head
And cursed, and took the bet, and dropt back dead.
We ate our breakfast lying on our backs
Because the shells were screeching overhead.

Wilfrid Gibson

THE BAYONET

This bloody steel
Has killed a man.
I heard him squeal
As on I ran.

He watched me come
With wagging head.
I pressed it home,
And he was dead.

Though clean and clear
I've wiped the steel,
I still can hear
That dying squeal.

Wilfrid Gibson

NOISE OF BATTLE

And all hours long, the town
Roars like a beast in a cave
That is wounded there
And like to drown;
While days rush, wave after
wave
On its lair.

An invisible woe unseals
The flood, so it passes beyond
All bounds: the great old city
Recumbent roars as it feels
The foamy paw of the pond
Reach from immensity.

But all that it can do
Now, as the tide rises,
Is to listen and hear the grim
Waves crash like thunder
through
The splintered streets, hear
noises
Roll hollow in the interim.

D H Lawrence

CARRION

It is plain now what you are. Your head has dropped
Into a furrow. And the lovely curve
Of your strong leg has wasted and is propped
Against a ridge of the ploughed land's watery swerve.

You are swayed on waves of the silent ground;
You clutch and claim with passionate grasp of your fingers
The dip of earth in which you body lingers;
If you are not found,
In a little while your limbs will fall apart;
the birds will take some, but the earth will take most your
heart.

You are fuel for a coming spring if they leave you here;
The crop that will rise from your bones is healthy bread.
You died – we know you – without a word of fear,
And as they loved you living I love you dead

No girl would kiss you. But then
No girl would ever kiss the earth
In the manner they hug the lips of men:
You are not known to them in this, your second birth.

No coffin-cover now will cram
Your body in a shell of lead;
Earth will not fall on you from the spade with a slam,
But will fold and enclose you slowly, you living dead.

Hush, I hear the guns. Are you still asleep?
Surely I saw you a little heave to reply.
I can hardly think you will not turn over and creep
Along the furrows trenchward as if to die.

Harold Monro

AT LAST CAME DEATH (*from* New Heaven and Earth)

IV

At last came death, sufficiency of death,
and that at last relieved me, I died.
I buried my beloved; it was good, I buried myself and was gone.
War came, and every hand raised to murder!
very good, very good, every hand raised to murder!
Very good,very good, I am a murderer!
It is good, I can murder and murder, and see them fall,
the mutilated, horror-struck youths, a multitude
one on another, and then in clusters together
smashed, all oozing with blood, and burned in heaps
going up in a foetid smoke to get rid of them,
the murdered bodies of youths and men in heaps
and heaps and heaps and horrible reeking heaps
till it is almost enough, till I am reduced perhaps;
Thousands and thousands of gaping, hideous foul dead
that are youths and men and me
being burned with oil, and consumed in corrupt thick smoke,
    that rolls
and taints and blackens the sky, till at last it is dark, dark as
    night, or death, or hell
and I am dead, and trodden to nought in the smoke-sodden tomb;
dead and trodden to nought in the sour black earth
of the tomb; dead and trodden to nought, trodden to
nought.

V

God, but it is good to have died and been trodden out,
trodden to nought in sour, dead earth,
quite to nought,
absolutely to nothing
nothing
nothing
nothing.

For when it is quite, quite nothing, then it is everything.
When I am quite trodden out quite, quite out,
every vestige gone, then I am here
risen and setting my foot on another world
risen, accomplishing a resurrection
risen, not born again, but risen, body the same as before,
new beyond knowledge of newness, alive beyond life,
proud beyond inkling or furthest conception of pride,
living where life was never yet dreamed of, nor hinted at,
here, in the other world, still terrestrial
myself, the same as before yet unaccountably new. . .

D. H. Lawrence

THE FALLING LEAVES

Today, as I rode by,
I saw the brown leaves dropping from their tree
In a still afternoon,
When no wind whirled them whistling to the sky,
But thickly, silently,
They fell, like snowflakes wiping out the noon;
And wandered slowly thence
For thinking of a gallant multitude
Which now all withering lay,
Slain by no wind of age or pestilence,
But in their beauty strewed
Like snowflakes falling on the Flemish clay.

Margaret Postgate Cole, November 1915

YOUTH'S OWN

Out of the fields I see them pass,
Youth's own battalion –
Like moonlight ghosting over grass
To dark oblivion.

They have a wintry march to go –
Bugle and fife and drum!
With music, softer than the snow
All flurrying, they come!

They have a solemn tryst to keep
Out on a starry heath;
To fling them down, and sleep and sleep
Beyond Reveille –   Death!

Since Youth has vanished from our eyes,
Who of us glad can be?
Who will be grieving when he dies
And leaves this Calvary?

John Galsworthy

TO MY BROTHER
(In memory of July 1st, 1916)

Your battle-wounds are scars upon my heart,
Received when in that grand and tragic "show"
You played your part
Two years ago,

And silver in the summer morning sun
I see the symbol of your courage glow –
That Cross you won
Two years ago.

Though now again you watch the shrapnel fly,
And hear the guns that daily louder grow,
As in July
Two years ago,

May you endure to lead the Last Advance
And with your men pursue the flying foe
As once in France
Two years ago.

Vera Brittain

VALLEY OF THE SHADOW

God, I am travelling out to death's sea,
I who exulted in sunshine and laughter,
Dreamed not of dying –   death is such waste of me!
Grant me one prayer: Doom not the hereafter

Of mankind to war, as though I had died not –
I who, in battle, my comrade's arm linking,
Shouted and sang, life in my pulses hot
Throbbing and dancing! Let not my sinking
In dark be for naught, my death a vain thing!
God, let me know it the end of man's fever!
Make my last breath a bugle call, carrying
Peace o'er the valleys and cold hills for ever!

John Galsworthy

I SHOUTED FOR BLOOD

I shouted for blood as I ran, brother,
Till my bayonet pierced your breast:
I lunged thro' the heart of a man, brother,
That the sons of men might rest.

I swung up my rifle apace, brother.
Gasping with wrath awhile,
And I smote at your writhing face, brother,
That the face of peace might smile.

Your eyes are beginning to glaze, brother,
Your wounds are ceasing to bleed.
God's ways are wonderful ways, brother,
And hard for your wife to read.

Janet Begbie

From TEN MEN IN A CRATER-HOLE

Ten men in a crater-hole, –
Orders – "Bar the way! –
You men hold that crater-hole,
Cost you what it may!"

Ten men in a crater-hole,
Facing a brigade;
Sworn to hold that crater-hole
Till the last man's dead.

* * *

Ten men in a crater-hole, –
Two hot Lewis guns, –
Great the toll of the crater-hole
On the close-packed Huns.

Ten men in a crater-hole,
Holding Death at bay;
Ten men in a crater-hole,
Scything human hay.

Nine men in a crater-hole,
Doing all men can;
Fine men in a crater-hole, –
"Join you soon, old man!"

Eight men in a crater-hole,
Faces hard as steel;
Great men in a crater-hole,
Fighting with a will.

Seven men in a crater-hole,
Cursing till all's blue;
Merry men in a crater hole
Giving Fritz his due.

Six men in a crater hole
Somewhat out of breath.
Four men from the crater-hole
Shaken hands with death.
* * *
Two men in a crater-hole
Fearless to the last:
Few men in a crater hole
Ever lived so fast.

One man in a crater hole,
Sticking it alone:
One great soul in a crater-hole,
Fed up, - well nigh done.

* * *
Ten men from the crater-hole,
Arm in arm they've gone;
Plain men from a crater-hole,
All their duty done.

Ten men from the crater-hole,
Up at G. H. Q. –
"Ten men, Sir, from a crater-hole, –
Done our best for You!"

Ten men from the crater-hole,
You have given your best
Great souls from the crater-hole,
Welcome to My rest!"

John Oxenham

The following verses, the hymn, *For the Men at the Front*, are reputed
to have sold eight million copies during the war.

HYMN: FOR THE MEN AT THE FRONT

Lord God of Hosts, whose mighty hand
Dominion holds on sea and land,
In Peace and War Thy Will we see
Shaping the larger liberty.
Nations may rise and nations fall,
Thy Changeless Purpose rules them all.

When Death flies swift on wave or field,
Be Thou a sure defence and shield!
Console and succour those who fall,
And help and hearten each and all!
O, hear a people's prayers for those
Who fearless face their country's foes!

For those who weak and broken lie,
In weariness and agony –
Great Healer, to their beds of pain
Come, touch, and make them whole again!

O, hear a people's prayers, and bless
Thy servants in their hour of stress!

For those to whom the call shall come
We pray Thy tender welcome home.
The toil, the bitterness, all past,
We trust them to Thy Love at last.
     O, hear a people's prayers for all
Who, nobly striving nobly fall!

John Oxenham

HOW THE PRESS REPORTED THE WAR

So great are the psychological resistances to war in modern nations, that every war must appear to be a war of defence against a menacing, murderous aggressor. There must be no ambiguity about whom the public is to hate. The war must not be due to a world system of conducting international affairs, nor to the stupidity or malevolence of all governing classes, but to the rapacity of the enemy. Guilt and guilelessness must be assessed geographically and all the guilt must be on the other side of the frontier. If the propagandist is to mobilize the hate of the people, he must see to it that everything is circulated which establishes the sole responsibility of the enemy.

H D Lasswell, *Propaganda Techniques in World War I*

Don't believe stories which you see in the papers about troops asking as a special privilege not to be relieved. We stick it, at all costs if necessary, as long as ordered, but everyone's glad to hand over to someone else. And anyone who says he enjoys this kind of thing is either a liar or a madman.

Captain Harry Yoxall, 18th Bn Kings Royal Rifle Corps [1]

An image of evil

It was not difficult to create an evil image for the Germans. Ruthless executions of civilians, old and young alike, were carried out in a number of towns and villages in Belgium. For five days at the end of August 1914 the university town of Louvain was the scene of executions and arson. About a fifth of the town was destroyed by fire.

---

1   Quoted in *Tommy Goes to War*, Malcolm Brown, p128.

TO THE GERMAN EMPEROR
(after the sack of Louvain)

Wherefore are men amazed at thee, thou Blot
On the fair script of Time, thou sceptred Smear
Across the Day? Thou wert divulged full clear –
Hell's sponsor –   long ago! Has earth forgot
Thy benison on a monster reeking hot
From shambles bloody as these, – thy orient peer,
Thy heart's mate, and infernal comrade dear?
His red embrace do men remember not?
Fall'n is thy fellow and withered from the scene:
Follow him thou! And when the hounds of doom
Rend thee, and for thy carrion there hath been
Fit dust-heap found, and no relenting broom,
Purged be Life's palace of thy trail unclean,
And Earth made bride-sweet with returning bloom.

William Watson

KULTUR: A DIALOGUE

Staff Officer.
Highness, yon babe his popgun fired.

Crown Prince.
No further pretext is required.
On, my brave Guards, and in God's name
Give old and young to sword and flame.

William Watson

The management of the press

When war was declared every national daily paper supported the action, and though there were to be some occasions when powerful, domineering, and opinionated newspaper proprietors were annoyed by the Government's conduct of the war, throughout the war they did all in their very considerable power to manipulate British opinion to support the war, endure hardship and suffering and provide the men needed to fight the battles.

Some owners were friendly with and close in ideals and outlook to key politicians. Some, it will be remembered, had helped to make the war possible by creating a climate of public opinion characterised by distrust, fear and hatred of Germany.

The most powerful newspaper proprietors were the Harmsworth brothers: Lord Northcliffe and Lord Rothermere. Northcliffe owned *The Times* (circulation in 1914, 183,000) and the *Daily Mail* (circulation in 1914, just under a million). Before the war, from May 1905 till February 1911, he had owned *The Observer* which was, for most of this time, edited by his friend , J L Garvin, who campaigned, as he saw it, to alert the country to the German threat. Rothermere owned the *Daily Mirror*, the *Sunday Pictorial* and the *Glasgow Daily Record*. Both owned numerous provincial newspapers. Northcliffe became Director of Propaganda to Enemy Countries: Rothermere Director of Propaganda to Neutral Countries.

However, in spite of the close relationship and common ideas of the government and newspaper proprietors, the Government considered it needed to control the content of newspapers directly, partly for sound military reasons and partly to manipulate opinion. It did this in two ways. First, it controlled the information about military activities that was made available to newspapers. Second, it operated a system of censorship. Both forms of control were the responsibility of the Press Bureau which was set up on 6th August, 1914.

In the first weeks the amount of information it provided about the war in France was so slim that the press clamoured for an opportunity to send correspondents to the action. This was turned down, but as a concession they were provided with an "eye witness" (Lt. Col. Sir Ernest Swinton) who was appointed by the Bureau. His reports were censored and then passed to Lord Kitchener for his personal approval. "Eyewitness's" guidelines were, "to tell as much of the truth as was compatible with safety, to guard against depression and pessimism, and to check unjustified optimism which might lead to relaxationof effort." [1]

Defying the rules

Guarding against depression meant lying about setbacks and failures. It may seem an inevitable policy for a country at war, but when the chief censor, the Head of the Press Bureau, F C Green defied his instructions, by urging *The Times* to print the truth about a crushing early defeat at the end of August 1914, morale was not weakened. In fact it led to an immediate enormous surge in recruitment which may have actually helped to prevent an early defeat of the Allies.

The report had been brought to *The Times*' offices by a special courier – a dispatch from Amiens dated August, 29. It had arrived too late for

1 *Eye Witness*, Lt Col Sir E Swinton, p53, quoted by Cate Haste in *Keep the Home Fires Burning*.

the Saturday edition of the paper. It told of British soldiers over-whelmed by numbers. It stated, "Our small British force could not stand before a volume so powerful, so immense . . . England should realise and realise at once that she must send reinforcements, and still send them. Is an army of exhaustless valour to be borne down by the sheer weight of numbers, while young Englishmen at home play golf and cricket? We want men and we want them now."

The Times published the report in a special Sunday edition, putting the story on the front page in place of the customary classified advertise-ments.

For his courageous and beneficial honesty F C Green was removed from his post.

Other developments

From April 1915 correspondents were allowed to visit the front line area where their movements were controlled and they were fed information by military press liaison officers.

Further censorship controlled the newspapers through the Defence of the Realm Act which set out the kinds of information which papers were and were not permitted to print. There was to be no information on movements of troops, ships, aircraft or location or description of war material; no statements likely to cause "disaffection" to the success of His Majesty's Forces or those of his allies, or his relations with for-eign powers; no statements likely to prejudice recruiting. If in doubt, articles had to be submitted for direct censorship by the Press Bureau.

With so little material to use it is hardly surprising that the papers were tempted into invention and exaggeration. So long as they showed the enemy as a barbarian and British soldiers as gentlemanly, fair, moderate and always suffering nothing worse than minor setbacks then the Government and its censors at the Press Bureau were content. The vilification of Germans and Germany was allowed to go to extremes of racial hatred. [1]

The Times on The Battle of the Somme

The first day of The Battle of the Somme, 1st July 1916, is famous as the greatest disaster in British military history. Twenty thousand

---

1   See *Keep the Home Fires Burning*, Cate Haste, p30, 31.

British men were killed on that first day, forty thousand were wounded. On 3rd July *The Times* stated in a preliminary report

"EVERYTHING HAS GONE WELL . . . Our troops have successfully carried out their missions, all counter-attacks have been repulsed and large numbers of prisoners taken."

Complete Success

A further report in The Times of 4th July was headlined 'FIRST DAY'S RESULTS' and came from "Our Special Correspondent, Press Camp, July 2." It claimed complete success for the Allies.

FIRST DAY'S RESULTS

It is now possible to get something like an accurate picture of the results of the first day's fighting in the battle which is now raging here; and the essential fact that stands out is that on the main part of the offensive both we and the French co-operating on our right won complete success . . .

The success of the advance on this main section of the front is most heartening. The enemy's losses at Fricourt and Montauban are known to have been immense.

OUR CASUALTIES

Today I have seen large numbers of German prisoners, including one batch of 470 at a single place. In all it is believed that to date we have taken about 3,000. I have also visited some of our wounded in the collecting stations. They are extraordinarily cheery and brave. It is gratifying to know (and I have gathered the same information at too many points to have any doubt of its accuracy) that an exceptionally large proportion of our casualties are very slight wounds, being injuries from shrapnel and machine-gun fire. Whatever our total casualties may be, the proportion of permanent disablements will be very small. . . our artillery fire had over most of the front been extremely destructive and very good. . . As always, however, there were places where individual bits of trench and stretches of the protecting barbed wire had miraculously escaped. Some of the latter caused our attacking infantry considerable losses.

In mid 1916 the general public had no way of knowing the facts, and armchair poets could go on imagining our gallant soldiers gloriously fighting for Justice, Right and Freedom. In this way the newspapers, censor and propagandists sent thousands of men to their deaths; or as they might say, in this way they won the war.

Men of conscience

Some journalists and newspaper proprietors must have felt qualms of conscience. Rothermere certainly seemed unhappy in a conversation he is reported as having with J L Garvin.

> You and I, Garvin, we haven't the pluck of those young lieutenants who go over the top. We're telling lies; we know we're telling lies; we don't tell the public the truth, that we're losing more officers than the Germans, and that it's impossible to get through on the Western Front. You've seen the correspondents shepherded by Charteris – they don't know the truth; they don't speak the truth and we know they don't.[1]

THE VISION SPLENDID

Here – or hereafter – you shall see it ended,
This mighty work to which your souls are set;
If from beyond – then, with the vision splendid,
You smile back and never know regret.

Be this your vision! – through you, Life transfigured,
Uplift, redeemed from its forlorn estate,
Purged of the stains which once its soul disfigured,
Healed and restored, and wholly consecrate.

Christ's own rich blood, for healing of the nations,
Poured through his heart the message of reprieve;
God's holy martyrs built on His foundations,
Built with their lives and died that Life might live.

Now, in their train, your blood shall bring like healing;
You, like the Saints, have freely given your all,
And your high deaths, God's purposes revealing,
Sound through the earth His mighty Clarion Call.

O, not in vain has been your great endeavour;
For, by your dyings, Life is born again,
And greater love hath no man tokened ever,
Than with his life to purchase Life's high gain.

John Oxenham, published March 1917

---

1   Quoted by Cate Haste from *C F G Masterman*, p296

PICARDY

When the trees blossom again;
When our spirits lighten –
When in quick sun and rain
Once more the green fields brighten;
Each golden flower those fields among,
The hum of thrifting bee,
Will be the risen flower and song
Of Youth's mortality.

When the birds flutter their wings,
When our scars are healing
When the furry-footed things
At night again are stealing;
When through the wheat each rippling wave,
The fragrance of flower breath
Will bring a message from the grave,
A whispering from death.

When the sweet waters can flow,
When the world's forgetting –
When once more the cattle low
At golden calm sun-setting;
Each peaceful evening's murmur, then,
And sigh the waters give,
Will tell immortal tale of men
Who died that we might live.

John Galsworthy

THIS IS NO CASE OF PETTY RIGHT OR WRONG

This is no case of petty right or wrong
That politicians or philosophers
Can judge. I hate not Germans, nor grow hot
With love of Englishmen, to please newspapers.
Beside my hate for one fat patriot
My hatred of the Kaiser is love true: –
A kind of god he is, banging a gong.
But I have not to choose between the two,
Or between justice and injustice. Dinned
With war and argument I read no more
Than in the storm smoking along the wind
Athwart the wood. Two witches' cauldrons roar.
From one the weather shall rise clear and gay;
Out of the other an England beautiful
And like her mother that died yesterday.
Little I know or care if, being dull,
I shall miss something that historians

Can rake out of the ashes when perchance
The phoenix broods serene above their ken.
But with the best and meanest Englishmen
I am one in crying, God save England, lest
we lose what never slaves and cattle blessed.
The ages made her that made us from dust:
She is all we know and live by, and we trust
She is good and must endure, loving her so:
And as we love ourselves we hate her foe.

Edward Thomas, 26 December 1915

Films for propaganda

In December 1915 the Wellington House Team launched the first (silent) propaganda film of the war, *Britain Prepared.* It was shown in
London daily till mid February. In August 1916 the film *The Battle of
the Somme* was shown simultaneously in thirty London cinemas and had
2000 bookings all over the country by October. – The creators of the
films may not have had a very clear idea of the responses they wanted
to elicit from their audiences. [1]

A WAR FILM

I saw,
With a catch of the breath and the heart's uplifting,
Sorrow and pride,
            The "week's great draw" –
The Mons Retreat;
The "Old Contemptibles" who fought, and died,
The horror and the anguish and the glory.

As in a dream,
Still hearing machine-guns rattle and shells scream,
I came out into the street.

When the day was done,
My little son
Wondered at bath-time why I kissed him so,
Naked upon my knee.
How could he know
The sudden terror that assaulted me? . .
The body I had borne
Nine moons beneath my heart,

[1]   See *Britain and the Two World Wars*, J Hunt and S Watson.

A part of me . . .
If, someday,
It should be taken away
To War. Tortured. Torn.
Slain.
Rotting in No Man's Land, out in the rain –
My little son . . .
Yet all those men had mothers, every one.

How should he know
Why I kissed and kissed and kissed him, crooning his name?
He thought that I was daft.
He thought it was a game,
And laughed, and laughed.

Teresa Hooley

THE WAR FILMS

O living pictures of the dead,
O songs without a sound,
O fellowship whose phantom tread
Hallows a phantom ground –
How in a gleam have these revealed
The faith we had not found.

We have sought God in a cloudy Heaven.
We have passed by God on earth:
His seven sins and his sorrows seven,
His wayworn mood and mirth,
Like a ragged cloak have hid from us
The secret of his birth.

Brother of men, when now I see
The lads go forth in line,
Thou knowest my heart is hungry in me
As for thy bread and wine:
Thou knowest my heart is bowed in me
To take their death for mine.

Henry Newbolt, 8 October 1916

THE PERSECUTION OF THE GERMANS

The Germans . . . here is a race which has for its chief fault
docility and a belief in teachers and rulers. For the rest, as all
who know it intimately will testify, it is a most civilised of
peoples. It is naturally kindly, comfort-loving, child-loving,

musical, artistic, intelligent. In countless respects German homes and towns and countrysides are the most civilised in the world.

H G Wells, 1914 [1]

Only two kinds of people

However the world pretends to divide itself, there are only two divisions in the world today – human beings and Germans.

Rudyard Kipling in the *Morning Post*, 22 June 1915.

In praise of hatred

Hatred, or, if my critics prefer it, righteous wrath, is the means to attain invincible resolve and it is as such that I recommend it. Lukewarm feelings can give only half-hearted results.

Arthur Conan Doyle in *The Times*, 16 January 1918.

Unofficial propaganda, condoned by politicians, created a burning animosity against Germany and against Germans living in England, even naturalised Germans and people with German-sounding names. Shocking racist statements were printed finding a ready response amongst a vicious-minded minority. The Northcliffe press (especially the *Daily Mail* and the *Weekly Dispatch*) and *John Bull* , edited and owned by Horatio Bottomley were amongst the most prominent of the campaigners. – The British Empire Union campaigned for the boycott of German goods.

Hiding one's German origins

As a direct result of the feeling that was generated against Germans many people, both famous and unknown, decided to change their names. The writer and poet, Ford Hermann Hueffer, changed his name to Ford Madox Ford. Robert von Ranke Graves called himself Robert Graves. The king renounced the dukedoms of Saxony and Sax-Coburg-Gotha and became plain English "Windsor". His brothers-in-law the Duke of Teck and Prince Alexander of Teck became Marquess of Cambridge and Earl of Athlone. The Battenburg cousins became Mountbatten. German shepherd dogs were renamed Alsations.

---

1   *The War That Will End War,* p 10.

The internment of enemy aliens

On 22nd October 1914, in response to the press campaign, the Cabinet ordered the arrest of all unnaturalised male Germans, Austrians and Hungarians between the ages of seventeen and forty-five. Internment camps were set up all over the mainland and on the Isle of Man. – One of the first tasks Robert Graves had in the army was to accompany forty German waiters in handcuffs and chains from Manchester hotels to their internment centre.

Charitable organisations which were set up to assist the destitute wives of internees were pilloried by the press.

Press abuse continued

On 7th May 1915 a German submarine sank an "innocent" British passenger liner, *The Lusitania*, in the war zone which it had declared round the British Isles (which then included the whole of Ireland). The Germans had warned of the risks of sailing in the war zone.

From the firing of the first of two torpedoes it took the *Lusitania* just twenty minutes to sink. One thousand one hundred and ninety eight passengers perished including 291 women, and 94 children. The dead included 128 Americans. Many of the bodies washed up on the south coast of Ireland.

What struck the public, encouraged, by the newspapers, was the horror of the civilian losses. It presented a wonderful opportunity for propagandists like Horatio Bottomley to lash the evil Germans for their monstrous act. The press campaign incited rioting, and looting of German shops and property.

> I call for a vendetta - a vendetta against every German in Britain – whether "naturalised" or not . . . You cannot naturalise an unnatural abortion, a hellish freak.´ But you can exterminate him.

> We have been very patient – patient with the Government, patient with the enemy . . . thousands and thousands of German savages are roaming at large in our midst – and all the time our brave honourable soldiers are being asphyxiated in the trenches; our wounded are being tortured; prisoners are being starved and insulted; unfortified towns are being bombarded; peaceful civilians – old men, women and children – are being murdered; trawlers and merchant vessels are being sunk; and now comes the crowning infamy of the *Lusitania* . . .

> I should welcome the formation of a National Council of Righteous Retribution – a National Vendetta, pledged to exterminate

every German-born man (God forgive the term!) in Britain – and
to deport every German-born woman and child . . .

As regards naturalised Germans they should be registered, made
to report themselves every day, and compelled to wear a distinc-
tive badge.

Horatio Bottomley in John Bull, 15 May 1915

Throughout the country demonstrations and riots erupted; German-
owned shops were smashed up.

A German shop in London's East End is smashed by rioting crowds,
12th May 1915.

Distinguished men with German connections were hounded by the press
– even Lord Haldane, simply because he had been partly educated in
Germany. He had been Minister for War until 1912, re-modelled the
army and founded the Territorials, yet was victimised by the press until, at the formation of a coalition government in May 1915, he was
dropped from office.

In Cornwall lived D H Lawrence with his German wife Frieda von
Richthofen – the cousin of the renowned fighter pilot, the Red Baron.
Lawrence complained vigorously to locals about the war and with a
German wife he was considered suspicious. Had he moved into this
coastal cottage in order to send signals to German U-boats in coastal
waters? A local boat was torpedoed. Perhaps Frieda's white scarf was
a signal, or the way she arranged washing on the line. To help

matters along a bit Lawrence took to singing German folk songs. Their
house was searched for incriminating documents on 12th October 1917
and although none was found the Lawrences were given three days to
get out of Cornwall. – Briefly they went to live in London, with
Hilda Doolittle, the wife of Richard Aldington.   Lawrence protested
to the war office about his treatment, asking permission to return to
Cornwall. His request was turned down and the Criminal Investigation
Department began to follow him. – This was the land of freedom, liberty and justice the British were fighting for. [1]

THE HALF-MAN

Sparing not age, sparing not youth,
They tore their way with wolfish tooth
Through human homes, through human hopes:
Not men, not men, but lycanthropes!*

Thus do the fabled monsters rear
Their heads anew; thus reappear
Old Shapes that free us and appal;
And the Half-Man is worst of all

William Watson

* lycanthrope - werewolf

A Clean Sweep
Mrs Britannia: "It has to
be done: so I might as
well do it first as last –
and so get rid of all the
dangerous microbes.

1   *Flame into Being,* Anthony Burgess, p81, 82.

LOVE AND FAREWELLS

LAST LEAVE (1918)

Let us forget tomorrow! For tonight
At least, with curtains drawn, and driftwood piled
On our own hearthstone, we may rest, and see
The firelight flickering on familiar walls.
(How the blue flames leap when an ember falls!)

Peace, and content, and soul-security –
These are within. Without, the waste is wild
With storm-clouds sweeping by in furious flight,
And ceaseless beating of autumnal rain
Upon our window pane.

The dusk grows deeper now, the flames are low:
We do not heed the shadows, you and I,
Nor fear the grey wings of encroaching gloom,
So softly they enfold us. One last gleam
Flashes and flits, elusive as a dream,

And then dies out upon the darkened room.
So, even so, our earthly fires must die;
Yet, in our hearts, love's flame shall leap and glow
When this dear night, with all it means to me,
Is but a memory!

Eileen Newton

UNDER THE SHADOW

Under the shadow of a hawthorn brake,
Where bluebells draw the sky down to the wood,
Where 'mid brown leaves, the primroses awake
And hidden violets smell of solitude;
Beneath green leaves bright-fluttered by the wing
Of fleeting, beautiful, immortal Spring,
I should have said, " I love you," and your eyes
Have said, "I too. . ." The gods saw otherwise.

For this is winter, and the London streets
Are full of soldiers from that far, fierce fray
Where life knows death, and where poor glory meets
Full-face with shame, and weeps and turns away.

And in the broken, trampled foreign wood
Is horror, and the terrible scent of blood,
And love shines tremulous, like a drowning star,
Under the shadow of the wings of war.

Edith Nesbit, first published December, 1915

LOVE, 1916

One said to me, "Seek Love, for he is Joy
Called by another name."
A Second said, "Seek Love, for he is Power
Which is called Fame."
Last said a Third, "Seek Love, his name is Peace."
I called him thrice
And the answer came, "Love now
Is christened Sacrifice."

May Wedderburn Cannan, August 1916

TRAIN

Will the train never start?
God, make the train start.

She cannot bear it, keeping up so long:
and he, he no more tries to laugh at her.
He is going.

She holds his two hands now.
Now, she has touch of him and sight of him.
And then he will be gone.
He will be gone.

They are so young.
She stands under the window of his carriage,
and he stands in the window.
They hold each other's hands
across the window ledge.
And look and look, and know that they may never
look again.

The great clock of the station –
how strange it is.
Terrible that the minutes go,
terrible that the minutes never go.

They had walked the platform for so long,
up and down, and up and down –

the platform, in the rainy morning,
up and down, and up and down.

The guard came by, calling,
"Take your places, take your places."

She stands under the window of his carriage,
and he stands in the window.

God, make the train start!
Before they cannot bear it,
make the train start!

God, make the train start!

The three children, there,
in black, with the old nurse,
standing together, and looking, and looking,
up at their father in the carriage window,
they are so forlorn and silent.

The little girl will not cry,
but her chin trembles.
She throws back her head,
with its stiff little braid,
and will not cry.

Her father leans down,
out over the ledge of the window,
and kisses her, and kisses her.

She must be like her mother,
and it must be the mother who is dead.
The nurse lifts up the smallest boy,
and his father kisses him,
leaning through the carriage window.

The big boy stands very straight,
and looks at his father,
and looks, and never takes his eyes from him.
And knows that he may never look again.

Will the train never start?
God, make the train start!

The father reaches his hand down from the window,
and grips the boy's hand,
and does not speak at all.

Will the train never start?

He lets the boy's hand go.

Will the train never start?

He takes the boy's chin in his hand,
leaning out through the window,
and lifts the face that is so young, to his.
They look and look,
and know that they may never look again.

Will the train never start?
God, make the train start!

Helen Mackay

THE SEND-OFF

Down the close darkening lanes they sang their way
To the siding-shed,
And lined the train with faces grimly gay.

Their breasts were stuck all white with wreath and spray
As men's are, dead.

Dull porters watched them, and a casual tramp
Stood staring hard,
Sorry to miss them from the upland camp.

Then, unmoved, signals nodded, and a lamp
Winked to the guard.

So secretly, like wrongs hushed-up, they went.
They were not ours:
We never heard to which front these were sent;

Nor there if they yet mock what women meant
Who gave them flowers.

Shall they return to beating of great bells
In wild train-loads?
A few, a few, too few for drums and yells,
May creep back, silent, to village wells,
Up half-known roads.

Wilfred Owen

Eleanor Farjeon's farewell to Edward Thomas

On 6th January 1917, Eleanor Farjeon went to the home of Edward and Helen Thomas to see him on his last leave before going to France.

> While we chatted, there was no sense of this being the last night; Helen kept her bravely smiling face, and it was still a continuation, not an ending. Presently she went upstairs to see to the bedrooms. I said good night to Edward and followed her, leaving him to do the last things in the house. But in my room at the head of the stairs, I knew it was an ending. I wished I had managed to break through the wave of shyness which had kept me from kissing him good night downstairs. Strong as it was, and for me so very deep, our friendship had remained undemonstrative from beginning to end. Now, as he came up the stairs, I opened my door, and said again "Good night, Edward," and lifted my face. We kissed, he said "Good night," and went on, and that was the real goodbye.
>
> Next morning after breakfast he went part of the way to Loughton Station with me, walking down the hill through Epping Forest to the foot, where we shook hands as usual. [1]

NOW THAT YOU TOO

> Now that you too must shortly go the way
> Which in these bloodshot years uncounted men
> Have gone in vanishing armies day by day,
> And in their numbers will not come again:
> I must not strain the moments of our meeting
> Striving each look, each accent, not to miss,
> Or question of our parting and our greeting,
> Is this the last of all? is this – or this?
>
> Last sight of all it may be with these eyes,
> Last touch, last hearing, since eyes, hands, and ears,
> Even serving love, are our mortalities,
> And cling to what they own in mortal fears: –
> But oh, let end what will, I hold you fast
> By immortal love, which has no first or last.
>
> Eleanor Farjeon

---

1   *Edward Thomas, the Last Four Years,* Eleanor Farjeon, p241.

NO ONE SO MUCH AS YOU

No one so much as you
Loves this my clay,
Or would lament as you
Its dying day.

You know me through and through
Though I have not told,
And though with what you know
You are not bold.

None ever was so fair
As I thought you:
Not a word can I bear
Spoken against you.

All that I ever did
For you seemed coarse
Compared with what I hid
Nor put in force.

My eyes scarce dare meet you
Lest they should prove
I but respond to you
And do not love.

We look and understand,
We cannot speak
Except in trifles and
Words the most weak.

For I at most accept
Your love, regretting
That is all: I have kept
Only a fretting

That I could not return
All that you gave
And could not ever burn
With the love you have,

Till sometimes it did seem
Better it were
Never to see you more
Than linger here

With only gratitude
Instead of love –
A pine in solitude
Cradling a dove.

Edward Thomas,
11 February 1916

How Helen Thomas remembered her parting from Edward

On the eleventh of January 1917 Edward Thomas said goodbye to his wife for the last time. For Helen this was an experience so terrible that she "did not know one could live through such agony." Three years later she recalled the occasion in a letter to her closest friend.

> Three years ago today Edward went away from me. The snow was deep on the ground and he soon disappeared in a thick fog, and we cooied to each other until we could not hear any more. I was left knowing I would never see him, never hear him, never hold him in my arms again. Tonight I think of all our life together, and I think of my life during these three years. Our life together was a restless sea, tide in, tide out, calm and glorious despair and ecstasy; never still, never easy, but always vivid and moving, wave upon wave, a wild deep glorious sea. Our life was terrible and glorious but always life. And I think of my life these

three years. And again it has been like a sea, calm and cruel, happy and despairing, just the same as always but without a harbour, without an anchorage, and I have been tired to death of its tossing to and fro on to this beach and that on to this rock and that. For life to me cannot be otherwise until that new life comes to me and I am gathered into my anchorage and him and get a calm. [1]

AND YOU, HELEN

And you, Helen, what should I give you?
So many things I would give you
Had I an infinite great store
Offered me and I stood before
To choose. I would give you youth,
All kinds of loveliness and truth,
A clear eye as good as mine,
Lands, waters, flowers, wine,
As many children as your heart
Might wish for, a far better art
Than mine can be, all you have lost
Upon the travelling waters tossed,
Or given to me. If I could choose
Freely in that great treasure-house
Anything from any shelf,
I would give you back yourself
And power to discriminate
What you want and want it not too late,
Many fair days free from care
And heart to enjoy both foul and fair,
And myself, too, if I could find
Where it lay hidden and it proved kind.

Edward Thomas, 9 April, 1916

Edward Thomas's last poem, *Out in the Dark*, was written on 24th December, 1916, a month before embarking for France and the front line.

---

1   Quoted in *Edward Thomas, a Critical Biography,* William Cook, p94, 95.

OUT IN THE DARK

Out in the dark over the snow
The fallow fawns invisible go
With the fallow doe;
And the winds blow
Fast as the stars are slow.

Stealthily the dark haunts round
And, when the lamp goes, without sound
At a swifter bound
Than the swiftest hound,
Arrives, and all else is drowned;

And star and I and wind and deer,
Are in the dark together, – near,
Yet far, – and fear
Drums on my ear
In that sage company drear.

How weak and little is the light,
All the universe of sight,
Love and delight,
Before the might,
If you love it not, of night.

Edward Thomas

IN TIME OF WAR

I dreamed (God pity babes at play)
How I should love past all romance,
And how to him beloved should say,
As heroes' women say, perchance,
When the deep drums awake –
"Go forth: do gloriously for my dear sake."

But now I render, blind with fear,
No lover made of dreams, but You,
O You – so commonplace, so dear,
So knit with all I am or do!
Now, braver thought I lack:
Only God bring you back – God bring you back!

Lesbia Thanet

THE WOUNDED RETURN

THE NURSE

Here in the long white ward I stand,
Pausing a little breathless space,
Touching a restless fevered hand,
Murmuring comfort's commonplace –

Long enough pause to feel the cold
Fingers of fear about my heart;
Just for a moment, uncontrolled,
All the pent tears of pity start.

While here I strive, as best I may,
Strangers' long hours of pain to ease,
Dumbly I question – *Far away*
Lies my beloved even as these?

Miss G M Mitchell,   August 30, 1916

NIGHT DUTY

The pain and laughter of the day are done,
So strangely hushed and still the long ward seems,
Only the Sister's candle softly beams.
Clear from the church nearby the clock strikes "one;"
And all are wrapt away in secret sleep and dreams.

They bandied talk and jest from bed to bed;
Now sleep has touched them with a subtle change.
They lie here deep withdrawn, remote and strange;
A dimly outlined shape, a tumbled head.
Through what far lands do now their wand'ring spirits range?

Here one cries sudden on a sobbing breath,
Gripped in the clutch of some incarnate fear:
What terror through the darkness draweth near
What memory of carnage and of death?
What vanished scenes of dread to his closed eyes appear?

And one laughs out with an exultant joy.
An athlete he – Maybe his young limbs strain
In some remembered game, and not in vain
To win his side the goal. – Poor crippled boy,
Who in the waking world will never run again.

One murmurs soft and low a woman's name;
And here a vet'ran soldier, calm and still
As sculptured marble sleeps, and roams at will
Through eastern lands where sunbeams scorch like flame,
By rich bazaar and town, and wood-wrapt snow-crowned hill.

Through the wide open window one great star,
Swinging her lamp above the pear-tree high,
Looks in upon these dreaming forms that lie
So near in body, yet in souls as far
As those bright worlds thick strewn on that vast depth of sky.

Eva Dobell

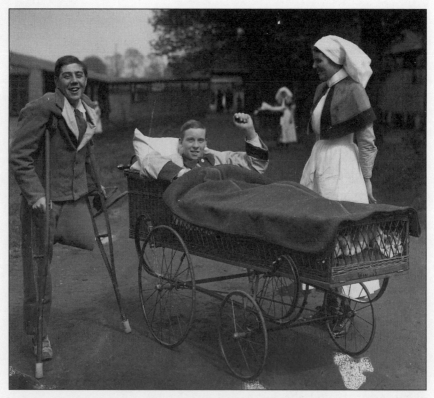

Young disabled soldiers at the Fourth London General Hospital.

PLUCK

Crippled for life at seventeen,
His great eyes seem to question why:
With both legs smashed it might have been
Better in that grim trench to die
Than drag maimed years out helplessly.

A child –   so wasted and so white,
He told a lie to get his way,
To march, a man with men, and fight
While other boys are still at play.
A gallant lie your heart will say.

So broke with pain, he shrinks in dread
To see the "dresser" drawing near;
And winds the clothes about his head
That none may see his heart-sick fear.
His shaking, strangled sobs you hear.

But when the dreaded moment's there
He'll face us all, a soldier yet,
Watch his bared wounds with unmoved air,
(Though tell-tale lashes still are wet),
And smoke his Woodbine cigarette.

Eva Dobell

WHAT REWARD?

You gave your life, boy,
And *you* gave a limb:
But he who gave his precious wits,
Say what reward for him?

One has his glory,
One has found his rest.
But what of this poor babbler here
With chin sunk on his breast?

Flotsam of battle,
With brain bemused and dim,
O God, for such a sacrifice
Say, what reward for him?

Winifred M Letts

BEREAVEMENT

This section, like many others in this book, cannot begin to tell of the
depths and scale of human emotion generated by this war. Bereavement
is common, but what sets the bereavement of the First World War apart
from the daily tragedies of a peacetime world is that over the whole of
Europe especially, but in other parts of the world too, there was a sense
that a whole generation had been lost –   nine or ten million men; and
many survivors searched in vain for the reason why.

In Britain 160,000 women lost their husbands, and 300,000 children lost their fathers.[1]

The literature actually generated by this tragedy is colossal. The mourning commemorated in war memorials throughout Europe and around the world shows the extraordinary scale and importance of the trauma inflicted by the First World War.

Christmas leave

Vera Brittain had been granted leave from her nursing duties for Christmas Day, 1915, and went, in great excitement to Brighton to await the evening boat train which was to bring Roland, her fiancé, home on Christmas leave. She waited in the lounge of the Grand Hotel for the telephone call that would bring news of his arrival.

By ten o'clock that night no news had come. She concluded that Christmas calls had overwhelmed the telephone system and went to bed, exhausted but unperturbed.

In the morning she was called to the telephone and rushed to hear the voice she had waited so long to hear. But the voice was not that of Roland. It was a message to say that he had died of wounds at a casualty clearing station on December 23rd. [2]

PERHAPS –
(To R A L . Died of wounds in France, December 23rd 1915)

Perhaps some day the sun will shine again,
And I shall see that still the skies are blue,
And feel once more I do not live in vain,
Although bereft of You..

Perhaps the golden meadows at my feet
Will make the sunny hours of Spring seem gay,
And I shall find the white May blossoms sweet,
Though You have passed away.

Perhaps the summer woods will shimmer bright,
And crimson roses once again be fair,
And autumn harvest fields a rich delight,
Although You are not there.

1   Ian Beckett in *A Nation in Arms*, p27.
2   Testament of Youth, p236.

Perhaps some day I shall not shrink in pain
To see the passing of the dying year,
And listen to the Christmas songs again,
Although You cannot hear.

But, though kind Time may many joys renew,
There is one greatest joy I shall not know
Again, because my heart for loss of You
Was broken, long ago.

Vera Brittain, February 1916

THE WIND ON THE DOWNS

I like to think of you as brown and tall,
As strong and living as you used to be,
In khaki tunic, Sam Brown belt and all,
And standing there and laughing down at me,
Because they tell me, dear, that you are dead,
Because I can no longer see your face.
You have not died, it is not true, instead
You seek adventure in some other place.
That you are round about me, I believe;
I hear you laughing as you used to do,
Yet loving all the things I think of you;
And knowing you are happy, should I grieve?
You follow and are watchful where I go;
How should you leave me, having loved me so?

We walked along the tow-path, you and I,
Beside the sluggish-moving, still canal;
It seemed impossible that you should die;
I think of you the same and always shall.
We thought of many things and spoke of few,
And life lay all uncertainly before,
And now I walk alone and think of you,
And wonder what new kingdoms you explore.
Over the railway line, across the grass,
While up above the golden wings are spread,
Flying, ever flying overhead,
Here still I see your khaki figure pass,
And when I leave the meadow, almost wait
That you should open first the wooden gate.

Marian Allen

THE MOTHER

If you should die, think only this of me
In that still quietness where is space for thought,
Where parting, loss and bloodshed shall not be,
And men may rest themselves and dream of nought:
That in some place a mystic mile away
One whom you loved has drained the bitter cup
Till there is nought to drink; has faced the day
Once more, and now, has raised the standard up.

And think, my son, with eyes grown clear and dry
She lives as though for ever in your sight,
Loving the things you loved, with heart aglow
For country, honour, truth, traditions high, –
Proud that you paid their price. (And if some night
Her heart should break –   well, lad, you will not know.)

May Herschel-Clarke, first published 1917

A GIRL'S SONG

The Meuse and Marne have little waves;
The slender poplars o'er them lean.
One day they will forget the graves
That give the grass its living green

Some brown French girl the rose will wear
That springs above his comely head;
Will twine it in her russet hair,
Nor wonder why it is so red.

His blood is in the rose's veins,
His hair is in the yellow corn.
My grief is in the weeping rains
And in the keening wind forlorn.

Flow sofly, softly, Marne and Meuse;
Tread lightly all ye browsing sheep;
Fall tenderly, O silver dews,
For here my dear Love lies asleep.

The earth is on his sealèd eyes,
The beauty marred that was my pride;
Would I were lying where he lies,
And sleeping sweetly by his side!

The spring will come by Meuse and Marne,
The birds be blithesome in the tree.
I heap the stones to make his cairn
Where many sleep as sound as he.

Katherine Tynan

The Death of Edward Thomas

During the evening of 9th April, 1917, Eleanor Farjeon wrote once more to Edward Thomas and posted the letter at Billingshurst Station on her way to her family's home in Fellows Road, London. She did not know then that Edward's wife, Helen, had written to her with "the news that broke her heart."

> I went blithely in ignorance to London, and in Fellows Road found an envelope addressed in Viola Meynell's delicate hand. The family was sitting at the supper-table; still standing I opened the letter.
>
> "My darling Eleanor, I can hardly bear this for you . . ."
>
> I made some sort of cry as I dropped the note. Somebody said, "What is it?" I said, "Edward," and went upstairs to my room where I went on standing in a state beyond feeling.
>
> The door opened and my mother came to me, and stood there with her mouth trembling and eyes full of tears. I heard myself saying to her very clearly, "Mother it was never as you feared with Edward and me." I say I heard myself, for I seemed separated from my body's movements and words and actions. I remember her saying, "Nellie – " pleadingly. After a little while we went back to the dining-room, and I sat down with the others. I never forgot Harry's quiet injunction the day our Father died: "We've got to eat, you know," at times when I've known I mustn't break down.

Helen visited her sister in Chiswick and wanted Eleanor to return with her to the Thomas's family home at High Beech, Loughton in Essex. They arranged to meet at Liverpool Street Station ticket barrier.

> I was waiting for her there when she arrived, not with the laughing face and hurrying steps with which she always ran a little to a meeting. She was very pale, and said "Eleanor" in a faint voice as we passed through, and found a corner seat in a carriage. She sat in it, and I by her, between her pale face and the incoming travellers. We held each other's hands. Suddenly in a great burst came her sobs and tears. "Don't let me cry, don't let me cry," she sobbed. I put my arms round her and held her

while she wept, and nobody looked. Presently she whispered "I
asked you to come because I thought I could comfort you – oh
Eleanor, you'll have to comfort me."

I stayed at High Beech, for the next two weeks. I slept with
her. Grief like hers was shattering thousands of homes all over
the world, but I had never before been identified with such grief.
My own seemed to be obliterated in it. I took responsibility, as
best I could, for the house and children; the meals and shopping,
and whatever has to be thought of in a home. After a fortnight
Irene, Helen's elder sister came, and I went back to Fellows Road.

THE FALLEN

Shall we not lay our holly wreath
Here at the foot of this high cross?
We do not know, perhaps a breath
Of our remembering may come
To them at last where they are sleeping,
They are quiet, they are dumb,
No more of mirth, no more of weeping,
Silent Christmas they are keeping;
Ours the sorrow, ours the loss.

Diana Gurney

WHEN THE VISION DIES

When the Vision dies in the dust of the market place,
When the Light is dim,
When you lift up your eyes and cannot behold his face,
When your heart is far from him,

Know this is your War; in this loneliest hour you ride
Down the roads he knew;
Though he comes no more at night he will kneel at your side
For comfort to dream with you.

May Wedderburn Cannan

Repression of feelings

Millions daily feared news of the death of a soldier close to them.
Apart from her fiancé, Roland Leighton, Vera Brittain had lost other
friends, killed in action. When, on June 16th, 1918, she read news
of heavy fighting in Italy where her brother was stationed, she feared
the worst. Of that time she wrote, "There was nothing to do in the midst
of one's family but practice that concealment of fear which the long

years of war had instilled, thrusting it inward until one's subconscious became a regular prison-house of apprehensions and inhibitions which were later to take their revenge."

Some days later she received news of her brother's death.

> There came the sudden loud clattering at the front-door knocker that always meant a telegram.
>
> For a moment I thought that my legs would not carry me, but they behaved quite normally as I got up and went to the door. I knew what was in the telegram   –   I had known for a week   - but because the persistent hopefulness of the human heart refuses to allow intuitive certainty to persuade the reason of that which it knows, I opened and read it in a tearing anguish of suspense.
>
> "Regret to inform you Captain E H Brittain, MC, killed in action Italy June 15th."
>
> "No answer," I told the boy mechanically, and handed the telegram to my father, who had followed me into the hall. As we went back into the dining-room I saw, as though I had never seen them before, the bowl of blue delphiniums on the table; their intense colour, vivid, ethereal, seemed too radiant for earthly flowers.
>
> Long after the family had gone to bed and the world had grown silent, I crept into the dining-room to be alone with Edward's portrait. Carefully closing the door, I turned on the light and looked at the pale, pictured face, so dignified, so steadfast, so tragically mature. He had been through so much – far, far more than those beloved friends who had died at an earlier stage of the interminable War, leaving him alone to mourn their loss.   Fate might have allowed him the little, sorry compensation of survival, the chance to make his lovely music in honour of their memory.   It seemed indeed the last irony that he should have been killed by the countrymen of Fritz Kreisler, the violinist whom of all others he had most greatly admired.
>
> And suddenly, as I remembered all the dear afternoons and evenings when I had followed him on the piano as he played his violin, the sad, searching eyes of the portrait were more than I could bear, and falling on my knees before it I began to cry "Edward! Oh, Edward!" in dazed repetition, as though my persistent crying and calling would somehow bring him back. [1]

---

[1]   Testament of Youth, p438.

An angry response

Three weeks exactly after her wedding, Ethel Bath's husband was
killed. His captain wrote her a sympathetic letter announcing her
husband's death.   She replied:

> It is small comfort to know he gave his life in a successful attack.
> His captain wrote that the success was entirely due to the mag-
> nificent way the men went forward led by their officers. He also
> said that of the five officers from the 10th only one was left . . .

> I am very proud of my boy but at the same time it grieves
> me dreadfully to think those boys are given such a small chance
> to show their grit. You will understand what I mean when I tell
> you he was only out 16 days in all, and he was attached to the
> Middlesex Regiment on Friday 6th, sent into the trenches the
> same afternoon, when he was killed. It all seems too quick to give
> them a chance.

LAMENT

The young men of the world
Are condemned to death.
They have been called up to die
For the crime of their fathers.

The young men of the world,
The growing, the ripening fruit.
Have been torn from their branches,
While the memory of the blossom
Is sweet in women's hearts;

They have been cast for a cruel purpose
Into the mashing-press and furnace.

The young men of the world
Look into each other's eyes,
And read there the same words:
Not yet! Not yet!
But soon perhaps, and perhaps certain.

The young men of the world
No longer possess the road:
The road possesses them.
They no longer inherit the earth:
The earth inherits them.
They are no longer the masters of fire:
Fire is their master;
They serve him; he destroys them.

They no longer rule the waters:
The genius of the seas
Has invented a new monster,
And they flee from its teeth.
They no longer breathe freely:
The genius of the air
Has contrived a new terror
That rends them into pieces.

The young men of the world
Are encompassed with death.
He is all about them
In a circle of fire and bayonets.

Weep, weep, O women,
And old men break your hearts.

F S Flint

HOW THE GERMANS STRENGTHENED BRITAIN'S RESOLVE TO FIGHT

1914

4th August   Germany invaded neutral Belgium. Before long, thousands of Belgian refugees were arriving in Britain.

2nd November   German battle-cruiser raid on Norfolk coast.

16th December   German battle cruisers shelled the English coast at Whitby, Hartlepool, and Scarborough.

1915

19th January   First Zeppelin attack on Britain. Bombs dropped on Kings Lynn, Norfolk. Raids continued along the coast and London for eighteen months.

18th February Germany announced that any ships found in the waters around Britain would be sunk on sight.   Used submarines to carry out this aim, until 4th August. – At the start of the war Britain was very dependant on imported food and the ships that carried it. Four fifths of Britain's wheat and two fifths of her meat came from overseas.

22nd April   Near Ypres the Germans used poison gas for the first time.

7th May   German submarine sank a passenger liner, the *Lusitania,* off Ireland with the loss of 1,198 lives, including 128 American.

30th July The Germans used flame-throwers against the British at Hooge, near Ypres.

1916

Germans continued Zeppelin bombing raids along the coast and on London. The raids reached a peak in the summer when aeroplanes began to be used instead of Zeppelins.

1917

1st February   Germany announced intention to sink all enemy and neutral ships around Britain, using her submarine fleet – and started to do so. – The effect on the thousands of ships which brought food and raw materials to Britain was stunning. A quarter of all ships leaving British ports were sunk by the U-boats.

(Only after Lloyd George had persuaded a reluctant Navy to sail in armed convoys did the losses dramatically reduce. Only four per cent of the 95,000 ships that sailed from British ports from January to November 1918 were sunk.)

25th May   Twin-engined German Gotha bombers made first big daylight raid on Britain.

31st December   Germans used flame-throwers at Cambrai.

1918

May   German bombing raid on military hospital complex at Étaples, killing nurses and patients.

THE END OF THE WAR

A shudder of fear went through the British nation when the Germans made their spectacular breakthrough in the Spring of 1918.

THE SOUL OF A NATION

The little things of which we lately chattered –
The dearth of taxis or the dawn of spring;
Themes we discussed as though they really mattered,
Like rationed meat or raiders on the wing; –

How thin it seems to-day, this vacant prattle,
Drowned by the thunder rolling in the West,
Voice of the great arbitrament of battle
That puts our temper to the final test.

Thither our eyes are turned, our hearts are straining,
Where those we love, whose courage laughs at fear,
Amid the storm of steel around them raining,
Go to their death for all we hold most dear.

New-born of this supremest hour of trial,
In quiet confidence shall be our strength,
Fixed on a faith that will not take denial
Nor doubt that we have found our soul at length.

O England, staunch of nerve and strong of sinew,
Best when you face the odds and stand at bay,
Now show a watching world what stuff is in you!
Now make your soldiers proud of you to-day!

Owen Seamen, published in *Punch*, 3 April 1918

A nation inconvenienced

Sir Owen had been mistaken, I reflected sorrowfully; repre-
senting the finer type of non-combatant whose mind was concerned with the larger aspects of the situation, he had ignored –
perhaps intentionally – the less disinterested crowd to whom the
"little things" went on mattering more than the Army's anguish.
The thunder might roll in the west as loud as it could, but in
spite of his noble verses, it would still be drowned in England
by the chatter about meat and milk.

Vera Brittain [1]

In her affluence it was easy for Vera Brittain to be above being concerned about the cost of meat and milk. For millions living in poverty
the cost of food was of more than passing concern. By July 1917 they
had seen food prices since the start of the war rise by a hundred and four
per cent. Prices were rising faster still in 1918.

1   *Testament of Youth*, p431.

LITTLE CROSSES IN THE SNOW

O endless little crosses in the snow, –
They are but tokens of our love for you,
    Our Brothers, Our Brothers!

"My life I gave to bring the world more light,
And you gave yours for what you deemed the Right, –
    My Brothers, My Brothers!

"Your woes were great, your sorrows multiplied,
I died for you, now you for Me have died, –
    My Brothers, My Brothers!

"But none of you is fallen from my hand;
Bravely you fell, now safe with Me you stand, –
    My Brothers, My Brothers!

"You through the Gate of Death have come to Life, –
My Peace for those who waged the goodly strife, –
    My Brothers, My Brothers!

"So not for you I sorrow, – not for you,
But for the Wrong from which this foul thing grew, –
    My Brothers, My Brothers!

"O Life, O Life, why still so deaf and blind,
When here in Me all healing ye may find? –
    My Brothers, My Brothers!"

John Oxenham

In 1919 Oxenham published his resounding celebration of the war, a thirty-two
page poem, *All Clear!*   A small taste of it must suffice.

ALL CLEAR!

    ... Right willingly they died,
Right joyfully they live,
For ever by Thy side,
Since Thou dost honour give...

All Clear! All Clear!
The evil days are gone,
The Prince of Peace is here
To claim His Throne.
All Clear! All Clear!
The evil days are gone...

John Oxenham

8

THE WOUNDED, THE DYING AND THE DEAD

Entertaining statistics –
When Asquith visited Field Marshal Haig in France

> After lunch we went into the garden for coffee and I turned on the Surgeon-General with his graphics, percentages etc, of sick and wounded to entertain the Premier.
>
> Field Marshal Haig, in his diary, 1 June 1915[1]

The wounded await transport to hospitals behind the lines.

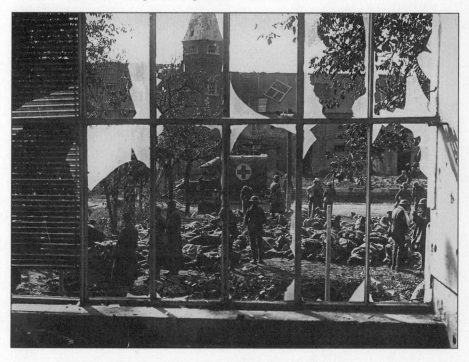

1   *The Private Papers of Douglas Haig, 1914-1919*, p94.

Many millions of men were wounded in the war and no one knows the true figure. If one assumes that twice as many were injured as died there would have been 16 to 20 million wounded. Many, of course, recovered sufficiently from wounds to return to suffer again.

WOUNDED SURVIVING IN BRITAIN

In Britain, by 1929 the Government had paid disability awards to 2.4 million men. For most of the men their suffering stayed with them and their families for the remainder of their lives.[1]

Twenty years after the war had ended and large numbers of the wounded had died the Government was still paying disability pensions to the following numbers of men: [2]

STILL SUFFERING FROM NEURASTHENIA (SHELL SHOCK)	25,000
HEAD INJURIES, MEN UNABLE TO WORK	15,000
PERMANENT DEAFNESS	11,000
PARTIAL BLINDNESS	8,000
TOTAL BLINDNESS	2,000
AMPUTATION OF ONE OR BOTH ARMS	3,600
WITHERED OR USELESS LIMB	90,000
ONE OR BOTH LEGS AMPUTATED	8,000
DISABILITY FROM FROSTBITE	2,200
EFFECTS OF GASSING	40,000

We could do nothing to help

. . . so I went out again into the open and walked along our line; a few heavies were still pounding about us, but a more terrible sound now reached my ears.

From the darkness on all sides came the groans and wails of wounded men; faint, long, sobbing moans of agony, and despairing shrieks. It was too horribly obvious that dozens of men with serious wounds must have crawled for safety into new shell-holes, and now the water was rising about them and, powerless to move, they were slowly drowning. Horrible visions came to me with those cries – of Woods and Kent, Edge and Taylor, lying maimed out there trusting that their pals would find them, and now dying terribly, alone amongst the dead in the inky darkness. And we could do nothing to help them; Dunham was

1   *A Nation in Arms,* Ian Beckett, p27.
2   *Roses of No Man's Land,* Lynn Macdonald.

crying quietly beside me, and all the men were affected by the piteous cries.

How long, I wondered, could this situation last . . .

Sometime later the survivors were relieved and began to pre-pare to make their way back to a rest camp.

The cries of the wounded had much diminished now, and as we staggered down the road, the reason was only too apparent, for the water was right over the tops of the shell-holes. From survivors came faint cries and loud curses. When we reached the line where the attack had broken we were surrounded by the men who earlier had cheered us on. Now they lay groaning and blaspheming, and often we stopped to drag them up on to the ridges of earth. We lied to them all that the stretcher-bearers were coming, and most resigned themselves to a further agony of waiting.

> From the diary of Captain Edwin Campion Vaughan,
> Royal Warwickshire Regiment, 27 August, 1917

Medical services – first day of the Somme

Near the fields of battle the medical services attempted to cope with an incredible work-load. On the first day of the Battle of the Somme one of the casualty clearing stations had been set up between Albert and Amiens. Tented wards were erected with space for 1000 patients. Ten thousand patients arrived in the first forty eight hours. One of the sur-geons wrote,

> Streams of ambulances a mile long waited to be unloaded. The whole area of the camp, a field of six acres, was completely covered with stretchers placed side by side, each with its suffer-ing or dying man. We surgeons were hard at it in the operating theatre, a good hut holding four tables. Occasionally we made a brief look around to select from the thousands of patients we had time to save. It was terrible. [1]

---

1   *Butchers and Bunglers of World War One*, John Laffin, p73.

DOES IT MATTER?

Does it matter? – losing your legs?. . .
For people will always be kind,
And you need not show that you mind
When the others come in after hunting
To gobble their muffins and eggs.

Does it matter? – losing your sight? . . .
There's such splendid work for the blind;
And people will always be kind,
As you sit on the terrace remembering
And turning your face to the light.

Do they matter?   –   those dreams from the pit? . . .
You can drink and forget and be glad,
And people won't say that you're mad;
For they'll know that you've fought for your country
And no one will worry a bit.

Siegfried Sassoon

DISABLED

He sat in a wheeled chair, waiting for dark,
And shivered in his ghastly suit of grey,
Legless, sewn short at elbow. Through the park
Voices of boys rang saddening like a hymn,
Voices of play and pleasure after day,
Till gathering sleep had mothered them from him.

About this time Town used to swing so gay
When glow-lamps budded in the light blue trees,
And girls glanced lovelier as the air grew dim, –
In the old times, before he threw away his knees.
Now he will never feel again how slim
Girls' waists are, or how warm their subtle hands.
All of them touch him like some queer disease.

There was an artist silly for his face,
For it was younger than his youth, last year.
Now, he is old; his back will never brace;
He's lost his colour very far from here,
Poured it down shell-holes till the veins ran dry,
And half his lifetime lapsed in the hot race
And leap of purple spurted from his thigh.

One time he liked a blood-smear down his leg,
After the matches, carried shoulder-high.
It was after football, when he'd drunk a peg,
He thought he'd better join. – He wonders why.
Someone had said he'd look a god in kilts,
That's why; and maybe, too, to please his Meg,
Aye, that was it, to please the giddy jilts
He asked to join. He didn't have to beg;
Smiling they wrote his lie: aged nineteen years.
Germans he scarcely thought of; all their guilt,
And Austria's, did not move him. And no fears
Of Fear came yet. He thought of jewelled hilts
For daggers in plaid socks; of smart salutes;

And care of arms; and leave; and pay arrears;
Esprit de corps; and hints for young recruits.
And soon, he was drafted out with drums and cheers.

Some cheered him home, but not as crowds cheer Goal.
Only a solemn man who brought him fruits
Thanked him; and then enquired about his soul.

*   *   *   *   *   *

Now, he will spend a few sick years in institutes,
And do what things the rules consider wise,
And take whatever pity they may dole.
Tonight he noticed how the women's eyes
Passed from him to the strong men that were whole.
How cold and late it is! Why don't they come
And put him into bed? Why don't they come?

Wilfred Owen

BLINDED

Wilfred Owen's poem, *The Sentry,* was based on an event in the following letter, in which he describes his initiation into the First World War. – He had been in France just twelve days.

> I can see no excuse for deceiving you about these last four days.
> I have suffered seventh hell. – I have not been at the front. –
> I have been in front of it. – I held an advanced post, that is, a
> "dug-out" in the middle of No Man's Land.

> We had a march of three miles over shelled road, then nearly
> three along a flooded trench. After that we came to where the
> trenches had been blown flat out and had to go over the top. It
> was of course dark, too dark, and the ground was not mud, not
> sloppy mud, but an octopus of sucking clay, three, four, and
> five feet deep, relieved only by craters full of water . . .

> Three quarters dead we reached the dug-out and relieved the
> wretches therein . .

> My dug-out held twenty-five men tight packed. Water filled it
> to a depth of one or two feet, leaving say four feet of air. One
> entrance had been blown in and blocked. – So far, the other
> remained.

> The Germans knew we were staying there and decided we
> shouldn't. Those fifty hours were the agony of my happy life.

> Every ten minutes on Sunday afternoon seemed an hour.

I nearly broke down and let myself drown in the water that was now slowly rising over my knees.

Towards 6 o'clock, when I suppose, you would be going to church, the shelling grew less intense and less accurate: so that I was mercifully helped to do my duty and crawl, wade, climb and flounder over No Man's Land to visit my other post. It took me half an hour to move about a hundred and fifty yards . . .

In the platoon on my left the sentries over the dug-out were blown to nothing . . . I kept my own sentries half way down the stairs during the most terrific bombardment. In spite of this, one lad was blown down and, I am afraid, blinded.

Letter to Susan Owen, 16 January 1917

THE SENTRY

We'd found an old Boche dug-out, and he knew,
And gave us hell; for shell on frantic shell
Lit full on top, but never quite burst through.
Rain, guttering down in waterfalls of slime,
Kept slush waist-high and rising hour by hour,
And choked the steps too thick with clay to climb.
What murk of air remained stank old, and sour
With fumes from whizz-bangs, and the smell of men
Who'd lived there years, and left their curse in the den,
If not their corpses . . .
                 There we herded from the blast
Of whizz-bangs; but one found our door at last, –
Buffeting eyes and breath, snuffing the candles,
And thud! Flump! Thud! Down the steep steps came thumping
and sploshing in the flood, deluging muck,
The sentry's body; then his rifle, handles
Of old Boche bombs, and mud in ruck on ruck.
We dredged him up, for dead, until he whined,
"O sir, my eyes – I'm blind – I'm blind – I'm blind."
Coaxing, I held a flame against his lids
And said if he could see the least blurred light
He was not blind; in time they'd get all right.
"I can't," he sobbed. Eyeballs, huge-bulged like squids',
Watch my dreams still; but I forgot him there
In posting next for duty, and sending a scout
To beg a stretcher somewhere, and floundering about
To other posts under the shrieking air.

Those other wretches, how they bled and spewed,
And one who would have drowned himself for good. –
I try not to remember these things now.
Let Dread hark back for one word only: how,
Half-listening to that sentry's moans and jumps,
And the wild chattering of his shivered teeth,
Renewed most horribly whenever crumps
Pummelled the roof and slogged the air beneath –
Through the dense din, I say, we heard him shout
"I see your lights!"   –   But ours had long gone out.

Wilfred Owen

THE ONE-LEGGED MAN

Propped on a stick he viewed the August weald;
Squat orchard trees and oasts with painted cowls;
A homely, tangled hedge, a corn-stalked field,
And sound of barking dogs and farmyard fowls.

And he'd come home again to find it more
Desirable than ever it was before.
How right it seemed that he should reach the span
Of comfortable years allowed to man!

Splendid to eat and sleep and choose a wife,
Safe with his wound, a citizen of life.
He hobbled blithely through the garden gate,
And thought: "Thank God they had to amputate!"

Siegfried Sassoon, August 1916

GAS ATTACKS

The first significant use of poison gas in war was on 22nd April 1915
when the Germans used it at Langemarck near Ypres, against French
Algerian troops. During the First World War various types of gas were
used – mustard, chlorine, phosgene, chloropicrin, prussic acid and
tear gas. The effects of some of these gases were hideous.

Mustard gas

This blistered the skin, made the eyes extremely painful and caused
vomiting. It burned into the bronchial tubes stripping off the mucous

membrane. The pain was so intense that most mustard gas victims had to be strapped to their beds where their slow and agonising deaths lasted for up to five weeks.

Vera Brittain, writing of her experiences of nursing gas cases in France, wrote,

> I wish those people who write so glibly about this being a holy war and the orators who talk so much about going on, no matter how long the war lasts and what it may mean, could see a case . . . of mustard gas – the poor things burnt and blistered all over with great mustard coloured suppurating blisters, with blind eyes . . . all sticky and stuck together, and always fighting for breath, with voices a mere whisper, saying their throats are closing and they know they will choke. [1]

Chlorine gas

> It produces a flooding in the lungs . . . a splitting headache, terrific thirst (to drink water is instant death), a knife edge pain in the lungs and the coughing up of a greenish froth off the stomach and lungs, ending finally in insensibility and death. The colour of the skin turns a greenish black and yellow, the tongue protrudes and the eyes assume a glassy stare.

> Lance Sergeant Elmer Cotton [2]

Gas attacks became common

It is possible to gain the impression that gas was only occasionally used in the war, and from bitter complaints, like Frankau's "Poison", that the Germans were solely responsible for the use of this hideous weapon. In fact one hundred and fifty thousand tons of gas were used in the war – most of it on the Western Front, and both sides used it. The main users of gas were Germany (68,000 tons), France (37,000 tons) and Britain (26,000 tons). [3]

---

1   *Testament of Youth*, Vera Brittain, p395.
2   *Tommy Goes to War*, Malcolm Brown, p106.
3   *Tanks and Weapons of World War One*, Edited by Bernard Fitzsimons, p19, 20.

DULCE ET DECORUM EST*

Bent double, like old beggars under sacks,
Knock-kneed, coughing like hags, we cursed through
sludge,
Till on the haunting flares we turned our backs
And towards our distant rest began to trudge.
Men marched asleep. Many had lost their boots
But limped on, blood-shod. All went lame; all blind;
Drunk with fatigue; deaf even to the hoots
Of tired, outstripped Five-Nines that dropped behind.

Gas! Gas! Quick, boys! – An ecstasy of fumbling,
Fitting the clumsy helmets just in time;
But someone still was yelling out and stumbling,
And floundering like a man in fire or lime . . .
Dim, through the misty panes and thick green light,
As under a green sea, I saw him drowning.

In all my dreams, before my helpless sight,
He plunges at me, guttering, choking, drowning.

If in some smothering dreams you too could pace
Behind the wagon that we flung him in,
And watch the white eyes writhing in his face,
His hanging face, like a devil's sick of sin;
If you could hear, at every jolt, the blood
Come gargling from the froth-corrupted lungs,
Obscene as cancer, bitter as the cud
Of vile, incurable sores on innocent tongues,
My friend, you would not tell with such high zest
To children ardent for some desperate glory,
The old Lie; Dulce et Decorum est
Pro patria mori.

Wilfred Owen

* The title: the first words of a Latin saying, Dulce et decorum est pro patria mori,
was popular with Roman conquerors, and at the start of the First World War. The
sense of it is, "It is a wonderful and great honour to fight and die for your country."

POISON

Forget, and forgive them – you say:
War's bitterness passes;
Wild rose wreaths the gun-pit to-day,
Where the trench was, young grass is;
Forget and forgive:
Let them live.

Forgive them – you say – and forget;
Since struggle is finished,
Shake hands, be at peace, square the debt,
Let old hates be diminished;
Abandon blockade,
Let them trade.

Fools! Shall the pard* change his skin
Or cleanse one spot from it?
As the lecher returns to his sin
So the cur to its vomit.
Fools! Hath the Hun
Earned place in the sun?

You who accuse that I fan
War's spark from hate's ember,
Forgive and forget if you can;
But, I, I remember
Men who face death
Choking for breath.

Four years back to a day –
Men who fought cleanly.
Killed say you? Murdered I say,
Murdered, most meanly,
Poisoned! . . . And yet,
You can forget.

Gilbert Frankau

Written 21 April 1919, four years after the introduction of poison gas by the
Germans near Ypres, and three years after the first use of gas by the British.
* leopard

FACING DEATH

IN FLANDERS FIELDS

In Flanders fields the poppies blow
Between the crosses, row on row,
That mark our place; and in the sky
The larks, still bravely singing, fly
Scarce heard amid the guns below.

We are the Dead. Short days ago
We lived, felt dawn, saw sunset glow,
Loved and were loved, and now we lie
In Flanders fields.

Take up our quarrel with the foe:
To you from failing hands we throw
The torch; be yours to hold it high.
If ye break faith with us who die
We shall not sleep, though poppies grow
In Flanders fields.

John McCrae

Written near Ypres in May, 1915, when McCrae, as a Canadian doctor, was
tending hundreds of mainly British gas victims. First published in *Punch*,
8 December, 1915.

SUCH IS DEATH

Such, such is Death: no triumph: no defeat:
Only an empty pail, a slate rubbed clean,
A merciful putting away of what has been.

And this we know: Death is not Life effete,
Life crushed, the broken pail. We who have seen
So marvellous things know well the end not yet.

Victor and vanquished are a-one in death:
Coward and brave: friend and foe. Ghosts do not say
"Come, what was your record when you drew breath?"
But a big blot has hid each yesterday
So poor, so manifestly incomplete.
And your bright Promise, withered long and sped,
Is touched, stirs, rises, opens and grows sweet
And blossoms and is you, when you are dead.

Charles Sorley, 12 June 1915

LIGHTS OUT

I have come to the borders of sleep,
The unfathomable deep
Forest where all must lose
Their way, however straight,
Or winding, soon or late;
They cannot choose.

Many a road and track
That, since the dawn's first crack,
Up to the forest brink,
Deceived the travellers,
Suddenly now blurs,
And in they sink.

Here love ends,
Despair, ambition ends;
All pleasure and all trouble,
Although most sweet or bitter,
Here ends in sleep that is sweeter
Than tasks most noble.

There is not any book
Or face of dearest look
That I would not turn from now
To go into the unknown
I must enter, and leave, alone,
I know not how.

The tall forest towers;
Its cloudy foliage lowers
Ahead, shelf above shelf;
Its silence I hear and obey
That I may lose my way
And myself.

Edward Thomas, November 1916

A PERPETUAL MEMORY

Broken and pierced, hung on the bitter wire.
By their most precious death the Sons of Man
Redeem for us the life of our desire −
O Christ how often since the world began!

Henry Newbolt, Good Friday, 1915

THE SLAUGHTER

A low estimate of the First World War death toll suggests

Victors –   The Allied Powers   – 5.1 million dead

Vanquished   –   The Central Powers – 3.5 million dead.

This amounted to an average of over five and a half thousand men killed every day of the war.

In the four years of The First World War three quarters of a million British men were killed. [1]

THE SOMME

Every battle had its awful death toll. History's worst first day was the first day of the Battle of the Somme, on 1st July 1916. A hundred and ten thousand British men attacked the Germans that day. Twenty thousand British soldiers were killed and forty thousand were wounded.   – In the second week, British losses were running at ten thousand per day.

Confident that the massive shelling of the German lines over seven days had virtually wiped out the German army of the Somme and that success would therefore be a walkover, Field Marshal Haig, a devout Christian, wrote to his wife shortly before the battle, "I feel every step of the plan has been taken with Divine help." [2]

In his diary, on 2nd of July, Haig wrote, "A day of downs and ups . . . The A G reported today that the total casualties are estimated at over 40,000 to date. This cannot be considered severe in view of the numbers engaged, and the length of front attacked."

Winston Churchill's view

> I view with the utmost pain, the terrible and disproportionate slaughter of our troops. We have not conquered in a month's fighting as much ground as we were expected to gain in the first two hours. We have not advanced two miles in a direct line at any point. Unless a gap of at least 20 miles can be opened, no large force can be put through. Nor are we making for any point of strategic or political consequence.   What are Peronne and Bapaume, even if we are likely to take them? The open country

1   *The First World War,* Martin Gilbert, p541.
2   *The Great War and Modern Memory,* Paul Fussell, p29.

towards which we are struggling by inches is capable of entrenched defence at every step and is utterly devoid of military significance. There is no question of breaking the line, of "letting loose the cavalry" in the open country behind or of inducing a general withdrawal of the German armies in the West. In personnel the results of the operation have been absolutely barren.

Memorandum, August 1916 [1]

Lloyd George's considered opinion

The wasteful prolongation of the Somme campaign after it had become clear that a break through the German lines was unattainable was a case where the Government might have intervened. It cost us heavily. The volunteers of 1914 and 1915 were the finest body of men ever sent to do battle for Britain. Five hundred thousand of these men, the flower of our race, were thrown away on a stubborn and unintelligent hammering away at what was then an impenetrable barrier. I strongly urged Mr Asquith and Sir William Robertson that the useless slaughter ought to be stopped. I am still of that opinion. The loss in men was irreplaceable, less in numbers than in quality. It was the first real disillusionment the new army suffered. Our losses were twice as great as those we inflicted . . . Much was lost, nothing was gained. [2]

Facing the slaughter

On that first day of the battle, Captain Leetham was attempting to tend the wounded when he came across a trench which shocked him.

The trench was a horrible sight. The dead were stretched out on one side, one on top of each other six feet high. I thought at the time I should never get the peculiar disgusting smell of the vapour of warm human blood heated by the sun out of my nostrils. I would rather have smelt gas a hundred times. I can never describe that faint sickening, horrible smell which several times nearly knocked me up altogether. To do one's duty, one was actually climbing over corpses in every position and when one trod on human flesh it sent a shudder down one's spine.[3]

No photographs of such scenes exist. Soldiers were not allowed cameras

1   *The World Crisis.*
2   *War Memoirs,* p2036.
3   *Tommy Goes to War,* p204.

at the front.   – Official photographers, for reasons of keeping up morale, were not allowed to photograph the vast numbers of dead, and the
photographs they did take were checked and destroyed if they set the
wrong tone. Of the five million photographs in the Imperial War Museum none of those of the First World War would give you the impression that there were ever more than a couple of dozen dead to be seen
at any one place.

The fearless dead

> Today our dead were being prepared for burial. Three chap-
> lains, representing different religious denominations, were in
> readiness. "My God,"said one of them to me, "how brave and
> devoted our dear soldiers boys are. Look at them now where
> they lie – every man with his face to the foe. They never fear
> death. To them it is simply one of the fortunes of war."

Morning Post, 6 July 1916

The rotting dead – taking over Dewdrop and Hazy trenches

> When the 2nd Battalion of the West Yorkshire Regiment took
> over the new line on 12th November and spent four days hold-
> ing it, they were overcome by the stench of the heaped-up dead
> at their backs. Dewdrop and Hazy were literally filled   with
> bodies, and around them corpses lay scattered on the tumbled
> earth. Under cover of darkness two burial parties were sent out,
> but they were so sickened by the task that they achieved little;
> the bodies were already disintegrating with putrefaction. The
> line advanced no further, and in such an exposed and unhealthy
> place, constantly under shellfire that pulverised the living and the
> dead alike, there was no choice but to leave the dead where they
> lay, gradually sinking into the mud and into oblivion.[1]

1   *The Roses of No Man's Land*, Lynn Macdonald, p180.

ANTHEM FOR DOOMED YOUTH

What passing-bells* for these who die as cattle? –
Only the monstrous anger of the guns.
Only the stuttering rifles' rapid rattle
Can patter out their hasty orisons.*
No mockeries now for them; no prayers nor bells;
Nor any voice of mourning save the choirs, –
The shrill, demented choirs of wailing shells;
And bugles calling for them from sad shires.

What candles may be held to speed them all?
Not in the hands of boys but in their eyes
Shall shine the holy glimmers of goodbyes.
The pallor of girls' brows shall be their pall;
Their flowers the tenderness of patient minds,
And each slow dusk a drawing-down of blinds.

Wilfred Owen

* passing bells   –   a bell tolled to announce someone's death to the world
* orisons   –   prayers; here, funeral prayers

A NIGHT ATTACK

The rank stench of those bodies haunts me still,
And I remember things I'd best forget,
For now we've marched to a green, trenchless land
Twelve miles from battering guns: along the grass
Brown lines of tents are hives for snoring men;
Wide, radiant water sways the floating sky
Below dark, shivering trees. And living-clean
Comes back with thoughts of home and hours of sleep.

Tonight I smell the battle; miles away
Gun-thunder leaps and thuds along the ridge;
The spouting shells dig pits in fields of death,
And wounded men are moaning in the woods.
If any friend be there whom I have loved,
God speed him safe to England with a gash.

It's sundown in the camp; some youngster laughs,
Lifting his mug and drinking health to all
Who come unscathed from that unpitying waste.
(Terror and ruin lurk behind his gaze.)
Another sits with tranquil, musing face,
Puffing his pipe and dreaming of the girl
Whose last scrawled letter lies upon his knee.

The sunlight falls, low-ruddy from the west,
Upon their heads; last week they might have died;
And now they stretch their limbs in tired content.

One says "The bloody Bosche has got the knock;
And soon they'll crumple up and chuck their games.
We've got the beggars on the run at last!"
Then I remembered someone that I'd seen
Dead in a squalid, miserable ditch,
Heedless of toiling feet that trod him down.
He was a Prussian with a decent face,
Young, fresh, and pleasant, so I dare to say.
No doubt he loathed the war and longed for peace,
And cursed our souls because we'd killed his friends.

One night he yawned along a half-dug trench
Midnight; and then the British guns began
With heavy shrapnel bursting low, and "hows"
Whistling to cut the wire with blinding din.
He didn't move; the digging still went on;
Men stooped and shovelled; someone gave a grunt,
And moaned and died with agony in the sludge.
Then the long hiss of shells lifted and stopped.

He stared into the gloom; a rocket curved,
And rifles rattled angrily on the left
Down by the wood, and there was noise of bombs.
Then the damned English loomed in scrambling haste
Out of the dark and struggled through the wire,
And there were shouts and curses; someone screamed
And men began to blunder down the trench
Without their rifles. It was time to go:
He grabbed his coat; stood up, gulping some bread;
Then clutched his head and fell.
                    I found him there
In the grey morning when the place was held.
His face was in the mud; one arm flung out
As when he crumpled up; his sturdy legs
Were bent beneath his trunk; heels to the sky.

Siegfried Sassoon, July 1916

THE DEAD SOLDIERS

I

Spectrum Trench. Autumn. Nineteen-sixteen.
And Zenith. (The Border Regiment will remember.)
A little north of where Lesboeufs had been.
(The Australians took it over in December.)
Just as the scythe had caught them, there they lay,
A sheaf of Death, ungarnered and untied:
A crescent moon of men who showed the way
When first the Tanks crept out, till they too died:
Guardsmen, I think, but one could hardly tell.
It was a forward slope, beyond the crest,
Muddier than any place in Dante's hell,
Where sniping gave us very little rest.
At night one stumbled over them and swore;
Each day the rain hid them a little more.

II

Fantastic forms, in posturing attitudes,
Twisted and bent, or lying deathly prone;
Their individual hopes my thought eludes,
But each man had a hope to call his own.
Much else? – God knows. But not for me the thought.
"Your mothers made your bodies: God your souls,
And , for because you dutifully fought,
God will go mad and make of half-lives wholes."
No. God in every one of you was slain;
For killing men is always killing God,
Though life destroyed shall come to life again
And loveliness rise from the sodden sod.
But if of life we do destroy the best,
God wanders wide, and weeps in his unrest.

Max Plowman

Somme satisfaction

Haig was well satisfied with the Battle of the Somme. In his Despatches, which were published in the *London Gazette* and written, he
said, for a public "to whom at all times the truth could be told" he
claimed that his three main objectives had been achieved: "Verdun had
been relieved; the main German forces had been held on the Western
Front; and the enemy's strength had been very considerably worn
down."

The total number of prisoners taken by us in the Somme battle

between the 1st July and the 18th November is just over
38,000, including 800 officers. During the same period we captured 29 heavy guns, 96 field guns and field howitzers, 136
trench mortars and 514 machine guns.

What Haig said was true, but in his summing up of the Somme battle
he didn't mention the British casualties except to praise the newly
trained soldiers sent "to replace wastage."

The British and British Empire casualties for the Battle of the Somme
amounted to 420,000 men. The French lost 200,000 men. The Germans
an uncertain number. Estimates range between 210,000 and 650,000.

The battle had been intended to make rapid progress through the German
lines. When it ended after five months of carnage, the British and
Empire forces had advanced about six miles and were still three miles
short of Bapaume which had been one of the first day's objectives. [1]

HOW LONG, O LORD?

How long, O Lord, how long, before the flood?
Of crimson-welling carnage shall abate?
From sodden plains in West and East the blood
Of kindly men streams up in mists of hate,
Polluting Thy clean air: and nations great
In reputation of the arts that bind
The world with hopes of Heaven, sink to the state
Of brute barbarians, whose ferocious mind
Gloats o'er the bloody havoc of their kind,
Not knowing love or mercy. Lord, how long
Shall Satan in high places lead the blind
To battle for the passions of the strong?
Oh, touch Thy children's hearts, that they may know
Hate their most hateful, pride their deadliest foe.

Robert Palmer

---

1   Martin Gilbert, p299.

THE LAST MINUTES OF LIFE

The Strange Death of Edward Thomas, 9 April 1917

Edward Thomas sailed from England on 30th January 1917. His death, ten weeks later, was quite extraordinary. The Battle of Arras was over for that day. The artillery had been used with great success with the first use of the creeping barrage. The Germans were in retreat and British soldiers were shouting and singing and dancing almost believing they had won the war. 2nd Lieutenant Edward Thomas stepped out of the dugout behind the artillery and leaned in the doorway filling his clay pipe. The Germans fired one last shell. It missed him, but came so close that the blast of air stopped his heart. There was not the slightest sign of injury. His pipe was unbroken. Only the papers in his pockets – some letters, a notebook, and Shakespeare's Sonnets – showed the effects of the blast. All were strangely creased as if subjected to some terrible pressure. He died, where he stood relaxed and confident, in an instant. [1]

From the Diary of Captain Robert Graves, Royal Welch Fusiliers

June 9th, 1915. The company had seventeen casualties yesterday from bombs and grenades. The front trenches average thirty yards from the Germans. Today, at one part, which is only twenty yards away from an occupied German sap, I went along whistling *The Farmer's Boy,* to keep up my spirits, when suddenly I saw a group bending over a man lying at the bottom of the trench. He was making a snoring noise, mixed with animal groans. At my feet lay the cap he had worn, splashed with his brains. I had never seen human brains before; I somehow regarded them as a poetical figment. One can joke with a badly-wounded man and congratulate him on being out of it. One can disregard a dead man. But even a miner can't make a joke that sounds like a joke over a man who takes three hours to die, after the top part of his head has been taken off by a bullet fired at twenty yard's range.

1   *Edward Thomas , the Last Four Years,* Eleanor Farjeon, p262/263.

CONSCIOUS

His fingers wake, and flutter, up the bed.
His eyes come open with a pull of will,
Helped by the yellow Mayflowers by his head.
The blind-cord drawls across the window-sill . . .
What a smooth floor the ward has! What a rug!
Who is that talking somewhere out of sight?
Three flies are creeping round the shiny jug . . .
"Nurse! Doctor!" – "Yes, all right, all right."

But sudden evening blurs and fogs the air.
There seems no time to want a drink of water.
Nurse looks so far away. And here and there
Music and roses burst through crimson slaughter.
He can't remember where he saw blue sky . . .
The trench is narrower. Cold, he's cold; yet hot –
And there's no light to see the voices by . . .
There is no time to ask . . . He knows not what.

Wilfred Owen

DIED OF WOUNDS

His wet white face and miserable eyes
Brought nurses to him more than groans and sighs:
But hoarse and low and rapid rose and fell
His troubled voice: he did the business well.

The ward grew dark; but he was still complaining
And calling out for "Dickie". "Curse the Wood!
It's time to go. O Christ, and what's the good?
We'll never take it, and it's always raining."

I wondered where he'd been; then heard him shout,
"They snipe like hell! O Dickie, don't go out . . ."
I fell asleep . . . Next morning he was dead;
And some Slight Wound lay smiling on the bed.

Siegfried Sassoon, July 1916

THE DYING SOLDIER

"Here are houses," he moaned,
"I could reach, but my brain swims."
Then they thundered and flashed,
And shook the earth to its rims.

"They are gunpits," he gasped,
"Our men are at the guns. Water! – Water! –
Oh, water! For one of England's dying sons."

"We cannot give you water,
Were all England in your breath."
"Water! – Water! – Oh, water!"
He moaned and swooned to death.

Isaac Rosenberg

IN THE TRENCHES

I snatched two poppies
From the parapet's ledge,
Two bright red poppies
That winked on the ledge.
Behind my ear
I stuck one through,
One blood red poppy I gave to you.

The sandbags narrowed
And screwed out our jest,
And tore the poppy
You had on your breast . . .
Down – a shell – O! Christ,
I am choked . . .safe . . . dust blind, I
See trench floor poppies
Strewn. Smashed you lie.

Isaac Rosenberg, 1916

Death of Graves reported in *The Times*

On 20th July 1916 Graves was captain of B Company of the Second
Battalion, Royal Welch Fusiliers, and in reserve for an attack on High
Wood (Bois des Fourneaux) near Bazentin. A German barrage killed
about one third of the Fusiliers before the attack got under way and
fragments of one shell hit Graves.

> I heard the explosion, and felt as though I had been punched
> rather hard between the shoulder-blades, but without any pain. I
> took the punch merely for the shock of the explosion; but blood
> trickled into my eye and, turning faint, I called to Moodie: "I've
> been hit." Then I fell. [1]

1   *Goodbye to All That*, p181.

One fragment split the bone in a finger. A piece of metal went through his thigh, near the groin; another piece went through his lung, entering below his right shoulder blade and coming out his chest two inches above the right nipple.

His wounds were dressed and he was put on a stretcher and taken to an old German dressing-station in Mametz Wood where he fell unconscious for twenty-four hours. Late that night Colonel Crawshaw visited the dressing station and was told Graves was done for. He wrote to Graves's mother, expressing his sorrow at the loss of a very gallant soldier. The letter arrived on 24th July, his twenty-first birthday. An announcement appeared in *The Times*, and people who were "on the worst terms" with Graves wrote "the most enthusiastic of condolences" to his mother.

On the morning of 21st July, when soldiers came to remove the dead, Graves was found to be still breathing. He was carried, screaming part of the way, to a tented field hospital. He remained on a stretcher in the heat of summer for five days before being transported in great agony on a train to a hospital in Rouen. – Two days later he was moved by hospital ship, arriving in London to be met by crowds who had gathered to cheer the wounded of the Somme home.

A CHILD'S NIGHTMARE

Through long nursery nights he stood
By my bed unwearying,
Loomed gigantic, formless, queer,
Purring in my haunted ear
That same hideous nightmare thing,
Talking, as he lapped my blood,
In a voice cruel and flat,
Saying for ever, "Cat! . . Cat! . . Cat! . . "

That one word was all he said,
That one word through all my sleep,
In monotonous mock despair.
Nonsense may be light as air
But there's Nonsense that can keep
Horror bristling round the head,
When a voice cruel and flat
Says for ever "Cat! . . Cat! . . Cat! . . "

He had faded, he was gone
Years ago with Nursery Land,
When he leapt on me again
From the clank of a night train,
Overpowered me foot and hand

Lapped my blood, while on and on
The old voice cruel and flat
Purred for ever "Cat! . . Cat! . . Cat! . ."

Morphia drowsed, again I lay
In a crater by High Wood:
He was there with straddling legs,
Staring eyes as big as eggs,
Purring as he lapped my blood,
His black bulk darkening the day,
With a voice cruel and flat,
"Cat! . . Cat! . . Cat! . ." he said,
        "Cat! . . Cat! . ."

When I'm shot through heart and head,
And there's no choice but to die,
The last word I'll hear, no doubt
Won't be "Charge!" or "Bomb them out!"
Nor the stretcher-bearer's cry,
"Let that body be, he's dead!"
But a voice cruel and flat
Saying for ever, "Cat! . . Cat! . . Cat! . ."

Robert Graves

THE LAST LAUGH

"O Jesus Christ! I'm hit," he said and died.
Whether he vainly cursed, or prayed indeed,
The bullets chirped, "In vain! vain! vain!"
Machine-guns chuckled, "Tut-tut! Tut-tut!"
And the big guns guffawed.

Another sighed, "O Mother, Mother! Dad!"
Then smiled at nothing, childlike, being dead.
And the lofty shrapnel-cloud
Leisurely gestured, "Fool!"
And the splinters spat, and tittered.

"My Love!" one moaned. Love languid seemed his mood,
Till, slowly lowered, his whole face kissed the mud.
And the Bayonets' long teeth grinned;
Rabbles of Shells hooted and groaned;
And the Gas hissed.

Wilfred Owen

CONTEMPLATING THE DEAD

FUTILITY

Move him into the sun –
Gently its touch awoke him once,
At home, whispering of fields unsown.
Always it woke him, even in France,
Until this morning and this snow.
If anything might rouse him now
The kind old sun will know.

Think how it wakes the seeds. –
Woke, once, the clays of a cold star.
Are limbs, so dear achieved, are sides
Full-nerved   –   still warm   –   too hard to stir?
Was it for this the clay grew tall?
– O what made fatuous sunbeams toil
To break earth's sleep at all?

Wilfred Owen

NOT DEAD

Walking through trees to cool my heat and pain,
I know that David's with me here again.
All that is simple, happy, strong, he is.
Caressingly I stroke
Rough bark of the friendly oak.
A brook goes bubbling by: the voice is his.
Turf burns with pleasant smoke;
I laugh at chaffinch and at primroses.
All that is simple, happy, strong, he is.
Over the whole wood in a little while
Breaks his slow smile.

Robert Graves[1]

---

1   Written following the death of Graves's friend, David Thomas.

Robert Graves had gone into Mametz wood, where every tree had been ripped off by the shells, and both German and British dead were lying everywhere, to take overcoats from the dead to use as blankets.

> Going and coming, by the only possible route, I passed by the bloated and stinking corpse of a German with his back propped against a tree. He had a green face, spectacles, close shaven hair; black blood was dripping from the nose and beard. [1]

A DEAD BOCHE

To you who'd read my songs of War
And only hear of blood and fame,
I'll say (you've heard it said before)
"War's Hell!" and if you doubt the same,
To-day I found in Mametz Wood
A certain cure for lust of blood:

Where, propped against a shattered trunk,
In a great mess of things unclean,
Sat a dead Boche; he scowled and stunk
With clothes and face a sodden green,
Big bellied, spectacled, crop-haired,
Dribbling black blood from nose and beard.

Robert Graves, July 1915

One is hardened by now

> Looking into the future one sees a holocaust somewhere: and at present there is – thank God – enough of "experience" to keep the wits edged (a callous way of putting it, perhaps).   But out in front at night in that no-man's land and long graveyard there is a freedom and a spur. Rustling of the grasses   and   grave tap-tapping of distant workers: the tension and silence of en-counter, when one struggles in the dark for moral victory over the enemy patrol: the wail of the exploded bomb and the animal cries of wounded men. Then death and the horrible thankfulness when one sees that the next man is dead: "We won't have to carry him in under fire, thank God; dragging will do:" hauling in one of the great resistless bodies in the dark, the smashed head rattling: the relief, the relief that the thing has ceased to groan: that the bullet or bomb that made the man an animal has now

---

1   *Goodbye to All That*, p175.

made the animal a corpse. One is hardened by now: purged
of all false pity: perhaps more selfish than before. The spiritual
and the animal get so much more sharply divided in hours of
encounter, taking possession of the body by swift turns.

Charles Sorley, letter to Arthur Watts, 26 August 1915

DEAD MAN'S DUMP

The plunging limbers* over the shattered track
Racketed with their rusty freight,
Stuck out like many crowns of thorns,
And the rusty stakes like sceptres old
To stay the flood of brutish men
Upon our brothers dear.

The wheels lurched over sprawled dead
But pained them not, though their bones crunched.
Their shut mouths made no moan.
They lie there huddled, friend and foeman,
Man born of man, and born of woman,
And shells go crying over them
From night till night and now.

Earth has waited for them
All the time of their growth
Fretting for their decay:
Now she has them at last!
In the strength of their strength
Suspended – stopped and held.

What fierce imaginings their dark souls lit!
Earth! have they gone into you?
Somewhere they must have gone,
And flung on your hard back
Is their souls' sack,
Emptied of God-ancestralled essences.
Who hurled them out? Who hurled?

None saw their spirits' shadow shake the grass,
Or stood aside for the half used life to pass
Out of those doomed nostrils and the doomed mouth,
When the swift iron burning bee
Drained the wild honey of their youth.

What of us, who flung on the shrieking pyre,
Walk, our usual thoughts untouched,

Our lucky limbs as on ichor fed,
Immortal seeming ever?
Perhaps when the flames beat loud on us,
A fear may choke in our veins
And the startled blood may stop.

The air is loud with death,
The dark air spurts with fire
The explosions ceaseless are.
Timelessly now, some minutes past,
These dead strode time with vigorous life,
Till the shrapnel called "an end!"
But not to all. In bleeding pangs
Some borne on stretchers dreamed of home,
Dear things, war-blotted from their hearts.

A man's brains splattered on
A stretcher-bearer's face;
His shook shoulders slipped their load,
But when they bent to look again
The drowning soul was sunk too deep
For human tenderness.

They left this dead with the older dead,
Stretched at the cross roads.
Burnt black by strange decay,
Their sinister faces lie
The lid over each eye,
The grass and coloured clay
More motion have than they,
Joined to the great sunk silences.

Here is one not long dead;
His dark hearing caught our far wheels,
And the choked soul stretched weak hands
To reach the living word the far wheels said,
The blood-dazed intelligence beating for light,
Crying through the suspense of the far torturing wheels
Swift for the end to break,
Or the wheels to break,
Cried as the tide of the world broke over his sight.

Will they come? Will they ever come?
Even as the mixed hoofs of the mules,
The quivering-bellied mules,
And the rushing wheels all mixed
With his tortured upturned sight,
So we crashed round the bend,
We heard his weak scream,

We heard his very last sound,
And our wheels grazed his dead face.

Isaac Rosenberg, 1917

* limbers – wagons

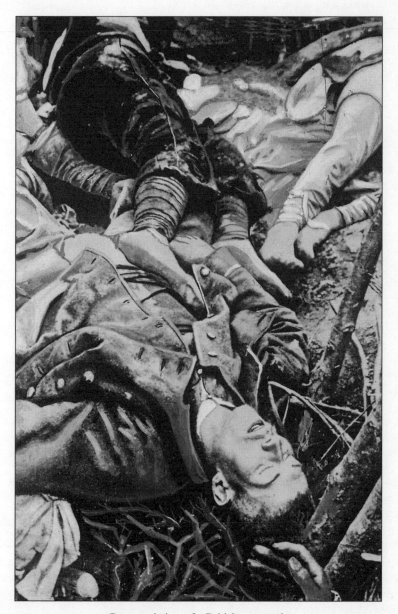

German victims of a British gas attack

SOLILOQUY I

No, I'm not afraid of death
(Not very much afraid, that is)
Either for others or myself;
Can watch them coming from the line
On the wheeled silent stretchers
And not shrink,
But munch my sandwich stoically
And make a joke when "it" has passed.

But – the way they wobble! –
God! that makes one sick.
Dead men should be so still, austere,
And beautiful,
Not wobbling carrion roped upon a cart...

Well, thank God for rum.

Richard Aldington

SOLILOQUY II

I was wrong, quite wrong;
The dead men are not always carrion.
After the advance,
As we went through the shattered trenches
Which the enemy had left,
We found, lying upon the fire-step,
A dead English soldier,
His head bloodily bandaged
And his closed left hand touching the earth,

More beautiful than one can tell,
More subtly coloured than a perfect Goya,
And more austere and lovely in repose
Than Angelo's hand could ever carve in stone.

Richard Aldington

Soldier with head beaten in.

Man of faith

Geoffrey Dearmer's faith helped him to survive and recover. Beyond
the death and destruction he could envisage a world renewed.

TWO TRENCH POEMS

THE STORM NIGHT

Peal after peal of splitting thunder rolls
(Still roar the howling guns, and star shells rise)
We perish, drowned in anger-blasted holes,
Give ear, O Lord! Our very manhood cries,
Shell-fodder yea – but spare our human souls
From fury-shaken skies!

RESURRECTION

Five million men are dead. How can the worth
Of all the world redeem such waste as this?
And yet the spring is clamorous of birth,
And whispering in winter's chrysalis
Glad tidings to each clod, each particle of earth.

So the year's Easter triumphs. Shall we then
Mourn for the dead unduly, and forget
The resurrection in the hearts of men?
Even the poppy on the parapet
Shall blossom as before when summer blows again.

Geoffrey Dearmer

I STOOD WITH THE DEAD

I stood with the Dead, so forsaken and still:
When dawn was grey I stood with the Dead.
And my slow heart said, "You must kill; you must kill:
Soldier, soldier, morning is red."

On the shapes of the slain in their crumpled disgrace
I stared for a while through the thin cold rain . . .
"O lad that I loved, there is rain on your face,
And your eyes are blurred and sick like the plain."

I stood with the Dead . . . They were dead; they were dead;
My heart and my head beat a march of dismay;
And gusts of the wind came dulled by the guns.
"Fall in!" I shouted; "Fall in for your pay!"

Siegfried Sassoon

9

REFUSING TO FIGHT –
PSYCHOLOGICAL STRESS –
BREAKDOWNS AND PROTESTS

NO WORD OF COMPLAINT FROM THE BRITISH

EPITAPH: NEUVE CHAPELLE

Tell them at home,
There's nothing here to hide:
We took our orders,
Asked no questions,
Died.

H W Garrod

How could they?

How could men continue, day after day, to carry on their horrific work in their horrific alien environment? Volunteer and conscript alike found himself daily in danger of maiming and death. All suffered the trauma of witnessing horror. Most were required to kill or "accidentally" mutilate other men.

The answer is, in part, that they were psychologically prepared by propaganda to believe that the enemy was the incarnation of evil; but more than that, men were simply trained to use weapons, to fight, to kill and were expected to cooperate fully as members of a fighting team, obeying orders at all times.

> The purpose of military morale is to get men to stay and die when all reason and every instinct tells them to flee and live. Its essence is the "organised abnegation of self." [1]

---

1   *Britain and the Great War 1914-1918,* J M Bourne, p216.

Military discipline was extraordinarily successful. For the most part men did what they were told. Winston Churchill, who fought for 6 months on the Western Front, claimed,

> No word of complaint ever arose from the fighting troops. No attack, however forlorn, however fatal, found them without ardour. No slaughter, however desolating, prevented them from returning to the charge. No physical conditions, however severe, deprived their commanders of their obedience and loyalty . . . [1]

The power of group psychology obliterated a lifetime of moral and intellectual development – only the calls of patriotism, racial hatred, the steadfast belief that the enemy must be defeated whatever the personal cost, and group loyalty, could argue against morality and rational self-interest. And these powerful motivators were reinforced by military traditions and demands. The army command expected from its officers, leadership by example; from all rank and file soldiers it expected discipline, cheerfulness in adversity, unquestioning obedience. Men who did not comply with army requirements were harshly and often brutally treated.

> Military crime – petty theft, drunkenness, insubordination, misuse of equipment, malingering, untidiness – was met with instant and frequently painful retribution. Cowardice, desertions and sleeping on duty could be capital offences. [2]

Apart from the death penalty the other loathed punishment was Field Punishment Number 1 which consisted of lashing the victim by ankles and wrists to the wheel of a gun carriage, arms and legs spread wide, for one hour each morning and evening for up to twenty-eight days, whatever the weather.

The Australian Government would not allow Australian troops to be subjected to the death penalty – yet Australian soldiers were renowned for their courage and fighting effectiveness.

SOLDIERS' MORALITY

For most of the troops in the front line, memories of home, the desire for civilised life and the desperate wish to be released from the hell of war must have often been in their minds. Was it weakness or strength that led some men to rebel against the war?

1   *The World Crisis 1911-1918*, (1931 edition), p634/5.
2   Bourne, p216.

The great majority of soldiers believed that the Germans had to be beaten.

> If anyone at home thinks of talks of peace you can truthfully say that the army is weary enough of war but prepared to fight for another 50 years if necessary, until the final object is attained . . . Our cause is right and certain in the end to triumph.

A letter from Lieutenant Harold Macmillan to his mother in 1916. He was seriously wounded some time later in the war. Prime Minister, 1957 - 1963.

R E Vernède, having been wounded in 1916 was offered a safe job working in the War Office, but believed so strongly in the need to oppose the Germans that he insisted on returning to the front line. – For Vernède, whilst believing in the rightness of his cause, there was bewilderment at the contrast between his actions and his moral principles.

A LISTENING POST

The sun's a red ball in the oak
And all the grass is grey with dew,
A while ago a blackbird spoke –
He didn't know the world's askew.

And yonder rifleman and I
Wait here behind the misty trees
To shoot the first man that goes by,
Our rifles ready on our knees.

How could he know that if we fail
The world may lie in chains for years
And England be a bygone tale
And right be wrong, and laughter tears?

Strange that this bird sits there and sings
While we must only sit and plan –
Who are so much the higher things –
The murder of our fellow man . . .

But maybe God will cause to be –
Who brought forth sweetness from the strong –
Out of our discords harmony
Sweeter than that bird's song.

R E Vernède, 1917

KILLING YOUR OWN MEN

SERGEANT-MAJOR MONEY

It wasn't our battalion, but we lay alongside it,
So the story is as true as the telling is frank.
They hadn't one Line-officer left, after Arras,
Except a batty major and the Colonel, who drank.

"B" Company Commander was fresh from the Depot,
An expert on gas drill, otherwise a dud;
So Sergeant-Major Money carried on, as instructed,
And that's where the swaddies began to sweat blood.

His Old Army humour was so well-spiced and hearty
That one poor sod shot himself, and one lost his wits;
But discipline's maintained, and back in rest-billets
The Colonel congratulates "B" company on their kits.

The subalterns went easy, as was only natural
With a terror like Money driving the machine,
Till finally two Welshmen, butties from the Rhondda,
Bayoneted their bugbear in a field-canteen.

Well, we couldn't blame the officers, they relied on
Money;
We couldn't blame the pitboys, their courage was grand;
Or, least of all blame Money, an old stiff surviving
In a New (bloody) Army he couldn't understand.

Robert Graves, 1917

Why I didn't shoot my men.

> We sorted ourselves out a bit at a line of dugouts half way up the
> opposite hill and then went forward again. When we crossed the
> brow of the hill we came under very heavy machine gun fire
> indeed, together with a hot fire of 5.9 shells. We started advanc-
> ing in short rushes. A 5.9 shell plumped into the middle of my
> platoon, followed by another. One man's body went hurtling
> over my head and dreadful groans came from where the shells
> fell. I shouted out to the platoon to advance, to get them on
> before more shells came. Some men of the line regiment who
> had appeared on our right started running back. I shouted out to
> them to halt, but they took no notice. I pulled out my revolver
> and very nearly shot at them, but I thought it wouldn't do any
> good, as they all had their backs to me so would have thought that

anyone hit was hit by a German bullet.   If I ran after them my
men might think I was running away. So I took my men on!

Lieutenant William St Leger (Killed 27th April 1918, aged 23.) [1]

FEAR

THE HERO

"Jack fell as he'd have wished," the Mother said,
And folded up the letter that she'd read.
"The Colonel writes so nicely." Something broke
In the tired voice that quavered to a choke.
She half looked up. "We mothers are so proud
Of our dead soldiers." Then her face was bowed.

Quietly the Brother Officer went out.
He'd told the poor old dear some gallant lies
That she would nourish all her days, no doubt.
For while he coughed and mumbled, her weak eyes
Had shone with gentle triumph, brimmed with joy,
Because he'd been so brave, her glorious boy.

He thought how "Jack," cold-footed, useless swine,
Had panicked down the trench that night the mine
Went up at Wicked Corner; how he'd tried
To get sent home, and how, at last, he died,
Blown to small bits. And no one seemed to care
Except that lonely woman with white hair.

Siegfried Sassoon

THE DEADBEAT

He dropped, – more sullenly than wearily,
Lay stupid like a cod, heavy like meat,
And none of us could kick him to his feet; –
Just blinked at my revolver, blearily; –
Didn't appear to know a war was on,
Or see the blasted trench at which he stared.
"I'll do 'em in," he whined. "If this hand's spared,
I'll murder them, I will."

1   *People at War 19-1918,* edited by Michael Moynihan.

A low voice said,
"It's Blighty, p'raps, he sees; his pluck's all gone,
Dreaming of all the valiant, that aren't dead:
Bold uncles smiling ministerially;
Maybe his brave young wife, getting her fun
In some new home, improved materially;
It's not these stiffs have crazed him; nor the Hun."

We sent him down at last, out of the way.
Unwounded; – stout lad, too, before that strafe.
Malingering? Stretcher-bearers winked, "Not half!"

Next day I heard the Doc's well-whiskied laugh:
"That scum you sent last night soon died. Hooray!"

Wilfred Owen

EVERYBODY WAS AFRAID

Everybody was afraid. If any man says he never felt fear, I don't care who he is, he's a liar. You all tried not to show it, but everybody felt the same. But when the whistle blew and you went over the top, your fears all went. You never thought about the danger once you were out there among it, but it was that waiting, waiting, waiting in the trenches to go over that got your wind up.

Rifleman F. C. White, 10th (Service) Battalion,
King's Royal Rifle Corps [1]

Scared like a rabbit.

Were we brave? I don't think we were brave. We had a job to do, and we did it. Of course, I used to be frightened some-times, like a scared rabbit.

Rifleman F. Scarbrow, 12th (Service) Battalion,
The Rifle Brigade. [2]

Self-wounding, Suicide, Desertion.

To be "windy" was one thing; to be "funky" was another. Windiness was almost universal and men "did their job" in spite of it; "funkiness'; meant shirking the job, and the majority

1   *The Roses of No Man's Land*, Lynn Macdonald.
2   *The Roses of No Man's Land.*

of infantrymen held "funk" in contempt. A funky man was an
outcast, a pariah. But a nervous temperament did not neces-
sarily exclude courage. It took considerable courage as well as
a degree of desperation to shoot off your trigger-finger, to blast
a hole in your foot, or even, as occasionally happened, to
commit suicide rather than face the ordeal of "going over the
top." Every soldier knew the consequences. He would be evacu-
ated to a special hospital and nursed under guard, until he was
sufficiently recovered to face court martial and the inevitable
punishment of imprisonment, or even death. The alternative was
to run away, and in cases of cowardice or desertion in the face
of the enemy, if no mitigating circumstances were proved, death
sentence was automatic.

Lyn Macdonald [1]

DESERTERS

I saved him from desertion, but . . .

The casualty clearing station moved up to the Ypres salient
just before the battle. We weren't expected to take in any
casualties until two days after the battle began, so the evening
before – which would be 29 July, the day before the troops
went into the line – it was a beautiful evening and I went for
a walk. I met a young officer and I recognised him. He'd been
one of my drill-sergeants in the Boys' Brigade years earlier
when he was only a boy, and we stopped and spoke. I said "What
are you doing here?" because I knew where his unit was and
this was some distance away. And then he broke down. He said,
"I can't face it." I said, "Well, there's only one alternative, isn't
there? You wouldn't want that." He said, "Yes I know that.
Don't think I don't know that. There are fifteen men in the cage
now, waiting to be shot."

We spoke together for a long time, and I tried to comfort
him. It seemed to help him, just to talk about it, which he
couldn't have done to anyone else, and eventually he calmed
down. I said, "Well, we must get you back to your unit." He
didn't argue. He agreed. It was about a five-mile walk back to
his battalion and I went with him, talking to him all the way
back, and I was able to get this dear lad back again. He was
killed the next day.

1   *The Roses of No Man's Land.*

I was very upset about it. I think it was simply disgraceful that there should have been a death penalty. How does the average man, in the heat of battle, tell the difference between a real nervous breakdown and cowardice? I don't think it should have any place in battle at all.

Captain the Reverend Leonard Pearson,
Chaplain at No.44 Casualty Clearing Station [1]

Official figures for executions in the British Army abroad in the First World War

112 - for desertion
14 - for cowardice
9   - for disobedience
1   - for sleeping on post
6   - for quitting post
3   - for casting away arms
14 - for striking or violence
163 - for murder[2]

It is accepted that many men were shot by their officers without appearing in court. – See, for example, Act 2, scene 2 of Sherriff's *Journey's End.*

Executed for getting drunk

These two men got drunk and they wandered away and got caught and were brought back and were charged with absenteeism on active service. If it had been in England they would have got seven days CB. They laughed it off. They thought wandering away was just something or nothing; but they were court-martialled and they were sentenced to be shot, subject to Sir Douglas Haig. He could have said no, but he didn't. So they were shot. They were described as being killed in action. Of course it was kept fairly dark, but their family got to know about it. – They didn't shoot any Australians. They would have rioted. They weren't like us. We were docile.

Private George Morgan, 10th Battalion West Yorkshire Regiment. [3]

In all Haig signed 253 death warrants.

---

1   *The Roses of No Man's Land.*
2   *Statistics of the Military Effort of the British Empire During the Great War.*
3   *Tommy Goes to War*, Malcolm Brown, p236.

Witnessing an execution

We were called to attention and the APM began to read: "Private So-and-so, you have been charged and found guilty of desertion in the face of the enemy. The verdict of the court martial is that you are to be shot at dawn." It was signed by Sir Douglas Haig.

Next morning the sun was shining and a touch of frost in the air. I was sent up the road to stop any traffic and being high up and on horseback I had a bird's eye view. I saw the man brought out to the post and the firing squad march into position, turn right and take up stand. I heard the report as they fired and saw the smoke from their rifles. Then they turned and marched off. The officer, with revolver in hand, inspected the body, then turned away. The dead man was then taken away in a blanket and buried in the small cemetery in the next field. It was over. I came down, but it didn't seem real.

The next one followed the same pattern, except the APM said, "Cowardice."

And the man said, "Never!"

Trooper Sydney Chaplin, 1st/1st Northamptonshire Yeomanry. [1]

THE DESERTER

"I'm sorry I done it, Major."
We bandaged the livid face;
And led him out, ere the wan sun rose,
To die his death of disgrace.

The bolt-heads locked to the cartridge;
The rifles steadied to rest,
As cold stock nestled at colder cheek
And foresight lined on the breast.

"Fire!" called the Sergeant-Major.
The muzzles flamed as he spoke:
And the shameless soul of a nameless man
Went up in the cordite smoke

Gilbert Frankau

---

[1]   *Voices and Images of the Great War,* Lynn Macdonald, p184.

THE EXECUTION OF CORNELIUS VANE

Le combat spirituel est aussi brutal que la bataille d'hommes; mais la vision de la justice est le plaisir de Dieu seul. – Arthur Rimbaud

Arraigned before his worldly gods
He would have said:
"I, Cornelius Vane,
A fly in the sticky web of life,
Shot away my right index finger.
I was alone, on sentry, in the chill twilight after dawn,
And the act cost me a bloody sweat.
Otherwise the cost was trivial – they had no evidence,
And I lied to the wooden fools who tried me.
When I returned from hospital
They made me a company cook:
I peel potatoes and other men fight."

For nearly a year Cornelius peeled potatoes
And his life was full of serenity.
Then the enemy broke our line
And their hosts spread over the plains
Like unleashed beads.
Every man was taken –
Shoemakers, storemen, grooms –
And arms were given them
That they might stem the oncoming host.

Cornelius held out his fingerless hand
And remarked that he couldn't shoot.
"But you can stab," the sergeant said,
So he fell in with the rest, and, a little group,
They marched away towards the enemy.

After an hour they halted for a rest.
They were already in the fringe of the fight:
Desultory shells fell about them,
And past them retreating gun teams
Galloped in haste.
But they must go on.

Wounded stragglers came down the road,
Haggard and limping
Their arms and equipment tossed away.
Cornelius Vane saw them, and his heart was beating wildly,
For he must go on.

At the next halt
He went aside to piss,
And whilst away a black shell
Burst near him:
Hot metal shrieked past his face;
Bricks and earth descended like hail,
And the acrid stench of explosive filled his nostrils.

Cornelius pitched his body to the ground
And crouched in trembling fear.
Another shell came singing overhead,
Nowhere near.

But Cornelius sprang to his feet, his pale face set.
He willed nothing, saw nothing, only before him
Were the free open fields:
To the fields he ran.

He was still running when he began to perceive
The tranquillity of the fields

And the battle distant.
Away in the north-east were men marching on a road;
Behind the smoke-puffs of shrapnel,
And in the west the sun declining
In a sky of limpid gold.

When night came finally
He had reached a wood.
In the thickness of the trees
The cold wind was excluded,
And here he slept a few hours.

In the early dawn
The chill mist and heavy dew
Pierced his bones and wakened him.
There was no sound of battle to be heard.

In the open fields again
The sun shone sickly through the mist.
And the dew was icy to the feet.
So Cornelius ran about in that white night,
The sun's wan glare his only guide.

Coming to a canal
He ran up and down like a dog
Deliberating where to cross.
One way he saw a bridge
Loom vaguely, but approaching
He heard voices and turned about.
He went far the other way,
But growing tired before he found a crossing,
Plunged into the icy water and swam.
The water gripped with agony;
His clothes sucked the heavy water,
And as he ran again
Water oozed and squelched from his boots,
His coat dripped and his teeth chattered.

He came to a farm.
Approaching cautiously, he found it deserted.
Within he discarded his sopping uniform, dried himself and donned
Mufti he found in a cupboard.
Dark mouldy bread and bottled cider he also found
And was refreshed.
Whilst he was eating,
Suddenly,
Machine-guns opened fire not far away,

And their harsh throbbing
Darkened his soul with fear.

The sun was more golden now,
And as he went –
Always going west –
The mist grew thin.
About noon,
As he skirted the length of a wood
The warmth had triumphed and the spring day was beautiful.
Cornelius perceived with a new joy
Pale anemones and violets of the wood,
And wished that he might ever
Exist in the perception of these woodland flowers
And the shafts of yellow light that pierced
The green dusk.

Two days later
He entered a village and was arrested.
He was hungry, and the peace of the fields
Dissipated the terror that had been the strength of his will.

He was charged with desertion
And eventually tried by court-martial.
The evidence was heavy against him,
And he was mute in his own defence.

A dumb anger and despair
Filled his soul.

He was found guilty.
Sentence: To suffer death by being shot.

The sentence duly confirmed,
One morning at dawn they led him forth.

He saw a party of his own regiment,
With rifles, looking very sad.
The morning was bright, and as they tied
The cloth over his eyes, he said to the assembly:
"What wrong have I done that I should leave these:
The bright sun rising
And the birds that sing?"

Herbert Read

OLAF

i sing of Olaf glad and big
whose warmest heart recoiled at war:
a conscientious object:or

his wellbelovéd colonel (trig
westpointer most succinctly bred)
took erring Olaf soon in hand:
but–though an host of overjoyed
noncoms (first knocking on the head
him) do through icy waters roll
that helplessness which others stroke
with brushes recently employed
anent this muddy toilet bowl,
while kindred intellects evoke
allegiance per blunt instruments–

Olaf (being to all intents
a corpse and wanting any rag
upon what God unto him gave)
responds, without getting annoyed
"I will not kiss your f.ing flag"

straightway the silver bird looked grave
(departing hurriedly to shave)

but–though all kinds of officers
(a yearning nation's blueeyed pride)
their passive prey did kick and curse
until for wear their clarion
voices and boots were much the worse,
and egged the firstclassprivates on
his rectum wickedly to tease
by means of skilfully applied
bayonets roasted hot with heat–
Olaf (upon what were once his knees)
does almost ceaselessly repeat
"there is some s. I will not eat"

our president, being of which
assertions duly notified
threw the yellowsonofabitch
into a dungeon, where he died

Christ (of His mercy infinite)
i pray to see; and Olaf, too

preponderatingly because
unless statistics lie he was
more brave than me:more blond than you.

E E Cummings

SIEGFRIED SASSOON DESERTS –
WAR HERO TURNED PROTESTER

Siegfried Sassoon won the Military Cross for bombing and capturing a German trench single handed in June 1916. In August he was invalided to England with trench fever.

He returned to France in February 1917. In April he was wounded in the shoulder and sent to hospital in England.

While convalescing he discussed his growing disillusionment with the war with Bertrand Russell who encouraged him to make a daringly defiant protest in an attempt to influence public opinion and the Government. Sassoon decided to refuse to fight and not only to send his refusal to his commanding officer, but also to publish it as widely as possible. He threw his Military Cross into the River Mersey.

He prepared a protest statement which eventually appeared in *The Times* on 31st July, 1917, and was read in Parliament.

He expected to be put on trial and possibly shot.

He was ordered to appear before a medical board at Chester. He failed to appear. The next time he was ordered to appear before the board he did appear. His friend, Robert Graves, argued that Sassoon had gone mad. He had "seen corpses in the street"; he wanted to shoot the Prime Minister, and Sir Douglas Haig; and he had an irresistible urge to go back to fight and get himself killed. – Whether or not the board was persuaded by these arguments it seemed to give them an idea for defusing the publicity Sassoon was beginning to receive. He was sent to a mental hospital – Craiglockhart Military Hospital in Edinburgh which specialised in treating victims of shell shock.

He was seen by the distinguished psychologist , Dr W H R Rivers, who wrote on his Medical Case Sheet, 23rd July, 1917,

> There are no physical signs of any disorder of the Nervous System. He discusses his recent actions and their motives in a perfectly intelligent and rational way, and there is no evidence of any excitement or depression. He recognises that his views of warfare are tinged by his feelings about the death of friends. . .

At the hospital he fortunately and significantly met Wilfred Owen, who was there with genuine shellshock. His conversations, and interest in Owen's poetry proved a tremendous stimulus to Owen.

After four months Sassoon began to feel guilty about not fighting alongside other soldiers. – He wrote:

> At the front I should find forgetfulness.   And I would rather be killed than survive as one who wangled his way through by saying that the War ought to stop.

On 26th November 1917 he left the hospital to return to the battlefront. He was sent to fight in Palestine and then back to France where, on 13th July 1918 he was shot in the head, by accident, by one of his own men. The bullet grazed, rather than entered, his head.

He was sent home again to England on sick leave for the remaining months of the war.

WILFUL DEFIANCE
OF MILITARY AUTHORITY
Sassoon's Protest Statement read in Parliament
30th July, 1917

> I am making this statement as an act of wilful defiance of military authority, because I believe that the War is being deliberately prolonged by those who have the power to end it. I am a soldier, convinced that I am acting on the behalf of soldiers.

> I believe that this war, upon which I entered as a war of defence and liberation, has now become a war of aggression and conquest. I believe that the purposes for which I and my fellow soldiers entered upon this War should have been so clearly stated as to have made it impossible for them to be changed without our knowledge, and that, had this been done, the objects which actuated us would now be attainable by negotiation.

> I have seen and endured the suffering of the troops, and I can no longer be a party to prolong those sufferings for ends which I believe to be evil and unjust.

> I am not protesting against the military conduct of the War but against the political errors and insincerities for which the fighting men are being sacrificed.

> On behalf of those who are suffering now I make this protest against the deception which is being practised on them. Also I believe that I may help to destroy the callous complacence with

which the majority of those at home regard the continuance of agonies which they do not share, and which they have not sufficient imagination to realise.

BANISHMENT

I am banished from the patient men who fight.
They smote my heart to pity, built my pride.
Shoulder to aching shoulder, side by side,
They trudged away from life's broad wealds of light.
Their wrongs were mine; and ever in my sight
They went arrayed in honour. But they died, –
Not one by one; and mutinous I cried
To those who sent them out into the night.

The darkness tells how vainly I have striven
To free them from the pit where they must dwell
In outcast gloom convulsed and jagged and riven
By grappling guns. Love drove me to rebel.
Love drives me back to grope with them through hell;
And in their tortured eyes I stand forgiven.

Siegfried Sassoon, Craiglockhart, 1917

SASSOON'S DIARY ENTRY, 19 JUNE 1917

I wish I could believe that Ancient War History justifies the indefinite prolongation of this war. The Jingoes define it as "an enormous quarrel between incompatible spirits and destinies, in which one or other must succumb." But the men who write these manifestos do not truly know what useless suffering the war inflicts.

And the ancient wars on which they base their arguments did not involve such huge sacrifices as the next two or three years will demand of Europe, if this war is to be carried on to a knock-out result. Our peace-terms remain the same, "the destruction of Kaiserism and Prussianism." I don't know what aims this destruction represents.

I only know, and declare from the depths of my agony, that these empty words (so often on the lips of the Jingoes) mean the destruction of Youth. They mean the whole torment of waste and despair which people refuse to acknowledge or to face; from month to month they dupe themselves with hopes that "the war will end this year."

And the Army is dumb. The Army goes on with its bitter tasks. The ruling classes do all the talking. And their words convince no one but the crowds who *are their dupes*.

The soldiers who return home seem to be stunned by the things they have endured. They are willingly entrapped by the silent conspiracy against them. They have come back to life from the door of death, and the world is good to enjoy. They vaguely know that it is "bad form" to hurt people's feelings by telling the truth about the war. Poor heroes! If only they would speak out; and throw their medals in the faces of their masters; and ask their women why it thrills them to know that they, the dauntless warriors, have shed the blood of Germans. Do not the women gloat secretly over the wounds of their lovers? Is there anything inwardly noble in savage sex instincts?

The rulers of England have always relied on the ignorance and patient credulity of the crowd. If the crowd could see into those cynical hearts it would lynch its dictators. For it is to the inherent weakness of human nature, and not to its promiscuous nobility, that these great men make their incessant appeals.

The soldiers are fooled by the popular assumption that they are all heroes. They have a part to play, a mask to wear. They are allowed to assume a pride of superiority to the mere civilian. Are there no heroes among the civilians, men and women alike?

Of the elderly male population I can hardly trust myself to speak. Their frame of mind is, in the majority of cases, intolerable. They glory in senseless invective against the enemy. They glory in the mock-heroism of their young men. They glory in the mechanical phrases of the Northcliffe Press. They regard the progress of the war like a game of chess, cackling about "attrition," and "wastage of man-power," and "civilisation at stake." In every class of society there are old men like ghouls, insatiable in their desire for slaughter, impenetrable in their ignorance.

Soldiers conceal their hatred of the war. Civilians conceal their liking for it.

"How vastly the spiritual gain of those who are left behind out-weighs the agony and loss of those who fight and die . . . the everlasting glory and exaltation of war." (From a review in *The Times Literary Supplement*.)

This is the sort of thing I am in revolt against. But I belong to "a war-wearied and bewildered minority" which regards "victory" and "defeat" as rhetorical terms with little precise meaning.

21 JUNE, 1917

A long statement of the war-aims etc by Belloc in *Land and Water* leaves me quite convinced. He argues from the point of view of British rectitude: and it is that which I am questioning. Worst of all, he argues on the assumption that "the next few months" will bring a military decision; he has done this since 1915, so one cannot put much faith in him.

I am revolting against the war being continued indefinitely; I believe that Carson, Milner, Lloyd George and Northcliffe intend the war to continue at least two more years. . .

It is obvious that nothing could be worse than the present conditions under which humanity is suffering and dying. How will the wastage and misery of the next two years be repaired? Will Englishmen be any happier because they have added more colonies to their Empire? The agony of France! The agony of Austria-Hungary and Germany! Are not these equal before God?

On 15th June Sassoon had sent copies of his protest to over a dozen friends acquaintances and famous people – including the novelist, Arnold Bennet, who, probably unknown to Sassoon, was employed by the British Government to write propaganda supporting the war.

Extract from Arnold Bennett's letter to Siegfried Sassoon, 20 July 1917

I think you are very misguided and that your position cannot be argumentatively defended . . . The point is that you are not in a situation to judge the situation. For you are not going to tell me that you have studied it in all its main bearings and branches. In my opinion a citizen is not justified in acting in such a way as will, so far as he is concerned, fundamentally thwart the desires of the majority as expressed by the accepted channels, unless he has with reasonable fullness acquainted himself with the facts of the case. If you were acting from an objection to all war, your position would be comprehensible and justifiable. But you are acting from an opinion that this particular war has reached a particular stage and that civilians have reached a particular degree of inhumanity. The overwhelming majority of your fellow citizens are against you. You may say that your action affects only yourself. Not so. It affects the whole State. You did not bind yourself as an officer on the understanding you should be free from obligation whenever you happened to conclude that the war ought to be over. You are arrogating to yourself

a right to which you are not entitled . . .   I rely on you not to
resent this epistle. Your suspicion is correct. The Army will ultimately lay it down that you are "daft." You aren't of course, but
that's how it will end. What is the matter with you is spiritual
pride.

Yours ever, AB

MENTAL BREAKDOWN

At first the condition of shell-shock and mental breakdown was not
accepted as an illness and it was not until 1917 that special centres were
set up on the Western Front to deal with severe cases of mental distress.
Many men, after a period of rest and quiet, were able to return to the
trenches. Others never recovered.

> In Britain, in addition to six peacetime hospitals that could deal
> with nervous disorders an additional six hospitals for officers
> and thirteen for other ranks were set up in 1917 and 1918 to deal
> entirely with those whose mental balance had been disturbed by
> their experiences in the trenches, and who had been sent home
> for ever. [1]

The Medical History of the War estimated that about 2 per cent of soldiers suffered from shell-shock - about 80,000 men driven temporarily
or permanently insane. [2]

Even those who would still be regarded as "normal" often changed their
personalities. Vera Brittain noted that her brother Edward who was
home on leave had changed. He had become, "unfamiliar, frightening
Edward, who never smiled or spoke except about trivial things, who
seemed to have nothing to say to me and indeed hardly appeared to no-
tice my return." [3]

Being shown the mad ward

Jeffrey Farnol was once being shown round a Base Hospital when
they came across what the doctor blithely called the "mad ward."
Farnol described a room full of men with "a vagueness of gaze, a
loose-lipped, too-ready smile, a vacancy of expression. Some there were
who scowled sullenly enough, others who crouched apart, solitary souls,

1 *First World War*, Martin Gilbert, p358
2 *Eye Deep in Hell*, John Ellis, p118
3 *Testament of Youth*, p356.

who, I learned, felt themselves outcasts: others who crouched in corners haunted by the dread of pursuing vengeance always at hand."

Philip Gibbs saw similar cases – such as the sergeant-major in Aveluy Wood, near Thiepval, who was "convulsed with a dreadful rigor like a man in epilepsy, and clawed at his mouth, moaning horribly, with blind terror in his eyes. He had to be strapped to a stretcher before he could be carried away."

In almost the same place he saw a Wiltshire boy standing outside a dugout; "shaking in every limb, in a palsied way. His steel hat was at the back of his head, and his mouth slobbered, and two comrades could not hold him still. These badly shell-shocked boys clawed at their mouths ceaselessly. It was a common dreadful action. Others sat in field hospitals in a state of coma, dazed, as though deaf, and actually dumb." [1]

Pathetic men

> They were pathetic, these shell-shocked boys, and a lot of them were very sensitive about the fact that they were incontinent. They'd say "I'm terribly sorry about it, Sister, it's shaken me all over and I can't control it. Just imagine, to wet the bed at my age!"
>
> I'd say, "We'll see to that. Don't worry about it." I used to give them a bedpan in the locker beside them and keep it as quiet as possible. Poor fellows, they were so embarrassed – especially the better class men.
>
> Sister Mary Stollard, QAIMNS, Becket's Park Military hospital, Leeds.
>
> They used to tremble a great deal and it affected their speech. They stammered very badly, and they had strange ideas which you could only describe as hallucinations. They saw things that really didn't exist, and imagined all sorts of things.
>
> Sister Henrietta Hall, St Luke's Military Hospital, Bradford.[2]

Sassoon's observations in Craiglockhart

> One became conscious that the place was full of men whose slumbers were morbid and terrifying – men muttering uneasily

1   *Eye Deep in Hell.*
2   *Roses of No Man's Land*, p220.

or suddenly crying out in their sleep. Around me was that under-
world of dreams haunted by submerged memories of warfare and
its intolerable shocks . . . Each man was back in his doomed
sector of a horror-stricken front line, where the panic and stampede of some ghastly experience was re-enacted among the livid
faces of the dead. [1]

Wilfred Owen – shell shock victim

On 17th March, 1917, Owen got concussion when he hit his head falling
through a floor into a deep cellar. He was moved into a makeshift
hospital quite near the front line where he stayed until returning to the
fight.

He reported to his mother in a letter of 4th April, "My long rest has
shaken my nerve," and he explained his shaky writing by saying that it
was because he had cut his hand on a tin of lobster.

That same day he went back into action near St Quentin, and for four
days and four nights he was out in the open in snow(!), and had no
sleep at all.

> Not an hour passed without a shell amongst us," he said in his
> next letter to his mother, "We lay in wet snow. I kept alive on
> brandy, and the fear of death, and the glorious prospect of the
> cathedral town just below us, glittering with the morning.

About a week later he returned to the action again, suffered more, and
was actually blown up. In his letter home on 25th April he wrote,

> Twice in one day we went over the top . . . I had some extraor-
> dinary escapes from shells and bullets. Fortunately there was no
> bayonet work, since the Hun ran before we got up to his trench
> . . . Never before has the battalion encountered such intense
> shelling as rained on us as we advanced in the open. The
> Colonel sent round this message the next day: "I was filled with
> admiration at the conduct of the battalion under heavy shellfire
> . . . the leadership of the officers was excellent, and the
> conduct of the men was beyond praise." The reward we got for
> all this was to remain in the line for 12 days. For twelve days I
> did not wash my face, nor take off my boots, nor sleep a deep
> sleep. For twelve days we lay in holes, where at any moment a
> shell might put us out.

---

1   *Sherston's Progress* in *Complete Memoirs of George Sherston*, p556.

I think the worst incident was one wet night when we lay up against a railway embankment. A big shell lit on top of the bank, just two yards from my head. Before I awoke, I was blown in the air right away from the bank! I passed most of the following days in a railway cutting in a hole just big enough to lie in, and covered with corrugated iron. My brother officer of B Company, 2/Lt Gaukroger lay opposite in a similar hole. But he was covered with earth, and no relief will ever relieve him.

On the 1st May his commanding officer noticed that Owen's speech was confused and that he trembled uncontrollably. He was sent to hospitals in France, then on to a hospital at Netley, Hampshire where he arrived on 16th June.

Owen meets Sassoon

On 26th June he arrived at Craiglockhart War Hospital, Edinburgh.

In mid August he met Siegfried Sassoon who was under medical supervision there. Owen who was already very impressed by Sassoon's war poetry showed some of his poems to Sassoon who criticised them for being "over luscious" and in some poems there was "an almost embarrassing sweetness of sentiment." Nevertheless, Sassoon recognised Owen's talent and encouraged him to write more, but in an earthy style.

Stimulated by Sassoon, Owen burst into poetic activity, attempting this more earthy style. His first poem was *The Deadbeat* And then, gathering enthusiasm, in one week he completed six poems, including *Disabled* and *Dulce et Decorum Est*.

Sassoon and Owen became firm friends, and through Sassoon, Owen met other writers including Robert Graves.

In October 1917 Owen was pronounced fit for light duties in the army. He was sent first to an army camp in Scarborough – on 24th November. – In March 1918 he was transferred to the army base in Ripon, Yorkshire. – He was declared fit for front line service on 26th August.

MENTAL CASES

Who are these? Why sit they here in twilight?
Wherefore rock they, purgatorial shadows,
Drooping tongues from jaws that slob their relish,
Baring teeth that leer like skulls' teeth wicked?
Stroke on stroke of pain, – but what slow panic,
Gouged these chasms round their fretted sockets?
Ever from their hair and through their hands' palms
Misery swelters. Surely we have perished
Sleeping, and walk hell; but who these hellish?

These are men whose minds the Dead have ravished.
Memory fingers in their hair of murders,
Multitudinous murders they once witnessed.
Wading sloughs of flesh these helpless wander,
Treading blood from lungs that had loved laughter.
Always they must see these things and hear them,
Batter of guns and shatter of flying muscles,
Carnage incomparable, and human squander
Rucked too thick for these men's extrication.

Therefore still their eyeballs shrink tormented
Back into their brains, because on their sense
Sunlight seems a blood-smear; night comes blood-black;
Dawn breaks open like a wound that bleeds afresh.
– Thus their heads wear this hilarious, hideous,
Awful falseness of set-smiling corpses.

– Thus their hands are plucking at each other;
Picking at the rope-knouts of their scourging;
Snatching after us who smote them, brother,
Pawing us who dealt them war and madness.

Wilfred Owen, May to July 1918

SURVIVORS

No doubt they'll soon get well; the shock and strain
Have caused their stammering, disconnected talk.
Of course they're "longing to go out again," –
These boys with old, scared faces, learning to walk.
They'll soon forget their haunted nights; their cowed
Subjection to the ghosts of friends who died, –
Their dreams that drip with murder; and they'll be proud
Of glorious war that shatter'd all their pride . . .
Men who went out to battle, grim and glad;
Children, with eyes that hate you, broken and mad.

Siegfried Sassoon, Craiglockhart, October 1917

THE MAD SOLDIER

I dropped here three weeks ago, yes – I know,
And it's bitter cold at night, since the fight. –
I could tell you if I chose. – No one knows
Excep' me and four or five, what ain't alive.
I can see them all asleep, three men deep,
And they're no where near a fire – but our wire
Has 'em fast as can be. Can't you see
When the flare goes up? Ssh! Boys; what's that noise?
Do you know what these rats eat? –   Body-meat!
After you've been down a week, an' your cheek
Gets as pale as life, and night seems as white
As the day, only the rats and their brats
Seem more hungry when the day's gone away –
An' they look as big as bulls, an' they pulls
Till you almost sort o' shout – but the drought
What you hadn't felt before makes you sore.
And at times you even think of a drink. . .
There's a leg across my thighs. – If my eyes
Weren't too sore, I'd like to see who it be.
Wonder if I'd know the bloke if I woke? –-
Woke? By damn, I'm not asleep. – There's a heap
Of us wond'ring why the hell we're not well. . .
Leastways I am –   since I came. It's the same
With the others. – They don't know what *I* do,

Or they wouldn't gape and grin. – It's a sin
To say that Hell is hot – 'cause it's not.
Mind you, I know very well we're in hell. -
In a twisted hump we lie – heaping high,
Yes! An' higher every day. – Oh, I say,
This chap's heavy on my thighs. – Damn his eyes.

E W Tennant

LAMENTATIONS

I found him in the guard-room at the Base.
From the blind darkness I heard him crying
And blundered in. With puzzled, patient face
A sergeant watched him; it was no good trying
To stop it; for he howled and beat his chest.
And all because his brother had gone west,
Raved at the bleeding war; his rampant grief
Moaned, shouted, sobbed, and choked, while he was kneeling
Half-naked on the floor. In my belief
Such men have lost all patriotic feeling.

Siegfried Sassoon

THE IMMORTALS

I killed them, but they would not die.
Yea! All the day and all the night
For them I could not rest nor sleep,
Nor guard from them nor hide in flight.

Then in my agony I turned
And made my hands red in their gore.
In vain – for faster than I slew
They rose more cruel than before.

I killed and killed with slaughter mad;
I killed till all my strength was gone.
And still they rose to torture me,
For Devils only die in fun.

I used to think the Devil hid
In women's smiles and wine's carouse.
I called him Satan, Balzebub.
But now I call him, dirty louse.

Isaac Rosenberg

THE SHOW

> We have fallen in the dreams the ever-living
> Breathe on the tarnished mirror of the world,
> And then smooth out with ivory hands and sigh.*
> — W B Yeats

My soul looked down from a vague height, with Death,
As unremembering how I rose or why,
And saw a sad land, weak with sweats of dearth,
Grey, cratered like the moon with hollow woe,
And pitted with great pocks and scabs of plagues.

Across its beard, that horror of harsh wire,
There moved thin caterpillars, slowly uncoiled.
It seemed they pushed themselves to be as plugs
Of ditches, where they writhed and shrivelled, killed.

By them had slimy paths been trailed and scraped
Round myriad warts that might be little hills.

From gloom's last dregs these long-strung creatures crept,
And vanished out of dawn down hidden holes.

(And smell came up from those foul openings
As out of mouths, or deep wounds deepening.)

On dithering feet upgathered, more and more,
Brown strings, towards strings of grey, with bristling spines,
All migrants from green fields, intent on mire.

Those that were grey, of more abundant spawns,
Ramped on the rest and ate them and were eaten.

I saw their bitten backs curve, loop, and straighten.
I watched those agonies curl, lift, and flatten.

Whereat, in terror what that sight might mean,
I reeled and shivered earthward like a feather.

And Death fell with me, like a deepening moan.
And He, picking a manner of worm, which half had hid
Its bruises in the earth, but crawled no further,
Showed me its feet, the feet of many men,
And the fresh-severed head of it, my head.

Wilfred Owen

* Owen misquotes Yeats who wrote, "burnished mirror."

Background to *The Show*

On the 19th January 1917 Wilfred Owen had written to his mother describing no-man's land – "pock marked like a body of foulest disease and its odour is the breath of cancer . . . I have not seen any dead. I have done worse. In the dank air I have perceived it, and in the darkness, felt. No-man's land under snow is like the face of the moon: chaotic, crater ridden, uninhabitable, awful, the abode of madness . . ."

SUICIDE

Usual sort of letter

On his first night in the front line Robert Graves came across a man, face down in the mud who refused to respond to orders. When Graves had a closer look with his torch he saw that the man had used his rifle to shoot himself through the head by putting the muzzle in his mouth and pushing the trigger with his toe.

Two Irish officers who came up told him that they had had several suicides recently and gave orders for the next of kin to be informed. "Usual sort of letter; tell them he died a soldier's death, anything you like. I'm not going to report it as suicide."

SUICIDE IN THE TRENCHES

I knew a simple soldier boy
Who grinned at life in empty joy,
Slept soundly through the lonesome dark,
And whistled early with the lark.

In winter trenches, cowed and glum,
With crumps and lice and lack of rum,
He put a bullet through his brain.
No-one ever spoke of him again.

You smug-faced crowds with kindling eye
Who cheer when soldier lads march by,
Sneak home and pray you'll never know
The hell where youth and laughter go.

Siegfried Sassoon

NOT EVERYONE SAID YES –
MUTINIES, STRIKES, PEACE DEMANDS

Whether it was fear, over-heated imagination, or just propaganda the German story was that she feared encirclement. The German state was not fifty years old at the start of the war, and her borders not long established. Russia might seize territory in the east, Britain in the north and France in the west. Germany had to act to protect her interests.

Whilst the majority in Germany appear to have accepted this theory, there quickly grew up within Germany an organised and powerful op-position to the war far greater than anything seen in Britain. The leading opponents were Rosa Luxemburg, a key figure among German Com-munists, and Karl Liebknecht, a Social Democrat politician.Their first protest action took place in 1916.

Anti-war agitation in Berlin

May Day 1916 was chosen for the first trial of strength . . . At eight o' clock in the morning a dense throng of workers – almost ten thousand – assembled in the square, which the police had already occupied well ahead of time.Karl Liebknecht's voice then rang out: "Down with the War! Down with the Government!" The police immediately rushed at him . . . For the first time since the beginning of the war open resistance to it had appeared on the streets of the capital. The ice was broken.

Paul Frolich

That same day anti-war demonstrations took place in Jena, Dresden and other German cities. [1]

On 28th June Karl Liebknecht was sentenced to two and a half years' hard labour for anti-war agitation. Fifty-five thousand munitions workers went out on sympathy strike.

Revolution in Russia

Throughout 1917, on the Eastern Front, the Russian Army was finding increasing difficulty in getting troops to obey orders. The Bolsheviks urged soldiers to disobey orders. Munitions workers went on strike. There were riots in the cities. On 10th March a general strike began in Russia. On the 12th 17,000 soldiers in Petrograd joined the demonstrators. On the 15th the Tsar, in response to appeals from his commanders, resigned and the Russian Revolution was under way.

The Killing Seemed Excessive

On 9th April British and Canadian forces launched attacks at Arras and Vimy Ridge. Over 39,000 men were killed in four days including 11,500 Canadians whose bodies were never identified. On April 14th for the first time, British generals complained to the Commander in Chief (Haig) of the terrible casualty rate.   He called a halt to the fighting the next day.

The French

Under General Nivelle the French launched an attack on 16th April against the Germans along the river Aisne.   Within 4 days he had lost 100,000 men, and French soldiers began to desert. So many were refusing to fight that Haig, partly to divert German attention from the area of the Aisne, ordered troops back into action near Arras, with severe losses. General Allenby again urged Haig to call a halt, but this time with no effect − except that he was himself ordered back to London.

The disastrous slaughter endured by the French carried their soldiers beyond breaking point. Anger at the way lives were simply poured away and also conditions of service in the French army led to a massive spontaneous rebellion.

---

1   *Voices from the Great War*, Peter Vansittart, p107.

One regiment went to the front bleating like sheep led to slaughter. Soon fifty-four divisions were refusing to obey orders. Many thousands deserted. Great stretches of the front were left undefended, though strangely the Germans never learnt this, and took no advantage of it. Laboriously Pétain restored discipline.

Over a hundred thousand soldiers were court martialled. Twenty-three thousand were found guilty, though   only   432   were sentenced to death and only 55 were officially shot. A good many more were shot without sentence. Another   250   were pounded to death by the artillery, according to Henri Barbusse. [1]

Peace initiatives

On 12th April 1917 two of the Central Powers, Austria and Bulgaria, approached Allies through diplomats in Switzerland in an attempt to start peace negotiations. They were rebuffed.

On July 19th 1917, at a meeting of the Reichstag in Berlin, a Peace Resolution was passed urging the government to work for a peace by agreement and a permanent reconciliation with no territorial acquisitions by Germany. But the German Chancellor chose to ignore the resolution.The next day the Kaiser vowed to destroy Britain's world domination.

The Russian Desertions

On the Eastern Front there were almost two million deserters by the beginning of May, yet the provisional government persisted in trying to carry on the war. Advances were made against Austrian and German forces, but on July 19th the Russian army went into sudden retreat with tens of thousands of soldiers running away.

On November 8th Lenin, now the new leader of Russia as a result of the Bolshevik Revolution, read out the Decree of Peace. Russia was effectively out of the war, and appealed to all nations to end the fighting. On December 15th agreement was reached between Bolsheviks, Turks, Romanians, Austrians and Germans and all fighting on the Eastern Front ended. Germany was now free to transfer tens of thousands of men and weapons to fight in France.

1   *The First World War – An Illustrated History*, A J P Taylor, p177.

The Italians

The Italians had fought and continued to fight with enormous courage and determination against the Austrians, but in early October, 1917, 70,000 Italian troops deserted.

The Canadians

The Canadians are famous for their heroism and success on the Western Front. In October and November of 1917 313,934 Canadians had been conscripted to fight in France. Of these 313,376 applied for exemption from service.

The English

No significant protest ever occurred on the Western Front, but there were problems back in England. A wave of strikes broke out. The winter of 1917/18 was very severe, and the effects of German submarines in sinking the food supplies coming to Britain were felt by everyone. For the rich there were higher prices: for the poor there was hunger and malnutrition. There were serious fuel shortages, too. Munitions workers in Barrow-in-Furnace went on strike in March. By May there were strikes in forty-eight towns with two hundred thousand workers on strike. Leaders of the strikes were imprisoned. Concessions were made. Eventually rationing was brought in. Full co-operation returned. – The strikes had not been against the war, but about the unequal way hardships were being shared.[1]

Lloyd George, who, in December 1916, had taken over from Asquith as Prime Minister had always been unhappy about Haig's great attacks on the Western Front. As 1917 came to a close he decided there should be no more grand attempts to break the German line in 1918. It was not simply the poets who protested at the slaughter. Lloyd George spoke of "stopping the useless waste of life in attacks in the West," and he and his cabinet decided to retain in England 607,000 available trained "A" category men to frustrate Haig's plans for further offensive actions. – They allowed him only 100,000 men to replace some of his losses. [2] – Winston Churchill, who was Minister of Munitions, wrote on December 29th, "Thank God our offensives are at an end. Let them traipse across the crater fields. Let them rejoice in the occasional placeless names and the sterile ridges."

1   Bourne, p209.
2   *Britain and her Army*, Correlli Barnett, p405, and Martin Gilbert, p384, 389.

The great majority of English still believed that the fight to beat the Germans must go on.

The Germans

In April 1917 300,000 workers went on strike in Berlin demanding higher wages and something better than starvation-level food rationing.

In July 1917 a mutiny broke out in the German navy. Men were arrested and imprisoned. Sympathy strikes took place. After trials two men were sentenced to death.

Bigger strikes
Strikes, far bigger than the strikes of April 1917, broke out in January 1918. Four hundred thousand workers went on strike in Berlin and half a million other workers joined them in the rest of Germany. Strikers protested about the war and starvation – people were now eating cats and dogs. Many strikers were drafted into the army. Martial law was declared. The strikes crumbled but the Government was losing its grip. Revolution was under way.

In the army
By August 1918 almost the entire German army was beginning to lose hope. Soldiers were conscious that their supply of fresh strong troops had dried up; they struggled to work and fight on rations that were very poor; and they believed that the Allies were daily increasing in strength. Many German soldiers refused to continue to fight. There were mass surrenders.

Further mutinies in the navy
Orders were given on 27th October 1918 to the German fleet to set sail to confront the British at sea. Many crews refused to put to sea, and those that did so soon returned.

In the end the revolt spread from the navy and army to industrial works and so helped to put an end to the war.

WILFRED OWEN'S PSYCHOLOGICAL JOURNEY

For most of the time he was in the army Wilfred Owen lived and fought as an outsider. By his upbringing, character, religion and philosophy he was totally unsuited to the role of a soldier. He was shy, unoffensive, bookish, introverted, unworldly, sensitive, caring and deeply Christian.

He tried conscientiously to do his duty and play his part. The action he saw and the experiences he had were about as extreme and traumatic as any experienced by other soldiers on the Western Front.

Shortly after Owen had been declared unfit for service because of his shell-shock he reflected in great anguish on the teachings of Christ which he and others were so blatantly ignoring. He wrote to his mother, describing himself as "a conscientious objector with a very seared conscience." [1]

In August in Craiglockhart War Hospital he came under the influence of Sassoon who had just made his famous protest. Owen, too, wanted to make his protest, yet he couldn't identify with pacifists. His principles were locked into conflict. His role as a soldier, and patriot demanded one thing: as a Christian, another. Knowing and believing Christ's teaching, with absolute clarity, he felt compelled to act in complete contradiction to his convictions. The psychological conflict within him could hardly have been greater.

In a letter in October 1917 he asserted, "I hate washy pacifists . . ." And then, echoing Sassoon's example, "Therefore I feel that I must first get some reputation for gallantry before I could successfully and usefully declare my principles."

In his poetry – even if he had not consciously acknowledged this in his time at the front line – he was now expressing the soldier's loss of moral feeling.

> Merry it was to laugh there –
> Where death becomes absurd and life absurder.
> For power was on us as we slashed bones bare
> Not to feel sickness or remorse of murder.

These lines are from *Apologia Pro Poemate Meo* which Owen wrote in October and November of 1917. In this same period he also wrote a more extended account of the soldier's loss of feelings in *Insensibility* which he worked on between October 1917 and January 1918: "Their senses in some scorching cautery of battle now long since ironed, can laugh among the dying unconcerned."

By April 1918 he had taken another crucial decision. He had decided to turn his back on life. Talking to his brother whilst home on leave he

---

1   For further details, see his letter to his mother, May 1917, printed on page 147.

said that he wanted to return to the front line. "I know I shall be killed. But it's the only place I can make my protest from." [1]

In July, encouraged by Robert Ross (best known as a friend and supporter of Oscar Wilde) and the poet, Osbert Sitwell, Owen began to plan a volume of his poems. For it he wrote his first quick, half-thought-out draft of a preface. Some idea of his thoughts about his role may be gleaned from this.

> Above all I am not concerned with Poetry.
>
> My subject is War, and the pity of War.
>
> The Poetry is in the pity.
>
> Yet these elegies are to this generation in no sense consolatory. They may be to the next. All a poet can do today is warn. That is why the true Poets must be truthful.

On 26th August he was declared fit for front line action and instructed to embark for France. He wrote to Sassoon, "Everything is clear now; and I am in hasty retreat towards the Front." Retreat from life, perhaps, or from himself.

Having joined the Manchesters close to the front line near Amien on 13th September his fear was beginning to show. He wrote to Sassoon, pathetically blaming him for his predicament.

> You said it would be a good thing for my poetry if I went back. That is my consolation for feeling a fool.
>
> This is what the shells scream at me every time: "Haven't you got the wits to keep out of this?"

Late afternoon on 1st October, and on through the night, the 96th Brigade of the Manchesters went into action near the villages of Joncourt and Sequehart, six miles north of St Quentin. There was "savage hand-to-hand fighting." At first the Germans were driven back, but they made repeated counter-attacks. Owen threw himself into his task. He wrote to his mother,

> I lost all my earthly faculties, and I fought like an angel . . . I captured a German Machine Gun and scores of prisoners . . I only shot one man with my revolver . . . My nerves are in perfect order.

---

1   Harold Owen, *Journey from Obscurity,* Volume III, p162, 163.

The psychological change in Owen's personality was now definitely confirmed in action. Before this time we do not know what attempts, if any, he made to kill the enemy. His identification with soldiers and the soldiers' role, and his abandonment of his Christian principles, was now complete. Showing his habitual concern for his mother's feelings he implied that he had killed only one man, but the citation accompanying the Military Cross which he was awarded for his actions that night make it clear that he used the machine gun to kill a large number of men. "He personally manipulated a captured machine gun in   an   isolated   position and inflicted considerable losses on the enemy. Throughout he behaved most gallantly."

He now rationalised his motives. In part, he was thinking as a soldier. Forgetting that he had been ordered there, he wrote,

> I came out in order to help these boys – directly by leading them as well as an officer can . . .

and then he added an idea which had long been with him, seeing himself once again as an outsider to the soldier's role,

> indirectly, by watching their sufferings that I may speak of them as well as a pleader can.

By killing men he crossed a moral divide between the good and the damned, and in so doing, surrendered his personality to the moral-numbness of front-line soldiers. The real Wilfred Owen no longer ex-isted. The Wilfred Owen who entered the war was dead. His behaviour was no longer the expression of his own will: he was part of a fighting brotherhood, a killing machine. He was impervious to fear, had no sen-sitivity. He had no self-regard, no self-respect – no self to lose.

From now on his behaviour could be totally reckless being sufficiently rewarded by surges of adrenalin and a sense of heart-warming cama-raderie. He wrote to his mother again on 8th October telling her this story of the aftermath of the battle when his company was still sur-rounded by the enemy.

> All one day we could not move from a small trench, though hour by hour the wounded were groaning just outside. Three stretcher bearers who got up were hit, one after one. I had to order no-one to show himself after that, but remembering my own duty. . . I scrambled out myself and felt an exhilaration in baffling the Machine Guns by quick bounds from cover to cover. After the shells we had been through, and the gas, bullets were like the gentle rain from heaven . . . Must write now to hosts of parents of Missing, etc . . .

Writing of the battle to Sassoon on 10th October he said, "I cannot say I suffered anything; having let my brain grow dull . . . My senses are charred."

Owen knew that the war was nearing its end. The Germans were in full retreat. The British soldiers were welcomed with joyful gratitude by the French, and he was really enjoying himself being part of a band of soldiers. In his last letter to his mother, written on 31st October, he describes the maty atmosphere in his billets, "The Smoky Cellar of Forester's House." Conditions were so cramped that he could hardly write for pokes, nudges and jolts. The room was dense with smoke. His cook was chopping wood and an old soldier peeled potatoes and dropped them in a pot splashing Owen's hand as he did so. It was a scene of perfect soldierly brotherhood, and Owen remarks on his lack of sensitivity to danger.

> It is a great life. I am more oblivious than alas! yourself, dear Mother, of the ghastly glimmering of the guns outside, and the hollow crashing of the shells.
>
> There is no danger down here, or if any, it will be well over before you read these lines.
>
> I hope you are as warm as I am; as serene in your room as I am here . . . Of this I am certain: you could not be visited by a band of friends half so fine as surround me here.
>
> Ever Wilfred x

His mind was now perfectly prepared for his final action. There were now no crucial military objectives, yet the crossing of the seventy feet wide Sambre and Oise Canal, just south of the tiny village of Ors was treated as such. The Germans held the east bank, and were well de-fended with machine guns. At 5.45 on the morning of 4th November, under a hail of machine gun fire, the Royal Engineers attempted to con-struct an instant bridge out of wire-linked floats so that Owen's brigade and 15th and 16th Lancashire Fusiliers could cross and destroy or cap-ture the enemy. Group after group of soldiers went forward and were killed or wounded. Wilfred Owen, standing at the water's edge, was encouraging his men when he was hit and killed.

Seven days later the war was over. Church bells rang throughout the country. As they were ringing in Shrewsbury, Susan and Tom Owen received the telegram announcing their son's death.

INSENSIBILITY

Happy are men who yet before they are killed
Can let their veins run cold,
Whom no compassion fleers
Or makes their feet
Sore on the alleys cobbled with their brothers.
The front line withers.
But they are troops who fade, not flowers,
For poets' tearful fooling:
Men, gaps for filling:
Losses, who might have fought
Longer; but no one bothers.

And some cease feeling
Even themselves or for themselves.
Dullness best solves the tease and doubt of shelling,
And Chance's strange arithmetic
Comes simpler than the reckoning of their shilling.
They keep no check on armies' decimation.

Happy are these who lose imagination:
They have enough to carry with amunition.
Their spirit drags no pack.
Their old wounds, save with cold, can not more ache.
Having seen all things red,
Their eyes are rid
Of the hurt of the colour of blood for ever.
And terror's first constriction over,
Their hearts remain small-drawn.
Their senses in some scorching cautery of battle
Now long since ironed,
Can laugh among the dying, unconcerned.

Happy the soldier home, with not a notion
How somewhere, every dawn, some men attack,
And many sighs are drained.
Happy the lad whose mind was never trained:
His days are worth forgetting more than not.
He sings along the march
Which we march taciturn, because of dusk,
The long, forlorn, relentless trend
From larger day to huger night.

We wise, who with a thought besmirch
Blood over all our soul,
How should we see our task
But through his blunt and lashless eyes?
Alive, he is not vital overmuch;

Dying, not mortal overmuch;
Nor sad, nor proud,
Nor curious at all.
He cannot tell
Old men's placidity from his.

But cursed are dullards whom no cannon stuns,
That they should be as stones.
Wretched are they, and mean
With paucity that never was simplicity.
By choice they made themselves immune
To pity and whatever moans in man
Before the last sea and the hapless stars;
Whatever mourns when many leave these shores:
Whatever shares
The eternal reciprocity of tears.

Wilfred Owen, October-November 1917

THE NEXT WAR

> War's a joke for me and you,
> While we know such dreams are true.
> Siegfried Sassoon

Out there we walked quite friendly up to Death, –
Sat down and ate beside him, cool and bland, –
Pardoned his spilling mess-tins in our hand.
We've sniffed the thick green odour of his breath, –
Our eyes wept, but our courage didn't writhe.
He's spat at us with bullets, and he's coughed
Shrapnel. We chorussed if he sang aloft,
We whistled while he shaved us with his scythe.

Oh, Death was never enemy of ours!
We laughed at him, we leagued with him, old chum.
No soldier's paid to kick against His powers.
We laughed, – knowing that better men would come,
And greater wars: when every fighter brags
He fights on Death, for lives; not men, for flags.

Wilfred Owen
Written in Craiglockhart War Hospital in late September
1917

10

THE END

The war came to an end when men refused to fight.

Attempts to achieve peace through negotiation before 1918 came to nothing. The Germans were determined to keep all the territory they had occupied. The Allies were equally determined that Germany should gain nothing by her aggression and that her military power should be totally crushed so that she would never fight again.

IT MIGHT HAVE ENDED IN SEPTEMBER, 1914

Peace proposals were discussed before the war started, and in the early days of the war President Woodrow Wilson of the United States was busy trying to find a peace formula. The newspaper the *Evening World*, published in New York on 17th September 1914, carried a stunning report, "based on the highest diplomatic authority," on the Kaiser's response to Wilson. The Kaiser appears, in these remarks to be a man of wisdom and vision, proposing a settlement remarkably close to that eventually agreed after over four years of warfare.

The Kaiser's main points:

Germany would not stop fighting so long as Britain continued daily to declare that the war must be a fight to the finish, until Germany had been crushed.

If the world at large hoped for disarmament then the crushing of Germans would be the poorest way to accomplish it: a crushed Germany would "repeat the era after the Napoleonic wars and arm every man, child, cat and dog in the Empire for the day of revenge."

Germany was willing to call the war a draw [!]. If this were agreed it would be the most conducive solution towards future peace in Europe and to disarmament. Complete victory on either side would not lead to stable conditions.

Germany would not agree to being dismembered. The German colonies might be discussed.

Germany's borders must not be interfered with by surrounding states. "Every man in the German Empire believes sincerely and honestly to-day that the war is one of self-defence against the hostile encroachment of Russia, France and England. Live and let live is the policy that Germany wishes its enemies to observe."[1]

AMERICAN PEACE MOVES

In November 1917 President Wilson put forward a proposal for a negotiated peace settlement. Only the ageing Emperor of Austria expressed interest in the idea, but unfortunately he died before the month was out.

In December Wilson invited the nations involved in the war to state their aims as a basis for negotiation. Politicians did not wish to be wholly frank on this matter and in the case of the Germans they would say nothing of their aims.

Wilson's significant move came on 8th January 1918 when he issued his fourteen point peace plan which included Germany returning all captured Russian territory, returning and restoring Belgium, and returning the area of Alsace and Lorraine which Germany seized in 1871. National armaments of all countries would be reduced to a minimum. National groups, including the Poles, would have self-determination. A "general association of nations" would be set up to safeguard the independence of all nations, great and small.

TURNING POINT

On 8th August, 1918, the German armies near Amien were suddenly turned back by Australian, Canadian, British and French troops. From then on they were in continual retreat and their faith in their ability to win the war was shattered. German soldiers refused to advance. There were mass surrenders. The German High Command was in a state of shock, and a new spirit of confidence began to develop in the Allied armies.

1   *Evening World*, New York, 17 September, 1914.

DEFEAT OF THE REBELS

The enemy forces are in wild flight.
Poor souls (you say), they were intoxicated
With rhetoric and banners, thought it enough
To believe and to blow trumpets, to wear
That menacing lie in their shakos.*

Enough: it falls to us to shoot them down,
The incorrigibles and cowards,
Where they shiver behind rocks or in ditches
Seek graves that have no headstones to them –
Such prisoners were unprofitable.

Now as our vanguard, pressing on,
Dislodges them from village and town,
Who yelling abandon packs and cloaks,
Their arms and even the day's rations,
We are not abashed by victory,

We raise no pitying monument
To check the counter-stroke of fortune.
These are not spoils: we recognize
Our own strewn gear, that never had been robbed
But for our sloth and hesitancy.

Robert Graves

* shakos – tall military headgear

The situation as seen by a German soldier

Our lines are falling back. There are too many fresh English
and American regiments over there. There's too much corned
beef and white wheaten bread. Too many new guns. Too many
aeroplanes.

But we are emaciated and starved. Our food is bad and mixed
up with so much substitute stuff that it makes us ill. The factory
owners in Germany have grown wealthy; – dysentry dissolves
our bowels. The latrine poles are always densely crowded; the
people at home ought to be shown these grey, yellow, miserable, wasted faces here, these silent figures from whose bodies
the colic wrings out the blood. . .

Our artillery is fired out, it has too few shells and the barrels are
so worn that they shoot uncertainly, and scatter so widely as even
to fall on ourselves. We have too few horses. Our fresh

troops are anaemic boys in need of rest, who cannot carry a pack, but merely know how to die. By thousands. . .

The summer of 1918 is the most bloody and the most terrible. The days stand like angels in blue and gold, incomprehensible, above the ring of annihilation. Every man here knows we are losing the war. Not much is said about it, we are falling back, we will not be able to attack again after this big offensive, we have no more men and no more ammunition.

Still the campaign goes on – the dying goes on –

Summer of 1918 – Never has life in its niggardliness seemed to us so desirable as now; – the red poppies in the meadows round our billets, the smooth beetles on the blades of grass, the warm evenings in the cool, dim rooms, the black, mysterious trees of the twilight, the stars and the flowing waters, dreams and long sleep – O Life, life, life!

Summer of 1918 – Never was so much silently suffered as in the moment when we depart once again for the front line. Wild, tormenting horrors of an armistice and peace are in the air, they lay hold on our hearts and make the return to the front harder than ever. . .

Summer of 1918 – Breath of hope that sweeps over the scorched fields, raging fever of impatience, of disappointment, of the most agonizing terror of death, insensate question: Why? Why do they make an end? And why do these rumours of an end fly about?

*   *   *

There are so many airmen here, and they are so sure of themselves that they give chase to single individuals, just as though they were hares. For every one German plane there come at least five English and American. For one hungry, wretched German soldier come five of the enemy, fresh and fit. For one German army loaf there are fifty tins of canned beef over there. We are not beaten, for as soldiers we are better and more experienced; we are simply crushed and driven back by overwhelming superior forces.

Behind us lay rainy weeks – grey sky, grey fluid earth, grey dying. If we go out, the rain at once soaks through our overcoat and clothing; – and we remain wet all the time we are in the line. We never get dry. Those who will wear high boots tie sand bags round the tops so that the mud does not pour in so fast. The rifles are caked, the uniforms caked, everything is fluid and dissolved, the earth, one dripping, soaked, oily mass in which lie yellow pools with red spiral streams of blood and into which the dead, wounded, and survivors slowly sink down.

The storm lashes us, out of the confusion of grey and yellow the hail of splinters whips forth the childlike cries of the wounded, and in the night shattered life groans painfully into silence.

Our hands are earth, our bodies clay and our eyes pools of rain. We do not know whether we still live.

Erich Maria Remarque in *All Quiet on the Western Front*. [1]

THE BRITISH PREPARE FOR VICTORY

WHAT'S THE USE OF WORRYING?

What's the use of worrying?
It never was worth while,
So pack up your troubles
In your old kit bag
And smile, smile, smile.

Popular soldier's song of the First World War

SMILE, SMILE, SMILE

Head to limp head, the sunk-eyed wounded scanned
Yesterday's *Mail*; the casualties (typed small)
And (large) Vast Booty from our Latest Haul.
Also, they read of Cheap Homes, not yet planned,
"For," said the paper, "when this war is done
The men's first instincts will be making homes.
Meanwhile their foremost need is aerodromes,
It being certain war has but begun.
Peace would do wrong to our undying dead, –
The sons we offered might regret they died
If we got nothing lasting in their stead.
We must be solidly indemnified.
Though all be worthy Victory which all bought,
We rulers sitting in this ancient spot
Would wrong our very selves if we forgot
The greatest glory will be theirs who fought,
Who kept this nation in integrity."

1   p 182-185.

Nation? – The half-limbed readers did not chafe
But smiled at one another curiously
Like secret men who know their secret safe.
(This is the thing they know and never speak,
That England one by one had fled to France,
Not many elsewhere now, save under France.)
Pictures of these broad smiles appear each week,
And people in whose voice real feeling rings
Say: How they smile! They're happy now, poor things.

Wilfred Owen, late September 1918.

GERMAN ARMY BELIEVED THE WAR WAS UNWINNABLE

On 29th September General Erich von Ludendorff, Second in Command of the German armies insisted there must be an immediate armistice, and on 12th October the German Government stated their acceptance of President Wilson's demands that they withdraw from France and Belgium. However, Field Marshal Paul Hindenburg, Chief of the German armies, declared that military success would improve the terms of an armistice. The German armies must fight on. – Very often they did so, inflicting heavy losses, but on October 17 British forces took Lille without firing a single shot.

Within the Austro-Hungarian Empire, during October 1918, national groups asserted their independence. Poland, Czechoslovakia, and Yugoslavia came into being

When, on 23rd October, the Italian and British armies advanced against Austro-Hungarian forces, the Austro-Hungarians deserted in huge numbers and returned home. The power of the Hapsburg Dynasty was gone for ever. Emperor Charles and his advisers knew they could not continue the war.

German forces, against this background, and in the face of continuing hunger and defeats against Allied forces in Northern France, doubted they could go on much longer. They knew that their enemy's armies were being reinforced with a steady flow of battle-fresh soldiers, the Americans. (In fact, the Americans were arriving at the rate of 10,000 per day.) The Germans had few reserves. – They did not know how doubtful the Allies were of sustaining their attack; nor how the Americans, in spite of significant success, were having problems with as many as 100,000 soldiers straggling behind their front lines where they should have been fighting; nor how ignorant the Allies were of the German weakness.

Further mutinies, protests, surrenders

On the same day that the the German fleet in Wilhelmshaven ceased to respond to orders (27th October 1918) Emperor Charles of Austria, after two of his divisions had refused to counter-attack against the Italians, telegraphed the Kaiser, "My people are neither capable nor willing to continue the war. I have made an unalterable decision to ask for a separate peace and an immediate armistice." [1]

On 30th October a German division on the Western Front refused to go forward and fight.

On the streets of Berlin people were calling for the German monarchy to be abolished. When the Kaiser was told of the demands on 1st November he said, "I wouldn't dream of abandoning the throne because of a few hundred Jews and a thousand workers."

On 2nd November the Hungarians declared themselves an independent nation.

On 3rd November, in Kiel, 3000 German sailors and workers raised the red flag of revolution. In the next two days they were joined by 20,000 soldiers and other sailors from Kiel, Bremen, Cuxhaven and Wilhelmshaven. Thousands travelled to Berlin and soldiers refused to fire on the rebels. – The Austrians signed an armistice.

When the Socialists in the Reichstag demanded the Kaiser's resignation, and he refused, they resigned and called for a general strike throughout Germany. More cities were flying the rebel flag. The will of the people had changed. They no longer submitted to the demands of their leaders; and this attitude continued to develop on the battlefield with disastrous effects.

In the one hundred days from the beginning of August the British, Canadian and other Dominion forces, together with the Belgian, French and American armies took 363,000 German prisoners and 6,400 guns – "a quarter of the German army in the field and half of all its guns." [2]

The Kaiser wanted to fight on. His military leaders said it was impossible. There was no hope of victory and it was senseless to sacrifice the lives of German soldiers when there could be no benefit. They refused to obey his orders. On 10th November the Kaiser left Germany, ignominiously, for neutral Holland.

1   *First World War,* Martin Gilbert, p485.
2   Martin Gilbert, p499.

Although in retreat in Belgium and France, the German army continued
to fight and never surrendered. Armistice negotiations were taking place
in a railway carriage in the forest of Compiègne. An armistice was
signed at ten past five in the morning of 11th November. The leading
German delegate, Mathias Erzberger said, "A nation of 70 million
suffers, but does not die."

Many German soldiers were disappointed when orders came to end
the fighting at 11 o'clock on the morning of 11th November, 1918.

VICTORY!

Even at the end, there was little sense of reality. The war had been a medieval battle,
and peace was an angel. – *Punch* cartoon, 20th November 1918.

ARMISTICE

NIGHTFALL

Hooded in angry mist, the sun goes down:
Steel-grey the clouds roll out across the sea:
Is this a kingdom? Then give Death the crown,
For here no emperor hath won, save He.

Herbert Asquith

THE END

After the blast of lightning from the east,
The flourish of loud clouds, the Chariot Throne;
After the drums of time have rolled and ceased,
And by the bronze west long retreat is blown,
Shall life renew these bodies? Of a truth,
All death will he annul, all tears assuage?
Or fill these void veins full again with youth,
And wash, with an immortal water, age?

When I do ask white Age, he saith not so:
"My head hangs weighed with snow."
And when I hearken to the Earth, she saith:
"My fiery heart shrinks, aching. It is death.
Mine ancient scars shall not be glorified,
Nor my titanic tears, the seas, be dried."

Wilfred Owen
Late 1916, with revisions October 1917 - January 1918

THE END

Round the great ruins crawl those things of slime;
Green ruins, lichenous and scarred by moss –
An evil lichen that proclaims world doom,
Like blood dried brown upon a dead man's face.
And nothing moves save those monstrosities,
Armoured and grey, and of a monster size.

But now, a thing passed through the cloying air
With flap and clatter of its scaly wings –
As if the whole world echoed from some storm.
One scarce could see it in the dim, green light
Till suddenly it swooped and made a dart

And brushed away one of those things of slime,
Just as a hawk might sweep upon its prey.

It seems as if the light grows dimmer yet —
No radiance from the dreadful green above,
Only a lustrous light or iridescence
As if from off a carrion-fly — surrounds
That vegetation which is never touched
By any breeze. The air is thick, and brings
The tainted, subtle sweetness of decay.
Where, yonder, lies the noisome river-course,
There shows a faintly phosphorescent glow.
Long writhing bodies fall and twist and rise,
And one can hear them playing in the mud.

Upon the ruined walls there gleam and shine
The track of those grey, vast monstrosities —
As some gigantic snail had crawled along.

All round the shining bushes waver lines
Suggesting shadows, slight and grey, but full
Of that which makes one nigh to death from fear.

Watch how those awful shadows culminate
And dance in one long wish to hurt the world.

A world that now is past all agony.

Osbert Sitwell

HOSPITAL SANCTUARY

When you have lost your all in a world's upheaval,
Suffered and prayed, and found your prayers were vain,
When love is dead, and hope has no renewal —
These need you still; come back to them again.

When the sad days bring you the loss of all ambition,
And pride is gone that gave you strength to bear,
When dreams are shattered, and broken is all decision -
Turn you to these, dependent on your care.

They too have fathomed the depths of human anguish,
Seen all that counted flung like chaff away;
The dim abodes of pain wherein they languish
Offer that peace for which at last you pray.

Vera Brittain,   September 1918

'AND THERE WAS A GREAT CALM'
(On the signing of the Armistice, November 11, 1918)

There had been years of Passion — scorching, cold,
And much Despair, and Anger heaving high,
Care whitely watching, Sorrows manifold,
Among the young, among the weak and old,
And the pensive Spirit of Pity whispered, "Why?"

Men had not paused to answer. Foes distraught
Pierced the thinned peoples in a brute-like blindness,
Philosophies that sages long had taught,
And Selflessness, were as an unknown thought,
And "Hell!" and "Shell!" were yapped at Lovingkindness.

The feeble folk at home had grown full-used
To "dug-outs," "snipers," "Huns," from the war-adept
In the mornings heard, and at evetides perused;
To day-dreamt men in millions, when they mused —
To nightmare-men in millions when they slept.

Waking to wish existence timeless, null,
Sirius they watched above where armies fell;
He seemed to check his flapping when, in the lull
Of night a boom came thencewise, like the dull
Plunge of a stone dropped into some deep well.

So when old hopes that earth was bettering slowly
Were dead and damned, there sounded, "War is done!"
One morrow. Said the bereft, and meek, and lowly,
"Will men some day be given to grace? yea, wholly,
And in good sooth, as our dreams used to run?"

Breathless they paused. Out there men raised their glance
To where had stood those poplars lank and lopped,
As they had raised it through the four years' dance
Of Death in the now familiar flats of France;
And murmured, "Strange, this! How? All firing stopped?"

Aye; all was hushed. The about-to-fire fired not,
The aimed-at moved away in trance-lipped song.
One checkless regiment slung a clinching shot
And turned. The Spirit of Irony smirked out "What?
Spoil peradventures woven of Rage and Wrong?"

Thenceforth no flying fires inflamed the grey,
No hurtlings shook the dewdrop from the thorn,
No moan perplexed the mute bird on the spray;

Worn horses mused: "We are not whipped to-day;"
No weft-winged engines blurred the moon's thin horn.

Calm fell. From Heaven distilled a clemency;
There was peace on earth, and silence in the sky;
Some could, some could not, shake off misery:
The Sinister Spirit sneered: "It had to be!"
And again the Spirit of Pity whispered, 'Why?'

Thomas Hardy, first published 11 November 1920

Terms of the Armistice

In 1914 George Bernard Shaw had warned, "Unless we are all prepared to fight Militarism at home as well as abroad, the cessation of hostilities will last only until the belligerents have recovered from their exhaustion."

By the terms of the armistice Germany agreed:

– to remove all troops and personnel from: Belgium, France, Luxembourg, Alsace, and Lorraine

– to remove all troops in the east that occupied Russia; to restore eastern frontiers to their 1914 status

– to return all prisoners and deported civilians from these areas

– to hand over their means of making war, including, 5,000 heavy guns, 25,000 machine guns, 1,700 aeroplanes, 5,000 railway engines, 150,000 railway wagons,   5,000 lorries, 10 battleships, and all their submarines

– to make good all damage and loss in Belgium and northern France.

PARIS, NOVEMBER 11, 1918
For G. A. H.

Down on the boulevards the crowds went by,
The shouting and the singing died away,
And in the quiet we rose to drink the toasts,
Our hearts uplifted to the hour, the Day:
The King – the Army – Navy – the Allies –
England – and Victory.

And then you turned to me and with low voice
(The tables were abuzz with revelry),
"I have a toast for you and me," you said,
And whispered "Absent," and we drank
Our unforgotten Dead.
But I saw Love go lonely down the years,
And when I drank, the wine was salt with tears.

May Wedderburn Cannan, first published 1919

ARMISTICE DAY, 1918

What's all this hubbub and yelling,
Commotion and scamper of feet,
With ear-splitting clatter of kettles and cans,
Wild laughter down Mafeking Street?

O, those are the kids whom we fought for
(You might think they'd been scoffing our rum)
With flags that they waved when we marched off to
war
In rapture of bugle and drum.

Now they'll hang Kaiser Bill from a lamp-post,
Von Tirpitz they'll hang from a tree . . .
We've been promised a "Land Fit for Heroes" --
What heroes we heroes must be!

And the guns that we took from the Fritzes,
That we paid for with rivers of blood,
Look, they're hauling them down to Old Battersea
Bridge
Where they'll topple them, souse, in the mud!

But there's old men and women in corners
With tears falling fast on their cheeks,
There's the armless and legless and sightless –
It's seldom that one of them speaks.

And there's flappers gone drunk and indecent
Their skirts kilted up to the thigh,
The constables lifting no hand in reproof
And the chaplain averting his eye . . .

When the days of rejoicing are over,
When the flags are stowed safely away,
They will dream of another wild "War to End Wars"
And another wild Armistice day.

But the boys who were killed in the trenches,
Who fought with no rage and no rant,
We left them stretched out on their pallets of mud
Low down with the worm and the ant.

Robert Graves, 1918

In November came the Armistice. . .   Armisitice-night hysteria
did not touch our camp much, though some of the Canadians
stationed there went down to Rhyl to celebrate in true overseas
style. The news sent me out walking alone along the dyke
above the marshes of Rhuddlan (an ancient battlefield, the Flod-
den of Wales), cursing and sobbing and thinking of the dead.

Robert Graves, *Goodbye to All That*

Hysteria swept the country. There was little sign of magnanimity in
victory: instead a mood of ruthless revenge. Countless public meetings were held at which the most popular cries were, "Make Germany
pay!" and "Hang the Kaiser!"

Armistice Celebrations in London
The revelry in Piccadilly Circus, as seen by the *Punch* artist, J H Dowd. –
Punch, 20th November 1918.

Vera Brittain recorded that night after night young people danced frantically at the Grafton Galleries while pictures of the Canadian soldiers' wartime agony hung accusingly on the walls. She said that it was these "nocturnal orgies" which shocked Alfred Noyes into writing *The Victory Ball.*

Victory Ball

> The older generation held up outraged hands in horror at such sacrilege, not understanding that reckless sense of combined release and anti-climax which set my contemporaries, who had lived a life-time of love and toil and suffering and yet were only in their early twenties, dancing in the vain hope of recapturing the lost youth that the world had stolen.
>
> Not having anyone left with whom to dance, I spent most of the bland and rather frightening days . . . roaming about London.

Vera Brittain [1]

THE VICTORY BALL

The cymbals crash,
And the dancers walk,
With long silk stockings
And arms of chalk,
Butterfly skirts,
And white breasts bare,
And shadows of dead men
Watching 'em there.

Shadows of dead men
Stand by the wall,
Watching the fun
Of the Victory Ball.
They do not reproach,
Because they know,
If they're forgotten,
It's better so.

Under the dancing
Feet are the graves.
Dazzle and motley,
In long white waves,
Brushed by the palm-fronds
Grapple and Whirl
Ox-eyed matron,
And slim white girl.

Fat wet bodies
Go waddling by,
Girdled in satin,
Though God knows why;
Gripped by satyrs
In white and black,
With a fat wet hand
On the fat wet back.

---

1   *Testament of Youth*, p469.

See, there is one child
Fresh from school,
Learning the ropes
As the old hands rule.
God, how the dead men
Chuckle again,
As she begs for a dose
Of the best cocaine.

"What do you think
We should find," said the shade,
"When the last shot echoed
And peace was made?"
"Christ," laughed the fleshless
Jaws of his friend,
"I thought they'd be praying
For worlds to mend,

Making earth better
Or something silly,
Like whitewashing hell
Or Piccadilly.
They've a sense of humour,

These women of ours,
Thes exquisite lilies,
These fresh young flowers!"

"Pish," said a statesman
Standing near,
I'm glad they keep busy
Their thoughts elsewhere!
We mustn't reproach 'em.
They're young, you see."
"Ah," said the dead men,
"So were we!"

Victory! Victory!
On with the dance!
Back to the jungle
The new beasts prance!
God, how the dead men
Grin by the wall,
Watching the fun
Of the Victory Ball.

Alfred Noyes

WHAT HAD BEEN ACHIEVED?

AN IMPERIAL ELEGY

Not one corner of a foreign field
But a span as wide as Europe;
An appearance of a Titan's grave,
And the length thereof a thousand miles.
It crossed all Europe like a mystic road,
Or as the Spirits' Pathway lieth on the night.
And I heard a voice crying,
This is the Path of Glory.

Wilfred Owen
September1915 - May 1916

Human failure

Ten million soldiers dead. Perhaps twenty million maimed. Perhaps twenty million children without fathers. Perhaps thirty million families bereaved, handicapped, distressed as a direct result of the fighting. Thousands of homes destroyed, land ruined. Mass deportation into slavery. Hundreds of thousands dead of starvation. One million Armenians massacred by the Turks. Triumph no-where. Human dignity, self-respect; torn to pieces. A monumental failure for mankind – a failure to speak and listen, to find common ground, to negotiate. A futile, illogical and mindless reliance on the use of force which dev-astated the user and victim alike, illustrating the fact that no other spe-cies is capable of causing horror and distress on such a scale. Man had created powers that collectively he had neither the intelligence nor the morality to control. Man had released a genie. – The signifi-cance of human foolishness and aggression had been hugely mag-nified by the technological powers at his disposal – military, scientific, and the media. The need for wisdom in national leaders became important as never before.

The century of war

More than a hundred million people died in wars in the twentieth cen-tury. The twentieth century was the century of war; and the First World War was merely an overture. Yet those who ordered their nations into action, and less still, those who so willingly obeyed the call to war had no clear concept of what it was meant to achieve. They fought for crudely nationalistic and personal reasons.

Once the British people had committed themselves to war to save Bel-gium (and Britain) from the German invasion they accepted extensions of the war without a murmur of protest. They found themselves fighting and dying in other parts of the world for reasons that probably made little sense. Britain declared war on Austria-Hungary, an Empire with whom we had no quarrel, on 12th August 1914, and on Turkey on 6th November. British troops fought in Africa, Palestine and Italy. No-one seemed to question this, yet tens of thousands died in these periph-eral wars.

Belgium

And did they save Belgium? Or did Belgium save France and Britain by absorbing the speed and force of the German attack?

At the end of the war her independence was restored, but only after she had first been devastated. Within weeks of marching into this neu-tral country savage reprisals had taken place against civilians who had attempted to harass the German forces. Scores of civilians including children, teenagers and old people had been rounded up and killed by firing squads. Villages, including churches, had been totally destroyed. Hostages had been seized by the German armies as a guarantee of "good behaviour" by Belgian communities. The Belgians were forced to pay for upkeep of the occupying forces.

Thousands fled the country. Seven hundred thousand men had been
deported to Germany as slave labourers. Famine had broken out which
had been relieved by charitable help from overseas – but even this
humanitarian aid had been less successful than it might because many
supply ships were sunk by German submarines. Hunger was everywhere. The birthrate fell by 75 per cent. The university city of Louvain
had been set on fire. The town of Ypres had been blasted to rubble.
Farmlands were ruined by trenches and shells.

Art treasures had been looted and shipped to Germany. Machinery
from factories was taken to Germany and what could not be moved
had been destroyed. Blast furnaces had been blown up; coal mines had
been flooded.

This was how the Allies saved Belgium, yet it was a basis for a
renewal of life. What would Belgium's fate have been without opposing
Germany?

The once magnificent centre of Ypres, with its cathedral and thirteenth century Cloth Hall
– 27th April 1918.

North Eastern France

This area suffered in ways similar to Belgium; four thousand and
twenty-two villages had been destroyed; twenty thousand factories had
been robbed of machinery and destroyed. In addition, hundreds of
thousands of acres of farmland, far more than in Belgium, had been

ravaged by trenches, shells, thousands of miles of barbed wire, the litter of corpses, the deadly debris of war. But for a time the enemy had been repulsed and the areas of Alsace-Lorraine returned to France after nearly fifty years of German occupation.

September 1918. A French farmer and his wife return to their home at Villers-Bretonneux, which was well away from the main area of the fighting.

Britain and the rest of Europe

Edward Grey's fear had been that if Germany won she would dominate France; that the independence of Belgium, Holland, Denmark, and perhaps Norway and Sweden would become "a mere shadow, a fiction," with all their labours at the disposal of a Germany that would dominate the whole of Western Europe; and this would be an intolerable situation for Britain.

It seemed that Edward Grey's war aims had been achieved. – The defence of Belgium and the crushing of militarism for ever was less successful.

America

America had wanted to remain neutral in the war, and was only reluctantly drawn in by the Allies. Her war dead were relatively few. The survivors returned home to ports devoid of cheering crowds. No-one knew of their courage or achievements. Yet America had been an important reason for the Allied victory. Furthermore it was President

Woodrow Wilson's 14 point plan which set the agenda for a peace settlement and which would have been more successful had it been interpreted in keeping with its spirit and clear intent.

America was strengthened by the war. It became the foremost world power.

The German perspective

> We cherish no illusions as to the extent of our defeat – the degree of our impotence. We know that the might of German arms is broken.

> Count Brockdorff-Rantzau,
> Head of German delegation at the Versailles Peace Conference.

The war continued after the signing of the armistice and the end to the fighting on 11th November. Britain continued to blockade German ports to stop food getting through. The belief and fear was that the Germans would revive to fight on or be able to weaken the punitive nature of the treaty which would be signed. The blockade, which had existed throughout most of the war, had helped to weaken and so defeat Germany. However, the blockade was not the sole reason for her food problems. These had been worse than Britain's partly as a result of her use of manpower. A far greater proportion of her workers worked in munitions and war related activities than in Britain and relatively fewer in agriculture.

Ultimately, it is believed, between half and three quarters of a million Germans died as a result of starvation brought about by the blockade. When, in the treaty negotiations that followed, Germany was branded as solely responsible for the war her representatives seized on the concept of "war guilt" and pointed to Britain's behaviour in continuing the blockade against a defenceless nation.

THE TREATY OF VERSAILLES – A PEACE TO END PEACE

In 1914 George Bernard Shaw anticipated the peace negotiations, and the claims and counter-claims of innocence and guilt.

> Neither England nor Germany must claim any moral superiority in the negotiations. Both were engaged for years in a race for armaments. Both indulged and still indulge in literary and oratorical provocation. Both claimed to be "an Imperial race" ruling other races by divine right. Both showed high social and political consideration to parties and individuals who openly

said that the war had to come. Both formed alliances to reinforce
them for that war. [1]

At Versailles Count Brockdorff-Rantzau, leader of the German team of
negotiators, said much the same thing, "During the last fifty years the
imperialism of all European states has chronically poisoned the international situation. The policy of retaliation and that of expansion, as
well as disregard of right of peoples to self-determination, contributed
to the disease of Europe, which reached its crisis in the world war."

Nevertheless, the victors unanimously agreed that Germany was
responsible for the war and because of this Germany was to pay for the
damage. This was an idea that had been stridently supported by the British press for years, especially the Northcliffe press which campaigned
for ever harsher treatment of Germany.   Rudyard Kipling had been an
early supporter of the punish-Germany faction in his self-pitying poem,
The Children. –   His only son had been killed in the Battle of Loos.

THE CHILDREN
("The Honours of War" – A Diversity of Creatures)

These were our children who died for our lands: they were dear in
our sight.
We have only the memory left of their home-treasured sayings and
laughter.
The price of our loss shall be paid to our hands, not another's
hereafter.
Neither the Alien nor Priest shall decide it. That is our right.
But who shall return us the children?

At the hour the Barbarian chose to disclose his pretences,
And raged against Man, they engaged , on the breasts that they bared
for us,
The first felon-stroke of the sword he had long-time prepared for us,
Their bodies were all our defence while we wrought our defences.

They bought us anew with their blood, forbearing to blame us,
Those hours which we had not made good when the Judgement
o'ercame us.

1   *Common Sense About the War*, supplement to New Statesman, 4 November,1914.

They believed us and perished for it. Our statecraft, our learning
Delivered them bound to the Pit and alive to the burning
Whither they mirthfully hastened as jostling for honour –
Not since her birth has our Earth seen such worth loosed upon her.

Nor was their agony brief, or once only imposed on them.
The wounded, the war-spent, the sick received no exemption:
Being cured they returned and endured and achieved our redemption,
Hopeless themselves of relief, till Death, marvelling, closed on
them.

That flesh we had nursed from the first in all cleanness was given
To corruption unveiled and assailed by the malice of Heaven –
By the heart-shaking jests of Decay where it lolled on the wires –
To be blanched or gay-painted by fumes – to be cindered by fires –
To be senselessly tossed and retossed in stale mutilation
From crater to crater. For this we shall take expiation.
But who shall return us our children?

Rudyard Kipling.
Written in 1917, when reparations were first discussed.

Public opinion in Britain and France fiercely supported Kipling's point
of view at the end of the war.

FOR THE APOSTLES OF "NO HUMILIATION"

(Certain people have proclaimed their opinion that the German nation ought
not to be humiliated.)

Rumours arrive as thick as swarming bees;
Our evening rags announce with raucous clamour
The latest wire, the semi-final wheeze
Transmitted by the fertile Rotterdammer,
Giving a local version
Of William Two's spontaneous dispersion.

They leave me cold. I care not how he pays
The heavy debt his deeds of wanton fury owe –
Whether he puts his orb to bed, or stays
On exhibition like an antique curio;
The reckoning we charge
Has to be settled by the Hun at large.

Here and elsewhere his advocates impute
Innocence to the Bosch – a gentle creature,
Too prone perhaps to lick the tyrant's boot,
But otherwise without a vicious feature;
They'd have our wrath abated;
Poor child, "he must not be humiliated."

Why not? Against his army's bestial crimes
He never lifted one protesting finger
The wrongs of Belgium drew his jocund rhymes;
Over the Hymn of Hate he loved to linger,
Pressing the forte pedal
And wore – for luck – the *Lusitania* medal.

He took a holiday for children slain,
And butchered women set his flags a-flutter;
Our drowning anguish served for light refrain
To beery patriots homing down the gutter;
On prisoners he spat,
The helpless ones, and thanked his Gott for that.

Had he but fought as decent nations fight,
Clean-handed, then we must have spared his honour;
But now, if Germany goes down in night,
'Tis he, not we, that puts that shame upon her,
Shame not of mere defeat,
But such that never our hands again can meet.

Why should his pride of race be spared a fall?
Let him go humble all his days for sentence.
Why pity him as just a Kaiser's thrall,
This beast at heart – though fear may fake repentance?
For me, when all is said,
I save my pity for the murdered dead

Owen Seaman.   Published in *Punch*, October 23, 1918.

Skin Germany Alive

> Saw Winston Churchill for a few minutes at the Ministry. Full
> of victory talk . . . One feels that England is going to increase
> in power enormously. They mean to skin Germany alive. "A
> peace to end peace!"

> Siegfried Sassoon, Diary, 6 November 1918

In Paris, the nucleus of a wild, international, pleasure-crazed crowd, the Big Four were making a desert and calling it peace. When I thought about these negotiations at all – which was only when I could not avoid hearing them discussed by Oxford dons or Kensington visitors – they did not represent at all the kind of "victory" that the young men whom I had loved would have regarded as sufficient justification for their lost lives. Although they would no doubt have welcomed the idea of a League of Nations, Roland and Edward certainly had not died in order that Clemenceau should outwit Lloyd George, and both of them bamboozle President Wilson, and all three combine to make the beaten, blockaded enemy pay the cost of the War. For me the "Huns" were then and always, the patient, stoical Germans whom I had nursed in France, and I did not like to read of them being deprived of their Navy, and their colonies, and their coal-fields in Alsace-Lorraine and the Saar Valley, while their children starved and froze for lack of food and fuel. So, when the text of the Treaty of Versailles was published in May, after I had returned to Oxford, I deliberately refrained from reading it; I was beginning already to suspect that my generation had been deceived, its young courage cynically exploited, its idealism betrayed, and I did not want to know the details of that betrayal.

Vera Brittain

The charge on Germany was set at £240,000,000,000, fifty-two percent to go to France, twenty two percent to Britain; ten percent to Italy, eight percent to Belgium, and eight per cent to the remaining Allies. Over the years the Germans succeeded in arguing the charge down. From 1923 to 1925 French tanks and troops occupied the Ruhr region of Germany because Germany had failed to keep up payments. The remaining payments were finally wiped out by the Treaty of Lausanne in 1932. Britain continued to settle her war debts with the USA, making the final payment in 1969.

At the Versailles conference the Germans had, at first, refused to sign the crippling and humiliating agreement. They were distressed by many of the articles in the two hundred page document. They bitterly resented the clause concerning the transfer of the three and a half-million German speaking population in Sudetenland to Polish rule.

In 1914, H G Wells, George Bernard Shaw, the Kaiser, and no doubt others, had warned that peace terms that were harshly punitive to Germany would provoke retaliation and revenge at the earliest opportunity. Of the big four who so disgusted Vera Britain, Lloyd George had tried in vain to soften the manifestly provocative terms being imposed on Germany. In proposals he put before the peace conference, the Fontainebleau Memorandum of March 1919, he asserted that:

You may strip Germany of her colonies, reduce her armaments to a mere police force and her navy to that of a fifth-rate power; all the same, in the end if she feels that she has been unjustly treated in the peace of 1919 she will find means of exacting retribution from her conquerors. The impression, the deep impression made upon the human heart by four years of unexampled slaughter will disappear with the hearts upon which it has been marked by the terrible sword of the great war.

The maintenance of peace will then depend on there being no causes of exasperation constantly stirring up either the spirit of patriotism, or justice or of fairplay. To achieve redress our terms may be severe, they may be stern and even ruthless, but at the same time they can be so just that the country upon which they are imposed will feel in its heart that it has no right to complain. But injustice, arrogance, displayed in the hour of triumph, will never be forgotten or forgiven.

For these reasons I am strongly averse to transferring more Germans from German rule to some other nation than can possibly be helped. I cannot conceive of a greater cause of a future war than that the German people, who certainly proved themselves one of the most vigorous and powerful nation's in the world, should be surrounded by a number of small states, many of them consisting of people who have never previously set up a stable government for themselves, but each of them containing large masses of Germans clamouring for re-union with their native land.[1]

The French accused Lloyd George of being an appeaser and with their friends over-ruled him. Lloyd George's voice could not hold back the tide of Allied opinion; it could not resist the pressure of press inspired opinion in Britain. He had been certain for a long time, not only that harshness would be counter-productive, but also that Germany was incapable of paying the astronomic sums of money being proposed. Ultimately Germany paid only approximately £2,500M. Had such a low figure been written into the treaty Lloyd George was certain that, "no Allied Ministry would have survived to sign it, for no Allied parliament at that time nor for several years afterwards would have sanctioned so low a figure."

The German delegation and Government were horrified by the treaty they were asked to sign. Only when threatened with an Allied inva-

---

1　From Lloyd George's summary in *The Truth About the Peace Treaties*. Gollancz, 1938.

sion of Germany did they, under protest, sign it. The German Government statement read,

> The Government of the German Republic has seen with consternation from the last communication of the Allied and Associated Governments, that the latter are resolved to wrest from Germany by sheer force even the acceptance of those conditions of peace which, though devoid of material significance, pursue the object of taking away its honour from the German people. The honour of the German people will remain untouched by any act of violence. The German people, after the frightful suffering of the last few years, lacks all means of defending its honour by external action. Yielding to overwhelming force, but without on that account abandoning its view in regard to the unheard of injustice in the conditions of peace the Government of the German Republic therefore declares that it is ready to accept and sign the conditions of peace imposed by the Allied and Associated Governments. [1]

It is strange that the Germans should complain about having things wrested from them by force; what did these innocents expect? – The real issue was the unacceptable nature of some of the treaty requirements which hurt and festered and were the seeds, as Lloyd George had foreseen, of the next war. – Germany had lost everything – except her will to survive, regenerate and assert herself again.

PEACE

I

I am as awful as my brother War,
I am the sudden silence after clamour.
I am the face that shows the seamy scar
When blood has lost its frenzy and its glamour.
Men in my pause shall know the cost at last
That is not to be paid in triumph or tears.
Men will begin to judge the thing that's past
As men will judge it in a hundred years.

Nations! whose ravenous engines must be fed
Endlessly with the father and the son,
My naked light upon your darkness, dread! –
By which ye shall behold what ye have done:
Whereon, more like a vulture than a dove,
Ye set my seal in hatred, not in love.

---

1   Quoted by Martin Gilbert, p517.

II

Let no man call me good. I am not blest.
My single virtue is the end of crimes.
I only am the period of unrest,
The ceasing of the horrors of the times;
My good is but the negative of ill,
Such ill as bends the spirit with despair,
Such ill as makes the nations' soul stand still
And freeze to stone beneath its Gorgon glare.

Be blunt, and say that peace is but a state
Wherein the active soul is free to move,
And nations only show as mean or great
According to the spirit then they prove. –
O which of ye whose battle-cry is Hate
Will first in peace dare shout the name of Love?

Eleanor Farjeon

How the press directed public opinion

> The Treaty of Versailles shocked me; it seemed destined to
> cause another war some day, yet nobody cared. While the
> most critical decisions were being taken in Paris, public inter-
> est concentrated entirely on three home-news items: Hawker's
> Atlantic flight and rescue; the marriage of England's reigning
> beauty, Lady Diana Manners; and a marvellous horse called The
> Panther – the Derby favourite, which came in nowhere.

Robert Graves [1]

MEMORIALS

Reburying the dead

For seven years after the war had ended, 5,000 men of the Imperial War
Graves Commission were employed in digging over the battlefields,
identifying the bodies where possible, and reburying the dead in more
than 2,000 British cemeteries – land given to Britain by the French
and Belgian Governments. – Today 500 gardeners still tend these
graves.

1   *Goodbye to All That*, p236.

Wherever the war had raged, and wherever soldiers had come from, memorials were erected. The largest memorials include the British at Thiepval in the Somme region, the Canadian at Vimy Ridge, near Arras, and the French at Douaumont near Verdun. At Ypres 54,896 names are inscribed on the massive Menin Gate memorial – the names of soldiers who died nearby but were not able to be identified. Yet the memorial proved too small. 34,984 names were left over. These were inscribed on a wall a few miles away at the British military cemetery at Tyne Cot, Passchendaele. The Menin Gate memorial was inaugurated by King Albert of the Belgians on 24th July 1927. The last post was sounded. Every evening since then and every evening "for all time" the last post will be sounded at the Menin Gate.

The Menin Gate Memorial, Ypres
Trumpeters sound the last post at 8pm, as they have done every evening since July 1927, and will do for all time.

ON PASSING THE NEW MENIN GATE

Who will remember, passing through this Gate,
The unheroic dead who fed the guns?
Who shall absolve the foulness of their fate, –
Those doomed, conscripted, unvictorious ones?
Crudely renewed, the Salient holds its own.
Paid are its dim defenders by this pomp;
Paid, with a pile of peace-complacent stone,
The armies who endured that sullen swamp.

Here was the world's worst wound. And here with pride
"Their name liveth for ever," the Gateway claims.
Was ever an immolation so belied
As these intolerably nameless names?
Well might the Dead who struggled in the slime
Rise and deride this sepulchre of crime.

Siegfried Sassoon

The Imperial War Graves Commission completed its task of cemetery building on 22nd July 1938. The Second World War began on 1st September 1939 when Germany invaded Poland to seize back Sudetenland.

Part of Tyne Cot Cemetery, Paschendaele –
11,908 graves and a wall of remembrance to 34,048 missing.

Near Verdun stands a grim tower, the Ossuary at Douaumont. The vaults beneath this tower contain the bones of 130,000 unidentified French and German soldiers who died nearby.

Today thousands of people visit the battlefield memorials in wonder and sadness at a human tragedy which casts its shadow over them, and which adds to their apprehension for the future of mankind.

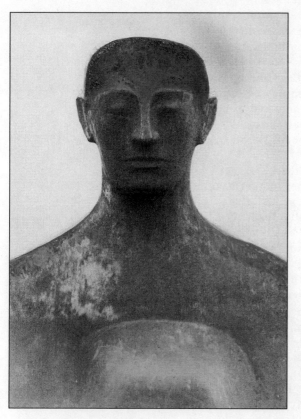

German Cemetery, Langemarck
One of four sculptures of German soldiers which stand as penitent sentinels on the edge of the cemetery.

RECONCILIATION

When you are standing at your hero's grave,
Or near some homeless village where he died,
Remember, through your heart's rekindling pride,
The German soldiers who were loyal and brave.

Men fought like brutes; and hideous things were done;
And you have nourished hatred harsh and blind.
But in that Golgotha perhaps you'll find
The mothers of the men who killed your son.

Siegfried Sassoon,   November 1918.

FORGOTTEN DEAD, I SALUTE YOU

Dawn has flashed up the startled skies,
Night has gone out beneath the hill
Many sweet times; before our eyes
Dawn makes and unmakes about us still
The magic that we call the rose.
The gentle history of the rain
Has been unfolded, traced and lost
By the sharp finger-tips of frost;
Birds in the hawthorn build again;
The hare makes soft her secret house;
The wind at tourney*comes and goes,
Spurring the green, unharnessed boughs;
The moon has waxed fierce and waned dim:
He knew the beauty of all those
Last year, and who remembers him?

Love sometimes walks the waters still,
Laughter throws back her radiant head;
Utterly beauty is not gone,
And wonder is not wholly dead.
The starry, mortal world rolls on;
Between sweet sounds and silences,
With new, strange wines her breakers brim:
He lost his heritage with these
Last year, and who remembers him?

None remember him: he lies
In earth of some strange-sounding place,
Nameless beneath the nameless skies,
The wind his only chant, the rain
The only tears upon his face;
Far and forgotten utterly
By living man. Yet such as he
Have made it possible and sure
For other lives to have, to be;
For men to sleep content, secure.
Lip touches lip and eyes meet eyes
Because his heart beats not again:
His rotting, fruitless body lies
That sons may grow from other men.

He gave, as Christ, the life he had –
The only life desired or known;
The great, sad sacrifice was made
For strangers; this forgotten dead
Went out into the night alone.
There was his body broken for you,

There was his blood divinely shed
That in the earth lie lost and dim.
Eat, drink, and often as you do,
For whom he died, remember him.

Muriel Stuart

* tourney –   a medieval tournament

Victory – an agonised cry – a French interpretation. Rodin's sculpture in a main street in Verdun.

GREAT MEN

The great ones of the earth
Approve, with smiles and bland salutes, the rage
And monstrous tyranny they have brought to birth.
The great ones of the earth
Are much concerned about the wars they wage,
And quite aware of what those wars are worth.

You Marshals, gilt and red,
You Ministers and Princes, and Great Men,
Why can't you keep your mouthings for the dead?
Go round the simple cemeteries; and then
Talk of our noble sacrifice and losses
To the wooden crosses.

Siegfried Sassoon

WHEN YOU SEE MILLIONS OF THE MOUTHLESS DEAD

When you see millions of the mouthless dead
Across your dreams in pale battalions go,
Say not soft things as other men have said,
That you'll remember. For you need not so.
Give them not praise. For, deaf, how should they know
It is not curses heaped on each gashed head?
Nor tears. Their blind eyes see not your tears flow.
Nor honour. It is easy to be dead.
Say only this, "They are dead." Then add thereto,
"Yet many a better one has died before."
Then, scanning all the o'ercrowded mass, should you
Perceive one face that you loved heretofore,
It is a spook. None wears the face you knew.
Great death has made all his for evermore.

Charles Sorley, September/October 1915

THE NEXT WAR

The long war had ended.
Its miseries had grown faded.
Deaf men became difficult to talk to,
Heroes became bores.
Those alchemists
Who had converted blood into gold
Had grown elderly.
But they held a meeting,
Saying,
"We think perhaps we ought
To put up tombs
Or erect altars
To those brave lads
Who were so willingly burnt,
Or blinded,
Or maimed,
Who lost all likeness to a living thing,
Or were blown to bleeding patches of flesh
For our sakes.
It would look well.
Or we might even educate the children."
But the richest of the wizards
Coughed gently;
And he said:
"I have always been to the front   –
In private enterprise.
I yield in public spirit

To no man.
I think yours is a very good idea –
A capital idea
And not too costly,
But it seems to me
That the cause for which we fought
Is again endangered.
What more fitting memorial for the fallen
Than that their children
Should fall for the same cause?"
Rushing eagerly into the street,
The kindly old gentlemen cried
To the young:
"Will you sacrifice
Through your lethargy
What your fathers died to gain?
The world *must* be made safe for the young!"

And the children
Went . . .

Osbert Sitwell, November 1918

HIGH WOOD

Ladies and gentlemen, this is High Wood,
Called by the French, Bois des Fourneaux,
The famous spot which in Nineteen-Sixteen,
July, August and September was the scene
Of long and bitterly contested strife,
By reason of its High commanding site.
Observe the effect of shell-fire in the trees
Standing and fallen; here is wire; this trench
For months inhabited, twelve times changed hands;
(They soon fall in), used later as a grave.
It has been said on good authority
That in the fighting for this patch of wood
Were killed somewhere above eight thousand men,
Of whom the greater part were buried here,
This mound on which you stand being . . .
                              Madame, please,

You are requested kindly not to touch
Or take away the Company's property
As souvenirs; you'll find we have on sale
A large variety, all guaranteed.
As I was saying, all is as it was.
This is an unknown British officer,

The tunic having lately rotted off.
Please follow me −   this way . . .
                the *path*, sir, *please.*

The ground which was secured at great expense
The Company keeps absolutely untouched,
And in that dug-out (genuine) we provide
Refreshments at a reasonable rate.
You are requested not to leave about
Paper, or ginger-beer bottles, or orange-peel,
There are waste-paper baskets at the gate.

Phillip Johnstone, 1918

Not High Wood, but there are many tours of the trenches available these days. Here are students from Ratcliffe College, Leicester, at Vimy Ridge near Arras on a sub-zero March afternoon.

MEMORIAL TABLET

Squire nagged and bullied till I went to fight,
(Under Lord Derby's Scheme). I died in hell -
(They called it Passchendaele). My wound was slight,
And I was hobbling back; and then a shell
Burst slick upon the duck-boards: so I fell
Into the bottomless mud, and lost the light.

At sermon-time, while Squire is in his pew,
He gives my gilded name a thoughtful stare;
For, though low down upon the list, I'm there;
"In proud and glorious memory" . . . that's my due
Two bleeding years I fought in France, for Squire:
I suffered anguish that he's never guessed.
Once I came home on leave: and then went west . .
What greater glory could a man desire?

Siegfried Sassoon, November 1918

Glory, honour, and courage

> I was always embarrassed by the words sacred, glorious, and
> sacrifice and the expression in vain. We heard them, sometimes
> standing in the rain almost out of earshot, so that only the shouted
> words came through, and had read them, on proclamations that
> were slapped up by billposters over other proclamations, now for
> a long time, and I had seen nothing sacred, and the things that
> were glorious had no glory and the sacrifices were like the dock-
> yards at Chicago if nothing was done with the meat except bury
> it. There were many words that you could not stand to hear and
> finally only the names of places had dignity . . . Abstract words
> such as glory, honour, courage, or hallow were obscene.

Ernest Hemingway [1]

Victory Crowns the Just

> Let all who trust justice to the arbitrament of war bear in mind
> that the issue may depend less on the righteousness of the cause
> than on the cunning and craft of the contestants. It is the teach-
> ing of history, and this war enforces the lesson. And the cost is
> prohibitive. It cripples all the litigants. The death of ten millions

---

1   Quoted by Peter Vansittart, *Voices of World War One*, p248.

and the mutilation of another twenty millions amongst the best young men of a generation is a terrible bill of costs to pay.

Lloyd George [1]

POETS WHO DIED IN THE WAR

Rupert Brooke − died 23rd April 1915 of blood poisoning following a mosquito bite. Age 28.

Julian Grenfell − died of wounds, 30th April 1915. Age 27.

Charles Hamilton Sorley −   killed 13th October 1915 in the Battle of Loos. Age 20.

Robert Palmer − killed 21st January, 1916, in Mesopotamia. Age 28.

William Noel Hodgson − killed 1st July 1916 on the first day of the Battle of the Somme. Age 23.

Alan Seeger − killed 4th July 1916 in the Battle of the Somme. Age 28.

Edward Wyndham Tennant − killed 22nd September 1916 in the Battle of the Somme. Age 19.

Arthur Graeme West − killed 3rd April 1917 by a sniper. Age 26.

Edward Thomas − killed 9th April 1917 in the Battle of Arras. Age 39.

Robert Ernest Vernède − killed 9th April, 1917 in an attack on Havrincourt Wood. Age 41.

Ewart Alan Mackintosh − killed 21st November, 1917 at Cambrai. Age 24.

John McCrae − died of pneumonia, 28th January, 1918. Age 46.

Isaac Rosenberg − killed 1st April 1918, on night patrol. Age 28.

Phillip Bainbrigge − killed 18th September, 1918. Age 27.

Wilfred Owen − killed 4th November, 1918. Age 25.

---

1   *War Memoirs*, Introduction, p ix.

THE KNIGHTED POETS

Owen Seaman   –   knighted 1914

Henry Newbolt   –   knighted 1915

William Watson   –   knighted 1917

John Galsworthy was offered a knighthood in 1918 but turned it down.

A P Herbert   –   knighted 1945

Herbert Read   –   knighted 1953

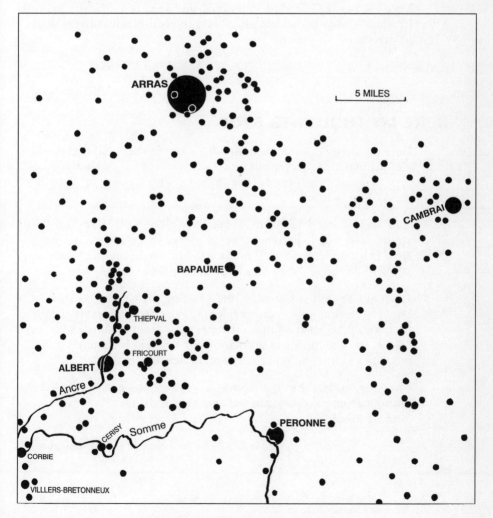

British Commonwealth Military Cemeteries.

11

AN ALIEN PEACE-TIME WORLD

Our power of feeling or caring beyond the immediate questions
of our own material well being is temporarily eclipsed . . . We
have been moved beyond endurance, and need rest. Never in the
lifetime of men now living has the universal element in the soul
of man burnt so dimly.

John Maynard Keynes [1]

HERE MY THOUGHTS STOP

Here my thoughts stop and will not go any farther. All that meets
me, all that floods over me are but feelings – greed of life,
love of home, yearning for the blood, intoxication of deliverance. But no aims.

Had we returned home in 1916, out of the suffering and the
strength of our experiences we might have unleashed a storm.
Now if we go back we will be weary, broken, burnt out, rootless,
and without hope. We will not be able to find our way any more.

It cannot be that it has gone, the yearning that makes our blood
unquiet, the unknown, the perplexing, the oncoming things, the
thousand faces of the future, the melodies from dreams and from
books, the whispers and divinations of women; it cannot be that
this has vanished in bombardment, in despair, in brothels.

I am very quiet. Let the months and years come, they can take
nothing from me, they can take nothing from me, they can take
nothing more.

Erich Maria Remarque [2]

1   Quoted by J M Roberts, *The Pelican History of the World*, p837.
2   *All Quiet on the Western Front,* p190.

Remarque had written his book, *All Quiet on the Western Front*, he said, "to tell of a generation of men who, even though they may have escaped its shells, were destroyed by the war."

A BETTER BRITAIN?

> The *Herald* spoiled our breakfast every morning. We read in it of unemployment all over the country due to the closing of munitions factories; of ex-service men refused reinstatement in the jobs they had left when war broke out, of market-rigging, lockouts, and abortive strikes. I began to hear news, too, of the penury to which my mother's relatives in Germany had been reduced, particularly the retired officials whose pensions, by the collapse of the mark, now amounted to only a few shillings a week. Nancy and I took all this to heart and called ourselves socialists.

> Robert Graves [1]

Generations Will Thank You

Field Marshal Earl Haig, having "won the war," became a national hero. He issued a statement thanking

> all ranks of the Army and non-combatant and auxiliary serv-ices, including the many thousands of women, who by devoted work in many capacities have assisted the victory of our arms so that generations of free people, both of your own race and all countries, will thank you for what you have done.

After the war he organised the Royal British Legion for the care and support of ex-servicemen. The poppies made by disabled ex-service-men carry, to this day, in their black centres the words "Haig Fund". When he died in 1928 huge crowds turned out to pay their respects at his lying in state in London and Edinburgh and at his funeral.

FOR A WAR MEMORIAL
Clifton College, 1914 - 1918

> From the Great Marshal to the last recruit
> These, Clifton, were thyself, thy spirit in deed,
> Thy flower of chivalry, thy fallen fruit
> And thine immortal seed.

Henry Newbolt

[1]   *Goodbye to All That*, p236.

With Mr Punch's grateful compliments to Field Marshal, Sir Douglas Haig. – Punch magazine's interpretation of the soldiers' view of Field Marshal Sir Douglas Haig, 27th November 1918.

A SHORT POEM FOR ARMISTICE DAY

Gather to take fierce degree
trim the lamp set out for sea
here we are at the workmen's entrance
clock in and shed your eminence.

Notwithstanding, work it diverse ways
work it diverse days, multiplying four digestions
here we make artificial flowers
of paper tin and metal thread.

One eye one leg one arm one lung
a syncopated sick heart-beat
the record is not nearly worn
that weaves a background to our work.

I have no power therefore have patience
These flowers have no sweet scent
no lustre in the petal no increase
from fertilising flies and bees.

No seed they have no seed
their tendrils are of wire and grip
the buttonhole the lip
and never fade

And will not fade though life
and lustre go in genuine flowers
and men like flowers are cut
and wither on a stem

And will not fade a year or more
I stuck one in a candlestick
and there it clings about the socket
I have no power therefore have patience.

Herbert Read

A DEAD STATESMAN

I could not dig: I dared not rob:
Therefore I lied to please the mob.
Now all my lies are proved untrue
And I must face the men I slew.
What tale shall serve me here among
Mine angry and defrauded young?

Rudyard Kipling

THE LAMENT OF THE DEMOBILISED

"Four years," some say consolingly. "Oh well,
What's that? You're young. And then it must have been
A very fine experience for you!"
And they forget
How others stayed behind and just got on –
Got on the better since we were away.
And we came home and found
They had achieved, and men revered their names,
But never mentioned ours;
And no one talked heroics now, and we
Must just go back and start again once more.

"You threw four years into the melting-pot –
Did you indeed!" these others cry. "Oh well,
The more fool you!"
And we're beginning to agree with them.

Vera Brittain

PRAEMATURI

When men are old, and their friends die,
They are not so sad,
Because their love is running slow,
And cannot spring from the wound with so sharp a
pain;
And they are happy with many memories,
And only a little while to be alone.

But we are young, and our friends are dead
Suddenly, and our quick love is torn in two;
So our memories are only hopes that came to
nothing.
We are left alone like old men; we should be dead –
But there are years and years in which we shall still
be young.

Margaret Postgate Cole

POETS AFTER THE WAR

Robert Graves

Not only did I have no experience of independent civilian life,
having gone straight from school into the army: I was still
mentally and nervously organized for war. Shells used to come
bursting on my bed at midnight, even though Nancy shared it
with me; strangers in daytime would assume the faces of friends
who had been killed. When strong enough to climb the hill behind
Harlech and revisit my favourite country, I could not help seeing it as a prospective battlefield.

I knew it would be years before I could face anything but a quiet
country life. My disabilities were many: I could not use a telephone, I felt sick every time I travelled by train, and to see more
than two new people in a single day prevented me from sleeping.
I felt ashamed of myself as a drag on Nancy, but had sworn on

the very day of my demobilisation never to be under anyone's orders for the rest of my life. Somehow I must live by writing.

Graves's marriage broke up. He quarrelled with all his friends, lived in self-imposed exile in Majorca, and had a strangely subservient fourteen year relationship with Laura Riding, married a second time and in all fathered eight children. In his later years he formed romantic attachments to a succession of women much younger than himself, his "muses" who inspired some of his celebrated love poetry. He wrote prolifically and successfully, lectured in Britain and America, and appeared on television.

As he lapsed into senility in the last ten years of his life, before he lost the power of speech, he talked often of the war. He was haunted by what he had done. He told everyone that he had murdered a lot of men.

Edmund Blunden

Gentle is what he seemed, but underneath he was troubled, a victim of frequent bouts of depression relieved by mad flurries of work as well as recourse to the bottle. His experience as a sensitive young infantry officer in the Great War haunted him all his life.

At the beginning of the Second World War he declared, "I still regard murder as murder no matter how boldly hidden up in steel helmets and rolls of honour."

Paul Fussell[1]

Ivor Gurney

Wounds, the effects of gassing, and shell-shock put Ivor Gurney in hospital. On 19th June 1918 he planned to commit suicide and wrote a suicide letter explaining his motive - "because I am afraid of slipping down and becoming a mere wreck." He didn't go through with it. The next day he admitted that he had "lost courage."

After the war he returned to study at the Royal College of Music. He was a talented composer. But, he suffered from depression and paranoia and was soon committed to mental hospital where he lived for the rest of his life. In 1926 he was "convinced he was being tortured by machines passing electrical currents through the ceiling and floor of his hospital room. In 1931 he believed he was being similarly persecuted by wireless speakers."[2] Believing the war was still going on and that he was fighting in it he continued to write poems about his experiences.

1 Writing in *The Sunday Times*, 2 December 1990.
2 James Methven, *The Ivor Gurney Society Journal*, 2000.

Siegfried Sassoon

After the war Sassoon became literary editor of the *Daily Herald* - the only paper which criticised the Versailles Treaty (according to Robert Graves). He dabbled in radical politics, dined out on his fame, and returned to his golf and his hunting. His chief task, however, was the writing of six volumes of autobiography which was the major task of his life, (although he maintained that his real biography was his poetry). But his mind was stuck in the war and he never wrote about the period of his life after 1920.

He married quite late in life, and had one son, George. His spiritual searchings led him in 1957 to become a Roman Catholic.

Herbert Read

During the war I used to feel that . . . comradeship which had developed among us would lead to some new social movement when peace came. I used to imagine an international party of ex-combatants, united by their common suffering, who would turn against the politicians and the profiteers in every country, and create a new order based on respect for the individual human being. But no such party came into existence. The war ended in despair in Germany, in silly jubilation in England, and in an ineffective spirit of retribution in France. The societies of ex-combatants that were formed in England devoted themselves either to jingo heartiness or to the organisation of charitable benefits. We left the war as we entered it: dazed, indifferent, incapable of any creative action. We had acquired only one new quality: exhaustion . . .

The political situation of 1919 offered no basis for allegiance or enthusiasm. The political parties were all in the hands of non-combatants, especially on the left; and deep within me was a feeling that I simply could not speak to such people, much less cooperate with them. It was not that I despised them: I even envied them. But between us was a dark screen of horror and violation: the knowledge of the reality of war. Across that screen I could not communicate. Nor could any of my friends who had had the same experience. We could only stand on one side, like exiles in a strange country.[1]

1   *Annals of Innocence and Experience.*

Vera Brittain

Her years as a nurse in military hospitals, and even more, the loss of her fiancé, brother and close friend left Vera Brittain in a state of shock. For eighteen months she felt close to mental breakdown.

> Only gradually did I realise that the War had condemned me to live to the end of my days in a world without confidence or security, a world in which every dear personal relationship would be fearfully cherished under the shadow of apprehension; in which love would seem threatened perpetually by death, and happiness appear a house without duration, built upon the shifting sands of chance.   I might, perhaps, have it again, but never should I hold it . . .

> After the first dismayed sense of isolation in an alien peace-time world, such rationality as I still possessed reasserted itself in a desire to understand how the whole calamity had happened, to know why it had been possible for me and my contemporaries, through our own ignorance and others' ingenuity, to be used, hypnotised and slaughtered. I had begun, I thought by feeling exasperated about the War, and I went on by ignoring it; then I had to accept it as a fact, and at last was forced to take part in it, to endure the fear and sorrow and fatigue that it brought me, and to witness in impotent anguish the deaths, not only of those who had made my personal life, but of the many brave, uncomplaining men whom I had nursed and could not save. But even that isn't enough. It's my job, now, to find out all about it, and try to prevent it, in so far as one person can, from happening to other people in days to come. Perhaps the careful study of man's past will explain to me much that seems inexplicable in this disconcerting present. Perhaps the means of salvation are already there, implicit in history, unadvertised, carefully concealed by the war-mongers, only awaiting rediscovery to be acknowledged with enthusiasm by all thinking men and women.

Vera Brittain [1]

Wilfred Owen

In the corner of a meadow, up a quiet lane, just north of the sleepy village of Ors in northern France lies the village cemetery. Within the cemetery, separated by a small hedge, is a tiny plot of land, one of the

---

[1]   *Testament of Youth,* p471.

smallest British military cemeteries in France. In the corner of this, third grave from the left, lies Wilfred Owen.

At the time of his death Owen was unknown to the general public, only five of his poems having been published in his lifetime. His work, when it began to be published, was derided by the literary lions of the day. It took many years for his stature as a poet to be recognised.

The first Wilfred Owen poems to be printed after his death appeared in the Sitwells' magazine *Wheels* published in 1919. The first edition of his poems appeared in 1920, edited nominally by Sassoon, with most of the work being done by Edith Sitwell. It contained just twenty three of his poems.

> Owen, and the rest of the broken men who rail at the old men who sent the young to die: they suffered cruelly, but in the nerves and not in the heart. – They haven't the experience or the imagi- nation to know the extreme of human agony . . . I don't think these shell-shocked war poems will move our grandchildren greatly – there's nothing fundamental or final about them.

Sir Henry Newbolt, in a letter to Lady Hylton, 2nd August 1924 [1]

Edmund Blunden's edition of 1931 contained fifty-nine poems.

By 1932 Owen was still not given even a mention in the *Oxford Com- panion to English Literature.*

> Wilfred Owen I consider unworthy of the poet's corner of a country newspaper . . . He is all blood, dirt and sucked sugar stick . . .

W B Yeats, in a letter to Dorothy Wellesley, 21st December 1936 [2]

> I have a distaste for certain poems written in the midst of the great war; they are in all the anthologies . . . I have rejected these poems . . . passive suffering is not a theme for poetry.

W B Yeats,
Introduction to The Oxford Book of Modern Verse, 1936

In 1963 C Day Lewis collected eighty of Owen's poems, and in 1983 came the definitive collection of all of Owen's poetic writing – 177 poems and fragments – edited and annotated by the poet and scholar, Jon Stallworthy.

1   *The Later Life and Letters of Sir Henry Newbolt,* edited by Margaret Newbolt, p 314.
2   *The Letters of W B Yeats,* edited by Allan Wade, p 874.

Today, Owen's reputation as a poet rests on his war poetry alone: one of the greatest poets in the English language.

The grave of
Wilfred Owen –
in the village cemetery, in
the corner of a field near
Ors, north eastern France,
not far from the border with
Belgium.

LATE DOUBTS ABOUT THE WAR

H G Wells, assessing his early First World War writing[1]

> I was intensely indignant at the militant drive in Germany . . .
> I shouted various newspaper articles of an extremely belligerent
> type . . . My own behaviour in 1914-15 is an excellent example
> of . . . the general inability to realise that a "sovereign state" is
> essentially and incurably a war-making state . . . The fount
> of sanguine exhortation in me swamped my warier disposition
> towards critical analysis and swept me along.

1   *Experiment in Autobiography.*

THE WARNINGS OF HISTORY

> The historian's rightful task is to distil experience for future
> generations, not to distill it like a drug. Having fulfilled his task
> to the best of his ability, and honesty, he has fulfilled his purpose.
> He would be a rash optimist if he believed that the next genera-
> tion would trouble to absorb the warning. History at least teaches
> the historian a lesson.
>
> Basil Liddell Hart, 1930 [1]

AN END OF DREAMS

**The Dada Movement, Anti-War, Anti-political, Art, and Gestures,
Protests from the Cabaret Voltaire, Zurich** (sic)

> No more painters, no more writers, no more musicians, no
> more sculptors, no more religions, no more republicans, no more
> royalists, no more imperialists, no more anarchists, no more
> socialists, no more bolsheviks, no more proletariat, no more
> democrats, no more bourgeois, no more aristocrats, no more
> weapons, no more police, no more countries, enough of all these
> imbecilities, no more of anything, nothing, nothing, nothing.
>
> Tristan Tzara, in the Manifesto of the Dada Movement [2]

TO A CONSCRIPT OF 1940

Qui n'a pas une fois désespéré de l'honneur, ne sera jamais un héros.
Georges Bernanos

A soldier passed me in the freshly fallen snow,
His footsteps muffled, his face unearthly grey;
And my heart gave a sudden leap
As I gazed on a ghost of five-and-twenty years ago.

I shouted Halt! and my voice had the old accustomed ring
And he obeyed it as it was obeyed
In the shrouded days when I too was one
Of an army of young men marching

1   *History of the First World War*, Preface.
2   Quoted by Peter Vansittart, *Voices from the Great War*, p99.

Into the unknown. He turned towards me and I said;
"I am one of those who went before you
Five-and-twenty years ago; one of the many who never returned,
Of the many who returned and yet were dead.

We went where you are going, into the rain and the mud;
We fought as you will fight
With death and darkness and despair;
We gave what you will give our brains and our blood.

We think we gave in vain. The world was not renewed.
There was hope in the homestead and anger in the streets,
But the old world was restored and we returned
To the dreary field and workshop, and the immemorial feud

Of rich and poor. Our victory was our defeat.
Power was retained where power had been misused
And youth was left to sweep away
The ashes that the fires had strewn beneath our feet.

But one thing we learned: there is no glory in the dead
Until the soldier wears a badge of tarnish'd braid;
There are heroes who have heard the rally and have seen
The glitter of garland round their head.

Theirs is the hollow victory. They are deceived.
But you, my brother and my ghost, if you can go
Knowing that there is no reward, no certain use
In all your sacrifice, then honour is reprieved.

To fight without hope is to fight with grace,
The self reconstructed, the false heart repaired."
Then I turned with a smile, and he answered my salute
As he stood against the fretted hedge, which was like white lace.

Herbert Read

OLIVER SINGING

Oliver's singing
Comes down to my study,
As I sit in the twilight
Poring the problem
Of this old battered planet,
This universe tragical,
Bloodily twirling.

Nearly all his small span
And through both of his birthdays
This senseless hell-fury,
This horror has hurtled,
Yet he lies in his cot,
Happy, sleepy and singing.

Thus – I muse – at the core
Of our battered old planet,
Something young and untainted,
Something gay and undaunted,
Like a bud in its whiteness
Like a bird in its joy,
Through the foul-smelling darkness,
Through the muck and the slaughter,
Pushes steadily forward,
Singing.

Israel Zangwill

Refugee children with a British soldier, near Tournai, 26 October, 1918.

WE ARE GETTING TO THE END

We are getting to the end of visioning
The impossible within this universe,
Such as that better whiles may follow worse,
And that our race may mend by reasoning.

We know that even as larks in cages sing
Unthoughtful of deliverance from the curse
That holds them lifelong in a latticed hearse,
We ply spasmodically our pleasuring.

And that when nations set them to lay waste
Their neighbours' heritage by foot and horse,
And hack their pleasant plains in festering seams,
They may again, – not warely, or from taste,
But tickled mad by some demonic force. –
Yes. We are getting to the end of dreams!

Thomas Hardy [1]

STRANGE MEETING

It seemed that out of battle I escaped
Down some profound dull tunnel, long since scooped
Through granites which titanic wars had groined.

Yet also there encumbered sleepers groaned,
Too fast in thought or death to be bestirred.
Then, as I probed them, one sprang up, and stared
With piteous recognition in fixed eyes,
Lifting distressful hands, as if to bless.
And by his smile, I knew that sullen hall, –
By his dead smile I knew we stood in Hell.

With a thousand pains that vision's face was grained;
Yet no blood reached there from the upper ground,
And no guns thumped, or down the flues made moan.
"Strange friend," I said, "here is no cause to mourn."
"None," said that other, "save the undone years,
The hopelessness. Whatever hope is yours,
Was my life also; I went hunting wild
After the wildest beauty in the world,
Which lies not calm in eyes, or braided hair,

---

[1]   One of Hardy's last poems.

But mocks the steady running of the hour,
And if it grieves, grieves richlier than here.
For by my glee might many men have laughed,
And of my weeping something had been left,
Which must die now. I mean the truth untold,
The pity of war, the pity war distilled.
Now men will go content with what we spoiled,
Or, discontent, boil bloody, and be spilled.
They will be swift with swiftness of the tigress.
None will break ranks, though nations trek from progress.
Courage was mine, and I had mystery,
Wisdom was mine, and I had mastery:
To miss the march of this retreating world
Into vain citadels that are not walled.
Then, when much blood had clogged their chariot-wheels,
I would go up and wash them from sweet wells,
Even with truths that lie too deep for taint.
I would have poured my spirit without stint
But not through wounds; not on the cess of war.
Foreheads of men have bled where no wounds were.

I am the enemy you killed, my friend.
I knew you in this dark; for so you frowned
Yesterday through me as you jabbed and killed.
I parried; but my hands were loath and cold.
Let us sleep now . . ."

Wilfred Owen   The Sambre Canal near Ors, where Wilfred Owen was
                               killed by machine gun fire on 4th November,1918.

BRIEF LIVES

POETS AND OTHER WRITERS

RICHARD ALDINGTON, 1892-1962.

Imagist poet, novelist and biographer, educated at Dover College and London University. Married Hilda Doolittle in 1913. Volunteered in 1914, but rejected on medical grounds. Accepted into army in June 1916. Friend of D H Lawrence. He suffered from gas and shell-shock. His celebrated war novel is *Death of a Hero* (1929).

HERBERT ASQUITH, 1881-1947.

Son of Henry Asquith, Prime Minister 1908-1916. Educated Winchester and Balliol College, Oxford. Captain in the Royal Artillery. Three brothers served in the army; Raymond was killed in 1916.

PHILLIP BAINBRIGGE, 1891-1918.

Educated at Eton and Trinity College, Cambridge. He was a teacher at Shrewsbury School till March 1917. Killed on 18th September, 1918.

HAROLD BEGBIE, 1871-1929.

Journalist and verse writer. Sent by the *Daily Chronicle* to America in 1914 to speak on the British view of the war.

ARNOLD ENOCH BENNETT, 1867-1931.

Prolific and financially very successful novelist, short-story writer, playwright, journalist and war-time propagandist. Began his working career as a solicitor working in his father's office in Hanley, Staffordshire. He became a friend of Lord Beaverbrook. He was active in propaganda work for the Government from the start of the war, eventually being put in charge of propaganda to France and finally becoming overall Director of Propaganda. His best known novels include *Anna of the Five Towns* (1902), *The Old Wive's Tale* (1908), *Clayhanger* (1910).

LAURENCE BINYON, 1869-1943.

Poet and Art Historian. He was born in Lancaster and educated at Trinity College, Oxford. He worked in the British Museum for forty years from 1893 with a brief spell in France working as a stretcher-bearer. His famous poem, *For the Fallen,* was written in the first weeks of the war. It is quoted every year in Remembrance Day Services throughout Britain.

EDMUND BLUNDEN, 1896-1974.

Born in Yalding, Kent and educated at Christ's Hospital School, then situated in London. He went directly from school into the army (in 1915) joining the Royal Sussex Regiment. He fought near Béthune and in the Battle of the Somme before moving to Ypres. He was gassed during the war and this had a permanent effect on his health. He was awarded the Military Cross. The majority of Blunden's war poems were written in the 1920's and published 1925 and 1928.

After the war he had a successful academic and literary career. He was Professor of Poetry, Oxford University 1966-1968.

BEATRIX BRICE-MILLER,

Accompanied the British Expeditionary Force at the start of the war.

ROBERT SEYMOUR BRIDGES, 1844-1930.

Poet, dramatist and critic. He was born in Walmer, Kent and educated at Eton and Corpus Christi College, Oxford. He practiced as a doctor until he was thirty-seven. He became Poet Laureate in 1913. In September 1914 he wrote a letter to *The Times* justifying the war as a "holy war" a "fight of good against evil". His verse, at this time, was imbued with the same vehement feeling. He worked for the Secret Bureau for Propaganda.

VERA MARY BRITTAIN, 1893-1970.

Born in Newcastle under Lyme, Staffordshire, and grew up in Macclesfield and Buxton.

Her *Testament of Youth* is one of the outstanding biographies of the First World War. She felt compelled to play a part, and worked as a VAD nurse in England, France (where her first task was looking after wounded German prisoners) and Malta. She was moved to the verge of a nervous breakdown by her experiences in the war and the loss of a close friend, her fiancé and brother. She wrote her *Testament of Youth* to record the effect of the war on her generation. Her interest in politics sprang from a desire to understand the causes of the war which, in turn, she hoped might help to prevent a recurrence of such a human catastrophe. She continued her biography in *Testament of Experience*.

As a pacifist, supporter of the League of Nations, and feminist she wrote prolifically and lectured in Britain, the USA and Canada.

RUPERT CHAWNER BROOKE, 1887-1915.

Georgian poet. Born at Rugby. Educated at Rugby School and King's College, Cambridge. He was an atheist and active Socialist. He was a friend of Edward Marsh and worked with him to prepare and promote the first *Georgian Anthology* of poetry. After travelling in Germany, and, following his nervous breakdown he went on a long tour to recuperate, taking in the USA, Canada, Honolulu, Samoa, Fiji, New Zealand, and Tahiti. – After hesitation about what course of action to take at the start of the First World War he joined the navy. He was a witness at the siege of Antwerp before writing his famous set of five sonnets called *1914*. Though he had seen the devastation and suffering created by the war he kept it all at an emotional distance from himself, denying the realities of war. He had a deeply confused personality – given to both ecstatic enthusiasm and suicidal doubt. Following a mosquito bite he died of acute blood poisoning on board ship on his way to Gallipoli, and was buried on the Greek Island of Skyros.

CLAUDE BURTON

Worked for Lord Northcliffe on *The Evening News* and *Daily Mail*. It is claimed that he wrote over 10,000 poems.

MARY WEDDERBURN CANNAN, 1893-1973.

Poet, journalist and librarian. Born in Oxford. Educated at Wychwood School. Worked as a VAD nurse before and during the war. She also worked for the Intelligence Service.

MARY POSTGATE COLE, 1893-1980.

Socialist writer on politics. Author of detective novels. Educated at Roedean, and Girton College, Cambridge.

EDWARD ESTLIN CUMMINGS, 1894-1962.

Born in Cambridge, Massachusetts. Educated at Harvard. Joined the American volunteer ambulance corps in France before the US entered the war. In 1917 he was imprisoned on suspicion (unfounded) of writing treasonable correspondence. He wrote several volumes of verse in which he delighted in his eccentric style and lack of punctuation, celebrating individualism and mocking the conventional.

WALTER DE LA MARE, 1873-1956.

Poet, novelist, short-story writer and author of children's books. Educated at St Paul's Cathedral Choristers School. Worked in the oil industry until he was thirty-five. A contributor to Georgian poetry anthologies. His poem, *The Listeners*, (1912) was one of the most popular poems in a 1995 BBC poll to discover "Britain's favourite poem." – A beneficiary of Rupert Brooke's will.

GEOFFREY DEARMER, 1893-

The last surviving English war poet – still alive and well (January 1996) and living in Kent. – He fought at Gallipoli, where his brother was killed, and on the Western Front. After the war he wrote poetry, plays, and novels. For a time he worked as a censor of plays presented on the London stage. He spent many years working for the BBC mainly as a contributor to, and director of, children's programmes.

EVA DOBELL, 1867-1963.

Born Cheltenham. Worked as a nurse during the war. Committed conservationist.

PARKE FARLEY
American contributor to *Poetry* magazine, Chicago.

ELEANOR FARJEON, 1881-1965.
Born in London. Well known as an author of children's stories. She was a close personal friend of Helen and Edward Thomas in the last few years of his life. She loved Edward, but knew that expressing her feelings to him would mean the immediate end of their friendship. They often visited each other and went on long country walks together. She typed his poems for him and submitted them, on his behalf, under the pseudonym of Edward Eastaway, to various publications. – Helen was aware of Eleanor's feelings towards Edward and was perfectly content with the situation, believing that it might help to make Edward a little happier.

FRANK STEWART FLINT, 1885-1960.
He served in the army in England for eleven months of the war. An imagist poet, and translator.

JOHN FREEMAN, 1880-1929.
Born in Dalton, Middlesex, he worked in the insurance business all his life but also published poetry and journalism.

FORD MADOX FORD, 1873-1939.
Born in Merton, Surrey. Educated University College School, London. Changed his name from Ford Hermann Hueffer. He served in the infantry during the war in the Royal Welch Regiment and was gassed. He wrote prolifically – novels and biography as well as being an imagist poet. He founded and edited *The English Review*, and later in Paris, *The Transatlantic Review*. His novels include *The Good Soldier* (1915) and *Parade's End, a war tetralogy, 1924-1928*.

GILBERT FRANKAU, 1884-1952.
Educated at Eton. Worked in the family tobacco business. Best-selling novelist *(World Without End*, 1943). Volunteered at the start of the war. He fought at Loos, Ypres and on the Somme. In spite of the bitter tone of some of his poetry he was an intense patriot and supporter of the war throughout. – At his own request, perhaps realising that he could not suppress the trauma much longer, he was transferred from the front line to staff work at the end of 1916 – propaganda in Italy. His brother, Jack, was killed in November 1917. He was invalided out of the war in February 1918 with shell-shock. – He served in the RAF as a Squadron Leader in World War II. – He married three times.

JOHN GALSWORTHY, 1867-1933.
Born Combe, Surrey. Educated at Harrow, and New College, Oxford. Very successful novelist and playwright. A deeply caring man, and social reformer. Nobel Prize for Literature, 1932.

HEATHCOTE WILLIAM GARROD, 1878-1960.
Worked in the Ministry of Munitions 1915 - 1918. Oxford Professor of Poetry 1923 - 1928.

JAMES LOUIS GARVIN, 1868-1947
Born in Birmingham. As a very influential campaigning journalist he did a great deal to establish a hostile public attitude to Germany before the First World War. His very close friendship with the First Sea Lord, Lord Fisher, provided him with inside information which helped him to promote with great success a major naval re-armament programme and make the naval arms race between Germany and Britain the dominating feature of the relationship between the two countries from 1908 to 1914.For many years Garvin was a close personal friend and political adviser to Lord Northcliffe, thereby having an influence on the whole Northcliffe press. Garvin became editor of the Sunday newspaper, the *Observer*, owned by Lord Northcliffe, in 1908, with the aim of raising circulation from 20,000 per week to 50,000. This he soon achieved. On 2nd August 1914 Garvin and the *Observer* urged Britain to fight "for the mastery of Europe." On 23rd July 1916 Garvin's only son, Gerard, was killed in the Battle of the Somme. Garvin wrote proudly of his son's sacrifice and "noble death." He remained editor and part owner of *The Observer* until 1942.

WILFRID WILSON GIBSON, 1878-1962.
Born Hexham. Educated privately. Social worker, poet and playwright. Friend of Rupert Brooke and Edward Marsh. Contributor to Georgian poetry anthologies which he helped to establish. He was keen to serve in the army during the war and was eventually accepted, in spite of poor eyesight, for duties in Britain. In his

later work he maintained a special interest in the lot of the working class and deprivation in English industrial society. – He was a beneficiary of Rupert Brooke's will.

ROBERT VON RANKE GRAVES, 1895-1985.

Born in London. Educated at Charterhouse. His mother was German. As a child he spent five summer holidays at his grandfather's home in Germany. Went straight from school into the Royal Welch Fusiliers at the age of nineteen. He became a friend of Sassoon, Nichols and Owen. In July 1916 shrapnel from an exploding shell pierced his lungs and he was invalided out of the front line with major injuries and shell-shock. His autobiography *Goodbye to All That* (1929) is the most racily readable personal account of the First World War. Highly regarded as a love poet.During his second marriage (to his loving and long-suffering wife Beryl) and as he grew older, he developed amorous, but doomed relationships with a series of attractive young women. – He was generous to a fault and commercially naive. – Oxford Professor of Poetry 1961-1966. His historical novels *I Claudius* and *Claudius the God* were best sellers. He lived most of his life in Majorca.

During his life he suppressed most of his war poems, probably because he was not happy with the quality of them.

JULIAN GRENFELL, 1888-1915.

Educated at Eton, and Balliol College, Oxford. He joined the army in 1910. He seemed to take a psychopathic joy in killing people. His poem *Into Battle* is said to be the most anthologised poem of the First World War. He died of wounds on 30th April, 1915, a few days after sending his poem to *The Times*.

IVOR GURNEY, 1890-1937.

Born in Gloucester. Educated at King's School Gloucester and the Royal College of Music. He wrote poetry and music from before the war. He volunteered to fight and was initially turned down because of his poor eyesight. He was gassed and wounded and returned to Britain. Mental illness developed. He was diagnosed as a paranoid schizophrenic in 1922. He was committed to mental hospital where he continued to write poetry and compose – sometimes believing that he was still taking part in the war. He died of tuberculosis.

THOMAS HARDY, 1840-1928.

Born at Higher-Bockhampton near Dorchester. Educated at a private school in Dorchester. His pre-war poetry was admired by Sassoon. *Wessex Poems* (1898), *Poems of Past and Present* (1901), *Times Laughing Stock* (1909) and the dramatic epic of the Napoleonic Wars, *The Dynasts* (1904 - 1908). Best known as a classic novelist. His novels include *Far from the Madding Crowd* (1874), *The Mayor of Casterbridge* (1886), *Tess of the D'Urbervilles* (1891). He staunchly supported the war until it was over. A member of the Fight for Right Movement and the Secret Bureau for Propaganda.

ALAN PATRICK HERBERT, SIR, 1890-1971.

Educated at Winchester, and New College, Oxford. Served at Gallipoli and on the Western Front in France. Wounded and invalided home in 1917. He wrote humour, verse, essays, musicals, musical criticism and novels. He became an independent MP for Oxford University, 1935-1950 and argued for plain, common sense language in the framing of laws, and the reduction of unnecessary bureaucracy.

WILLIAM NOEL HODGSON, 1893-1916.

Educated at Durham School and Christ Church, Oxford. He volunteered in 1914, was awarded the military cross in 1915 and killed on the first day of the Battle of the Somme, 1916.

TERESA HOOLEY, 1888-1973.

Born at Risley Lodge, Derbyshire.

ALFRED EDWARD HOUSMAN, 1859-1936.

Born in Fockbury, Worcestershire. Educated at Bromsgrove School and St John's College, Oxford. He became a celebrated classical scholar and popular poet. His best known work is *A Shropshire Lad* (1896).

DAVID JONES, 1895-1974.

Born in Kent. He volunteered in 1915 and served with the Royal Welch Fusiliers till the end of the war. He was a successful artist and worked with Eric Gill. *In Parenthesis* was first published in 1937.

RUDYARD KIPLING, 1865-1936.
Born in Bombay. As a small child he was sent to England (Southsea) to be educated. He was desperately miserable for some years. He was principally educated at the United Services College, Westward Ho! Before the war he favoured re-armament. He was vigorous in his opposition to Germany. After his only son was killed in the Battle of the Loos, in September 1915, Kipling's confident and simple verse faltered briefly. He is best known for his classic children's books – especially the *Jungle Books* (1894, 1895). He was awarded the Nobel Prize for Literature in 1907. During the First World War he was Director of Propaganda to the British Colonies.

DAVID HERBERT LAWRENCE, 1885-1930.
Born in Eastwood near Nottingham. Major British novelist. When conscription was introduced Lawrence was called for a medical inspection at Bodmin Barracks which he failed. He suffered considerably at the hands of authority. He was hounded on suspicion of being a German collaborator (because his wife was German) and was prosecuted for obscenity for his novel, *The Rainbow*. He was expelled from Cornwall in 1915 and went into self-imposed exile from Britain in 1919. He died of tuberculosis, which had troubled him for most of his life.

WINIFRED M LETTS, 1882-1971.
Born in Ireland. Worked as a Voluntary Aid Detachment nurse in England during the war.

ROSE MACAULAY, DAME, 1881-1958.
Educated Oxford High School and Somerville College, Oxford. Essayist, poet, and prize-winning novelist.

EWART ALAN MACKINTOSH, 1893-1917.
Educated St Paul's, and Christ Church, Oxford. Volunteered in 1914 joining the Seaforth Highlanders. Awarded the Military Cross 1916. Wounded and gassed at High Wood during the Battle of the Somme, during the same year. After his return to the trenches in October 1917 he was killed on 21st November at Cambrai.

JOHN MASEFIELD, 1878-1967.
Born in Ledbury, Herefordshire. Started his career as a sailor; worked in America. Worked for the Government as a propagandist in America during the war. He also served on a hospital ship at Gallipoli and served with the Red Cross in France. Poet, dramatist. Children's fiction writer. Poet Laureate from 1930.

JOHN McRAE, 1872-1918.
Born in Canada. Educated at McGill University. Although a doctor originally he fought on the Western Front in the artillery. *In Flanders Field*, one of the most famous poems of the war, was written during the Second Battle of Ypres. He was put in charge of the No 3 General Hospital at Boulogne before being appointed Medical consultant to all the British Armies in France. He died of pneumonia, on 28th January, 1918, before taking up the appointment.

HAROLD MONRO, 1879-1932.
Born in Belgium. Educated at Radley and Caius College, Cambridge. Opened the famous Poetry Bookshop in London and published all five volumes of Georgian Poetry. He was medically unfit for the front line service but performed anti-aircraft duties in 1916 before working in the War Office.

GEORGE GILBERT AIMÉ MURRAY, 1866-1957.
Born in Sydney, Australia. Arrived in England at the age of eleven. Educated Oxford. Classical scholar, widely known as a translator of Greek plays. Professor of Greek at Oxford 1908. He stood unsuccessfully for Parliament as a Liberal. A close friend of John Galsworthy. After initial doubts he supported the war. He was a keen supporter of The League of Nations and first President of the United Nations Association General Council.

EDITH NESBIT, 1858-1924.
Born in London. Socialist and writer of children's stories.

HENRY NEWBOLT, SIR, 1862-1924.
Born in Bilston, Staffordshire. Educated at Clifton College, Bristol and Corpus Christi College, Oxford. Barrister, then professional poet. Keenly interested in naval matters he wrote the official British naval history of the war. Best selling imperialist poet. Establishment literary figure.

ROBERT NICHOLS, 1893-1944.

Educated Winchester and Oxford. He was in the trenches for only a few weeks before being invalided out with shell-shock and syphilis in 1915, never to return. Worked for Ministries of Labour and Information. He was a friend of Brooke and Sassoon. Georgian poet.

ALFRED NOYES, 1880-1958.

Educated Exeter College, Oxford. Prolific poet.

WILFRED EDWARD SALTER OWEN, 1893 - 1918.

Born Oswestry, Shropshire. Educated at Birkenhead Institute and Shrewsbury Technical College. Fromthe age of nineteen Owen wanted to be a poet and immersed himself in poetry, being especially impressed by Keats and Shelley. He wrote almost no poetry of importance until he saw action in France in 1917. He was deeply attached to his mother to whom most of his 664 letters are addressed. (She saved every one.) He was a committed Christian and became lay assistant to the vicar of Dunsden near Reading 1911-1913 – teaching Bible classes and leading prayer meetings – as well as visiting parishioners and helping in other ways. From 1913 to 1915 he worked as a language tutor in France.

He felt pressured by the propaganda to become a soldier and volunteered on 21st October 1915. He spent the last day of 1916 in a tent in France joining the Second Manchesters. He was full of boyish high spirits at being a soldier. Within a week he had been transported to the front line in a cattle wagon and was "sleeping" 70 or 80 yards from a heavy gun which fired every minute or so. He was soon wading miles along trenches two feet deep in water. Within a few days he was experiencing gas attacks and was horrified by the stench of the rotting dead; his sentry was blinded, his company then slept out in deep snow and intense frost till the end of January. That month was a profound shock for him: he now understood the meaning of war. "The people of England needn't hope. They must agitate," he wrote home. (See his poems *The Sentry* and *Exposure*.)

He escaped bullets until the last week of the war, but he saw a good deal of front-line action: he was blown up, concussed and suffered shell-shock. At Craiglockhart, the psychiatric hospital in Edinburgh, he met Siegfried Sassoon who inspired him to develop his war poetry. He was sent back to the trenches in September, 1918 and in October won the Military Cross by seizing a German machine-gun and using it to kill a number of Germans. On 4th November he was shot and killed near the village of Ors. The news of his death reached his parents home as the Armistice bells were ringing on 11 November.

JOHN OXENHAM, 1852-1941.

Popular novelist and poet.During the First World War his poetry sold over a million volumes, showing him to be the most popular poet at that time. His hymn, *For the Men at the Front*, is reputed to have sold eight million copies.

ROBERT PALMER, 1888-1916.

A cousin of Edward Grey, the Foreign Secretary. Educated at Winchester and Oxford. A deeply religious man. He had embarked on a very promising career in the legal profession before volunteering in August, 1914. – He was killed in action in Mesopotamia on 21 January, 1916

MAX PLOWMAN, 1883-1941

Born in Tottenham. His experiences on the Somme turned him into a committed pacifist. Like Siegfried Sassoon, having been wounded and invalided home, he resigned his commission. – He joined the pacifist organisation, the Peace Pledge Union, becoming Secretary, 1937-1938. He wrote an account of his war experiences in *A Subaltern on the Somme*, under the pseudonym, of Mark VII.

JESSIE POPE, 1868- 1941.

Born in Leicester. Educated at Craven House, Leicester and North London Collegiate School. Popular journalist and versifier. Regular contributor to *Punch*, *The Daily Mail*, and *The Daily Express*. Owen originally addressed *Dulce et Decorum Est* to her.

HERBERT READ, SIR, 1893-1968.

Born in Kirbymoorside, Yorkshire, the son of a farmer. Educated at Leeds University. Before the war he was a Socialist, and internationalist, yet he volunteered in January 1915, joining the Yorkshire Regiment. Promoted to rank of captain. He was a natural leader and derived great satisfaction from his role. He was courageous, and daring. Awarded the Military Cross, and the DSO - an award just short of the Victoria Cross. - His 21-year-old brother, Charles, was killed in France in October, 1918. - He married the girl he had loved since before the war, in 1919. Leading art critic. Anarchist theorist. Distinguished academic career. - A complex and brilliant man. - Knighted 1953.

ERICH MARIA REMARQUE, 1898-1970.

Born in Osnabruck and served in the German army in the First World War. His novel about his war experience, *All Quiet on the Western Front* was published in 1929 and became an immediate success, selling two and a half million copies, world-wide, within eighteen months. Copies were publicly burned in Germany because of its "defeatist attitudes." Remarque lived in Switzerland from 1929-1939, then, disgusted by the Nazis, he moved to the USA where he became a naturalised citizen.

ISAAC ROSENBERG, 1890-1918.

Born in Bristol, educated in London's East End and Slade School of Art. He was an artist and engraver as well as a poet, but finding no work he volunteered in October 1915. Killed 1 April 1918.

SIEGFRIED LORRAINE SASSOON, 1886-1967.

Born in Kent. Educated at Marlborough, and Clare College, Cambridge. He was a keen sportsman, loving cricket and fox-hunting. He was the first war poet to volunteer - 3 August 1914. Disillusion set in slowly. His first critical poem, *In the Pink*, was written in February 1916. He was the only English disillusioned First World War poet who made an effort to be politically effective.

As a captain in the Royal Welch Fusiliers he met and became a friend of Robert Graves. He became wildly angry at the death of one of his friends and fought recklessly, winning the Military Cross. He was wounded in the shoulder and later was shot in the head accidentally by one of his own men. The wound was a graze, but serious enough to put him out of the action for good from July 1918. It was when convalescing from his shoulder wound in the summer of 1917 that he made his famous protest about the war. As a result of this he was sent to

Craigiockhart War Hospital in Edinburgh. There he met and encouraged Wilfred Owen with his poetry. He began to feel guilty about not fighting alongside his old comrades and returned to active service in November 1917.

After the war he became literary editor of the *Herald,* returned to his country pursuits and wrote a number of autobiographical books. He married and had one son. He became a Roman Catholic in 1957.

OWEN SEAMAN, SIR, 1861-1936.

Educated at Shrewsbury and Clare College, Cambridge. Professor of Literature at Newcastle (1890). Editor of *Punch* (1906-1932). He was encouraged to write for the war effort by the Government's Secret Bureau for Propaganda.

ALAN SEEGER, 1888-1916.

Born in New York. Educated at Harvard. After graduating he lived in Greenwich Village for two years by sponging off his friends. He was aimless, anti-social and scruffy. His parents sent him to continue his studies in Paris. He saw the war as a liberation from the dullness of everyday life. On its outbreak he rushed to join the French Foreign Legion. He dreamed of leading heroic charges in the thick of battle. He was killed at Belloy-en-Santerre on the fourth day of the Battle of the Somme, 4 July, 1916.

ROBERT SERVICE, 1874-1958.

Born in Preston, Lancashire. Travelled and worked in Canada as a journalist. A prolific writer of verse. He was an ambulance driver in the First World War.

GEORGE BERNARD SHAW, 1856-1950.

Irish dramatist, journalist, Socialist. In his time one of the most successful literary figures. He stood alone among the literary elite in his highly critical and qualified support for the war - expressed in his pamphlet *Common Sense About War* (first published as a special supplement in *The New Statesman*). He was awarded the Nobel Prize for Literature, 1925.

OSBERT SITWELL, 1892-1969.

He was born in London and educated at Eton. He joined the army in 1912 serving with the Brigade of Guards. He was invalided out in 1916. He wrote novels, short stories, travel books and autobiographies. He was the brother of Edith and Sacheverell Sitwell and a friend of T S Eliot, Ezra Pound and Wyndham Lewis.

CHARLES HAMILTON SORLEY, 1895-1915.

Born in Aberdeen. Educated at Marlborough, University College, Oxford, and for six months in Germany at Schwerin and Jena. He loved Germany and hated the idea of the war and fighting for England. Consciously yielding to psychological pressure he enlisted in 1914, joining the Suffolk Regiment. He was promoted to Captain in August 1915 and killed in the Battle of Loos, 13 October 1915, at the age of twenty.

MURIEL STUART, ? -1967.

Born in London. Thomas Hardy described her poetry as "superlatively good."

EDWARD WYNDHAM TENNANT, 1897-1916.

Educated at Winchester. Met Osbert Sitwell in the trenches, and was a friend of Raymond Asquith, a son of the Prime Minister. He was killed in the Battle of the Somme, 22 September, 1916 at the age of nineteen.

EDWARD THOMAS, 1878-1917.

He was born in London and educated at St Paul's School, and Lincoln College, Oxford. His first book was published when he was eighteen and in the next eighteen years he wrote over 30 books and thousands of articles and reviews. In spite of his output he was treated meanly by publishers and was often troubled by a shortage of money. He was a friend of Gordon Bottomley, Walter de la Mare, Lascelles Abercrombie, Harold Monro, Eleanor Farjeon, the Meynells and friend and spokesman for the American poet, Robert Frost. It was Frost who encouraged Thomas to write poetry. Starting in December 1914 and finishing in December 1916 Thomas wrote 144 poems – mainly about the English countryside, weather, the seasons – all of them written in England, in a straight, unadorned style – a number of them darkly influenced by the war. His poetry was rejected as fast as it was submitted to newspapers and periodicals, using his pseudonym, Edward Eastaway. He was a shy, self -effacing man who suffered from depression and came close to suicide. Having volunteered for the front, after eighteen months training, he went to France with the Royal Garrison Artillery at the end of January 1917. He was killed ten weeks later, on 9th April, leaving a wife and three children.

WALTER JAMES REDFERN TURNER, 1889-1946.

Born Melbourne, Australia. Served in the Royal Artillery 1916-1918. Novelist, essayist, journalist.

KATHARINE TYNAN, 1861 - 1931.

Born in Clondalkin, County Dublin. Educated Siena Convent, Drogheda. During the war she had a son serving in Palestine and another in France. Friend of W B Yeats.

ROBERT ERNEST VERNÈDE, 1875-1917.

Educated at St Paul's School and St John's College, Oxford. Volunteered in September 1914. Wounded, invalided home. Although offered a safe job in England he insisted on returning to the trenches in December 1916. He was killed the same day as Edward Thomas.

WILLIAM WATSON, SIR, 1858-1935.

Born in Burly-in-Wharfedale, Yorkshire. Prolific and popular poet, intensely patriotic during the war.

HERBERT GEORGE WELLS, 1866-1946.

Prolific science fiction writer, novelist, journalist; best-selling and highly regarded author. He began the war by giving his absolute support for it but soon began to be critical.

As the war progressed he began to see the behaviour of Britain as every bit as bad as that of Germany. He spoke for reconciliation and the idea of a League of Nations to meet and settle disputes by discussion.

In spite of criticisms of the conduct of the war Wells nevertheless continued to support it and do journalistic work on behalf of the Secret Bureau for Propaganda.

His novels include: *The War of the Worlds*; *The Invisible Man*; *The Time Machine, Ann Veronica* – an early feminist novel; *Love and Mr Lewisham*; *Mr Britling Sees It Through* (1916) – a semi-autobiographical novel, set in the First

World War period, which was very popular with soldiers.

ARTHUR GRAEME WEST, 1891-1917.

Educated at Blundell's and Oxford. Enlisted with the Public School's Battalion in February 1915. He grew to hate the war, and lost his faith in God. He was convinced he should protest or desert but could not find the courage to do so. He was killed by a sniper's bullet, 3 April, 1917 at Bapaume. His war diary, *The Diary of a Dead Officer*, which contained his poetry, was published in 1919.

WILLIAM BUTLER YEATS, 1865-1939.

Eminent Irish poet and playwright.

ISRAEL ZANGWILL, 1864-1926.

Born in London. Educated in Plymouth, Bristol and London University. Zionist, poet, playwright, novelist. Associated with the Secret Bureau for Propaganda.

IMPORTANT FIGURES IN THE FIRST WORLD WAR

ALBERT I, 1875-1934

King of Belgium, 1903-1934. A true hero of the First World War. He refused the Germans free passage through Belgium. Ordered the destruction of all bridges and tunnels in the path of the German army and the opening of the sluice gates at Nieuport at high tides, thereby flooding the land around the river Yser all the way from the coast to Dixmuide. The culverts in drainage ditches into the Yser south of Dixmuide, almost to Ypres were blocked causing a waterlogging of the land which made it impassable by the German army, in all for a distance of about twenty miles. This barrier helped to protect the Chanel ports, but drew the German attack south to the Ypres, Messine, Armentières region. King Albert personally commanded the remnants of his army on a daily basis and was often in the front line. He held back his meagre forces, refusing to commit them to the disastrous onslaught that the British Empire and the French forces felt compelled to wager, until the last few weeks of the war when he commanded the Belgian and French

army in the final successful offensive in northern Belgium. – He was a conservationist, hated blood-sports, read two books a day. He was a practical mechanic, loved cars, motorbikes, planes and ballooning. – He was killed at the age of fifty-eight in a climbing accident.

NORMAN ANGEL, SIR, 1872-1967

Born Holbeach, Lincolnshire. Economist and pacifist. He made out a convincing (and accurate) case that in a major war between economic powers victor and vanquished alike would suffer economic disaster and that the major powers were economically interdependent. – Businesses, (except arms manufacturers, and military suppliers) had much to lose and nothing to gain from a war. He presented his ideas in *The Great Illusion* (1909) which had, by 1913, undergone ten reprintings and been translated into German, French and Russian. – He was awarded the Nobel Peace Prize in 1933.

HERBERT HENRY ASQUITH, FIRST EARL OF OXFORD AND ASQUITH, 1852-1928.

Born in Morley, Yorkshire.Educated Balliol College, Oxford. Liberal politician. Prime Minister from 1908 till December 1916, when he was ousted by supporters of Lloyd George. During his period of power the Liberal Government founded Britain's welfare state, reformed the armed forces, increased spending on battleships, and took a step towards greater democracy by reducing the power of the House of Lords. He was wrestling, unsuccessfully, with the problem of home rule for Ireland when the outbreak of theFirst World War saved him from political disaster.

Lloyd George considered Asquith to be a brilliant speaker, and a brilliant judge of other men's ideas, but without any ideas of his own.

Sometimes the pressures of politics led him to excessive drinking. His relationship with Venetia Stanley saved him form this problem and rescued him from despair. He married twice and had seven children. Four sons served in the war, one of whom, Raymond, was killed. Arthur, a friend of Rupert Brooke, was wounded four times and had a leg amputated below the knee. His daughter, Violet, was also a friend of Rupert Brooke.

HORATIO WILLIAM BOTTOMLEY 1860-1933.

Born Bethnal Green, London. Brought up in an orphanage. His first job was as an errand boy. He became a very successful financier, journalist, public speaker and anti-German propagandist. For ten years he was a Member of Parliament. He founded the weekly paper *John Bull* in 1906 which was virulent and racist in its championing of the war. – In 1922 he was found guilty of fraud and imprisoned. He died in poverty.

SIR EDWARD CARSON, 1854-1935.

Conservative MP for Dublin University, 1892-1918. First Lord of the Admiralty. – Member of the War Cabinet, 1917-1918.

SIR WINSTON LEONARD SPENCER CHURCHILL, 1874-1965.

Born Blenheim Palace, Woodstock, Oxfordshire. Educated at Harrow, and Sandhurst Military Academy. His long and extraordinary career cannot be adequately summarised here. – As a soldier he experienced hand-to-hand fighting against the Dervishes at Obdurman. He was a war correspondent during the Boer War, when he was captured. He soon escaped. He became a Member of Parliament in 1906 and was soon holding cabinet positions. In 1911 he became First Lord of the Admiralty. He encouraged Rupert Brooke to join the navy. Following the disastrous failure of the Gallipoli campaign he resigned and became a Captain in the army serving in the front line in France. In 1917 he became Minister of Munitions. One aspect of this work was the promotion of the idea of tank warfare and his facilitation of the production of thousands of tanks. He was a critic of Haig's conduct of the war on the Western Font. – In the 1930's he was out of politics. In the Second World War, as Prime Minister, he was the inspirational leader of the British. He was an historian of distinction. Relevant here is *The World Crisis*, published in 4 volumes 1923-1929.

DAVID LLOYD GEORGE, FIRST EARL OF DWYFOR, 1863-1945.

Born in Manchester. As an orphan at the age of two he moved to Llanystumdwy near Criccieth North Wales where he was brought up by his uncle, a shoemaker. He was educated at the village Church of England School. As Chancellor of the Exchequer he brought in old age pensions (1908), and National Insurance (1911). He was a pacifist up to the outbreak of the war. He was Prime Minister from December 1916 till 1922, succeeding in maintaining the nations support for the war to the end, but behind the scenes he was bitterly unhappy with Haig's conduct of offensives. He quarrelled with Lord Northcliffe. At the end of the war the pressure of public opinion in Britain, stirred up by Northcliffe newspapers and other propagandists the Government had encouraged and the French desire for vengeance, worked against his wisdom in seeking more realistic and acceptable terms for reparations from Germany in the Treaty of Versailles. – Hitler described him as "the man who won the war." – He had four children. Both of his sons served in the war.

EDWARD GREY, FIRST VISCOUNT GREY OF FALLODON, 1862-1933.

Educated Winchester and Balliol College, Oxford. Foreign Secretary 1905 - 1916. His actions and decisions took Britain and the British Empire into the war. He resigned because of failing eyesight. An expert on ornithology and fly-fishing.

FIELD MARSHAL SIR DOUGLAS HAIG, FIRST EARL HAIG OF BEMERSYDE, 1861-1928.

Born in Edinburgh into the Haig whisky making family.Educated at Clifton College, Bristol; Brasenose College, Oxford; and the Royal Military College, Sandhurst. Through his wife's court connections was a friend of the king (George V). He became Commander-in-Chief of the British forces in France in December 1916. He faced a formidable enemy, brilliantly trained, organised and well equipped. His military response had to cope with a new kind of warfare in often appalling physical conditions. Few men in history have ever been called upon to exercise command over so many – Ultimately about three million men. – Accusations of "remoteness" were inevitable. He co-ordinated the troops of many nations, worked in co-operation with the French and Belgian armies and had to hold the line during times when the French forces were all but spent. He had also to cope with less than the full confidence of Lloyd George and the British War Cabinet. He was ruthless, imperturbable, unimaginative and believed himself to be a devout Christian. His reports of his work – however disastrous the results – always dwelt on elements of success and overlooked failures and disasters. He was positive to the point of mendacity. His plans of attack are easily criticised mainly for the approach of pushing more and more men forward towards enemy machine guns, regardless of the slaughter, to gain just a few hundred yards of line, "wear-out" the enemy and divert German pressure from other areas. He was in charge of some of the world's greatest ever military disasters. Only towards the end did he work out alternative approaches in strategy and learn to incorporate a new weapon – the tank.

Ultimately, in military terms, he was successful, though external factors, such as the arrival of American troops and the starving of the German nation by means of a naval blockade, played a part, too. Although France's General Foch became Supreme Commander of the Allied Forces in March 1918, in Britain Haig was credited with winning the war and became a national hero. In 1919 he was made an Earl and Parliament voted him £100,000. He was awarded the Order of Merit. In 1920 public subscriptions raised the money to buy for him Bemersyde Mansion and Estate.

After the war he devoted himself to promoting the welfare of ex-servicemen. The Remembrance Day poppies still bear his name.

RICHARD BURDON HALDANE, 1ST VISCOUNT HALDANE, 1856-1928.

Educated in Edinburgh and Götingen. A member of Asquith's Liberal cabinet. Reformed the organisation of the British Army and established the Territorial Army.

THE KAISER - SEE WILLHELM II.

HORATIO HERBERT KITCHENER, LORD, 1850-1916.

An Irishman, born near Ballylongford, County Kerry. Educated in Switzerland and The Royal Military Academy, Woolwich. He served in the army in Palestine, Cyprus, Egypt and the Sudan. He was Commander-in-Chief in South Africa, a hero of the Boer War. Asquith made him Secretary of State for War on 7th August , 1914. For some time Kitchener ran the war effort, expecting from the start that it would be a long war. He raised a remarkable volunteer army with his

recruiting campaign. – Such was the high esteem that he was held in by the nation that when Northcliffe, through the *Daily Mail*, set out to discredit him, the only result was a loss of ciculation for the *Mail*. – He was killed in June, 1916, when HMS Hampshire, on which he was travelling on a mission to Russia, struck a mine off the Orkneys, and sank, with the loss of all on board.

KARL LIEBKNECHT, 1871-1919.

German politician and member of the Reichstag from1912-1916. He campaigned, with Rosa Luxemburg, against Germany's military action gaining a great deal of support. He was imprisoned for his efforts. After the war on January 6th 1919, 10,000 Marxist supporters gathered in Berlin intent on revolution. Liebnecht and Luxemburg were murdered by right-wing para-military forces.

ROSA LUXEMBURG, 1871-1919.

Born in Poland she moved to Berlin in 1908. She became the leader of the Spartacus League with Karl Liebknecht, campaigning with him and sharing his fate.

EDWARD HOWARD MARSH, SIR, 1872-1953.

Private Secretary to Winston Churchill for 23 years. Did a great deal to encourage young poets and painters – including Isaac Rosenberg, Rupert Brooke, W W Gibson, Robert Graves, Edmund Blunden, D H Lawrence, Paul Nash and Stanley Spencer. Edited the five Georgian poetry anthologies between 1912 and 1922 which promoted new poetry very successfully and gave rise to the term, difficult to define, of Georgianism. Knighted in 1937.

ALFRED MILNER, FIRST VISCOUNT MILNER, 1854-1925.

Member of the War Cabinet. Secretary of State for War 1918 - 1919. He was born in Germany.

EDWIN SAMUEL MONTAGU, 1879-1924.

Educated Cambridge. Liberal MP 1906-1922. Minister of Munitions 1916. Married Venetia Stanley 1915.

NICHOLAS II, 1868-1918, EMPEROR OF RUSSIA.

His mother, Marie Dagmar, and the mother of England's George V, Alexandra, were sisters – the daughters of King Kristian IX of Denmark. Nicholas and his entire family were murdered by revolutionaries.

WILLIAM HALSE RIVERS, 1864-1922.

Born near Chatham, Kent. Anthropologist, psychologist, and neurophysiologist. He lectured at Cambridge. He was the psychologist at Craiglockhart War Hospital, Edinburgh who was responsible for Siegfried Sassoon. After the war he was a personal friend of Robert Graves and his family when they lived near Cambridge.

BERTRAND RUSSELL, THIRD EARL RUSSELL, 1872-1970.

Educated at Trinity College, Cambridge. Outstanding mathematician and philosopher. His pacifist views and opposition to the First World War lost him his fellowship at Cambridge in 1916 and led to his imprisonment. He supported and encouraged Siegfried Sassoon in his rebellion against military authority. He supported Britain's efforts in the Second World War and campaigned prominently against nuclear weapons in the 50's and 60's being imprisoned again in 1961 for his part in a demonstration. He wrote prolifically and was awarded the Nobel Prize for Literature in 1950.

BEATRICE VENETIA STANLEY, 1887-1948

Daughter of the 4th Baron Stanley of Alderley. Best friend of Violet Asquith, the daughter of Henry Asquith. By 1912 Asquith had begun to develop a special affection for her, which, by 1914, had developed into an obsessive love. The relationship came to an abrupt end when, on 11th May, 1915, Venetia announced her engagement to Edwin Montagu. After Venetia's death her daughter found, in her mother's papers, over five hundred letters from Asquith to her mother, in which he confided his political problems, and military secrets; sought her advice; expressed his longings to see her and his undying love.

WILLHELM II (THE KAISER), THIRD GERMAN EMPEROR AND NINTH KING OF PRUSSIA, 1859-1941.

Born in Berlin, the eldest son of Prince Frederick and Victoria (daughter of Queen Victoria). He loved army pageant. He dismissed, as Chancellor, Bismarck, "the architect of modern Germany," in 1890. In 1908 he had a nervous breakdown and from then on lacked firm and absolute control of policy. He was in love with the idea of extending Germany's imperial power and expanding Germany's navy. With little thought he gave complete support to Austria-Hungary in its demands on Serbia in 1914.
In discussing Germany's entry into the First World war he soon gave way to the wishes of his generals, and it was they, rather than the Kaiser, who directed Germany's war machine.

When his generals forced him to give up his title and power on 9th November 1918 he fled to Holland and lived first at Amerongen and then Doorn near Arnheim.

THOMAS WOODROW WILSON, 1856-1924.

Born in Virginia, the son of a Presbyterian minister. Educated at Princeton and John Hopkins. A Democrat he became President of the USA in 1912, maintaining a neutral stance with regard to the First World War. Re-elected in 1916 promising to keep America out of the war. In 1917 events persuaded him to change his mind.

He proposed the 14-point peace plan which became the basis of the Treaty of Versailles. He was unable to gain the Senate's approval for the treaty. He championed the League of Nations, but was unsuccessful in gaining the Senate's approval for this, too. Brought in the notorious prohibition of alcohol regulations in 1920.

GLOSSARY

A D C – aide-de-camp, an officer serving as a personal assistant to a senior officer.

Allemands – soldiers' slang for Germans.

Allies – The Triple Entente – France, Britain and Russia and their allies, including the countries of the British Empire, Italy, Serbia, Japan and eventually, America.

Armistice – an agreement, between opposing armies, to stop fighting so that terms for a peace agreement can be worked out.

army – the land forces of a country but also a subdivision of these. By 1918, Britain's army in France, was divided into 5 armies, each under its own General. Each army consisted of 4 corps (except the 4th Army, which had 3 corps). Typically there were 4 divisions in a corps. In addition, by 1918, there were 3 cavalry divisions, a communications division, the Royal Air Force, and the Tank Corps.

battalion – a military unit consisting of about 1,000 men (4 companies).

battery – a group of field guns.

Blighty – the soldiers' name for England (or Britain) and, sometimes, home.

a blighty – a wound serious enough to require the soldier to be removed to Britain.

Bosches – soldiers' slang for Germans.

brigade – about 4,000 men (divided into four battalions).

Central Powers – Germany, Austria-Hungary, Turkey, and their allies.

coal-box – a kind of First World War explosive shell.

company – a military unit consisting of 200 to 250 men, under the command of a captain. Within a company there would be 4 platoons.

conscription – compulsory military service.

counter attack – an attack made by one side in response to an attack by the opposing side, the usual aim being to regain lost ground.

Craiglockhart War Hospital – situated in Edinburgh. One of the psychiatric hospitals to which shell-shock cases were sent. Many patients were in the care of the eminent psychologist, W H Rivers. Wilfred Owen was an inmate from 26th June 1917 to 3rd November 1917 and wrote a number of his poems there. Siegfried Sassoon was in Craiglockhart from 21 July 1917 till 27th November 1917 after "wilfully defying military authority."

division – a unit of the army consisting of about 19,000 men – 12,000 infantry (divided into 3 brigades), 4,000 artillery, and 3,000 in supporting roles (medical, food, construction, transport, etc).

duck boards – planks put across the bottoms of trenches or wet or boggy ground to stop soldiers sinking into water or mud.

dud – a shell or bullet which fails to explode; an ineffective person.

elegy – a poem expressing sadness, especially regretting a death.

Eton – an English public school.

England – Many poets spoke as if the war was between only England and Germany. By "England" they meant "Great-Britain" – including the whole of Ireland. Haig, who commanded the British army in France in the latter part of the war, was a Scotsman; Kitchener, who was Minister for War, was an Irishman: and Lloyd George, though born in in Manchester, was raised in Wales. – See also, allies.

fascined (line) – embankments made using bundles of long sticks.

field gun – a heavy gun used in battle – most commonly mounted on a pair of large wheels, though sometimes on a metal platform or specially constructed railway wagon. Field guns fire shells and are operated by two or more men.

fire-step – a ledge running along a trench onto which soldiers stepped to fire on the enemy. See the drawing on page 111.

five-nine – a German shell, 5.9 inches (15 centimetres) in diameter. To the poets most shells were five-nines although there was a wide range of other sizes.

franc-tireur – a sniper or guerrilla fighter.

Fritz – soldiers' slang for a German.

Gallipoli – at the eastern end of the Mediterranean, a peninsula in north west Turkey where the Allies attempted to invade Turkey in 1915. The attacks were mismanaged and resulted in appalling loss of life and the resignation of the First Sea Lord, Winston Churchill.

Georgians – usually taken to be the forty poets who contributed to the five poetry anthologies edited by Edward Marsh between 1911 and 1922. The idea for the first anthology was worked out at a luncheon party at which Marsh, Rupert Brooke, John Drinkwater, W W Gibson and Harold Monro were present. At this time they considered that they were bringing a new realism to poetry, and putting on "a new strength and beauty". They were hostile to late Victorian poets like Henry Newbolt and William Watson. Yet in retrospect, Georgian poetry seems insular, unadventurous, dreamy, rural, impersonal, nostalgic – often concerned with the pleasant aspects of England, unaware of or indifferent to realities. Some poets who were included did not fit in with the general style – including D H Lawrence and Isaac Rosenberg. Others sometimes mistakenly classed as Georgians were never included in the anthologies. These include Edward Thomas, Charles Sorley and Wilfred Owen, although both Thomas and Owen were friendly with accepted Georgians. – Academics still debate who should and should not be classed as Georgian so the term has limited usefulness as a label for poets.

howitzer – a short barrelled field gun (or cannon) which, because of the low velocity of its shells, had to fire steeply upwards.

Hun – soldiers' slang for a German.

imagism – a movement which has had a considerable influence on modern poetry written in English. See "imagist".

imagist – a member of the imagist school of poetry which was founded as a movement in 1912 by American poet Ezra Pound, and F S Flint, although in 1908 T E Hulme and Edward Storer had written poetry according with imagist principles. Imagist writers aimed to express themselves with a rigorous succinctness, con-

centrating particularly on verbal images. The rhythm of their lines was composed "in the sequence of the musical phrase, not in sequence of a metronome." Imagists included in this volume are Ford Madox Ford, Richard Aldington, D H Lawrence (who was published in Georgian anthologies, too), Herbert Read, and F S Flint.

Jingoism – strident, obtrusive and intellectually weak patriotism.

Junker – a country gentleman or member of the aristocracy particularly associated with protecting his privileges and narrow-minded, short-sighted, aggressive nationalism. A term most often applied by the British to such people in Germany, although George Bernard Shaw took delight in applying it to the appropriate people in Britain.

Kaiser – a German emperor – the best known being Kaiser Wilhelm II (1888-1918). See *Brief Lives*.

Krupp – the German family of steel and armament manufacturers – major beneficiaries of two world wars.

Kruppism – promotion of the idea of the need to have strong armaments and vast armies to maintain, according to the promoters' arguments, peace.

lament – a poem regretting a death.

last post – a short bugle call played at military funerals.

Lewis gun – an early, American designed, British machine gun.

Loos, Battle of – a battle which took place between 25th September and 8th October 1915. The occasion on which the British first used gas. The obvious first rule of gas warfare (only use it when the wind is blowing towards your enemy) was ignored. The hopelessness of the British assault and the wholesale slaughter of the troops moved the Germans to stop firing in pity. The poet Charles Sorley, the son of Rudyard Kipling and Raymond, the son of Asquith, the Prime Minister, were killed in this battle.

Marlborough College – an English public school.

Maxim – an early machine gun, invented in Britain by American-born Sir Hiram Stevens Maxim.

M C – Military Cross – a British military award for conspicuous bravery.

Menin Gate – stone and brick war memorial gateway that stands astride the road to Menin on the eastern side of Ypres. Completed in 1927 it commemorates some of the dead whose remains were never found or identified in the Ypres/Passchendaele area. Men from England, Scotland, Wales, Ireland, Canada, New Zealand, India and Africa are recorded.

militarism – a belief in a need for increasing military power, the building up of armies and weaponry: the belief that the military or military ideals should dominate political decisions.

militarist – a supporter of militarism.

minenwerfer – big, German trench mortar

Montreuil – small town near the coast in northern France. Headquarters of Field Marshal Sir Douglas Haig for the Battle of the Somme – forty miles from the scene of the main fighting.

mortar – a field gun with a short, wide barrel, loaded at the muzzle.

mufti – civilian clothes.

parados – earth piled on top of the rear wall of a trench.

parapet – the low earth or sand-bag wall thrown up or built up along the top of a trench on the side nearest the enemy.

Passchendaele – a small village in Belgium, six miles east of Ypres. Today it is known by the Flemish name of Passendale. Hundreds of thousands of German, French, British and Empire soldiers died as the Allies advanced to capture the village (November 1917). They held it till April 1918.

platoon – a small fighting unit, a subdivision of a company, usually consisting of 50 to 60 men, commanded by a lieutenant. Platoons were divided into sections of 10 to 15 men commanded by sergeants.

pluck – guts, courage.

Poet Laureate – a poet appointed, for life, as the official poet of the English Royal Court.

posted – guns posted – positioned.

Prussia – the former German state of north Germany which was the militarist driving force for German expansion until 1871 when the German Empire was established.

Prussianism – aggressive militarism – especially in Germany, but the term was also applied to a similar ethos recognizable in England before and during the First World War.

public school – the name given by the English to private schools, independent of the state – usually residential – which charge fees and to which the upper class and rich send their children.

Reichstag – German parliament.

Remembrance Day – the second Sunday in November, being the Sunday nearest 11th November, the date of the ending of the First World War. The day when the dead of two world wars are remembered in formal ceremonies in cities, towns and villages throughout Great Britain.

rum – a drink frequently served to soldiers to bolster courage before they went over the top.

sap – a trench extending directly towards the enemy line.

shells – like a large bullet – filled with explosives, poison gas, or inflammable materials. Typically 4" (10 cm) to 8" (20 cm) in diameter, although there were some much larger. The most extraordinary shell used in the First World War was 8.26" in diameter. It was fired by a gun built by Krupps and nicknamed Big Bertha. Three hundred and sixty-seven of these shells were fired over seventy miles, with a trajectory which reached an altitude of twenty four miles, and landing on Paris between 23 March and 9 August 1918.

Somme – a department in northern France which shares its name with the river which flows through it. The scene of the Battle of the Somme.

Somme, Battle of the – a disastrous British military success fought in the Somme region from 1st July 1916 till 18th November 1916. The first day, with 20,000 British dead and 40,000 British wounded, is said to be the world's greatest ever single-day battlefield loss.

stand-to – to take up a position to be ready to fight; dawn and dusk (when front line soldiers needed to be especially ready to repel an attack, and therefore stood-to).

swaddies – soldiers' slang for "soldiers".

Tommy or Tommy Atkins – a colloquial name for a British soldier.

Transvaal – a province of South Africa which became a British colony in 1902.

trench mortar – the smallest of the mortars, easily portable.

Tsar – Emperor of Russia - the last one, with his family, was assassinated in 1917.

U-boat – German submarine.

V A D – Voluntary Aid Detachment – the volunteer nurses.

Victoria Cross – the highest British military award for bravery.

Vimy Ridge – a high hill, three miles north of Arras, bitterly contested and finally claimed by Canadian and Scots troops at a huge cost of lives. Today the site of the principal Canadian War Memorial in France commemorating over 60,000 Canadian war dead

Western Front – the area in which fighting took place in the four hundred miles between the Channel coast of north eastern France and Belgium, and Switzerland. Fighting took place in many other areas including the Eastern Front which was primarily between Germany and Russia.

whizz-bang – a shell which made a whizzing noise before it exploded showering high velocity iron shot onto its victims.

wire – the barbed wire entanglements which both sides used to protect their trenches. The use of high explosive shells before an attack was intended to blast gaps in the wire. The British used large numbers of shrapnel shells in the early stages of the war which were ineffective against barbed wire.

wiring party – a group of soldiers sent to repair or set up barbed wire defences.

Ypres – a small historic town in Belgium. An extraordinary amount of the fighting took place in the flat farmland to the east of this town in the First World War as the Allies mounted their vigorous defence. It was only briefly occupied by the Germans. – Today one can still admire the wonderful thirteenth century Cloth Hall which stands in the market place. Unfortunately it is not the original. It, like the rest of Ypres, was blasted to rubble by German shells. The replica was completed in 1961.

zeppelin – cylindrical gas-filled airship carrying passengers (and bombs, in the First World War) in a substantial cage suspended below it.

BIBLIOGRAPHY

ANTHOLOGIES

Billy the Kid, an Anthology of Tough Verse, edited by Michael Baldwin. Hutchinson Educational, 1963.

Some Corner of a Foreign Field, edited by James Bentley. Little, Brown and Company, 1992.

The Martial Muse, edited by Alan Bold. Wheaton, 1976.

An Anthology of War Poems, Frederick Brereton. Collins, 1930.

Lost Voices of World War I, edited by T Cross. Bloomsbury, 1988.

Poetry of the World Wars, edited by Michael Foss. Michael O'Mara Books, 1990.

The Poetry of War, 1914-1989, edited by Simon Fuller. BBC Enterprises / Longman, 1989.

The Bloody Game, edited by Paul Fussell. Scribners/Macdonald, 1990.

Up the Line to Death, edited by Brian Gardner. Methuen, 1976.

The War Poets, edited by Robert Giddings. Bloomsbury, 1988.

Peace and War, edited by Michael Harrison and Christopher Stuart-Clark. Oxford, 1989.

In Time of War, edited by Anne Harvey. Penguin, 1987.

Poetry of the Great War, edited by Dominic Hibberd and John Onions. Macmillan, 1986.

Poetry of the First World War, edited by Edward Hudson. Wayland, 1988.

Poetry of the First World War, edited by Maurice Hussey. Longman, 1967.

War Poetry, edited by D L Jones. Pergamon, 1968.

Poetry 1900 -1975, edited by George Macbeth. Longman, 1979.

Anthology of War Poetry, 1914 -1918, edited by Robert Nichols. Nicholson & Watson, 1943.

Ardours and Endurances, edited by Robert Nichols. Chatto & Windus, 1917.

The Muse in Arms, edited by E B Osborn. John Murray, 1918.

Men Who March Away, edited by I M Parsons. Hogarth Press, 1987.

Scars Upon my Heart, edited by Catherine Reilly. Virago, 1981.

The Penguin Book of First World War Poetry, edited by Jon Silkin. Penguin, 1979.

The Oxford Book of War Poetry, edited by Jon Stallworthy. Oxford 1984.

Never Such Innocence, A New Anthology of Great War Verse. edited by Martin Stephen, Buchan & Enright, 1988.

An Anthology of War Poetry, edited by Julian Symons. Penguin, 1942.

Lads, Love Poetry of the Trenches, edited by Martin Taylor. Constable, 1989.

The War Poets, edited by Michael White. Jarrold, 1992.

The Valiant Muse, edited by Frederick W Ziv. Putnam, New York, 1936.

INDIVIDUAL POETS

Collected Poems of Rupert Brooke, with a memoir by Edward Marsh. Sidgwick and Jackson, 1928.

E E Cummings, Complete Poems, 1913-1962. Harcourt, Brace, New York, 1980.

A Pilgrim's Song, Geoffrey Dearmer. John Murray, 1993.

The City of Fear, and Other Poems, Gilbert Frankau. Chatto, 1917.

The Poetical Works of Gilbert Frankau, Volume 2. Chatto and Windus,1923.

The Collected Poems of John Galsworthy. Heinemann, 1934.

Poems about War, Robert Graves. Introduced by William Graves. Cassell, 1988.

Collected Poems of Ivor Gurney. Oxford, 1982.

The Works of Thomas Hardy. Wordsworth Poetry Library, 1994.

In Parenthesis, David Jones. Faber & Faber, 1937.

The Works of Rudyard Kipling. Wordsworth Poetry Library, 1994.

Collected Poems, Harold Monro. Cobden-Sanderson, 1933, Duckworth, 1970.

Voices, Edith Nesbit. Hutchinson, 1922.

Selected Poems of Henry Newbolt, edited by Patric Dickinson. Hodder & Stoughton, 1981.

Wilfred Owen, War Poems and Others, edited by Dominic Hibberd. Chatto & Windus, 1973.

The Poems of Wilfred Owen, edited by Jon Stallworthy. The Hogarth Press, 1985.

Wilfred Owen, the Complete Poems and fragments, edited by Jon Stallworthy. Published jointly by Chatto & Windus, The Hogarth Press and Oxford University Press, 1983.

Hearts Courageous, John Oxenham. Methuen, 1918.

All Clear, John Oxenham. Methuen, 1919.

Collected Poems, Herbert Read. Faber & Faber, 1966.

Collected Works of Isaac Rosenberg, edited by Ian Parsons. Chatto & Windus, 1984.

The War Poems, Siegfried Sassoon, Edited by Rupert Hart-Davies. Faber & Faber, 1983.

Selected Poems, Old and New, Osbert Sitwell. Duckworth, 1943.

The Collected Poems of Charles Hamilton Sorley, edited by Jean Moorcroft Wilson. Cecil Woolf, 1985.

Robert Service, Collected Poems. Benn, 1930.

The Works of Edward Thomas. Wordsworth, 1994.

Edward Thomas, Selected Poems and Prose, edited by Michael White. Penguin, 1981.

The Man Who Saw and Other Poems Arising out of the War, William Watson. John Murray, *1917.*

BIOGRAPHIES, COLLECTED LETTERS, AND DIARIES.

H H Asquith Letters to Venetia Stanley, edited by Michael and Eleanor Brock. Oxford University Press, 1980 and 1985.

Men and Power, 1917-1918, Lord Beaverbrook. Hutchinson, 1956.

Undertones of War, Edmund Blunden. Cobden-Sanderson, 1930. Collins 1978.

Testament of Youth, Vera Brittain. Victor Gollancz, 1933. Virago, 1978.

Vera Brittain, a Life, Paul Berry and Mark Bostridge. Chatto and Windus, 1995.

The Letters of Rupert Brooke, edited by Sir Geoffrey Keynes. Faber & Faber, 1968.

Rupert Brooke, His Life and Legend, John Lehmann. Weidenfeld & Nicholson, 1980.

Song of Love, The Letters of Rupert Brooke and Noel Olivier, edited by Pippa Harris. Bloomsbury, 1991.

Rupert Brooke, The Splendour and the Pain, John Frayn Turner. Breese Books, 1992.

The Flower of Battle, Hugh Cecil. Secker and Warburg, 1995.

The Observer and J L Garvin, J M Gollin. Oxford, 1960.

Goodbye to All That, Robert Graves. Penguin, 1960.

Robert Graves, Life on the Edge, Miranda Seymour. Doubleday, 1995.

Robert Graves, Martin Seymour-Smith. Bloomsbury, 1995.

Ivor Gurney, War Letters, edited by R K R Thornton. Hogarth Press, 1984.

Lord Haig, George Arthur. Heinemann, 1928.

Private Papers of Douglas Haig, edited by Robert Blake. Eyre & Spottiswoode, 1952.

Flame into Being, the Life of D H Lawrence, Antony Burgess. William Heinemann, 1985.

Journey from Obscurity – the Life of Wilfred Owen 1893-1918, Harold Owen. Oxford, 1964.

C F G Masterman, L Masterman. Nicholson & Watson, 1939.

Greater Love, Letters Home 1914-1918, edited by Michael Moynihan. W H Allen, 1980.

People at War, edited by Michael Moynihan. David & Charles, 1988.

The Later Life and Letters of Sir Henry Newbolt, Edited by Margaret Newbolt. Faber, 1942.

Wilfred Owen, Collected Letters, Edited by Harold Owen and John Bell. Oxford, 1967.

Wilfred Owen, Jon Stallworthy. Oxford, 1974.

Wilfred Owen, Merryn Williams. Seren Books, 1993.

Annals of Innocence and Experience, Herbert Read. Faber, 1940.

Diaries 1915-1918, Siegfried Sassoon, edited by Rupert Hart-Davis. Faber & Faber, 1983.

Siegfried's Journey, 1916-1918, Siegfried Sassoon. Viking Press, USA, 1946.

Siegfried Sassoon: Poet's Pilgrimage, Dame Felicitas Corrigan. Gollancz, 1973.

Complete Memoirs of George Sherston, Siegfried Sassoon. Faber & Faber, 1937. (Includes *Memoirs of a Fox-Hunting Man, Memoirs of an Infantry Officer, Sherston's Progress*.)

Edward Thomas, A Critical Biography, William Cook. Faber & Faber, 1970.

Edward Thomas, the Last Four Years, Eleanor Farjeon. Oxford, 1979.

Some Desperate Glory – the Diary of a Young Officer, Edwin Campion Vaughan. Frederick Warne, 1981.

Experiment in Autobiography, H G Wells, Gollancz, 1934.

HISTORIES

Britain and Her Army 1509-1970, Correlli Barnett. Penguin, 1970.

A Nation in Arms, edited by Ian Beckett and Keith Simpson. Tom Donovan,1985.

Tommy Goes to War, Malcolm Brown. J M Dent & Sons, 1978.

Britain and the Great War, 1914-1918, J M Bourne. Edward Arnold, 1989.

World Crisis, Winston Churchill. Butterworth, 1927.

The Donkeys, Alan Clark. Hutchinson, 1961. Pimlico, 1991.

Ourselves, 1900-1930, Irene Clephane. The Bodley Head, 1933.

Eye Deep in Hell, John Ellis. Croom Helm, 1976.

Ypres in War and Peace, Martin Marix Evans. Pitkin Pictorials, 1992.

Tanks & Weapons of World War I, edited by Bernard Fitzsimons. Phoebus, 1973.

First World War, Martin Gilbert. Weidenfeld & Nicholson, 1994.

Sir Douglas Haig's Despatches, edited by J H Boraston. Dent, 1978.

History of the First World War, Basil Liddell Hart. Faber & Faber, 1930.

Keep the Home Fires Burning, Propaganda in the First World War, Cate Haste. Allen Lane, 1977.

World War One, Robert Hoare. Macdonald Educational, 1973.

The Age of Empire, 1875-1914, E J Hobsbawm. Weidenfeld & Nicholson, 1987.

The Age of Extremes, Eric Hobsbawm. Michael Joseph, 1994.

Britain and the Two World Wars, Jocelyn Hunt and Sheila Watson. Cambridge, 1990.

On the Origins of War and the Preservation of Peace, Donald Kagan. Hutchinson, 1995.

British Butchers & Bunglers of World War One, John Laffin. Allan Sutton, 1988.

Propaganda Techniques in World War I, Harold D Laswell. Kegan Paul, 1927, The M I T Press, Cambridge, Massachesetts, 1971.

The Viking Atlas of World War I, Anthony Livesey. Viking, 1994.

The Truth About the Peace Treaties, David Lloyd George. Victor Gollancz, 1938.

War Memoirs, David Lloyd George. Odhams Press, 1938.

1914-1918, Voices and Images of the Great War, Lyn Macdonald. Michael Joseph, 1988.

The Roses of No Man's Land, Lyn Macdonald. Michael Joseph, 1980.

They Called it Passchendaele, Lyn Macdonald. Michael Joseph, 1978.

Treitschke and the Great War, Joseph McCabe. T Fisher Unwin, November, 1914.

The Deluge, British Society and the First World War, Arthur Marwick. Open University Press, Macmillan, 1965.

Shot at Dawn, Julian Putkowski and Julian Sykes. Leo Cooper, 1989.

The Pelican History of the World, J M Roberts. Penguin, 1980.

From Vienna to Versailles, L C B Seaman. Routledge, 1955.

Common Sense About the War, George Bernard Shaw. Special Supplement of the New Statesman, 4 November, 1914.

Hot Blood & Cold Steel, Andy Simpson. Tom Donovan, 1993.

Contemporary Accounts of the First World War, John Simkin. Tressell Publications, 1981.

First World War, A J P Taylor. Penguin, 1963.

History of World War I, edited by A J P Taylor. Octopus, 1978.

Dear Old Blighty, E J Turner. Michael Joseph, 1980.

Voices from the Great War, Peter Vansittart. Jonathan Cape, 1981.

The War that will End War, H G Wells. Frank & Cecil Palmer, October, 1914.

The Experience of World War I, J M Winter. Macmillan, 1988.

Statistics of the Military Effort of the British Empire During the Great War, HMSO. 1922.

GENERAL BOOKS AND FICTION

Under Fire, Henri Barbusse, 1917. Translated by W Fitzwater Wray. Dent Everyman, 1926 and 1988.

The Riddle of the Sands, Erskine Childers.Granada, 1979.

The Invasion, William Le Queux. Everett, 1906.

Chambers Biographical Dictionary, edited by Magnus Magnusson. W & R Chambers, 1990.

The Oxford Companion to English Literature, 1985.

The Cambridge Guide to Literature in English, 1988.

New Penguin Dictionary of Quotations. Viking, 1992.

Disenchantment, C E Montague. Chatto, 1922, Penguin, 1968.

All Quiet on the Western Front, Erich Remarque. Translated by A W Wheen. Putnam, 1929. Pan/Picador, 1990.

In Praise of Idleness, Bertrand Russell. Unwin Books, 1960.

Common Sense About the War, George Bernard Shaw. Special Supplement of the *New Statesman*, 4 November 1914.

Journey's End, R C Sherriff. Heinemann, 1929, 1993.

A Country Calendar, Flora Thompson. Oxford, 1979.

Mr Britling Sees it Through, H G Wells. Cassell, 1916.

The War That Will End War, H G Wells. Frank Palmer, 1914.

Quaker Faith and Practice, The Yearly Meeting of the Religious Society of Friends (Quakers) in Britain, 1995.

LITERARY CRITICISM

Heroes' Twilight: A Study of the Literature of the Great War, Bernard Bergonzi. Constable, 1965. Carcanet, 1996.

The Great War and Modern Memory, Paul Fussell. Oxford, 1975.

Poetry of the First World War, a Selection of Critical Essays, edited by Dominic Hibberd. Macmillan, 1981.

English Poetry of the First World War, John H Johnston. Princeton University Press, 1964.

A Map of Modern English Verse, John Press. Oxford, 1969.

Out of Battle, the Poetry of the Great War, Jon Silkin. Oxford, 1978.

Literature and History VII, Spring, 1978. English Men of Letters, 1914-1916, D G Wright.

Notes on Selected Poems of Wilfred Owen, B Uttenthal. Longman York Press, 1986.

Poetry of World War I, Textwise, Felicity Currie. The Critical Forum, 2003.

NEWSPAPERS AND MAGAZINES

Evening World - New York, 17 September 1914.

John Bull

The Daily Mail

History Today

The Morning Post

The Nation

New Age

New Internationalist

The New Statesman

Poetry - Chicago

Punch

The Sunday Pictorial

The Sunday Times

The Times

INDEX - INCLUDING TITLES OF POEMS

Titles of poems are shown in capitals

POEMS
LISTED IN AUTHOR ORDER

Page numbers of poems can be found in the main index.

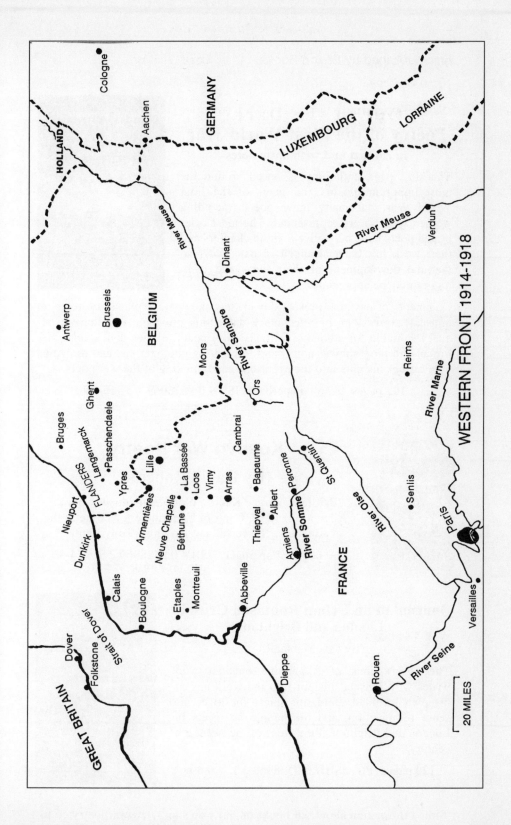

Also published by Saxon Books

Out in the Dark
Poetry of the First World War
in context and with basic notes

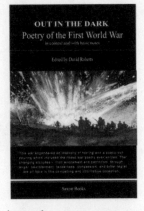

This 192 page anthology is based around the most important poems and poets of the First World War, but many other poets (including women writers) are represented. The most celebrated poets have been given whole chapters and their work has been arranged in date order so that the development of their ideas and techniques may be appreciated

Comments of past and present day critics, and basic explanatory notes on unusual expressions or vocabulary make this poignant anthology especially valuable for students. Extracts from poets' diaries and letters, historical and biographical notes, and fascinating photographs, and drawings give further insights into the experience and thinking of the war poets.

192 pages 9"x6" Paperback ISBN 0 9528969 1 5 £7-99

Kosovo War Poetry
By David Roberts

"Brilliant," Bruce Kent. "Wonderful anti-war book," Alice Mahon MP, Chair of Committee for Peace in the Balkans. "Powerful and moving," Tony Benn.

60 pages Paperback ISBN 0 9528969 2 3 £4-99

Journal of an Urban Robinson Crusoe
London and Brighton

By Des Marshall

The observations of a genuine outsider who writes with unusual insight into the workings of his own troubled mind, his quest for love, his sense of rejection, and the people he meets in London and Brighton at the close of the twentieth century.

120 pages PB ISBN 0 9528969 3 1 £6-99

More information about our books on our web site: www.warpoetry.co.uk